Collingwood Public Library

OUR
SCANDALOUS
SENATE

D1044368

OTHER BOOKS BY J. PATRICK BOYER

Another Country, Another Life: Calumny, Love, and the Secrets of Isaac Jelfs (Toronto: Dundurn, 2013)

Raw Life: Cameos of 1890s Justice from a Magistrate's Bench Book (Toronto: Dundurn, 2012)

Solitary Courage: Mona Winberg and the Triumph over Disability (Toronto: Blue Butterfly Books, 2010)

Local Library, Global Passport: The Evolution of a Carnegie Library (Toronto: Blue Butterfly Books, 2008)

A Passion for Justice: How 'Vinegar Jim' McRuer Became Canada's Greatest Law Reformer [revised paperback edition] (Toronto: Blue Butterfly Books, 2008)

A Man & His Words (Toronto: Canadian Shield Communications & Dundurn Press, 2003)

Leading in an Upside-Down World [contributing editor] (Toronto: University of Guelph & Dundurn Press, 2003)

"Just Trust Us": The Erosion of Accountability in Canada (Toronto: Breakout Educational Network & Dundurn Press, 2003)

The Leadership Challenge in the 21st Century [contributing editor] (Guelph: University of Guelph, 2002)

Accountability and Canadian Government (Guelph: University of Guelph, 2000)

Boyer's Ontario Election Law (Toronto: Carswell Publishing, 1996)

A Passion for Justice: The Life and Legacy of J.C. McRuer. (Toronto: University of Toronto Press & The Osgoode Society, 1994)

Direct Democracy in Canada: The History and Future of Referendums (Toronto: Dundurn Press, 1992)

The People's Mandate: Referendums and a More Democratic Canada (Toronto: Dundurn Press, 1992)

Hands-On Democracy: How You Can Take Part in Canada's Renewal (Toronto: Stoddart, 1993)

La democratie pour tous: Le citoyen...artisan du renouveau Canadien (Toronto: Stoddart, 1993)

Local Elections in Canada: The Law Governing Elections of Municipal Councils, School Boards and Other Local Authorities (Toronto: Butterworths, 1988)

Election Law in Canada: The Law and Procedure of Federal, Provincial and Territorial Elections. 2 vols. (Toronto: Butterworths, 1987)

Money and Message: The Law Governing Election Financing, Advertising, Broadcasting and Campaigning in Canada (Toronto: Butterworths, 1983)

Lawmaking by the People: Referendums and Plebiscites in Canada (Toronto: Butterworths, 1981)

The Egalitarian Option: Perspectives on Canadian Education [contributing author] (Toronto: Compass Books, 1975)

OUR
SCANDALOUS
SENATE

J. PATRICK BOYER

DUNDURN
TORONTO

Copyright © J. Patrick Boyer, 2014

All rights reserved. No part of this publication may be reproduced, stored in a retrieval system, or transmitted in any form or by any means, electronic, mechanical, photocopying, recording, or otherwise (except for brief passages for purposes of review) without the prior permission of Dundurn Press. Permission to photocopy should be requested from Access Copyright.

Editor: Dominic Farrell
Design: Jennifer Scott
Cover design: Carmen Giraudy
Cover image: Michel Loiselle/123RF Stock Photos
Printer: Webcom

Library and Archives Canada Cataloguing in Publication

Boyer, J. Patrick, author
        Our scandalous Senate / J. Patrick Boyer.

Issued in print and electronic formats.
ISBN 978-1-4597-2366-5 (pbk.).--ISBN 978-1-4597-2367-2 (pdf).--ISBN 978-1-4597-2368-9 (epub)

1. Canada. Parliament. Senate--Corrupt practices. 2. Canada. Parliament. Senate--Reform. 3. Political corruption--Canada. 4. Scandals--Canada. 5. Legislators--Canada. I. Title.

JL86.C67B69 2014   328.71'0766   C2014-901029-X   C2014-901030-3

1   2   3   4   5   18   17   16   15   14

We acknowledge the support of the Canada Council for the Arts and the Ontario Arts Council for our publishing program. We also acknowledge the financial support of the Government of Canada through the Canada Book Fund and Livres Canada Books, and the Government of Ontario through the Ontario Book Publishing Tax Credit and the Ontario Media Development Corporation.

Care has been taken to trace the ownership of copyright material used in this book. The author and the publisher welcome any information enabling them to rectify any references or credits in subsequent editions.

J. Kirk Howard, President

The publisher is not responsible for websites or their content unless they are owned by the publisher.

Printed and bound in Canada.

Visit us at
Dundurn.com
@dundurnpress
Facebook.com/dundurnpress
Pinterest.com/dundurnpress

Dundurn	Gazelle Book Services Limited	Dundurn
3 Church Street, Suite 500	White Cross Mills	2250 Military Road
Toronto, Ontario, Canada	High Town, Lancaster, England	Tonawanda, NY
M5E 1M2	LA1 4XS	U.S.A. 14150

*This book is joyfully dedicated
to my bride*

Elise Marie Boyer

"tout, tout, tout!"

CONTENTS

We Don't Have $37 Million and Two Years

In 2012, Canada's auditor general reported on his review of a number of Senate expense claims revealing that several senators didn't have the necessary documents to support their travel and living expenses. Subsequent investigation followed into what the news media quickly dubbed "the Senate expenses scandal." A small handful of Canada's 105 senators had claimed expenses that seemed problematic, mostly under a housing allowance but also for meals and, in one case, air fares. The claims had been duly approved and paid under the Senate's own uncertain rules and lax administrative hand. Later, an independent audit suggested the senators in question gave themselves an unwarranted bonus. They were ordered to repay the money. Embarrassed, the senators protested they'd done nothing wrong. Two at least asserted that the housing charges had been pre-cleared. One even started a court challenge against the Senate to quash the repayment order.

The disputed claims were not new; indeed, they had been made, processed, and paid on an ongoing basis for a number of years. The senators in question alleged the rules were unclear, the forms confusing, and the auditor's review "a flawed process." A couple paid the money back. One appeared to do so. A garnishee order or two would complete the restitution of funds owed by another senator.

That skeletal outline does not, as every Canadian knows, even begin to cover all the moving parts and conflicting pressures that would cause this sorry saga to blossom into a serialized political scandal that's now lasted more than two years. The Senate expenses scandal obsessed Canadians and sent our parliamentary life spinning down an unfamiliar path.

Although I would like this book to be as current and comprehensive as possible, to show how the Senate expenses scandal became the phenomenon it did, my second goal has been at odds with this first one. I would like, just as much, to address the even more puzzling Senate scandal — the continuing existence of this relic institution itself.

If I'd waited for more pieces of the Senate expenses puzzle to fall into place, *Our Scandalous Senate* would have been delayed by months or even years because the end of the current scandal is still not in sight. As Senator Mike Duffy, a leading actor in this morality play, accurately said in an October 30, 2013, email to me, this affair is "multi-layered and complex." Sorting everything out definitively would require a full public inquiry to find the plot and weave together this bizarre political debacle's many conflicting narratives.

But unlike the exhaustive reports produced by the Gomery Commission's more than $37 million two-year investigation into the Sponsorship Scandal, or earlier royal commission reports on other big Canadian political scandals, no integrating evidence-based public investigation into the Senate expenses scandal is underway. Bob Rae called for one, when he was still Liberal leader, but his suggestion was turned down. As a result, no comprehensive official document will ever be produced.

Moreover, significant developments that are separate from but relate to the Senate expenses scandal continue to unfold according to their own uncertain timetables:

- ► If, when the RCMP completes its investigations, criminal trials ensue, evidence provided at them will put a new gloss on current interpretations and keep the scandal alive for many more months. Some criminal charges have already been laid, such as those against suspended Senator Patrick Brazeau and former Senator Mac Harb, who were charged by the RCMP on February 4, 2014, as I finished this book;
- ► When Canada's auditor general, Michael Ferguson, completes his audit of each senator's expenses, other problems may come to light. Dealing with them, one way or another, will likely extend the run of this current Senate scandal. A preliminary report was expected, but the full audit is not likely before the end of 2014;

► When the Supreme Court of Canada delivers answers to questions from the Harper government about changing the Senate of Canada or even abolishing it within the framework of the Constitution, the justices will clarify matters for yet another round in the 140-year quest to do something about Parliament's upper house;

► When the Conservative Party takes stock of what transpired with the Senate expenses scandal and how the developments altered the party's performance capacity in national public life, pressures for change will be felt;

► When the 2015 general election takes place and the party leaders present Canadians with their divergent remedies to Canada's problematic Senate, the long-running expenses scandal will surely be as prominent in their speeches then as it is in our minds now;

► When central players who face legal constraints in the current Senate drama become free to speak, their statements, political acts, and published memoirs will give the expenses scandal future life by shedding light on matters still a mystery today.

Despite the fact that all those elements are still in play, something that makes the rendering of a definitive account of the Senate expenses scandal impossible, I decided not to wait until the final ding-dong of the last evening bell fades to silence at twilight. I want this book's historical perspective and timely lessons available when Senate reform is on the agenda and in our minds.

As the Senate scandal explodes, Canada's major news organizations catalogue on their constantly updated websites wherever the bits and pieces land. This invaluable resource of parading news remains a work-in-progress because fresh developments, from revelations of more senatorial slip-ups to the laying of criminal charges by the RCMP, are steadily added to the list, while prior entries are revised to incorporate fresh information that casts different light on previously reported facts. Thanks to the way digitally recorded and paper-printed communications complement each other now, *Our Scandalous Senate* does not try to imitate what media websites do superbly: serve as detailed record-keepers for this evolving saga. Instead, this book seeks to synthesize the jumble of recent events into the larger story of which they are part — the continuing existence of this relic institution and its detrimental impact on the democratic well-being of our country.

The present-day Senate expenses fiasco and the century-old challenge posed by Parliament's upper house are inextricably entwined, two faces of the same thing: the unfinished business of what to do about our scandalous Senate.

CHAPTER 1

Anatomy of a Scandal

We can learn a lot about a place from the kind of scandal it generates. From 2012 to 2014 our attention has been held in fascinated disbelief watching the Senate of Canada, an exception in just about everything, spinning at the centre of a unique scandal.

Typically, a scandal requires three elements: a nefarious deed being done, knowledge of the act becoming public, and people who hear the news becoming scandalized by it. But such a barebones anatomy does not begin to outline what happened with the Senate expenses scandal. It began smouldering when news came to light that claims for reimbursement of expenses by several senators were being reviewed by the independent auditing firm Deloitte. As the months passed, what had seemed like a minor accounting issue flared into a national obsession as the circle of scandal spread outward, important public careers ended, investigations deepened, and a desire to abolish the Senate escalated. It reached a point by the end of 2013 that the government seemed so embattled by the ongoing scandal the prime minister's press secretary had to issue a denial of the rumour that he was going to leave office.

A relatively small scandal had become a major national one. It dominated media coverage, overtook the national conversation, and distracted attention from a raft of other initiatives by the Harper government. Procedures conflicted, rules were bent, "solutions" turned out to be counter-productive. One senator, unable to repay his contested expenses for lack of funds, found his salary garnisheed by the Senate to recoup the amount, but then was suspended by senators without pay, an action that, in the process, defeated their own plan to get the money back. That's how surrealistic it all became.

The Senate's unique institutional status, when combined with its outdated administrative operations, made Parliament's upper house the epicentre of a national scandal so far beyond normal that the whole fiasco became as stunning an aberration in the realm of political ethics as the Senate itself is in the life of our country.

The Senate is not an isolated entity. Like all institutions, it functions in relation to other institutions, to the individuals who serve it and are molded by it, and to the political culture of which it is an expression and which it in turn influences.

So the "Senate expenses scandal" is a much bigger story than the "breaking news" reports about Mike Duffy or Pamela Wallin, Stephen Harper or Nigel Wright. It is a window onto the state of public affairs in contemporary Canada, through which can be seen the role of journalism, the power of the Official Opposition, the nature of the Prime Minister's Office, political party fund-raising, police work, and the cumulative effects of the failure to modernize our country's senior legislative assembly.

If only viewed in a narrow context — Did senators Mac Harb and Patrick Brazeau scam the public over fraudulent housing claims? Why did Senator Wallin pay back so much money while claiming the process that flushed out her improper billing was "flawed"? What did Senator Duffy have on the prime minister that caused his chief of staff, Nigel Wright, to inappropriately protect him? — the Senate expenses scandal might not have warranted such intense interest. After all, this story of greed and political backroom deals seems somewhat routine in relation to other news of the day: the deadly train wreck at Lac Mégantic in Québec; a stunning rise of flood waters in heavily populated parts of Alberta and Ontario; Canada's new trade treaty with the Europeans; the government's claim of Canadian Arctic sovereignty all the way to the North Pole. Foreign wars, natural disasters, genocide in Syria, Iran's nuclear program, government spying operations — on and on ran news from a larger universe busy with transcending matters. Yet the Senate expenses scandal resiliently outlasted news of most of these other developments. Clearly something deep was stirring.

Even when considered alongside other Canadian political scandals of the time, the expense claims of several members of Parliament's upper house might have seemed fairly colourless news. The hard-core political corruption being exposed by stunning revelations at the Charbonneau Commission's inquiry into how Québec's construction industry and provincial political parties were infiltrated by organized crime got only intermittent coverage beyond Québec's own media, which carried the story with a true sense of the gravity of this situation. When scandal erupted over Canada's electronic espionage on Brazil, a friendly nation and important trading partner, it stayed news for only a brief time. The smouldering scandal over the string of unsolved murders and disappearances of Aboriginal women in Canada could not generate enough shame to prod any government to launch a public inquiry into the matter. In Ontario, the billion dollar cost — a figure calculated by the province's auditor general — of the McGuinty government's decision to abort construction of two generating plants to win nearby seats during a provincial election, seemed to gain modest traction, but mostly just within the province.

The only Canadian news triggering comparable intensity of public outrage, garnering as much national attention, indeed, even creating reaction around the globe, was, oddly enough, a matter of *municipal* government — the unending circus of controversy Toronto's mayor Rob Ford proved capable of generating. In Canada's scandal department, Mr. Ford alone could distract attention from the Senate expenses fiasco.

Mayor Ford's court cases and shocking revelations not only competed with the Senate scandal, they even upstaged scandals and criminality of other mayors during the same period. In Montreal, Mayor Gerald Tremblay resigned after a public inquiry into corruption of the city's construction industry included the accusation he'd turned a blind eye to illicit campaign financing of his political party. When stepping down in November 2012, saying he was doing so "for the good of the city," the mayor denied the allegations.

His successor, Michael Applebaum, promised to combat corruption at city hall. But just seven months later, he too stepped down when charged with some fourteen corruption offences, including fraud and conspiracy, in June 2013. Mr. Applebaum also maintained his innocence, declaring as he departed, "I have never taken a penny from anybody." In November 2013, Denis Coderre, who'd resigned earlier in the year as Liberal MP for

Montreal's Bourassa riding, ran for mayor. The public remained skeptical, with continuing testimony flowing from the Charbonneau Commission about kickbacks and illegal party financing at the municipal level, but Denis Coderre weathered attacks from his opponents about his party's ties to members of the corruption-ridden, and since dissolved, Union Montréal Party, and was elected Montreal's new mayor.

In Laval, Mayor Gilles Vaillancourt resigned in November 2012 after twenty-three years in office, following raids by the province's anti-corruption squad throughout the city, including upon his own home. Mr. Vaillancourt was accused of getting kickbacks on construction contracts but denied the allegations. Police reported after the raid that, unlike incriminating paper currency that could be made to disappear in a panic as police were spied coming to the front door, Canada's new plastic bills do not flush down toilets.

Meanwhile, in Ontario, London's mayor, Joe Fontana, was ordered, on October 28, 2013, to stand trial on criminal charges of fraud under $5,000, breach of trust by a public official, and uttering forged documents. A year before, the London *Free Press* had published allegations the former federal cabinet minister and Liberal MP for London North Centre had used more than $20,000 in cheques from the Government of Canada to pay for his son's wedding reception at the Marconi Club banquet hall, first with a deposit of $1,700, then with nearly $19,000 more. The RCMP, unable to get enough evidence to lay charges for the larger amount, proceeded with the smaller. The mayor denied wrong-doing, refused repeated calls to resign, and vowed to fight and clear his name before the November 2014 municipal elections.

On the surface, four senators getting reimbursed money they were apparently not entitled to, contrasted with contemporaneous issues of organized crime, murder, espionage, electoral calumny, and criminal charges against incumbent mayors, makes the tempest involving Parliament's upper house seem *relatively* innocuous. The fact that it was not, and that it could spin into a national political scandal of such *gravitas*, brings us forceably back to the central problem of the Senate and the truer nature of its activities.

* * *

The expenses scandal was, and remains, a giant maze.

Everybody strode around in the maze with purposeful intent, but nobody could find a way out of its ever-twisting labyrinth. That much, at least, was understandable. As the Senate scandal, so the Senate itself: it is a clear and present reality that nobody really comprehends, despite all the narratives and interpretations in circulation to explain it.

What became even more inexplicable for Canadians, however, and a nightmare for those directly implicated, were not the facts themselves, but what became of them. So many players straying around this tortured course gave so many changing characterizations of events that we had the sensation of observing a drama unfolding through the lens of a kaleidoscope. With each twist, the pattern of "facts" became new. No prior arrangement of them ever reappeared; nothing was ever quite the same. As a result, it was certainly not a story that got stale. The Senate expenses scandal took, and still takes, new form almost every week.

Beyond peoples' chagrined outrage, and in addition to all the confusing stories, what also intrigued us about this odd affair, month after month, was its mystery. The scandal did not die because people kept waiting for an explanation that made sense. The country's prime minister stubbornly refused to give one.

On any given day, hard questions begged for answers. Why did a bright and ethical person like Nigel Wright, chief of staff to the prime minister of Canada, do such a dumb and improper thing as secretly pay Mike Duffy's $90,000 debt to the Senate? Why was the Prime Minister's Office even making itself an agent for the Senate's recoupment of Mike Duffy's ineligible expenses? How was Senator Duffy able to stipulate that he'd comply with the order to repay, provided that his reputation was not impaired and he would not be out of pocket at the end of it all? Why did Mr. Duffy get secret help repaying his expenses, and even his legal bills, but not the two other Conservative senators whom the same prime minister had appointed and who faced repayment orders too? What leverage did Mike Duffy have on Prime Minister Stephen Harper that Patrick Brazeau and Pamela Wallin did not? Troubling curiosity would not let us give up our wait for answers.

* * *

Yet, likely the deepest cause of all that accounts for our seemingly inexplicable attachment to the Senate scandal is our subconscious antagonism toward the institution itself.

Discomfort about the Senate, a feeling that has existed for more than a century, has generated decades of reform proposals. They have cost Canadians unquantifiable time, money, and distraction. But all that enterprise and expense has produced no change. As time has passed and memories have faded, the countless Senate reform proposals have slipped away, to vanish like water poured down a drain. Who today knows of Prime Minister Robert Borden's plan for a national referendum on the Senate in 1914, Prime Minister Pierre Trudeau's goal of converting the Senate to a House of the Federation in the 1970s, Prime Minister Brian Mulroney's Herculean negotiations to make the Senate elected, more effective, and equitably representative of the entire country, especially Western Canada? All have disappeared down the same drain.

The deeper impulse that propelled those and other failed efforts at Senate reform endured, however, and not on the cold pages of history books or dusty parliamentary committee reports but in some troubled part of our collective consciousness. Our negative feelings about Parliament's upper house had not disappeared. They'd just gone underground, waiting for a chance to resurface.

The Senate expenses scandal gave that opening. The highly contentious handling of senators' expense claims, combined with our outrage that already privileged senators got greedy about taking even more money from the public treasury, dredged up this muted recollection that we were unhappy about the Senate before, and harboured deep visceral antagonism toward this superfluous and costly institution still.

Because the theatre for this morality play was the antiquated Senate itself, the whole affair became an especially embarrassing reminder of our political impotence in trying to rid ourselves of the ill-fitting upper house, even lacking the ability, despite more than a century of talk about it, to reform the place. The expense claims scandal could not have provoked the same high-voltage outrage from citizens, nor the unexpected chain of responses from those running the government, nor the obsessive interest of Canada's news media, had it unfolded on any other stage.

Many Canadians, freshly scandalized, used phrases their ancestors voiced decades earlier, decrying anew Parliament's upper house as a "bastion of privilege," a "waste of taxpayers' money," and an "affront to democracy." This resurfacing sentiment helped push the Senate expenses fiasco beyond any normal scandal's contours.

For many scandals, the ignominious end comes quickly. An errant individual's career evaporates over sexual impropriety or financial skulduggery, sometimes for theft or for substance abuse. The personal flameout seldom makes it into the history books, perhaps only getting dishonourable mention in a university text like one I wrote, *Corruption, Scandal, & Political Ethics*, to illustrate some academic principle.

But every now and then, a scandal breaks through that barrier of personal failure and individual misstep. It becomes a really big deal, taking on a life of its own powerful enough to change the course of public affairs.

The 1873 "Pacific Scandal" erupted after Conservative Prime Minister John A. Macdonald got $360,000 in election campaign funds from the intended builder of the government-sponsored railway to British Columbia. The "Beauharnois Scandal" of 1931 shocked Canadians when Prime Minister Mackenzie King's Liberals took a $700,000 bribe and King himself an all-expenses paid holiday in Bermuda, the payments coming from Beauharnois Light, Heat & Power Company in exchange for the right to change the St. Lawrence River's flow when building a hydro power station west of Montreal. The "Sponsorship Scandal" of 2004 undermined Prime Minister Jean Chrétien's Liberals when it was revealed his government had paid Liberal-controlled firms and ad agencies in Québec $2 million in contracts without a proper bidding process, another $250,000 to top up one contract for no additional work, and $1.5 million for no services performed beyond making kick-backs to the Liberal party.

Scandals like those implicated governing political parties. They made it into the history books as seismic events that rocked and defeated governments, shifted political values, changed public expectations, and became turning points in our country's evolution for the reforms they triggered.

How could those few senators, padding their expense claims, have imagined they were likewise setting off a series of events leading inexorably to a final solution for the Senate of Canada?

CHAPTER 2

Taking a Risk with Celebrity Senators

The Senate of Canada is an odd place for famous people to end up. "An ornament to the legislature" is sometimes how a renowned public personality from a non-political field is described by those seeking a diplomatic turn of phrase for an exotic bird landed among the Senate's flock of seasoned politicians. Quite often the reason for the celebrity's surprise appearance is a complete mystery — is there some childhood connection with the prime minister, perhaps, or could it be some personified tribute to Canada's secular religion, a symbolic veneration of hockey through senatorial beatification of one of the game's star players?

Frank Mahovlich, for instance, left Timmins to become famous as "The Big M" in a blue Toronto Maple Leaf's jersey many years ago, but in 1998, Prime Minister Jean Chrétien persuaded Mahovlich to trade up and don the red maple leaf as a Liberal senator. During his ensuing fourteen-year season in Parliament's second legislature, Mahovlich's low-profile performance failed to match his efforts on ice, which had put him into the Hockey Hall of Fame. He fit quietly into the senators' club, where rules were seldom more onerous than "sip your Scotch slowly and keep out of trouble." He made few headlines, and certainly no bad ones.

When he skated into the sunset in January 2013, fellow senators bid seventy-five-year old Frank farewell. Needful of some noteworthy references for their tributes, they spoke about his accomplishments at the hockey rink winning six Stanley Cups, rather than any goals he'd scored in the political arena. Nobody even remembered Frank getting an assist on any of the plays in parliamentary match-ups. Only the Liberals' leader in the Senate, the astute Nova Scotia lawyer James Cowan, realized it would benefit his party to recall one or two of Senator Mahovlich's upper chamber breakaways.

"While he was never the first to intervene in committee hearings," remarked Cowan kindly, "his thoughtful, probing questions always cut to the heart of issues and concerns of witnesses who appeared before us." Cowan was drawing on his recollection of meetings of the Fisheries Committee, on which at one time he'd sat with Mahovlich. Fisheries was a natural fit for Maritimer Cowan, less so for the son of a northern Ontario gold mining town, although the Liberals' celebrity senator did ask about more than just what the testifying fishermen used for bait. "For me, Frank Mahovlich represents, by his quiet dignity, by his thoughtful remarks, and by his faithful attendance to his duties in committee and in the chamber, a fine example of a first-class senator." Indeed, what more could be expected?

For his own last play, departing Senator Mahovlich took an unaccustomed brief turn around the upper house ice. He thanked Jean Chrétien for appointing him, his assistants and research staff, his wife, Marie, and "everyone in the Senate and, indeed, in Parliament. I would like to bid *adieu* to the Senate and leave with these final words: I have had a wonderful time. Thank you."

No requirement obliges senators to make public statements, or to remain in the spotlight. Most make negligible public impact, regardless of what they may believe about their newfound importance, once they've taken a seat inside Parliament's upper house. It's just that for celebrity senators, switching from big star attention to lacklustre performance, the contrast seems more noticeable.

Like Prime Minister Chrétien, Mr. Harper has plucked stars from the world of sports. His new senators in 2009 included Canada's female athlete of the twentieth century, as voted by the Canadian Press and Broadcast News, and a highly respected hockey figure who spent more than two decades behind NHL benches coaching the Québec Nordiques, Detroit Red Wings, St. Louis Blues, and Montreal Canadiens, often deep into the playoffs.

Nancy Greene of British Columbia became famous as Canada's snowflake darling in the 1968 Olympic Winter Games in Grenoble. Claiming gold and silver medals for her downhill triumphs, she showed the world that a Canadian had the right stuff to break the Europeans' lock on alpine skiing. Internationally, Nancy won overall World Cup titles in 1967 and 1968, and her total of fourteen World Cup victories and Olympic medals is still a Canadian record. Here at home, during her nine-year skiing career, Nancy won seventeen Canadian championship titles. Then she promoted amateur sport and ski tourism, helped develop Whistler-Blackcomb and Sun Peaks, and in 1994 became Sun Peaks Resort's skiing director. Her star status also continued to sparkle as Chancellor Emeritus of Thompson Rivers University in Kamloops, an Officer of the Order of Canada, a member of both the British Columbia and Canada Sports Halls of Fame, and of Canada's Walk of Fame.

Jacques Demers led the Canadiens to a Stanley Cup championship in 1993, was twice awarded the Jack Adams trophy for coach-of-the-year, and in 1999 began his popular broadcasts analyzing Canadiens games as a commentator on RDS Television, a position that drew richly on his insider's knowledge of the sport. Soon after being inducted into the Senate of Canada, Demers made known that he had achieved his career successes despite being effectively illiterate, highlighting not only the challenges of literacy but how a determined individual can fashion a worthwhile career by inventing ways to overcome hurdles, including unseen ones. Neither Demers nor Nancy Greene had political backgrounds, yet both seemed as adept as Frank Mahovlich in learning the rulebook for this new sport of senatorship. Whenever they did make news, which was infrequently, the story was not controversial.

The risk with a celebrity senator, though, is that instead of fading blandly away, he or she will continue to earn controversial headlines. After all, stars achieve notoriety precisely for *not* being like everybody else. In 2012, Parliamentary Press Gallery interest in problems over at the Senate was *only* tweaked because some disputed expense claims had been submitted by senators whom Prime Minister Harper had personally selected for their value as national celebrities.

Born in Charlottetown on May 27, 1946, Michael Dennis Duffy was driven to reach out to others.

Even before becoming a teen, he'd told his chums he wanted to become a radio reporter on Parliament Hill. At age sixteen, he was an active ham radio operator, and in his teens, he worked as a disc jockey on CFCY, playing many records from his own collection on air. After completing high school, he opened a fall season at St. Dunstan's College, but burning to become a news reporter, Duffy quickly lost patience dallying around college classrooms studying humanities, so quit and simply crossed town to start reporting for the Charlottetown *Guardian*. In 1964, he traversed the Northumberland Straight to work for a mainland radio station in Amherst, Nova Scotia.

Burning for politics in the excitement of Centennial Year, Duffy used his 1967 vacation time and all his savings to get to the Progressive Conservative national leadership convention at Maple Leaf Gardens in Toronto with press accreditation, a sampler of his unabated determination to report major developing political stories. His next career move was further in the Ottawa direction, getting him from Amherst as far as Montreal's CFCF as an assignment editor. By 1971, he finally landed where he'd said since a youth he would be — in Ottawa — working as a political reporter. Duffy had a job with CFRA radio.

Three years later, Duffy joined the Canadian Broadcasting Corporation. Joyfully working out of CBC's Parliament Hill bureau, he covered politics for radio listeners between 1974 and 1977 before engineering a switch to *The National* newscast, becoming the CBC's lead television reporter on Parliament Hill. He covered most major stories of the Trudeau, Clark, and Mulroney years, becoming well known and recognized across Canada as a national political journalist. But Mike Duffy also worked as a foreign correspondent, covering the fall of South Vietnam in April 1975 for the CBC, one of the last journalists to leave Saigon before North Vietnamese troops and Viet Cong insurgents swarmed into the city.

Back home, he settled into a rewarding life as a reporter. His personal life was in flux, however; he divorced his first wife in the early 1980s but remarried a few years later. The change was matched by a professional change of partners, too. Shifting networks in 1988, Duffy crossed over to private television's CJOH-TV in Ottawa as host of a new *Sunday Edition* public affairs program, which aired until 1999. Leaving the CBC for a more prominent role at CTV was not unmitigated joy. He rankled at being kept further down the pecking order than the network's well-respected Ottawa political reporter Craig Oliver, and he'd also upset his former close friends and colleagues at CBC Television, men like Peter Mansbridge and Brian Stewart, who felt Duffy had deserted the ship that first sailed him into prominence.

At CTV, Duffy progressed to become host and interviewer with CTV Newsnet, forerunner of the CTV News Channel. An avid interest in political doings and his cherubic ways when meeting others soon made him a parliamentary insider, easily able to entice prominent cabinet ministers onto his name-bearing shows, first *Countdown with Mike Duffy* and later, *Mike Duffy Live*. Duffy was a gregarious egalitarian, as readily on a first-name basis with all the security guards and secretaries on The Hill as with senior ministers of the Crown. His personal routes into and around the parliamentary precincts exceeded those of anybody else I know. On his travels, he picked up a great deal of info from improbable sources, which he integrated and stored away. Who knew what secrets he acquired about those who wield power in Canada?

Often Mike Duffy broadcast from the foyer immediately outside the House of Commons, impressive as a set for his TV show, but also highly convenient as a place for ministers and other prominent politicians to get wired with a microphone and slide onto a stool in front of the camera. Like a P.E.I. lobster fisherman with a procession of fine specimens entering his well-placed trap, Duffy was easily able to catch worthy interviewees and dispatch over the country's airwaves a steady stream of live insider reports on the politics of the nation. Despite many setbacks, he'd determinedly engineered himself into the position he had aspired to from boyhood. The people he interviewed were the players who moved the country's government and shook our politics, but the fact they would come and go on the TV screen while Mike Duffy's was the constantly recurring face gave him national recognition and clout in political Ottawa.

As one who intermittently had a Duffy "interview," I was seduced by his easy-going manner of questions, his rounded face that seemed uncharacteristic of television personalities, and his unthreatening manner. An Ontarian, I was acclimatized to an earnest approach to all issues, no matter how large or small. Duffy's "down home" style reflected Prince Edward Island's more relaxed manner and the Island's down-to-earth dialogue. Off Parliament Hill and across Canada, the man's pleasing ways accounted for Duffy's enduring appeal. Television viewers found him as easy to take as comfort food. He was disarming. His enthusiasm was contagious. The twinkle in his eye never left you sure who was fooling whom.

After arriving on Parliament Hill in the early 1970s, Mike Duffy lived mostly in the National Capital Region. In 2003, he and wife Heather bought a home next to the Kanata Golf and Country Club for $293,000. He continued to bask in his popularity and influence, acquiring plenty of inside stories about Ottawa's major players and sharing them, a celebrity raconteur, with colleagues in such power venues as Mama Teresa's and Hy's restaurants.

Duffy developed a taste, as befits a celebrity, for expensive cars and good clothes. In a tax court case, according to Jonathan Gatehouse of *Maclean's* "Duffy had made some inventive attempts to lower his tax burden," including a claim his wardrobe of costly clothes actually consisted of "uniforms" belonging to the CTV network. It was not an implausible contention, since he needed them when appearing on-camera, but as Gatehouse notes, "Revenue Canada disagreed and presented him with a bill for $21,000."

Duffy attempted to parlay his celebrity standing into even higher acceptability with Canada's establishment in a number of ways, such as by gaining investiture into the Order of Canada. His orchestrated campaign suffered irreparable damage, however, at the hands of *Frank* magazine. The publication was repeatedly, and tiresomely, on Duffy's case — calling him "the Puffster," running unflattering photos, noting his dwindling audience ratings, and once designating him "Eyesore of the Year." Then a headline called Mike Duffy "A Fat-Faced Liar" after the broadcaster spread word he was going to the United States to speak in Durham at North Carolina's renowned Duke University, but, as *Frank* disclosed, his true destination was instead a weight-loss clinic in the state. His prospects for the prestigious Order of Canada, which he'd evidently tried not once but three times to achieve, were apparently scuppered by this ongoing attack from *Frank*. Prime Minister Chrétien privately confided to Duffy that this sort of publicity had thwarted his nomination to the Order. Duffy sued *Frank* and won, reported Jonathan Gatehouse in *Maclean's*, "an apology and a $30,000 out-of-court settlement."

Despite this acrimonious history with *Frank*, when Duffy later became embroiled in behind-the-scenes power struggles at CTV, he did not hesitate to leak information about his rivals to the magazine. Now he would gratefully use his former nemesis as a new ally in serious battle to protect his reputation and livelihood. Clearly, Mike Duffy's career-honed survival instinct enabled him to adapt for self-protection and change his stance dramatically if the stage upon which he played his starring role shifted.

The issues that percolated at this time between Duffy and CTV concerned disputes over expenses and contract provisions. When his personal behaviour was caricatured by fellow journalist John Fraser, or criticized by another journalist, Don Martin, or complained about formally by CTV producer Carl Langelier, Duffy was swift to strike back, either personally or through his lawyers. Colleagues learned to give his sensibilities wide berth. Complaints went uninvestigated. Transgressions remained unpunished. Even the Parliamentary Press Gallery, whose constitution prohibits members from using their position on The Hill to gain any benefit "except through journalism," ignored Duffy's decades-long campaign for the benefit of a prime ministerial appointment to the Senate. Rather than enforcing their only rule on ethical conduct, the journalists of the Press Gallery treated Duffy's breach of their constitution as a joke.

In a country where thousands crave a seat in the Senate, Mike Duffy was unrivalled as Canada's most ardent supplicant for appointment to the upper house. Everyone surmised that if he had any path into the Red Chamber, it would be across the red soils of Prince Edward Island. But the island province with just four Senate seats knows only infrequent vacancies. For Duffy's progress, an incumbent P.E.I. senator had to hit retirement age seventy-five or die in office. "Every time Mike Duffy shakes my hand," quipped Prince Edward Island Senator Heath Macquarie, "he takes my pulse!"

Over his many years on Parliament Hill, some half-dozen different prime ministers received Duffy's barrage of appeals. Most everyone working around Parliament Hill referred to him, either with a chuckle or dismissively, as "the Senator."

Brian Mulroney, aware of the standing joke, shocked reporters the day he announced that he'd been trying for years to persuade Mike Duffy to accept a seat in the Senate but the broadcaster had turned the prime minister down flat. Following a pause of stunned disbelief, Mulroney chuckled delivering his punch line, "It's the speakership of the Senate he wants, or nothing at all. These guys from P.E.I. sure know what to hold out for!"

In the 1990s, it was Jean Chrétien's turn to face the incessant battery of pitches by the wannabe senator. The former PM told the Charlottetown *Guardian* on October 30, 2013, that at least "a hundred times" he'd been ambushed. "When he was in the lobby of the House of Commons, he would say, 'Hi prime minister. I'm ready, I'm ready!'"

Mr. Chrétien refused the plea each time it was made. "I had the good judgment not to name him, I guess." The Liberals did, however, examine the possibility. When asked by the PM, Liberal MP for Charlottetown Shawn Murphy volunteered a comment that squelched the possibility: Duffy "couldn't be considered an Islander" because he'd not lived in Prince Edward Island since the 1960s. Mike Duffy's pleas were not taken seriously by anybody except, perhaps, "the Senator" himself.

Duffy was unrelenting, however, and following the Liberal loss of power, he turned his attention to the new Conservative government. In the run-up to in the national general election of October 2008, when Prime Minister Harper's minority Conservative government was seeking re-election and the Liberals were led by Stéphane Dion, Duffy broadcast an interview the Liberal leader recorded in the Halifax studio of a CTV affiliate.

The interview started badly. The party's leader displayed hesitancy with some English words and appeared not to quite understand the opening question. A number of re-starts were recorded on camera. Normally such failed beginnings get cut, giving viewers a better impression. That this standard practice would be followed was apparently the understanding between the interviewer, the Liberal leader, and his advisers — in short, CTV would put together and broadcast the best of the interview, leaving any evidence of ineptness on the cutting room floor. But when Duffy saw raw footage of the entire interview, he could not wait to broadcast the halting missteps and re-takes. Whether dismayed or amused, Canadians across the country, in the course of making up their mind about whom to vote for, saw many replays of a seemingly incompetent person who aspired to be prime minister. Mr. Harper, whose campaign was faltering, met reporters that night to add scorn.

The damage Mike Duffy inflicted on Mr. Dion's campaign was measurable. Stephen Harper won the October 2008 general election and formed another government, still a minority but with an increased number of seats. A panel at the Canadian Broadcast Standards Council concluded that journalist Duffy violated broadcasting codes and ethics by airing the "false starts" of the Liberal leader's interview, ruling he "was not fair, balanced, or even handed."

Two months later, on December 22, the reinstated prime minister gave "the Senator" his most cherished Christmas present ever, a real seat in the Senate of Canada.

Pamela Wallin flew out of Wadena, Saskatchewan, a town of a thousand people bordering the great wetlands of Quill Plain, where she was born on April 10, 1953.

By 1994, the townspeople had swelled so proud of their famous daughter of Swedish descent in a community mostly derived from Swedes, Ukrainians, Norwegians, Poles, and Germans that they renamed main street *Pamela Wallin Drive* and painted in big letters, below the name WADENA on the municipal water tower, their happy boast: *Home of Pamela Wallin.*

Becoming renowned enough to get your name on a town water tower first requires going out into the bigger world and making something of yourself. Wallin first went to Moose Jaw to complete high school at Central Collegiate Institute and earn money working at the Co-Op, then moved on to Regina where, at age twenty, she graduated from the University of Saskatchewan with a degree in psychology and political science. After a brief stint in Regina with a Saskatchewan government program to counsel adults making their own way in society, she next went northeast to Prince Albert and landed work at the nearby Saskatchewan Federal Penitentiary, a maximum security facility built in 1911 on the site of a residential school for Indian children. Wallin had become a political activist and feminist, and her work with the male prisoners was to improve their links with waiting and impoverished wives on the outside.

Collingwood Public Library

Like most Saskatchewanians, Wallin held strong political views. She'd also inherited deep values about "service to country" from her adored father, Bill, who'd flown valiantly as an RCAF pilot in World War II. Her teen years coincided with radical student protest against the existing order of things, and when she signed on with the NDP, Wallin affiliated herself with its most radical element, the "party within the party" formally named the Movement for an Independent Socialist Canada but popularly dubbed "The Waffle."

Waffle members formed a militant faction trying to shift the already left-wing New Democratic Party further to the political left. The movement mirrored the sixties, combining campus radicalism, feminism, Canadian nationalism, general left-wing nationalism, and a quest for a more democratic Canada. Its 1969 *Manifesto for an Independent Socialist Canada* offered a critique of the "American Empire" and sparked much-needed debate about American control over Canada's economy. There was extensive U.S. ownership of Canadian business and resources, and deep concern over the emergence of a branch-plant economy — felt not only by The Waffle but also by Liberals like economic nationalist Walter Gordon and many "Red Tory" Progressive Conservatives, myself included. The Waffle advocated nationalization of Canadian industries to rescue them from American control. Before The Waffle was expelled from the NDP, its ideas influenced party policy and, in turn, Liberal Party programs. Prime Minister Trudeau, dependent on NDP members of Parliament to support his minority government after 1972, obliged by creating Petro-Canada and the National Energy Policy to assert Canadian control over the energy sector, and the Foreign Investment Review Agency to limit foreign ownership generally and, in particular, American takeovers of Canadian companies. With all of this, Pamela Wallin was more than sympathetic.

In 1974, leaving behind her social work at the penitentiary, Wallin began a career in journalism with the news division of CBC Radio in Regina. Her lefty credentials appealed to those in charge of hiring, as did her ability to ask big questions of callers to the *Radio Noon* show. After four years' experience in radio, she joined the Ottawa bureau of Canada's largest circulation daily, the *Toronto Star.* With the benefit of those two years in print journalism, which introduced her to political Ottawa, Wallin switched back to broadcasting, but now in television rather than radio. She was hired by CTV in 1980 to co-host the network's *Canada AM* show alongside Norm Perry. The stuff of fame was now hers.

Wallin also hosted CTV's Sunday public affairs show *Question Period,* which was where I first met her, at CTV's Agincourt studio in northeast Toronto. I had just authored a new book on referendums. Wallin interviewed pollster Martin Goldfarb and me on whether, and when, it's better to take the public's pulse through plebiscites than polls. I was impressed by the informed, concise, and pointed direction in which she navigated the topic, giving her viewers value on an important but seldom considered topic. Pamela Wallin's interviewing skills blended a personable manner with pertinent inquiry.

In 1985, CTV named her the network's Ottawa bureau chief, a powerful position but a behind-the-scenes role. Longing for on-air reporting, after a while Wallin rejoined *Canada AM.*

By now she was famous. Magazine articles featured the beautiful woman with the brains and nerve to go after stories in Canada and around the world. To a rising number of young women hoping for a career in media and communications, Pamela Wallin served as a role model, going where no path had been and blazing a trail. In the arena of Canadian politics, however, some leading figures felt it was them, more than any trail, Wallin was marking.

Wallin had a lengthy televised interview with Liberal Party leader John Turner on her *Question Period* show that aired January 13, 1988. She repeatedly asked him about his alleged drinking problem. No matter how he answered, she returned to the topic of "long liquid lunches" or whether it was true that he "liked his drink" or whatever other way she could frame the allegation that he was an alcoholic unfit to be prime minister. She herself did not think this contentious interview any model for younger journalists to emulate, and later said so in her memoirs.

Prime Minister Brian Mulroney was another who took umbrage at her reporting style. The first time anyone with power to appoint Pamela Wallin to the Senate proposed doing so came at the height of the intense debate over Canada's comprehensive trade treaty with the United States in 1988. Although Wallin considered her controversial coverage of issues raised by the Free Trade Agreement "a valid examination of questions that needed answers," Mr. Mulroney was irked by the negativity of her reporting, as Wallin would later write and as I heard at the time as a member of his parliamentary caucus.

"Maybe I should just appoint Wallin to the Senate," he proposed, as a way of curbing what he considered her relentless attack on the trade initiative. Dalton Camp, a long-time Tory insider and past president of the Progressive Conservative Party of Canada who was working at this time in the Privy Council Office, tried to discern whether Mulroney was joking or hatching an ill-advised plan. Not taking any chances, Camp squelched the idea, reminding the PM "what an even bigger pain Wallin would be inside the fold as a Tory-appointed senator."

If Pamela Wallin zeroed in on issues in ways political leaders disliked, that was just the quality of her journalism, which, when also factoring in her good looks and nation-wide popularity, made the CBC covet her. In a highly publicized 1992 coup, the Canadian Broadcasting Corporation hired Wallin away from CTV. The public broadcaster wanted her star status to boost and reposition the network's entire approach to television news programming.

That fall, Pamela Wallin and Peter Mansbridge went on air as co-hosts of *Prime Time News*, featuring both news and interviews. The trail blazer had now become the first Canadian woman to co-anchor a nightly national television newscast. By 1994, CBC Television news, juggling for better ratings, rejigged the format so Mansbridge read the news after which Wallin hosted a magazine segment of interviews and special stories. It seemed a demotion. In 1995 Canadians and other news media were stunned when, as the result of further backstage struggles, the CBC replaced Wallin with Hanna Gartner. Non-CBC broadcasters, newspapers, and magazines across the country were full of the story. Wallin herself was now news.

Sidelined at the height of her career by CBC's humiliating dismissal, she retreated home to recover. In Wadena, she found her legion of loyal supporters boycotting the CBC. She took her bearings, then responded by creating Pamela Wallin Productions and successfully launched a daily interview series, *Pamela Wallin Live*, which CBC Newsworld, and intermittently CBC's main network, carried over the next four years. The engaging series featured Wallin interviewing newsmakers, celebrities, and other personalities with clarity and intimacy akin to CNN's popular *Larry King Live*. She was famous again. Young women once more were inspired by her example of resiliency, first in getting to the top, and then finding ways of staying there.

Wallin was again a media success, but her life would make an unexpected change at this point. Following the horrors of the 9/11 attack on New York and Washington, when the world was aching to help wounded, devastated America, Canadians were at the forefront. In the early rush to support New Yorkers, a "Canada Loves New York" rally was pulled together in Manhattan. Prime Minister Jean Chrétien, who'd just come off a U.S. trade mission and was mindful of new opportunities for Canadian businesses in the conveniently close American markets, was present. So was Canada's athletic foreign minister John Manley, who ran New York City's marathon. A key rally organizer was their fellow Liberal Jerry Grafstein, mastermind of many campaign victories who'd been strategically placed in the Senate of Canada. The deeply moving, star-studded tribute in still-reeling New York City drew some twenty-six thousand Canadians, many travelling south by train, plane, and motor vehicles, including thirty-three buses from Toronto alone. The emotionally searing event with its throng of performing Canadian celebrities was hosted by popular Canadian television personality Pamela Wallin.

Prime Minister Jean Chrétien, immediately grasping the importance of embracing this new connection between Canadians and Americans, did not hesitate to appoint Ms. Wallin as Consul General of Canada to New York. Her mission was to knit together as many new relationships as possible in cultural projects, commercial initiatives, and foreign policy. Canada's prime minister and foreign affairs minister both, having seen her skills on full display at the "Canada Loves New York" rally, embraced her potential to open doors in New York the way nobody else could.

Wallin was in her element, providing lavish entertainment, having her own car and driver, and staging an unending parade of prestigious receptions featuring notable Canadians to attract New York's biggest players. She forged a wide array of important American contacts, opening doors for other Canadians. Among numerous Canadians witnessing this tour-de-force on behalf of our country was John S. Elder, Q.C., a prominent Toronto lawyer who four times accompanied clients to Wallin's receptions to develop new business. "She was one very impressive lady," he recalled in 2014. "She could make things happen."

Canada's consul general was leading a heady, exhilarating life in Manhattan, deploying an over-the-top style compared to other Canadian diplomatic pushes that, in comparison, were long on frugality but short on results. In 2005, Wallin bought an oversized studio unit at 118 East 60th Street, a proper "white glove" address with covered circular driveway, doorman, and concierge. The high-end custom renovations to her thirty-fourth-floor Lenox Hill residence rendered it as charming as it was functional.

Her expenses were a contentious subtext, but this was not news. At the CBC, where money flowed and budget management was so loose that at one point program director Trina McQueen had to face the public and explain some $28 million was missing and nobody could trace it, Wallin learned nothing about restraint with public dollars. For Toronto power lunches, to which other movers and shakers arrived by taxicab, she was delivered by a CBC limousine, and later fetched and whisked away by the shiny black vehicle. When she had her own production company, it was standard industry practice to run all expenses through it, since they related one way or another to the TV shows she was creating and selling. Now in Manhattan as consul general with a specific mission from the PM to forge new Canadian-American business links, she just shifted from high gear into overdrive. Wallin excelled in her social and cultural task of bringing American high-rollers into a Canadian orbit, creating a positive glow about Canada by imparting the sense that our country had verve on a par with New York's.

Officials in the Department of External Affairs "had their hair on fire," as one insider told me, trying to control Pamela Wallin's spending, driving departmental comptrollers to complain to the Prime Minister's Office that she was throwing around money like no other diplomat even knew how. This apparent concern for financial rectitude disguised their real agenda, however. Wallin was getting results that bread-and-butter career diplomats could not even dream about, and jealousy was a factor. But appointment of a non-diplomat to a foreign posting was an especially sore point. The reason for complaining directly to the PMO about Pamela Wallin's expenses was that it was a choice way to rap Mr. Chrétien's knuckles under the pretence of financial management.

While that sideshow played out, though, Wallin would continue in what by now had become an indelible pattern in her successful career — incurring costs while getting the job done and, as an after-thought, either tossing receipts to somebody else to process or accumulating them to deal with "someday" as part of her never-finished paperwork. What a nuisance!

Two other patterns had emerged that were by this stage also definable hallmarks of the Wallin style: air travel and a whirlwind work schedule. Wallin could never have had the career she did without civil aviation. Wadena is a fine town, with the best wildfowl festival anywhere, but, two hours east of Saskatoon, it is not a crossroads of the world. From her teen years when she left town for high school, then university, then working at the penitentiary, next getting into broadcasting, Wallin was operating within the province, travelling by bus or driving her own car. After that, getting from Saskatchewan to the next places she worked, in Ottawa and Toronto, or flying down to Buenos Aires to cover the Falklands War for CTV, was only possible by airplane. Across Canada and around the world, Wallin's continuing career in television reporting put her into aircraft travelling with prime ministers, covering dramatic developments, and staying connected with the many people in her peripatetic life. As colleagues and friends routinely joked, "Pam lives on an airplane."

She knew airport facilities like the layout of her own home. She knew airline schedules by heart. She commuted between Ottawa and Toronto for many years as a national broadcaster, and added New York flights to the circuit, first as consul general and after 2006 as senior adviser on Canadian affairs to the president of the Americas Society and the Council of the Americas. Pamela Wallin continued flying to New York for three days' work a week from Toronto, and then from Ottawa after becoming a senator in 2008. This pattern was maintained for two more years, as she continued to hold this position while also working as a parliamentarian. As a senator, of course, she was also now flying to other spots in Canada and abroad — as she had always done with CTV and CBC — to pursue her work.

Wallin not only lived on airplanes but found this form of travel ideal for her habitual networking with our country's movers and shakers. She also used flights as her airborne office. "As I settled in for my third flight of the week," she wrote in 2009 for her Foreword to a book I was publishing of Patricia M. Boyer's newspaper columns, "I found that rare moment of quiet and calm, and therefore the opportunity to peruse a collection of columns written by my friend Patrick Boyer's mother." Pamela Wallin penned a reflective and uplifting message for the book. The quality of her effort was matched by her generosity in reading the manuscript and adding her prominent name to *The March of Days: Optimistic Realism through the Seasons of Life*, in tribute to a fellow woman journalist with Saskatchewan roots, my mother.

Her capacity for work overwhelmed many people. Sometimes I thought Wallin should just take a break and sort out her priorities. She seemed to be doing so much and, being constantly on the go, raced against herself as much as the clock. But this pattern was deep-seated. At university, she'd been involved in so many projects that "my life was one unending blur." In broadcasting, she'd rise in the middle of the night to prepare the early morning telecast. In the urgency of her stop-watch-tight routines, Wallin's need for efficiency often led her to say to others, "I'll do it myself." She knew how because over her career she'd learned just about every task that journalism incorporates, and she understood it would be fastest in the brief time available to complete something crucial — check a source, cue up some audio — herself. But often, colleagues instead heard her to be saying, "I can do it better than you." She could perform miracles, yet sometimes in an off-putting way.

In July 2006, completing her half-decade mission as consul general in New York, Wallin joined the board of Gluskin Sheff & Associates, a small but prosperous Bay Street investment and wealth management firm. The following month she became a director of Bell Globemedia, multimedia owner of the *Globe and Mail* newspaper and CTV television network. In 2007, she added the Calgary-based exploration company Oilsands Quest, Inc. to her roster of directorships. In March 2007, she became Chancellor of the University of Guelph. In 2008, adding a couple more corporate directorships, Wallin joined the board of Porter Airlines and Jade Tower, an antenna site and tower company. She became a member of the advisory board of BMO Harris Bank, and the board of an obscure entity called Ideas Council. With income and honorariums from these many positions, Wallin was financially very comfortable.

She worked just as hard in charitable organizations for which she received no payment, co-chairing the National Strategy Council for the

Mazankowski Alberta Heart Institute, and other volunteer boards such as the Ontario Institute for Cancer Research and the Nature Conservancy of Canada. She became a volunteer member of the Advisory Council of Breakout Educational Network, a non-profit public policy organization that I'd founded in 1995 with Manitoban Kitson Vincent.

Along the way, Wallin garnered some fourteen honorary doctorates and fifteen national and international awards, including being inducted into the Canadian Broadcasting Hall of Fame, receiving a national Visionary Award, being awarded the Toastmasters' "Golden Gavel," and twice being recognized by Queen Elizabeth for her public service and achievements.

If Canada had a celebrity, it was Pamela Wallin. Her work in New York had added an important international affairs component to her already impressive life. In 2007, Prime Minister Harper asked her to serve as a member of his independent advisory panel on Canada's mission in Afghanistan, a high-level group chaired by John Manley. Their work concluded in 2008. In February that year, Pamela Wallin was inducted into the Order of Canada, our country's highest civilian honour.

By year end, Prime Minister Harper asked Pamela Wallin if she believed in Senate reform. When she said "Yes," he invited her to become a member of his Conservative caucus as a senator. The people of Wadena took even greater pride in seeing her name on their water tower.

Born November 11 in 1974 in the Québec town of Maniwaki, Patrick Brazeau grew up off-reserve with his father, Marcel, an Aboriginal Canadian, living over his father's grocery store, Dépanneur Brazeau.

Originally, Maniwaki was on land that formed part of the Kitigan Zibi Anishinabeg Reserve, where Patrick's grandmother had been born, a full-status Algonquin Indian. Since then, the municipality had been carved out of the reserve and developed adjacent to it. When Patrick's grandmother fell in love with a non-native and married him, she was forced off the reserve. The Indian Act stipulated that native women who married non-natives forfeited their Indian status and had to quit their reserved homeland. The policy was designed to contain Indians, not see them multiply in number. She was, to Canadian law, no longer an Indian.

In 1985, the Mulroney government amended the Indian Act to end this discrimination against Indian women. Among the many thousands touched by this reform was the Brazeau family in Maniwaki. The Indian Act change applied not only to Indian women but their families, too. Eleven years after he'd been born Algonquin, Patrick Brazeau became an Indian in law as well as in fact.

Patrick's father did not want to move back to the reserve because he had his store in town and was conveniently settled in Maniwaki. The Kitigan Zibi reserve is large. It borders on Maniwaki at its southwest edge, is bounded along its western edge by the Eagle River, the Desert River to its north, and the Gatineau River on its east, making the heavily forested 184 square kilometers, with its many lakes and streams, the biggest Algonquin Nation in Canada, both in area and in population. Today, about half of Kitigan Zibi's three thousand members live off the reserve, while the others enjoy a well-developed community of grocery stores and hardware markets, a gas station, elementary and secondary schools with a library accessible to all, and gift shops. The reserve's sense of oneness is further strengthened by a local radio station, a day-care facility, the community hall, a health centre, police department, youth centre, the wildlife centre, and an educational and cultural centre.

As a young person growing up in Maniwaki, Patrick would daydream about his life and future, but in 1985 he had to confront a defining reality he faced as an Indian in Canada. He'd been an Algonquin *non-status Indian* living off reserve one day, and the next, because of Parliament's change to the Indian Act, he'd become an Algonquin *status Indian* living off reserve. The rights he'd acquired overnight imparted a lesson in absurdity to young Patrick. Its impact would become manifest over the coming two decades, in his radical reinterpretation of established Canadian policy governing Aboriginal peoples.

Part of young Brazeau's view resulted from the fact his theoretical upgrade in legal status meant next to nothing in real terms. The Government of Canada funded the system of reserves, and, generally speaking, chiefs within that structure along with their families and supporters were among the principal beneficiaries. Off-reserve natives like the Brazeaus, despite now gaining Indian status, were effectively excluded from this system and its financial benefits. Few spoke up for off-reserve natives, despite the fact they considerably outnumber their on-reserve counterparts. If democracy incorporated majority rule, and if fair government provided the greatest good for the greatest number, then the Indian Act system, in Patrick Brazeau's eyes, was neither democratic nor fair.

Patrick could do nothing about the situation at the time, though, and so he simply lived his life. He became fluent in Algonquin, French, and English. Strong and athletic, he played hockey and trained in karate. After graduating from local schools, Patrick went to Ottawa and enrolled at HMCS *Carleton*, a unit of the Canadian Forces Naval Reserve, which each year trains about 230 sailors. Next, he completed studies in social sciences at Gatineau's CEGEP, Heritage College. Then his desire to realign human rights, Aboriginal issues, and the outdated and dysfunctional regime imposed by the Indian Act led him to the University of Ottawa to study civil law.

In 2001, Brazeau abandoned legal studies for work with the Native Alliance of Québec, an affiliate of the Congress of Aboriginal Peoples, which represents native Canadians living off-reserve. He now saw a more direct way to advance Aboriginal interests, working for repeal of the Indian Act and implementing a new structure for First Nations' governance that would be more respectful of all indigenous communities.

Working at CAP exhilarated Patrick. Other people found him clear-spoken and intelligent. His powerhouse appearance — strong face, radiator smile, athletic build, piercing blue eyes, and long black hair — also helped attract others to him, and even gave Brazeau easy extra income as a model. As an appealing spokesperson for the organization, Patrick was named vice-chief in 2005.

The congress, of which he was now a chief, represents the interests of nine provincial and territorial affiliates, whose members include more than eight hundred thousand off-reserve Indian, Inuit, and Métis people. Such a voice as CAP's causes tensions within the Aboriginal community, however; the Assembly of First Nations, whose chiefs and band council governments speak for some 630 First Nations communities living on reserves, see themselves as the true lineal inheritors of Aboriginal rights connected to the land, and, thus, as the legitimate voice for Aboriginal peoples in Canada. Because over half of Canada's status and non-status Indians don't live on reserves, though, CAP says their interests are not effectively represented by the Assembly of First Nations. Many, it noted, did not choose to become dispossessed, but for generations had been driven into limbo by the Indian Act or forced to make the difficult decision of leaving their reserves to escape the poverty found there and to earn a livelihood or make a career. Moreover, because most of the $9 billion spent each year by the Government of Canada on Aboriginal programs and services goes to the reserves, CAP says this imbalanced allocation short-changes the off-reserve majority of Canadian Aboriginals. The two First Nations organizations are strong rivals.

On November 25, 2005, the Liberal government of Paul Martin, having spent a year and a-half consulting CAP, AFN, other national Aboriginal groups, and provincial and territorial governments, agreed at a meeting in Kelowna to boost funding in a big way. There would be an additional $5.1 billion over five years to improve housing, education, health services, and economic development for Aboriginal peoples.

Three days later, Prime Minister Martin's government was defeated in the Commons and a general election called for January 23, 2006. The PM made the so-called "Kelowna Accord" a centrepiece of his campaign. It embodied stark differences between Liberal and Conservative philosophy, respectively represented by Mr. Martin and Stephen Harper, leader of the Official Opposition. The Liberals, devoted to meeting Aboriginal interests by providing for specific aching needs, believed spending more money was essential. The Conservatives, devoted to the general imperative of reducing Canada's national debt, believed $9 billion a year was plenty. Instead of spending more money, already in short supply for a Canadian government with crippling annual deficits, Stephen Harper believed deeper change was needed. The Conservatives wanted to ensure that public funds already committed led to better results in the lives of First Nations peoples, and as part of that, would seek to establish financial accountability in band-council governance, along lines similar to the budget discipline required of municipal governments. The Conservatives would "support the principles and objectives" of the Kelowna Accord, said Mr. Harper, but would not commit to spend another $5.1 billion.

Stephen Harper's senior policy adviser, American-born and American-educated political scientist Tom Flanagan, had come to believe it necessary to revamp Aboriginal governance and the reserve system. In his 2000 book entitled *First Nations? Second Thoughts,* the political scientist at the University of Calgary described the reserve system as "anomalous and dysfunctional." He said, "Governments should help the reserves to run as honestly and efficiently as possible, but should not flood them with even more money." He added that government should focus attention and money on improving the lives of the eight hundred thousand Aboriginals who live off the reserves. In this, Tom Flanagan and the Congress of Aboriginal Peoples held carbon copies of each other's position.

On January 10, less than two weeks before voting day in the 2006 general election, Stephen Harper called for "a realignment of federal Aboriginal expenditures to include appropriate and adequate distribution of resources in order to accommodate the needs of off-reserve and non-status Indians." Only days before balloting began, CAP endorsed the Conservatives. A letter signed by National Chief Dwight Dorey and Vice-Chief Patrick Brazeau called Mr. Harper's position a "promising and respectful alternative to the status quo." On election night, January 23, Conservatives gathered in a Calgary hotel, and among those present, celebrating with prime minister–elect Stephen Harper the party's breakthrough victory at the polls, was Chief Dorey.

This Conservative-Congress alliance, founded on mutual agreement about a fundamental Canadian policy, meant the Congress of Aboriginal Peoples's voice in Ottawa would now be heard more attentively than that of its rival, the Assembly of First Nations. In November 2006, the Harper government increased CAP's annual budget from $5 million to $6.3 million, ensuring the Congress would have the resources needed for their common cause.

The Conservatives had gained strong backing from one of Canada's main Aboriginal groups, which meant the Harper government could take fresh approaches to Aboriginal issues "without appearing to be indifferent to native suffering," noted Ira Basen of CBC News, "or supporting the assimilationist positions advanced by Tom Flanagan." Even though CAP had been at the Kelowna conference, added Basen, "the Accord itself was a one-page document that no one had actually signed their names to," a fact that allowed the new government to say it was not bound by the agreement, making it easier for "Patrick Brazeau to help Stephen Harper drive a stake into it."

In February 2006, National Chief Dwight Dorey stepped down, and Brazeau's swift ascent continued as he was promoted to the position of acting chief. At CAP's annual convention that November, delegates keen for a new direction formalized the move, unanimously electing Patrick Brazeau their national chief.

From this country-wide platform, Chief Brazeau accelerated his radical campaign to dismantle the Indian reserve system across Canada, abolish the Indian Act, and reconstitute the traditional Aboriginal nations.

Chief Brazeau, speaking to a parliamentary committee about the Accord in November 2006, the same month his organization received significant increased funding from the Conservative government, said that while the process for the agreement seemed to be inclusive, the reality was that "Kelowna provided false hope for grassroots people — real people, in real need — while enriching organizations and the Aboriginal elite." The chief echoed the Conservative critique that the accord did not demand enough accountability for the billions of dollars that would flow to First Nations, nor break down how much would stay on reserves or go to natives living off reserves.

"The reserve system as we know it is broken and needs to be replaced," Brazeau had already told Ron Corbett in a 2007 Ottawa *Citizen* feature article. "Billions of dollars are poured every year into that system and what do we have to show for it? Reserves that are scandals, that's what."

Chief Brazeau's bold campaign to advance his message of a new day for Canada's First Peoples incorporated filmed messages, newspaper op-ed features, radio and television interviews, speeches, work at the United Nations, and addresses to such international conferences as a Chilean gathering on problems facing "urban indigenous peoples." Everywhere in Canada he told audiences that "anybody serious" about solving the problems on Canada's reserves "needed to get rid of a lot of chiefs."

The Indian Act should be replaced by "more progressive legislation," Brazeau argued, not only to reconstitute true Indian Nations, but also "to reflect the tenets of modern-day governance." Such reforms were needed "to end the status quo which overwhelmingly supports a system of Indian Reserves where poverty and hopelessness remain pervasive."

In tandem with abolishing the Indian Act, Chief Brazeau advocated the amalgamation of many First Nations communities "to restore the traditional Aboriginal nations," consolidating the 633 native communities in Canada into perhaps sixty or eighty. Why did it make sense to keep living on the scattered parcels of mostly marginal land onto which non-Aboriginals had relegated them? He envisaged how the ten Algonquin reserves in Québec and Ontario would become one, with something similar for the Cree people, the Mohawks, and other Indian nations across the land.

Upon re-establishing the traditional structure of Aboriginal societies, to help harmonize these communities among themselves and create First Nations that were no longer divided and weakened but indigenous nations of self-reliant peoples, Patrick Brazeau envisaged a far more rational and responsive allocation of the nearly $10 billion in federal funding going to Aboriginal programs and services in Canada every year. This would include substantial redirection of resources to natives living off reserve: a large, ignored, generally impoverished, and trouble-plagued component of Canadian society.

"The lion's share of the federal government's more than $9-billion investment in Aboriginal programs and services supports the system of Indian Act reserves," Chief Brazeau reminded policy makers in an op-ed explanation of his program for the Ottawa *Citizen*. "Yet Statistics Canada census data show that 79 percent of Canada's Aboriginal peoples live away from reserve communities." In the article, the chief complimented Prime Minister Stephen Harper for having "committed" his Conservative government to addressing this imbalance. The chief knew his goal of fundamental reordering of Canada's governance structure for Aboriginal peoples would require a prime minister's full support.

The Prime Minister's Office, tasked with developing the Conservative government's revamped approach to First Nations, which included band council financial management and budget accountability similar to that of municipal councils across Canada, took due note of Chief Brazeau's clearly articulated agenda. It was rare to find an Aboriginal leader with clear-eyed analysis and candid expression of views about a fundamental Canadian issue that, in political Ottawa, was a toxic topic. It was also encouraging that Chief Brazeau's program coincided on key points with recommendations of the PM's senior adviser, Tom Flanagan.

Right on cue, many chiefs across Canada, whose positions derive from the status quo that brash young Brazeau was vigorously challenging, responded in an orchestrated attack. Their power and income, flowing from the Indian Act and existing patterns of federal government funding, would be undermined if such radical ideas gained traction, let alone ever got implemented. Brazeau's message was that Canada's Aboriginal communities needed to be brought under "the tenets of modern-day governance." Representatives of band councils and the Assembly of First Nations leadership flooded Indian and Northern Affairs Minister Jim Prentice with letters. They also began a wider campaign to derail Patrick Brazeau, knowing the easiest way to stop a message is to discredit its messenger.

As radical and threatening as CAP's national chief appeared, Patrick Brazeau had not come up with his plan to overcome the stagnant life for many of Canada's Aboriginal peoples on his own. Nor, for that matter, had Tom Flanagan. A decade earlier, the largest study ever conducted into the Aboriginal condition in Canada had reached similar conclusions. The Progressive Conservative government of Brian Mulroney had not been content only to restore full legal status to Indian women and their families, but had more boldly laid the groundwork for far-reaching changes by launching a full-scale Royal Commission on Aboriginal Peoples. Its final report, which reached Parliament in November 1996, recommended dismantling the reserve system and reconstituting Canada's traditional Aboriginal nations.

These proposals had been distilled from years of hearings in First Nations communities across Canada, and included active participation by respected elders. Yet strong opposition to such change by those entrenched in and benefiting from the existing system, when combined with the Liberal government's reluctance to move ahead with recommendations of a review it had not initiated, consigned the ideas to oblivion — at least until Chief Patrick Brazeau gave them fresh wings.

As Ron Corbett noted, "Aboriginal people in Canada are an increasingly young, displaced, populace. Yet when the federal government funds Aboriginal programs and services, it continues to pour eight dollars out of every nine into a reserve system that was devised in the nineteenth century. To people like Patrick Brazeau, that's like maintaining a fleet of wooden ships when the *Bismarck* is bearing down on you."

Clearly, Brazeau knew the stakes were high and that the status quo could easily lead to real instability. This view found further support elsewhere; Canada's security and intelligence services were warning the Government of Canada about rising threats within the country from militant First Nations groups, and internationally recognized insurgency expert Lieutenant-Colonel Douglas Bland, retired from the Canadian Forces, was writing his warning on the same subject, a novel entitled *Uprising*, which I published in 2010.

For Patrick, it was obvious that the kind of change he sought required political action at the centre. Increasingly, he entertained the idea of pursuing that course of action himself. "I may take a stab at federal politics some day and run for elected office in the mainstream," he explained to Corbett near the end of their interview. "I've thought about that."

While working for fundamental change, CAP's national chief also focused on specific measures that supported his vision of Aboriginal people acting in society to achieve their goals, not only on a tribal basis, but as individuals. Brazeau sought to inculcate a vital sense of personal responsibility for one's own future because he felt strongly about self-sufficiency for Aboriginal peoples as individuals, not only as communities, which is particularly important for the majority of isolated natives living off-reserve. He fought to repeal section 67 of the Canadian Human Rights Act because it stipulated that communal rights under the Indian Act superseded the rights of individuals under the Canadian Human Rights Act. Brazeau argued this impeded the individual human rights of Aboriginals and was particularly detrimental to Aboriginal women. In this stance, CAP's national chief was supported editorially by the *National Post*, the *Globe and Mail*, and other major organs of public opinion.

On June 20, 2008, Chief Brazeau happily applauded passage of the Harper government's Bill C-21, which repealed section 67. Viewing this as another step toward the larger goal of reforming Aboriginal governance, he suggested this extension of human rights protection by the Harper government "will ultimately lead to the dismantling of the Indian Act itself."

Before the year was out, Prime Minister Stephen Harper invited the highly visible spokesperson for marginalized Aboriginal Canadians to become a senator. It was one of the PM's most strategic appointments.

CAP's national chief could continue to press, with whatever additional resources and status the Senate of Canada offered, alternative views that challenged positions held by Liberals and the Assembly of First Nations.

Chief Brazeau, who had contemplated federal politics "one day," radiated his sunniest smile and agreed.

Prime Minister Harper believed the lustrous presence of Mike Duffy, Pamela Wallin, and Patrick Brazeau would enhance the Conservative Party and even, as a side-effect, the Senate itself.

In a tightly controlled Parliament, moreover, he reasoned that senators, like MPs in the House of Commons, no longer needed to possess much legislative prowess. If their attendance in committee was sufficient to provide quorum, and if they supplied the expected votes in committee and in the chamber whenever summoned by the Conservative whip, that would suffice as far as Senate duties mattered.

Lacking prior political experience would not serve as a hindrance to being a member of Canada's highest legislative chamber because any decisions it made about legislation would continue to be orchestrated from the Prime Minister's Office. No real thinking or independent action as law-makers was required, or even wanted. The three celebrity senators could devote themselves instead and to much better purpose advancing the Conservative Party and Conservative policies in Canada's wider reaches beyond Parliament Hill.

The prime minister had yet to discover how taking a chance on famous self-starters would be like gambling with the family's grocery money.

CHAPTER 3

Senators in Free-Float

No other prime minister has taken bigger risks in Senate appointments than Stephen Harper. Yet as he has demonstrated — forging a new political party by merging two, claiming Canadian Arctic sovereignty all the way to the North Pole, negotiating a full-frontal trade treaty with the European Community — reward awaits leaders bold enough to take big risks. Launching individuals with large public personas on a mission to expand the Conservative Party from the novel staging area of the Senate of Canada might also pay substantial rewards, too.

But getting to this point required the PM to work himself out of a major conundrum.

Before becoming prime minister he'd strongly and frequently asserted his clear view that senators should be elected. Consistent with this position, after forming a Conservative government in 2006 he'd refused to appoint any. Vacancies in the upper house had, as a result, piled up for three years. The shortage of active members had been making it hard for the Senate, especially in its thinly populated committees, to even give the appearance of working. Yet Mr. Harper still refrained from appointing senators, waiting for a new era when Canadians would elect members of Parliament's upper house instead, although his government's legislative initiatives for this, launched with enthusiasm in 2006, had met resistance and not yet become law.

Facing defeat by a coalition of opposition parties in the Commons, the prime minister looked at the bigger picture and swiftly filled all vacancies. Eighteen new Conservative senators, including his trio of celebrities, were officially sworn in in January 2009, almost doubling the party's total to thirty-eight. Partisan critics needed no prodding to claim in public that his appointments contradicted the prime minister's pledge to make the upper chamber an elected body. In private, every politician understood that thwarting the opposition parties as he was now doing, trying to make the best of an awkward situation, was an instinctive survival move any prime minister would make. But to include high-voltage stars in his roster of senators was a new departure. That is what really raised eyebrows among political savants.

A "celebrity senator" would be a high-risk senator.

As national chief of the Congress of Aboriginal Peoples, Patrick Brazeau stood uniquely apart, and not just because he was the youngest senator in Canada. Tattooed and pony-tailed, holder not only of a black belt in karate but of radical views on Aboriginal governance, the new Conservative senator would gain attention in ways others could not and dared not.

As political broadcasters turned senators, Pamela Wallin and Mike Duffy faced their own unique hazards. They became targets of focused attention from their former journalist colleagues because of special interest, envy, or old scores to settle. With contemporary news media having developed a narcissistic self-interest, ever primed to report on themselves or examine media relations, it was guaranteed that any awkward or disconcerting story about such prominent journalism personalities as Pamela Wallin or Mike Duffy would get big play. While quite a few reporters are secretly hungry for the power and paycheque that accompanies being a press spokesperson for government, many other journalists feel that colleagues who "go over" to government or political parties betray journalism's code of detached and balanced observation and resent how such deserters tend to undermine their own credibility as independent reporters. There could always be payback for those who traded a television studio for a Senate office.

Even when still journalists, Pamela Wallin and Mike Duffy had each achieved notoriety not only for reporting the news, but, controversially, for *being* the news, just like Patrick Brazeau. If the best predictor of future performance is past behaviour, the Conservatives had reason to be anxious about their new stars. Special safeguards, from effective time-management supervision to proper financial accountability, would need to be in place as the Conservative Party began to deliberately and continuously thrust these big-name senators into the public eye to benefit its partisan interests.

In the weeks between the December 22, 2008 public announcement that he was going to the Senate and his official swearing-in ceremony on January 26, 2009, Chief Brazeau suggested that remaining as national chief of the Congress of Aboriginal Peoples would allow him to serve as a valuable bridge between the Senate and the First Nations' leadership.

That was sort of the idea the PM had, initially, as well. Such continuity would not be out of step, after all, with the tradition of allowing senators to retain prior affiliations with public policy organizations and special interest groups, continue their connections to private companies, and even acquire lucrative new directorships on corporate boards while serving as members of the Senate. Senators are not precluded from simultaneously holding paid positions outside Parliament. They need only disclose any roles for which they earn more than $2,000 annually, and do not even have to say how much they earn from each position.

But critics of an Aboriginal leader affiliating himself with the Conservatives were quick to decry this prospect of the senator remaining chief. The fact he was Patrick Brazeau, despised ruffler of headdress feathers of many establishment chiefs, ensured a hot new onslaught of criticism to discredit him even before he could give his maiden speech in the Senate. Overlooking any benefit that blending his two roles may have entailed, they complained that, as chief and senator, Brazeau would collect two six-figure publicly funded salaries. That was all it took to stir outrage.

So it was. Taking his cue from the PMO, which was busy damping down criticisms about several of the new senators in the prime minister's surprising about-face gang appointment, Patrick Brazeau dutifully resigned as chief of the Congress of Aboriginal Peoples the day after becoming a senator.

Two days before his swearing-in, and to complete his constitutional requirements for office, Patrick Brazeau also bought land worth $10,800 at Chertsey in his Québec Senate district of Repentigny.

* * *

Pamela Wallin's place of residence became an issue shortly after Prime Minister Harper named her a Saskatchewan senator on December 22, 2008. Wallin responded by saying her visits to Wadena and the property she owns in the municipality satisfied the residency requirement.

When questions about this persisted, following her swearing in on January 26, 2009, an effort was made, in concert with the PMO, to close down further discussion about the residency requirement. Her executive assistant, Shelley Clark, informed news media that Senator Wallin "would be making no further comment on this issue," adding that "the Senate Speaker and Prime Minister's Office are satisfied that all requirements have been met."

Political scientist Howard Leeson in Regina expressed skepticism, saying Pamela Wallin lived in New York and Toronto and had not lived in Saskatchewan for decades. "Senators are full members of Parliament, whose salaries are paid for by taxpayers, so it's not unreasonable to ask about their basic qualifications," he told reporters. A former head of the University of Regina's political science department who'd joined the Canadian Plains Research Centre, Leeson added that although "residency" is not spelled out in the Constitution, it typically could be evidenced by being able to vote, qualifying for a health card, and filing tax returns in the province. "Simply owning property and visiting Wadena once a month wouldn't seem to fit the bill," he suggested, though confirming it was "up to the Senate itself to make that determination." He told reporters he'd written to the Senate but had been unable to get clarification.

The reason nobody connected with Parliament's upper house was forthcoming in answering Professor Leeson was quite simply that there was no clear policy in place to tell him about, as Senator David Tkachuk, chair of the Senate's Internal Economy Committee, would later confirm. A second good reason was that the PMO had unequivocally asserted that the prime minister's new Senate appointees satisfied all requirements of office. Nobody running the Senate wanted to publicly contradict the all-powerful PMO.

On her appointment to the upper house, Senator Wallin pledged that as soon as the provincial government set up a voting system for Saskatchewanians to elect senators, she'd resign and seek election to her seat. Not only was that stance consistent with the private commitment the prime minister had extracted from his new Senate appointees to support Senate reform, but it was the kind of forthright public statement people had come to expect from Wallin. So it came as no surprise.

What did surprise many, however, was her acceptance of a senatorship as a Conservative. During her long career as a broadcast journalist, Wallin had covered all parties and maintained the necessary political neutrality. Like the CBC's Don Newman and the *Globe and Mail's* Jeffrey Simpson, Wallin did not vote in federal elections when working in Ottawa, knowing that to mark a ballot required making a choice and that doing so would make it harder to regain the objectivity true journalism demands.

Moreover, before starting into journalism with CBC Radio in the 1970s, Wallin had been a member of the NDP. And when she departed journalism years later in the 1990s, it was to accept a diplomatic appointment from Liberal Prime Minister Jean Chrétien. Reinforcing the sense that the former New Democrat now had an affinity for the Grits was the fact she'd worked closely with Liberal foreign affairs minister John Manley to host the "Canada Loves New York" post-9/11 rally in Manhattan, and that she and Liberal senator Jerry Grafstein had been jointly honoured in 2003 by the Canadian Society of New York for their ongoing devotion to strengthening ties between Canada and the United States. Although Consul General Wallin's work in New York as a partisan-neutral diplomat kept her away from party affiliations, her personal history suggested that if she had any at all, they'd likely be with the NDP or Liberals.

Yet Wallin had reached a station in life where the direction of the Conservatives and the opportunities for public service as a senator enabled her to step vigorously into her new role. She would be effective for Stephen Harper's party, not in the folksy but persistent manner of Mike Duffy, but as a suave and seductive spokesperson, especially with urbanites in places like Toronto, where she'd lived for years.

Between the pair, Wallin and Duffy could cover both sides of the street on their upbeat march to sell political conservatism.

Prince Edward Island's newest senator charged heavily out of the starting gate.

Just days after he'd been sworn in, I began receiving Tory-partisan emails from ebullient "Mike Duffy, Conservative Senator." As a former PC member of Parliament, the Conservative's candidate against Michael Ignatieff in the 2008 general election, and an intermittent financial contributor to Conservatives over the decades, my name and address were evidently in the party's database.

Had the Grits named Duffy to the upper house, I smiled, my Liberal friends would have been receiving these exhortations instead. At first it seemed that a procession of prime ministers — Trudeau, Clark, Trudeau again, Turner, Mulroney, Campbell, Chrétien, and Martin — had missed real opportunity by not getting Duffy onside. Sure, there was the adage "Be wary of one who wants something too greatly." But if you were a Tory, Senator Duffy was great!

Duffy's pent-up lust for being in the Senate of Canada — never a joke, in his mind — was now re-channelling him from being Canada's most ardent supplicant for a senatorship into Canada's most assertive partisan in the Red Chamber. His skills were those of a communicator. His talent in politics was to "get the message out." The prime minister had found his personal paladin. The two were seen on countless stages together in an unending flash of photo-ops, and provincial Progressive Conservative leaders were soon just as pleased as the national party leader to bask in the celebrity glow radiating from "the Senator," whose presence nobody could miss or mistake.

Duffy's urgent political messaging included frequent appeals for campaign donations. I began to sense, though, that these were being scripted by someone else, and sent from an office other than the senator's own. However such early donor appeals may have been orchestrated behind the scenes for the closely run Conservative money-vacuuming operation, soon enough the powers-that-be decided that personal contact with Senator Duffy would work better than continuing his avalanche of emails.

He began appearing across Canada, a magnet drawing people to public events and party gatherings, a Maritime Midas turning local fund-raising opportunities into lucrative events helping Conservatives amass a bulging campaign war chest. Yes, Senator Duffy was great!

In the meantime, the prime minister, his government having survived, developed the same fondness for using the Senate all his predecessors had. Among other appointees that year was Conservative campaign chair Doug Finley. One might have imagined a person running the party's disciplined election-ready machinery as a full-time paid job from the Senate would see the necessity of coordinating his Senate colleague's time and allocating Mike Duffy's expenses in ways to ensure immunity from partisan counter-attack. Basic adherence to conflict of interest rules would have been a starting point too. Payment of constant campaigner Duffy's expenses by the Conservative Party rather than the public treasury, another.

It is hard to be a celebrity; even harder, a celebrity senator.

In the House of Commons, members represent people who have chosen them over other candidates because of who they are as individuals and what they stand for politically. They also have an intense connection to a particular electoral district. Their supporters volunteer to work for them because great effort is needed for re-election campaigns. MPs have a public identity. Constituents admire MPs for their authentic qualities, such as their accomplishments as a job-creating entrepreneur, a fine educator, a respected lawyer, an innovative food-producer, a resilient unionist, an ardent civil libertarian, or an advocate for society's vulnerable members. They do not want their MP to change but to remain true to character. All the while, MPs must engage forces, both partisan and parliamentary, that render them more like each other, buffing off their individuality. They run for election under a common logo and using approved "messages" they are forced to stick with, and in the Commons they vote in unison, while struggling to preserve some vestige of their individual personality that got them into Parliament in the first place.

For senators, most all of this is absent.

The pressures to perform and remain actively connected to a specific community do not exist. Able to hold office to age seventy-five, free from any concern about being fired, with no imperative to get re-elected, senators free-float in time and space, the Chris Hadfields of Canadian politics.

So a senator merely carries on, being who he or she was before, miming their prior life on a new stage. That's what made it impossibly hard for a good man and a great hockey player like Frank Mahovlich — no ice surface. And very difficult for talented queen of skiing Nancy Greene — no downhill slopes. Patrick Brazeau remained true to himself when he climbed into a boxing ring with Justin Trudeau for a worthy cause. Pamela Wallin continued to play herself, but looked so out of place in the becalmed upper house that she dubbed herself "an activist senator." Mike Duffy, too, remained just who he always had been, with no incentive to change and no need to, either.

The Senate can swallow whole those not sufficiently well defined by strong character. But those already larger than life can attract in Canada's political arena all the attention of a gravity-free, camera-performing astronaut in space.

Senator Wallin was not cutting back, but becoming more active than ever, thanks to the freedom of action offered by the Senate. Her 1998 memoir *Since You Asked* made clear that Wallin never shied away from work, but in fact was addicted to it and defined by it. "Doing it all" summed up her hectic, frenetic, and upwardly mobile pace.

Before long she was active in Conservative Party outreach, lending her name and panache to a variety of party events across the country. She continued to hold her prestigious and remunerative positions on boards of directors, carried on with her wide-ranging charitable work, and remained active as chancellor of the University of Guelph and as senior consultant to the president of the Americas Society in New York. She participated in conferences on the status of women, not only in Canada but internationally. It was a full agenda, fuller than most could handle, and certainly more demanding than senators in Canada normally take on.

In the Senate, however, she was equally engaged. Wallin took up chairing the Committee on National Security and Defence, and served at the same time as a member of the Senate's Foreign Affairs and International Trade Committee. Both were natural progressions, building on her prior roles with Prime Minister Harper's Advisory Panel on Afghanistan and as Canadian consul general in New York, and drawing too on the interest in military matters she'd absorbed hearing her adored father talk about his experiences in the RCAF, her experience as honorary colonel of the Royal Canadian Air Force as a mentor and role model for military personnel at Ottawa headquarters, and her role as advisor to Breakout Educational Network on projects pertaining to the essential link between the Canadian Forces and citizens. She had more invitations than could be fitted into her crammed itinerary, despite long hours and frequent flights.

From his new Senate platform, Patrick Brazeau continued his outspoken critique of behaviour and attitudes he felt detrimental to First Nations' progress, arguing Canadian Aboriginals should not expect to be supported by taxpayers, "to sit back, wait for the government to give me handouts. Maybe be on welfare, maybe drink, maybe take up drugs."

Such direct talk, drawn from his personal observations and experiences, rankled many. So would his later criticism of the "Idle No More" protests and the liquid-only "hunger strike" by Chief Theresa Spence of Attawapiskat Reserve during which, Brazeau suggested, the Cree chief actually gained weight.

Few in the Canadian south or in our country's cities, remote from the desolate western shore of James Bay in northeast Ontario, had much direct information about the on-going difficulties of Attawapiskat. But anyone following public issues was familiar with impressionistic reports of sickness, moulding homes, sewage contamination, lack of work, and the reasons for a blockade on the reserve's road to a nearby mine. Many Canadian eyes were thus opened when, a couple of months later, on May 14, 2013, CBC Television's Terry Milewski presented a mini-documentary about the thriving Cree community Oujé-Bougoumou on James Bay's *eastern* shore, in Québec.

"Little noticed by the world outside," said Milewski, "the Cree of northern Québec are writing a startlingly different story than their cousins on the western shore of James Bay, with self-government, revenue-sharing, decent schools, and new development. Mining companies are welcomed instead of blockaded. And no hunger strikes." The forty-year struggle by Québec's Cree is paying off, he observed, noting how the reserve's neat streets "feel like they're on a different planet than Attawapiskat. If the stop signs weren't in Cree, you'd think the rows of warm, solid homes were in a suburb down south. Shiny new courthouses, band offices, recreation centres, and police stations are being completed. There's no crisis to summon reporters from Toronto or Montreal."

The veteran CBC reporter contrasted this prospering and healthy self-governing First Nation in Québec with its troubled Ontario twin, so recently publicized through the protest of Chief Spence. This enabled some CBC viewers to connect the dots and realize that Senator Brazeau, despite his undiplomatic critique, might be onto something.

In the main, however, the Algonquin's hard-edged views neither resonated with non-Aboriginal Canadians weighed down by historic guilt about First Nations, nor sat well with the chiefs whom Brazeau considered part of a government-reserve nexus that, despite good individuals, was corrupt systemically. Those wanting to discredit Patrick Brazeau stepped up their campaign.

AFN leaders pointed to high spending and poor accounting at CAP as belying what Brazeau espoused, to which the PMO and others countered that these had been Congress problems before Patrick Brazeau became national chief, not during his time as leader. In Ottawa, Canadian Press reporter Jennifer Ditchburn zeroed in on Senator Brazeau's attention to work, as measured by his attendance at meetings.

As a multi-cultural society, Canada comprises a variety of social values that do not uniformly mesh; not all communities have elevated the alarm clock and day-planner to the same life-controlling status. Moreover, a comprehensive evaluation of senators' behaviour patterns reveals that, although quite a few are hard-working and deeply devoted, many display lax performance — a number work by means other than sitting at committee meetings, and many *non-Aboriginal* senators are notoriously missing in action. Such caveats did not prevent reporter Ditchburn from combing the Senate's attendance register, however, to report that Senator Patrick Brazeau had been absent from 25 percent of the Senate's seventy-two sittings between June 2011 and April 2012, 31 percent of the meetings of the Human Rights Committee, of which he was deputy-chair, and 65 percent of meetings of the Senate's Standing Committee on Aboriginal Peoples, of which he was a member.

Jennifer Ditchburn displays quick intelligence and a good grasp of details in her reporting, and in 2013 she emerged as one of CBC Television's reliable commentators on the Senate expenses scandal's unfolding segments. That she earned the enmity of Patrick Brazeau for reporting those statistics about his attendance is hardly surprising, though. She had framed his performance according to narrow tests of parliamentary life and a traditional view that sitting in meetings is a measure of giving value.

Brazeau's greater realism and quicker insight led him to understanding that whatever transpired in these meetings mattered little because their outcome had already been determined in the Prime Minister's Office. Repeal of section 67 of the Indian Act had not been sparked by some initiative taken by a parliamentary committee, he understood, but by a prior decision reached in the PMO. Nor did reporter Ditchburn's tidy time-tally acknowledge that a young and energetic senator, not yet socialized into the routines of long-serving parliamentary veteran senators who dutifully show up and get attendance stars beside their name, would render much greater public service by rebelling, at some level, against those acclimatized to equate attendance with accomplishment.

Indeed, accounting for these more nuanced yet substantive factors, one should be amazed that Brazeau attended three-quarters of the Senate's sessions, two-thirds of the Human Rights committee meetings, and one-third of the Aboriginal Peoples committee gatherings. This is especially so because news reports about Patrick Brazeau in this period suggest that difficulties in his personal and family life were complicating his performance, at least at the Senate. He told reporters his attendance problems were caused by personal and private problems. Journalists gratuitously added that "he refused to elaborate," without acknowledging that if he had, his personal problems would no longer be private and his life would become even more complicated.

In any case, the Senate forum is not the only place a member works. In an arena removed from the Senate's precincts, as noted, the Conservative senator and the Liberal Party's Justin Trudeau faced off in a boxing ring on March 31, 2012, for a celebrity match that raised $230,000 for the Ottawa Regional Cancer Foundation — a beneficial accomplishment no other parliamentarians equalled. For losing, Brazeau cut off his pony-tail and hoped for a return bout.

Also outside the Senate during this same period, Senator Brazeau worked in service to the Conservative Party, as he'd been asked by the

PMO and party leaders to do, raising election campaign money by speaking at party fund-raising events. People wanted to meet the colourful Aboriginal senator, a man of growing reknown for his barely controlled intensity and plain speaking.

Celebrity senator Patrick Brazeau was someone to be heard because he stood apart from the herd.

Mac Harb, in contrast, was something of a loner and an organization man, certainly not a politician with the large national following of a celebrity.

But his Liberal Party loyalty and his steadfast support for Jean Chrétien through the internecine party warfare waged by Chrétien forces against the partisan troops of leadership rival Paul Martin had caused the grateful prime minister to thank the Ottawa MP with a Senate seat in September 2003. Mr. Harb thus was able to look forward to the prospect of another quarter century of highly remunerative and pleasant work close to home.

Born in Chaat, Lebanon, on November 10, 1953, Mahmoud Harb immigrated to Canada to study at the University of Ottawa. After graduating, he worked as an engineer at Northern Telecom and taught at Ottawa's Algonquin College. In 1985 he launched what would stretch into a twenty-eight-year career in public office, getting himself elected to Ottawa City Council and rising to become the city's deputy mayor in 1987 and 1988.

Next came election to the House of Commons in 1988. "Mac" Harb was elected the MP for Ottawa Centre riding, and everything else about him was Ottawa-centric, too. Ottawa was where he'd earned his university degree, worked as a professional, taught community college students, got active in municipal government, and lived.

It was when he became an MP that Mac Harb and I first became acquainted. I admired the ability of the Liberal Party to attract Canadians of different national origins and respected Mac himself for his detached perspective on national affairs, which I felt stemmed from both his more objective perspective as a clear-eyed immigrant and his technical pragmatism as an engineer.

The Liberal Party Mac entered was one torn by leadership rivalries, and he sided with Jean Chrétien and supported his bid to replace John Turner in 1990. For the next fifteen years in the Commons, Mac remained a quiet Chrétien loyalist. Then, for a decade in Parliament's upper house following his 2003 Senate appointment, he dutifully supported Liberal measures and opposed Conservative ones.

A couple of times, though, he took his own initiative on special issues, enjoying the freedom to float and be true to his own values and concerns. In 2006 Senator Harb brought forward a private member's bill to establish and maintain a national registry of medical devices, noting in his remarks that one in ten Canadians had some form of medical implant. "Perhaps in this chamber, fellow senators," he added, looking around at his aging colleagues, "the ratio is slightly higher."

Just how well his humour was received is not revealed in the Senate *Hansard* report, but Harb's acknowledgement of the aging and ailing population in Canada's upper house, with senators' increasing demands and dependence on Canada's health care system, would recur as a theme in 2013 when both senators Duffy and Wallin, speaking against their removal from the Senate because of the expenses scandal, stressed their personal need for medical coverage due to heart ailments and cancer problems, respectively. In voting to oust them, the senators, not without a measure of self-interest, would let them retain health care coverage.

Senator Harb's second legislative effort focused on the East Coast seal hunt. He expressed his anger over an annual slaughter of marine mammals of negative net benefit to Canada given the little amount of food produced, a declining market for sealskins, and hefty government subsidies to support its uneconomic operation. He viewed the slaughter as especially barbaric because it occurs at the height of whelping season, with mothers nursing the young, unlike the deer hunting season, which takes place in autumn when fawns are weaned and neither mother nor offspring so vulnerable. However, the seal hunt is fervently embraced within Canada by certain segments of society.

Against that background, Senator Harb entered the fray with a bill in March 2009 to restrict the hunt to those with Aboriginal treaty rights. A couple of years later he returned with a different bill to ban the commercial seal hunt. Next, in May 2012, he made a third try, with a bill opposing the annual hunt. Such proposals are disdained by a significant majority of parliamentarians, but Senator Harb was prepared to take heat over the issue because of his beliefs, which were bolstered by his research and understanding of marine science. He was recognized for his efforts by the hard-line animal rights organization PETA, or People for the Ethical Treatment of Animals. Given political alignments and PETA's extremism, it was a mixed blessing for Harb to be honoured by the U.S.-based organization as its "Canadian Person of the Year."

Mike Duffy's elevation to the upper house sparked criticism from Islanders because of his lack of familiarity with P.E.I. issues and his questionable validity as a senator, both arising from the fact he was not living on the Island.

Although he'd grown up in Charlottetown and started his career in Prince Edward Island, Duffy had left the island in his youth and had lived many years in Ontario. When the Liberals contemplated putting him in the Senate as one of theirs, they balked after ascertaining that Duffy's absence from the Island since the mid-1960s meant he was no longer considered much of an Islander in Prince Edward Island itself. Giving him a Senate seat would not be a smart appointment politically, despite how people on Parliament Hill perceived him.

Retired University of Prince Edward Island law professor David Bulger weighed in with his view that, despite reassurances to the contrary from Conservative Senate Leader Marjory LeBreton and the prime minister's chief of staff, Nigel Wright, Duffy's lack of Island residency invalidated his senatorship because the Constitution requires a senator to be resident in the province he represents.

Again the PMO took a hand in dampening critics. To address this residency challenge, Prime Minister Harper's office announced in January 2009 that Duffy would move back to Charlottetown "where he owned a home with his brother, but would likely also keep his Ottawa home." Significantly, it was not Senator Duffy who sought to assuage concerns about his qualifications. Instead, the PMO spoke for him. At least this suggested someone in the PMO had been detailed to watch over and protect the PM's new celebrity senators, a smart move given the specific and hostile attention they would get from everybody dissatisfied with Conservatives being in power— a sizable, talented, and influential contingent.

So strongly did Duffy now identify with the Conservatives, and so deeply did he want to push back against entrenched anti-Conservative attitudes of many Canadian journalists, that he began to carry the battle to his former Parliamentary Press Gallery colleagues and slam journalism schools for churning out leftist graduates.

In March 2010, speaking to Nova Scotia Conservative party members at Amherst, Senator Duffy attacked the journalism program at University of King's College in Halifax, and other schools of journalism, for exposing students to Noam Chomsky and critical thinking. "When I went to the school of hard knocks, we were told to be fair and balanced," Duffy was quoted in the Amherst *Daily News*. "That school doesn't exist anymore. Kids who go to King's, or the other schools across the country, are taught from two main texts." According to Duffy, they are *Manufacturing Consent*, Noam Chomsky's book on mainstream media, and books on the theory of critical thinking.

"When you put critical thinking together with Noam Chomsky, what you've got is a group of people who are taught from the ages of eighteen, nineteen, and twenty that what we stand for — private enterprise, a system that has generated more wealth for more people because people take risks and build businesses — is bad," Senator Duffy was reported saying. He then told Conservatives they had nothing to apologize for because most Canadians are not "on the fringe where these other people are."

A similar message had been delivered in 2002 by seasoned reporter Anthony Westell in his book *A Life in Journalism,* in which he examined "News Versus Truth" and said the role of journalists is to report the news not make the news. But Westell wrote reflectively, and without Duffy's newfound combativeness. The senator was casting seeds of resentment over the fertile terrain of Canada's newsrooms where they would sprout, once the seasons changed.

* * *

Pamela Wallin, sworn in as a Canadian senator representing Saskatch-ewan, owned property in Wadena, the hometown she returned to at Christmas, the place her parents and sister still lived. A Wadena perspec-tive was a counterpoint lens through which she tried to view national issues to determine their relevance to Canadians outside her immediate political and media circles in Ottawa, Toronto, and New York. Being in Saskatchewan helped her remain grounded in who she truly was.

Yet coming home also reminded the Conservative senator of where she'd first entered politics as a radical New Democrat.

Movement across the political spectrum is not uncommon. Brazeau had wanted to enter into "mainstream" federal politics, and while his statements supported initiatives by Conservative prime minister Harper, he'd also left the door open to the Liberal's, noting how Stéphane Dion had "an open mind" on Aboriginal questions.

Duffy's movement on the spectrum was more like that of a slalom skier adept at veering left or right to the Liberals or Conservatives, reflecting perhaps his more traditional and pragmatic Maritime political philosophy.

Pamela Wallin's case was quite different and, because fewer women have prominent public careers, her transition through political philoso-phy stood out more starkly.

Her shift was as dramatic as that of, say, Barbara Amiel, who tran-sitioned from Communism as a young woman to being a forcefully articulate exponent of right-wing philosophy several decades later, moving from her initial opening with CBC Radio to her platform as newspaper and magazine columnist in Canada and Britain in tandem with husband Conrad Black. In a similar vein, Wallin started political involvement in the anti-American socialist Waffle, opening her media career in a small role with CBC Radio in Regina, and ended up a pro-American Conservative senator. Both women became public figures and chronicled their progress in mid-life memoirs —*Confessions* in the case of Amiel, *Since You Asked* from the pen of Wallin.

For each, early years of hard work in low-paying jobs gave way eventually to high living and mass media roles in which they influenced public thinking. Many Canadians learned the background details of both —Amiel's multi-thousand-dollar shopping sprees for handbags and shoes, Wallin's condominiums in New York and Toronto — and shook their heads in a response located somewhere between shock and envy.

But it was Pamela Wallin, not Barbara Amiel, whom Prime Minister Harper appointed to the Senate, and because of her position in public office, it was she whose spending came under greater scrutiny. That was the peril of being a celebrity senator: there was no option but to carry on the way you've been performing, to float free and stay true to what made you the star you are.

Celebrities who become politicians may either be "parachuted" candidates who are landed by the party that recruited them into safe ridings where they can easily win election to the House of Commons, or appointees dropped into the Senate with even less hassle.

Whichever route is chosen to turn these star public personalities into parliamentarians, they share a common denominator of being accustomed to media attention. They know what it's like to have their personal life scrutinized. The best have acquired almost instinctive techniques for self-preservation, and learned ways to preserve a buffer zone of privacy. What they have much less familiarity with is the way government works, especially on the inside, and particularly in the continual byplay between journalists and politicians.

"Politics and the media play the same symbiotic game and each needs — and uses — the other," wrote Pamela Wallin in 1998. "But," she added, "there are rules."

It is one thing to acknowledge rules, another to comprehend their application — or to think that because you know what the rules are from the media side of the ramparts, you understand how they work on the political side. The real problem for a great many senators, something that is magnified in the case of those who are celebrities, is that they are simply not politicians.

Although some Canadians envisage a utopia of non-partisan senators, including Liberal leader Justin Trudeau who unveiled a plan in January 2014 to appoint members to the upper house free from party affiliation, we want hockey players who know how to skate and legislators adept in the fundamentals of politics, skills developed by being active in the game. A problem for many of Canada's senators is their lack of well-honed skills needed to work as legislators and to survive the political arena's unique demands. In the same way, the apparent understanding journalists and public commentators exude about government and politics lacks an essential foundation of experience inside parties, campaigns, and governments.

One might think a journalist would know better than anyone how reporters sniff out stories and, therefore, why extra care is needed to not misstep or deliver a juicy morsel of news to those waiting around with notebooks and cameras. But such logic does not fit reality. The fact that the two most media-savvy senators in Canadian history, Pamela Wallin and Mike Duffy, did so many things to encourage, and even provoke, members of the Parliamentary Press Gallery by their actions and practices suggests that perhaps a different law governs: the more familiar one is with the news media, the less one heeds a politician's instinctive wariness of journalists.

Another problem facing free-floating star senators who have a sense of entitlement is their assumption that others will tend to grunt-work and minor details.

Many senators — not just Indian chiefs, highly paid hockey players, and network star broadcasters, but also corporate executives and senior officials — have been accustomed to others handling the "details" of arranging travel, paying service accounts, keeping up with financial administration, filing accurate expense accounts, and collecting appropriate reimbursements. In their prior careers, somebody else looked after a lot of things necessary for them to do their jobs, like arranging limousines, air travel, hotels, working the telephones, reserving restaurant tables, picking up dry cleaning, buying clothing, organizing personal grooming, massages, and shopping for food and liquor. Those coming from Canada's big television news networks had become accustomed to the pattern that lots of people were always around to look after things.

Even if the star performer or top person in a hierarchy is the one pushing cash at people, gaining the goodwill that such munificence provides, it is some "underling" who has to collect a receipt, jot down a note about the payment, or later be handed a clutch of the star's receipts to process through the reimbursement regime. In 2013, a former employee of Senator Colin Kenny went public with her complaint that she'd spent a lot of time looking after his expenses, booking personal activities, delivering and fetching his cleaning, and the like. In the corporate world, personal assistants do all this, and more, for senior executives all the time. In the Senate, however, employees are paid from public dollars, with the general understanding they are being engaged in public business. But the Senate's "honour system," combined with uncertain rules and long tolerated practices, created a murky realm of tacit compliance and wilful abuse.

The Senate and its code of financial conduct, if problematic in the case of Senator Kenny, were especially ill-equipped to mesh a star senator's acquired sense of entitlement with public expectations for accountability in spending money. Moreover, the distinction between personal affairs and public activities, being foggy, was hard for senators themselves to adhere to. They were, most all of them, on the public dime and using parliamentary facilities and services while conducting private business, continuing professional roles, and doing partisan political organizing. Life was one glorious blur as a senator free-floated through it.

Whatever problems were brewing behind the scenes, however, for the first couple of years the public verdict on Stephen Harper's picks of celebrity senators was that, once again, the prime minister really knew what he was doing.

For the Conservative Party's biennial conference in June 2011, delegates to the event at Ottawa's impressive new convention centre were delighted, and television viewers across Canada entranced, to see two very familiar broadcasters who for years had sent them parliamentary news and reports of political developments from the nation's capital over CBC and CTV airwaves. Pamela Wallin and Mike Duffy basked in enthusiastic partisan approbation at centre stage, co-hosting the national Conservative convention in Ottawa.

CHAPTER 4

The Elements of Scandal Combine

In the spring of 2012, Canada's auditor general, Michael Ferguson, released an audit report on several senators' claims for expenses. In some cases, he noted on June 13, Senate administration did not have documents to support claims for travel and living expenses.

For anyone working inside Parliament familiar with Senate administration, this revelation was not news; it was a common thing, a picayune detail. But to someone unconditioned by senatorial norms, this matter of missing paperwork for expenses approved and paid was, well, scandalous. Even so, accounting sloppiness could not have become fodder for a titanic battle in Canadian politics unless other elements were also converging to make a truly major scandal.

Behind the stone-piled walls in the east end of the Parliament Buildings, the Senate of Canada is controlled by its all-powerful Standing Committee on Internal Economy, Budgets, and Financial Administration. The Senate's administrators report to this committee. Almost everyone refers to it as "the Internal Economy Committee" to conveniently shorten the long name; this subliminally leads to the overlooking of its role in supervising budgets and financial administration — a case of terminology revealing truth.

To appreciate the depth of the problems in the financial administration at the Senate, a comparison with Parliament's other house provides a quick lesson. Over at the House of Commons, in the west end of the Parliament Buildings, MPs come and go quickly — the result of Canada having the highest turnover rate of elected representatives in any of the world's democracies. The financial administrators are permanent employees with real power who take a firm hand in budget management. With passing years, they continue in office and get to know everything about the operations and weaknesses of parliamentarians. They lead each new intake of fresh MPs onto the approved financial pathways and become their firm guides along the journey. They have sharp pencils, even sharper eyes.

When a rule came in back in the 1980s that MPs could not hire family members, two of my colleagues winked as each one hired the other's daughter to work in their offices for the summer. The Commons Budget Office could not be hoodwinked by such a ruse, because its employees knew what to watch out for and also had a comprehensive system in place for cross-checking and verifying all aspects of an MP's expenses. The small scandal that resulted created red faces for the two Ontario MPs and loss of jobs for their girls, while serving as a morality play for all MPs: Never mock the budget rules or the financial administrators who enforce them.

Back in the Senate, in stark contrast, the appointed parliamentarians enjoy extended longevity in office while the hired staff come and go. The culture of lax budget control, which is the result, had already become well entrenched in the days when senators held office for life. The absence of administration was camouflaged by hallowed pretence of the Senate's "honour system."

The mythical "system" — it was actually an absence of system — continued to be the Senate's operating cultural norm, even after the 1960s when the rules were changed so that senators could no longer hang around past age seventy-five, simply because it was embedded in the very fabric of the place and because new senators appeared on the scene just a few at a time, sometimes even one by one through a lone appointment. These scattered novices acclimatized themselves to long-established practices. They did not question the existing order — three readings needed for a legislative bill to pass, no expense chits needed for submitting a reimbursement bill — any more successfully than a novitiate entering the priesthood might challenge the intimidating power and dumb inertia of a system that had lumbered along for centuries. Even with mandatory retirement, most senators remain on Parliament Hill for decades. New arrivals acclimatize. There are plenty of old hands to teach inductees the ropes.

All of this means that senators can intimidate the staff ostensibly running budget operations. They do so with ease. Unlike the Commons, members of the Senate have an upper hand over those trying to impose modern administrative procedures and controls. "I'll still be here long after you're gone," one senator asserted in one such showdown, forcing a staff administrator to relent. While not always expressed quite so bluntly, this attitude is part of the operating culture of the Senate. Its members are in charge of themselves and run this public institution more like their private club.

Reinforcing this order of things is the fact senators are appointed by the prime minister. Around Parliament Hill, the wish of a prime minister is as potent as a military commander's order to a subordinate. Few working on The Hill, including staff at the Senate, are immune from this deference to power. Even with two factors that can offset somewhat this fear of the PM — being of a different political party, and supposedly having some independence as a senator — the reality is that budget officers and financial administrators working for the Senate have little incentive to stir things up, for example, by trying to impose tighter control over spending, or by causing embarrassment to the prime minister over the "minor" financial sloppiness of his appointees.

It is not the case that most of the financial issues that arise in connection with the Senate are the result of deliberate attempts to cheat the system. Senators are good people who've had fascinating lives before reaching the upper house, and whose life experiences make each one abidingly interesting as an individual. Any Canadian fortunate enough to do so is enriched by the educational experience of conversing with a senator. Each has so much to teach. Many have rich contributions to make to public affairs, and try gamely through the muted channels of the Senate to do so. Few of them, though, have been administrators seasoned in running a large, diverse, tradition-bound organization spending $92,500,000 a year in a politically contentious environment.

The result is that those appointed to advance partisan interests focus their attention on political organization and fund-raising; those appointed in recognition of their past accomplishments devote themselves mostly to basking in such glory as the Senate offers; those appointed to get them out of cabinet or remove them from some other public role where they have become an impediment to the prime minister generally resign themselves to drawing a generous salary and accepting that their future is behind them; and the ones with years of senatorship ahead who want to promote a worthy cause of special personal importance devote themselves to that. With all those subtractions from a total membership of 105, a relatively small number of senators remains available for, or is even interested in, dedicating energy and time to the internal economy, budgetary, and administrative matters of the place.

It is mostly the "political" senators, previously distinguished by devotion to party and elections, who want to be on the Internal Economy Committee. They have been drawn to power and its exercise in the past, and remain that way still. As a consequence, those running the upper house as members of the Internal Economy Committee tend to look at things less through the lens of a chartered accountant or a professor of public administration and more through the eyes of instinctive power wielders serving the best interests of their party, while in the process seeking the least embarrassment or controversy for the institution they are running. As members of the Senate's most powerful committee, they are "players" in Ottawa's power game.

And among those players, the three most pivotal when the expenses scandal exploded were senators David Tkachuk, George Furey, and Carolyn Stewart-Olsen, with Conservatives Tkachuck and Stewart-Olsen indispensable in arranging the elements of an explosive scandal.

Senator David Tkachuk of Saskatchewan became known to Canadians, when the expenses scandal broke, as chair of the committee.

A down-to-earth man who earned his B.A. from University of Saskatchewan in the 1960s and followed that with teaching, David found politics a bigger draw by the 1970s. He became a member of the provincial Progressive Conservative Party when it was as flat as a field of Prairie wheat after a summer's heavy hailstorm. He set about rebuilding the party from the ground up, turning it into an effective political force that carried Grant Devine into office. David accompanied Saskatchewan's new premier to the Regina Legislative Buildings as his principal secretary.

Mr. Tkachuk's commitment to the PC cause extended into the national realm as well. After becoming chair of the John Diefenbaker Society in 1992, he arranged funding to keep the former prime minister's papers at the University of Saskatchewan's John G. Diefenbaker Centre.

In June the next year, a grateful Brian Mulroney appointed Tkachuk to the Senate. In 1997, from the Senate, he co-chaired the Progressive Conservative national election campaign, and in 2005 Conservative leader Stephen Harper named him "Senate Chair" for the general election that took place in 2006, when the Conservatives formed a national government. Senator David Tkachuk had earned his respected reputation in Conservative Party circles.

Liberal Senator George Furey of Newfoundland and Labrador had plenty of experience with Senate administration by the time the elements of the Senate expenses scandal came together, having himself chaired the committee from October 2004 to March 2010. He was now deputy chair of the Internal Economy Committee, in keeping with the tradition of partisan balance.

George Furey had also started his career as teacher, but after leaving the profession, he went on to qualify to practise law in 1984, specializing in labour arbitration at his St. John's firm. He also volunteered with community groups, and served on professional boards and provincial commissions. The pull of politics was strong. In 1989, he had a senior role in the provincial Liberal election campaign that brought Clyde Wells to power, and in 1995 chaired Brian Tobin's leadership campaign as the federal minister of fisheries and oceans became the province's new premier. He then chaired the Liberal landslide victory campaign in the ensuing general election.

On the federal front, George Furey was equally impressive, co-chairing successful general election campaigns in Newfoundland and Labrador for Prime Minister Chrétien in 1993 and 1997. In August 1999, Mr. Chrétien brought campaign organizer Furey closer to hand, placing him on the public payroll in the Senate of Canada from where he chaired the Liberal's 2000 general election win in the province. From 2012 on, when the Senate expenses issues began to grow complicated, Senator Furey would by instinct as an administrator, lawyer, and partisan maintain a close watch on Liberal interests and keep his colleagues informed, but keep his public profile low.

Joining them on the Internal Economy Committee, Senator Carolyn Stewart-Olsen played a pivotal role developing the Senate expenses scandal. Born in Sackville, New Brunswick, Carolyn Stewart became a registered nurse, working at hospitals in her home province, then in Québec and Ontario. By 1986, she'd become head nurse of ambulatory care at Ottawa's Grace Hospital, and later served as nursing manager for four primary health care departments at Carleton Place Hospital. As her twenty-year nursing career specializing in emergency and trauma care progressed, Carolyn witnessed enough wasteful practices in public administration and health care spending to make her receptive to Preston Manning's trumpet call for stringent fiscal management and accountability. Bureaucratic duplication, waste of money, and practices that put institutions and professionals ahead of patients could all be surgically removed, she believed, if the right person held the scalpel.

In 1993, Carolyn turned from nursing to politics, first volunteering in the Reform Party's communications office, then being hired on staff as a press aide working under Preston Manning, who now was leading a major party in the Commons with fifty-two MPs. She continued through the turbulent emergence of Reform's first successor party, the United Alternative, and then its second, the Canadian Alliance. When Stockwell Day, an MP who'd been Alberta's Progressive Conservative finance minister, defeated Manning for the Alliance leadership, Carolyn lost her job. Still dedicated to the Reform cause, she began working for Deborah Grey, the first Reform MP to have been elected and also a Manning loyalist. By 2001, Carolyn emerged as press aide to the "Democratic Representative Caucus," a dissident group of MPs, including Grey, who'd bolted from the third version of Reform, the Alliance, as led by Mr. Day.

As Carolyn Stewart-Olsen came to know Medicine Hat MP Monte Solberg, another of the dissident Alberta MPs in the group, she formed a productive working relationship with Alison Stodin, a skillful Parliament Hill staffer hired by Mr. Solberg when he'd first arrived in Ottawa as a freshly elected Reform MP in 1993 carrying a book of political science definitions as part of a crash-course on Parliament.

Stodin quickly became a trusted, respected, and reliable resource to Solberg, Stewart, and other neophyte Reformers on The Hill, imparting what she knew about the Commons Order Paper, drafting parliamentary resolutions, researching issues by tapping directly into the resources of the Parliamentary Library, printing and mailing free reports to constituents, ordering supplies, and the intricacies of House of Commons budget administration. Her prior years with Progressive Conservative riding associations in her hometown of Hamilton, her university studies in politics, on-going reading of books on political philosophy, and her years of dedicated work for several parliamentarians made Stodin an indispensible human pillar supporting Reform's parliamentary presence. Carolyn and Alison worked effectively together.

The following year, 2002, when Stephen Harper challenged Stockwell Day for the leadership of the Alliance, Carolyn Stewart-Olsen signed on as Mr. Harper's press secretary in what became a successful campaign. During their battle to prevail, a strong bond of loyalty and mutual respect was forged between the two. It fused even stronger in 2004 when Stephen Harper campaigned for, and won, the leadership of the reconstituted Conservative Party of Canada. Stewart-Olsen was frequently in contact with the party leader and had more ready access to Mr. Harper than even political staffers senior to her. When Mr. Harper became prime minister in 2006, she followed him into the PMO as his press secretary and director of strategic communication. In August 2009, the PM announced that Carolyn Stewart-Olsen, a resident of New Brunswick, where she and her husband have a home at Cape Spear, would become a senator. Prime Minister Harper now had a tested and trusted confidant in the upper house, an active supporter seasoned in the backrooms of parliamentary politics. She joined Senator Tkachuk on the Internal Economy Committee's smaller, and even more powerful, steering committee, where delicate decisions needed to be taken on how to handle the problematic expenses of Stephen Harper's celebrity senators.

In 2010, veteran journalist Peter Worthington made one of his formidable forays into the operations of Canadian public affairs by recommending, in the *Toronto Sun*'s December 22 edition, that the Senate of Canada needed "a watchdog." It was his way of saying the Internal Economy Committee was coming up short, that independent eyes were needed to ensure senators complied with rules and did not waste public money.

Although Worthington's slant on issues was often at odds with the conventional wisdom prevailing in Canadian political circles, on this issue he was the exponent of a fairly widely held view. Anyone who paid attention knew the Senate did not meet present-day standards in any department. The puzzle was that anybody would even waste their time or talent bothering to mention it. Especially for so skilled a marksman as Peter Worthington, the hoary Senate seemed too easy a target.

But in the eyes of the Internal Economy Committee's chair David Tkachuk, Worthington's in-bound missile required some counter-fire. "One matter that has drawn media attention, and which unfortunately has been misinterpreted, concerns the manner in which our expenses are approved," the senator responded.

"Senators," Tkachuk explained, "are responsible and accountable for their expenses." He was referring, of course, to the long-established "honour system" whereby members of the upper house submit chits, or stubs, or receipts, or scrawled notes, or nothing at all, then declare that the spending was for "Senate business" on a covering sheet and sign it. Tkachuk claimed that this system of individual accountability and responsibility was backed up by a strong administrative regime. "The Senate also has rules and limits to govern what is paid, and a vigorous process that ensures only legitimate and reasonable expenses are paid."

That process involved expense claims being reviewed by the Senate's Finance Directorate of accountants and bookkeepers. These employees, Tkachuk explained, "ensure that each expense passes the test of the Senate administration's rules before payment is made," adding that each claim was "reviewed line-by-line by two separate financial officers." If they found "anything questionable," Tkachuk as chair of the Internal Economy Committee would submit it to a committee of three other senators for review, "before payment was made."

The system was so rigorous, apparently, that if this committee of three senators was not satisfied, chairman Tkachuk would take the questionable expense before a committee of fifteen other senators to defend the expense. He added that senators sometimes even referred an expense issue to outside auditors for independent review. The powerful senator than confidently concluded that the Senate's own internal process of "a second set of eyes examining our expenses" was "more stringent and onerous" than any "second-level sign off involving auditors" would be.

While Senator Tkachuk dished out such public reassurances, behind the scenes this "stringent and onerous" verification process continued to examine the submitted expense claims of senators Duffy, Wallin, Harb, Brazeau and several others who would later come under scrutiny for seeking improper reimbursements or submitting claims unsupported by proper documentation. But at the time, following "line-by-line review by two separate financial officers," the Senate approved and paid them all. This had actually been going on for years.

In his response to Peter Worthington, the chair of the Internal Economy Committee further noted how "the auditors found no evidence of wrongdoing. Most of the problems concerned paperwork and documentation, and we are attending to these problems." He concluded with a final gratuitous salvo, "Senators are dedicated to moving forward in making the institution more accountable to the Canadians they serve, and will continue to strive to manage public funds conscientiously and carefully as we carry out our duties as parliamentarians."

It was after two more years of this conscientious and careful management that the auditor general of Canada released a report on his audit of Senate administration, stating the upper house had "a reasonable financial management framework in place." Because "reasonable" was obviously less than "first-rate," the auditor general recommended that "Senate Administration should ensure it has sufficient documentation to clearly demonstrate that expenses are appropriate" and "should bring to the attention of the Internal Economy Committee any cases in which the Administration believes that required documentation is not sufficient to clearly demonstrate that expenses are appropriate."

In response to that revealing recommendation, the Senate, still cocooned in its traditional culture of budget management, defensively asserted that it had "clearly defined rules for processing expense claims that are rigorously enforced. As in the private sector, the senator signs his or her expense claim form and attaches the receipts, according to strict rules and guidelines."

In broader terms, through various public statements between 2010 and 2012, Senator Tkachuk further asserted that for senators' expenses, "rules and limits govern what is paid," a "vigorous process ensures only legitimate and reasonable expenses are paid," and that "strict rules and guidelines" were in place and operating.

By this time, another twenty-four months of expense claims by senators who would subsequently be driven from office on the grounds they'd made false or inappropriate claims had been submitted, reviewed, approved, and paid. The most rigorous part of the Senate's administrative process appeared to be its ability to cut cheques.

Almost any organization with sizeable amounts of money on tap will spring leaks. Employees may make mistakes on the paperwork, greed could entice one or two to float claims that will enrich them, and every now and then a fraudster might test how successfully he can scam the operation.

If the funds are not earned by an organization's own hard efforts, but simply turned over from taxpayer revenues each year — for instance to a government department, Crown corporation, or body like the Senate of Canada — a further insidious element may also creep in. Many in government today view public money almost as being what economists call a "free good." The numbers are abstract. Figures appear on a screen rather than printed on physical currency that is seen and touched and is able to impart a tangible sense of value.

A reckless attitude about dollars emerged during the 1970s that would be abhorrent to an earlier era, when Prime Minister King's finance minister James Ilsley treated money raised through taxes as a "trust fund" he and others in government operated, with a fiduciary duty, on behalf of the Canadian people. Such frugality gave way to an "Easy come, easy go!" outlook, a transition over several decades that included structural removal of safeguards. Financial controls were loosened, budgets swelled, national debt soared. I explore the causes for this in book-length detail in *"Just Trust Us": The Erosion of Accountability in Canada* and also *Hands-On Democracy: How You Can Take Part in Canada's Renewal*.

Throughout it all the Senate carried on with its antiquated honour system and loose financial administration, and so, as if in some perverse nightmare, the rest of public sector spending seemed to be finally catching up with senatorial standards of practice.

There have been, fortunately, several countervailing forces.

Partisans, auditors, and reporters were poised to curb those ripping off Senate money or just mindlessly splashing it away. Examining how the expenses of senators were being handled in practice, each would ensure, in their different ways, that the latent potential of the Senate expenses scandal would become real.

The "partisans" in the Senate are the Liberals and Conservatives who, from the upper house's inception in the 1800s, have populated the place and run it.

Although they sometimes glow about the collegial bond they share and the reputed bi-partisan nature of their committee work, the truth is a large majority of senators arrive on the job as devoted and instinctive partisans. In moving to the Senate, they may become more relaxed, but they do not generally become less political. Each Tory or Grit habitually suspects the motives of his or her opposite numbers and keeps a trained eye on them while smiling pleasantly.

Counting on partisan rivalry to enhance accountability is as astute as it is economic, because sharp eyes and sensitive ears are necessarily present where the action takes place and law enforcement officers are generally absent. The practice has been embedded in Canadian political culture since the 1800s when two judges (one a Liberal appointee, the other Conservative) heard disputed election cases under the Dominion Controverted Elections Act, and in the statutorily enshrined tradition of appointing scrutineers from rival political parties at polling stations in elections, still in effect today under the Canada Elections Act. In the Commons, an Opposition MP chairs the Public Accounts Committee. In the Senate, opposing partisans are chair and deputy chair of the Internal Economy Committee.

Even so, partisans are only dependable for accountability to the extent they themselves are not complicit in some subversion of proper administration. Senators, working together and often forming friend-ships with colleagues, abetted by late night conversation over drinks or dinner, may gradually discover where each has skeletons buried. A truce of non-disclosure may be declared in certain cases, producing a tacit conspiracy of silence among fellow political players.

Looking the other way also fosters "the culture of entitlement" among senators, a number of whom feel they are owed whatever benefits they choose to claim. As a result, senators lose a sense of perspective and acquire a relatively lax approach to expenses. When confronted with the seeming transgressions in the expenses scandal, a number of senators, both Liberal and Conservative, would be outspoken about the expense claims of senators Harb, Duffy, Brazeau, and Wallin. But in the main, the partisans in the Senate were least effective in curbing abuses of any of those who might have transgressed.

Rather it was partisans in the Commons, primarily the NDP, acting as the Official Opposition and on principle opposed to the Senate's existence, who were the most effective politicians trying to cope with the issue. They, at least, kept the scandal alive, giving time for others to do their more effective work.

This is where auditors, the second force for bringing financial mismanagement and budget skullduggery to light, help keep behaviour in line. In the process, these arms-length vigilantes added a major new element to the emerging scandal of Senate financial administration.

In addition to reviews of Senate administration such as the auditor general of Canada carried out in 2012, the Senate itself retains professional auditing firms for dispassionate evaluation from time to time, as Senator Tkachuk noted in answering Peter Worthington. Between 2005 and 2012, outside auditors got the call nine times, principally to review overall spending, but also to examine several specific expenditures.

Typically, the auditor's report on findings is generally worded, its recommendations cast in broad terms of process, and the Senate's response one of saying that it agrees, is already implementing the proposed improvements, and remains dedicated to protecting public funds. Auditors are more regulators than revolutionaries in terms of what happens at the Senate, but nevertheless their presence does from time to time have a sobering, if not a corrective, effect.

A crucial third element among those investigating the Senate expenses scandal is the cadre of reporters covering Parliament for various news organizations. They would emerge as the most unsettling players amidst the Senate's process of financial oversight and ethical vigilance. Without journalists, the problems at the Senate could not have been become the national preoccupation they did.

The Parliamentary Press Gallery, and the news organizations it feeds across Canada, transported the details out of Senate committee rooms and over the country's airwaves, into newspapers, and onto hand-held screens.

Robert Fife, Ottawa bureau chief for CTV News, became an early and authoritative chronicler of the snags that several senators had hit with their expense claims. In March 2012 he broke stories about senators Mac Harb and Patrick Brazeau being under the gun for money the Senate had paid them as an allowance for housing costs and meals. From then on, he became a leading Ottawa reporter for this story, steadily broadcasting new developments over the months to come, often the first to do so.

Mr. Fife is a seasoned political reporter who'd started in the par-liamentary bureau of NewsRadio in 1978 and moved to UPI and next Canadian Press in the 1980s, emerging as a newspaper columnist for Sun Media and then the *National Post* before moving into television with CTV. He acquired an abiding interest in scandalous aspects of politics, in 1991 co-authoring a book entitled *A Capital Scandal: Politics, Patronage and Payoff — Why Parliament Must Be Reformed*. Robert Fife also has further media clout as executive producer of *Power Play*, CTV's daily political affairs show from Ottawa that is the permanent replacement for *Duffy Live*, which ended when Mike Duffy left the network to become a senator at the end of 2008.

Robert Fife's background knowledge of Parliament Hill, his fertile network of contacts, his national media platform as a network broad-caster, and his lead in scooping Senate scandal news all combined to make him a natural recipient for anyone at the Senate wanting to leak information about newsworthy senators who were overstepping ethical bounds on their expenses.

Fife reported as early as April 2013 that Nigel Wright had provided Mike Duffy some $90,000 to pay back the challenged expense claims. He also reported that there was another part of the deal, one of Duffy's conditions; that condition specified that the Senate's Internal Economy Committee would go easy on Duffy in its report, and that the Steering

Committee — controlled by senators Tkachuk and Stewart-Olsen — would whitewash whatever the Deloitte report said after auditing the P.E.I. senator's claims.

Whether Mr. Fife's source was a member of the Internal Audit Committee, or a Senate staffer, or someone else, is hard to confirm. Fife himself sticks to his understandable practice of never giving interviews about his journalism. Protecting sources is as crucial as it is challenging. When the RCMP asked him for copies of emails or other documents about the deal between Nigel Wright and Mike Duffy, which the CTV bureau chief had been reporting about authoritatively, he took a pass. It was not the role of journalists to do the work of the police. The work of all reporters continued, instead, to be to keep adding whatever new information they could to the story, giving it shape as a genuine political scandal.

In the days to come, senators offering "no comment" when scrummed, Prime Minister Harper being peppered with precise questions from Opposition Leader Mulcair, allegations in RCMP affidavits sworn to justify court orders for access to peoples' private records — all would provide the Parliamentary Press Gallery with content to keep the story alive.

The politically rewarding nightly play Mr. Mulcair's inquisition gave him and the NDP on national television would reinforce and extend a closed loop of spiralling fascination about the scandal. The intimacy and immediacy of live-streaming, unfiltered commentary, and trending tweets would lift the scandal like nothing in Canada before, causing CBC's Peter Mansbridge to marvel on-air when being interviewed by CBC's Ian Hanomansing about the scandal, or when himself hosting discussions with panels of insiders and political observers, over "how this story has legs."

The connectivity of traditional news channels and individuals participating with tweets, real-time opinion surveys, and ready online access to financial records, RCMP affidavits, and auditors' reports would create a cybernetic connection continuously feeding upon and reinforcing itself. People with cameras in their phones who captured developing scenes of the human drama — Mike Duffy walking by people in uncharacteristic sphinx-like silence, Patrick Brazeau coming down the steps of a Gatineau courthouse — and uploaded them, would often see their clip broadcast repeatedly over the major networks.

* * *

If Canada's biggest political scandals erupt when an individual reporter persists in investigating, pushing ahead when auditors wilt, prodding relentlessly after law-enforcement agencies fade, it is often because he or she has clues nobody else does.

Supporting journalistic scrutiny are the so-called "whistle-blowers" who enter the scene unpredictably. Some "go public" and gain notoriety, burning their bridges and ensuring that they will never be able to return to their place of work, even picketing Parliament Hill or giving television interviews, the way Pascale Brisson did when publicly ventilating her complaints about her employer, Liberal senator Colin Kenny, in 2013.

Other tipsters demand secrecy and journalists are as resolved to protect them. In 2004, Ottawa *Citizen* reporter Juliet O'Neill received a dossier of privileged documents related to Maher Arar, a Syrian-born Canadian, and refused to disclose to the RCMP her source of information after her story about the extent of Mr. Arar's alleged terrorist involvement was published. That brought the Mounties, armed with search warrants, in an 8 a.m. raid to her residence and the newspaper's offices to seize notebooks, computer hard drives, files, and other records, and led to subsequent litigation on the constitutionality of such seizures.

No journalist knows when a tipster may intentionally spill information: a loose-lipped official may slip a secret after one drink too many in some relaxed setting distant from Ottawa's chilly norms of secrecy; an anonymous email might arrive; or an unmarked envelope could come sliding under the office door. While "leads" to a story are normal, these special insider sources are random. Big journalistic scoops often hinge on a whistle-blower.

As intriguing as this role of journalists and their secret spies can be, such espionage is not the only dimension to whistle-blowing in Ottawa. Some insiders go not to the press but up the chain of command for redress of a wrong they discover being done. During the early 1980s, Bernard Payeur, a financial systems analyst in the Department of Foreign Affairs, discovered that staff had defrauded taxpayers of more than $7 million and that the practice had been underway for some time. He told senior departmental officials, expecting the fraud would be stopped and the culprits held to account. A decade later, Allan Cutler, a senior procurement manager at Public Works and Government Services, noticed irregularities in spending Sponsorship Program funds in Québec, which he reported to his superiors. In both cases, officials tried to cover up the abuses and launched a campaign of reprisal against the civil service whistle-blowers.

Going over the head of those directly implicated, hoping to reach someone high enough in the hierarchy to act responsibly, is the preferred choice of many imbued with the corporate values of their organization.

In the case of the Senate expenses scandal, the whistle-blowing of Pamela Wallin's assistant Alison Stodin would be credited for moving the issue from one of internal Senate management to an independent audit by Deloitte, the subsequent public unravelling of the expenses fiasco, and its ultimate investigation by the RCMP.

No fiction writer could credibly concoct all the shocking twists and improbable developments that kept unfolding around this national scandal over some thirty months. And few if any would imagine plotting such a riveting human story in so arcane a venue as Canada's hoary Senate. Yet in real life, that is precisely where the elements combined.

CHAPTER 5

Ignition

After Auditor General Michael Ferguson's mid-June 2012 report embarrassed Senate administrators over lack of supporting documentation for expense claims by two of seven senators he'd audited, those fingered felt the blowback. They scrambled to shore up the unsupported claims. It was a matter of reputation.

But it wasn't just the individuals the auditor general's findings had made to look incompetent. The Senate itself did not wear this well, nor did the Harper Conservative government, pledged as it was to eradicate wasteful public spending. True, the amounts were like pennies compared to the billions of taxpayers' dollars wasted in bungled defence procurements, but Canadians chatting at Tim Hortons could more readily latch onto amounts closer to their own budgets than those incomprehensible gazillions of dollars. News reports about senators' expenses began to upset people. Reporters looked for more Senate wrongdoings and found enough to keep the story going.

For the individual senators impugned in the developing scandal, each case was unique. But collectively, I said in a CBC Radio interview, they revealed a "culture of entitlement" that had become part of the Senate. That explained why some senators, already well paid by the upper house and earning additional income in the private sector, felt they could acquire even more money through spurious reimbursement claims. With not one such case but a number, I suggested, greed was being incubated, rather than extinguished, by the Senate's own privileged patterns of operation.

The Senate itself displayed a "pattern" of corruption. More than avaricious individuals were involved. The Senate's style of administration had enabled this problem that was now coming to light. The news was not about a single event, but multiple acts over time in which the Senate itself was complicit.

The issue was not just whether Patrick Brazeau had pulled a fast one by claiming an in-law's Maniwaki apartment as his "permanent home." That bit of evidence was also a clue about something more questionable in the institutional practices of the Senate.

Besides the Parliamentary Press Gallery's inquisitive reporters, a nation of citizens was now watching ever more attentively. Reporters like CTV's Robert Fife and the Ottawa *Citizen*'s Glen McGregor looked deeper and found the problem was not just missing taxi chits or non-existent restaurant receipts. Senator Pamela Wallin's air travel claims stood out like a mountain peak against the Prairie flatlands of other senators' flight costs. Senator Mike Duffy claimed money for days he could not have been on "Senate business" because Parliament had been dissolved for a general election or he was vacationing in Florida, and some of his meal claims covered repasts he'd eaten at home.

Having publicly asserted to Peter Worthington that, "as in the private sector," a senator "attaches receipts, according to strict rules," the Internal Economy Committee's chair Senator David Tkachuk wanted some paper filing, urgently, to justify or correct the humiliating lapses. Still, the chairman was uneasy. He hoped no payments had been made for amounts the Senate should not have reimbursed from public funds, especially to prominent Conservatives senators.

His fellow Saskatchewanian's travel claims were high, even for a senator who "lives on an airplane." Tkachuk knew the costs for his own flights between Ottawa and their same home Prairie province. Pamela Wallin announced she would review her claims, in light of the fact the forms and rules were so "confusing," sounding the same note Senator Duffy was now playing about being confounded by a simple reimbursement form. Both of them had been able, as political broadcasters, to unravel from Parliament Hill the gnarled complexities of national politics and government policies for their television audiences. Now, as senators, they were stumped by a standard claims form.

Senator Wallin needed help, certainly, and underscoring the urgency was the fact the person handling administration in her Senate office had departed. Government Senate Leader Marjory LeBreton, trying to help Conservative caucus members in difficulty over their expenses, opened her bulging file of resumés. One person seeking Senate employment was especially promising. Alison Stodin's sterling references attested to her solid experience as a Hill veteran who was honourable and, among many skills, adept at financial administration.

Why would such a talented individual be looking for work at the Senate? Back in 2006 Stodin, working with MP Monte Solberg and eager for new experience, had gone with the Alberta MP to help run his minister's office when he'd been appointed to cabinet. But when Stolberg left politics after a few short years, Stodin had felt swallowed up by the departmental labyrinth where she'd remained, missing the political action of The Hill that had first drawn her to Ottawa as a politically active young woman with a university degree. She already knew the Commons, so, ever interested in something new, she applied to Parliament's other house. In late June 2012 Marjory LeBreton arranged a Senate contract for Stodin to work for Senator Wallin.

LeBreton and Stodin had dedicated their careers to politics, primarily in attentive loyal service to senior elected representatives and party leaders. Each believed instinctively that rules governing senators' expenses were not just administrative guidelines but a regime to protect the public interest. Stodin, as an individual endowed with deep political intelligence, was to help Senator Wallin administratively and in particular to clear up her expenses problem by meshing receipts, travel stubs, and other records with the rules and forms of the Senate Budget Office. Everyone concerned knew the flame had to be extinguished. The consequences of not doing so were too great.

As haze settled over Ottawa, and Parliament Hill sat abandoned to summer heat and busloads of tourists, Stodin settled down at the start of July 2012 to take advantage of the season's minimal interruptions. She started in to clear up the senator's expenses backlog. Stodin found the stale and littered money trail a confusing challenge, in arrears and in a mess, but this was condition normal for Wallin. The paperwork details that first became a by-product of her hectic life at CTV, and later with CBC, got out of hand during her years as consul general in New York, and had now reached maturity in the Senate, where her pile of travel and expense records accumulated as the unattended detritus of a stellar career.

Stodin sorted through the records and unbilled costs, making piles and writing notes, but still found them a confusing challenge to fit within applicable categories and rules. Over five weeks she interacted with her new senator employer mostly by telephone and through email, with little opportunity for bonding, let alone direct clarifications of expense details.

The core issue was not Pamela Wallin's "primary residence" in Saskatchewan, a cottage she lived in during her times in the province, but how her travel to and from Saskatchewan for this purpose was complicated by the fact Wallin also had residences in Toronto and New York where she often stayed, and worked, sometimes for days, en route to or from Wadena.

The way the Senate administers the commuting costs of its members is not by budgeting dollars for individual senators but by allocating each of them sixty-four travel points for the year. A point is used up for each round-trip to and from the senator's primary residence, wherever in Canada it may be. This plan provides equality. A senator from Toronto or St. John's or Vancouver or Wadena would each use up a single point for a return flight, notwithstanding the difference in distance and price. Whatever the actual cost of a senator's trip, be it $300 or $1,300, the Senate Budget Office pays the amount from its general fund for all senatorial travel. If a senator needed to go elsewhere in the country than home or to his or her own province or territory, the points could be used for that, too, but with some adjustment. For a longer distance than normal for that senator, or for a trip with many legs and stopovers, a number of additional travel points would get used up in the process. Figuring out just how many is an accounting art.

Pamela Wallin might sometimes fly home from Ottawa to Saskatoon via Halifax and Toronto, with layovers of several days in both intermediate cities where she had work that included Senate duties, and claim it as one point for a trip to her province. Normally, such a multi-leg, multiple-day flight might consume three or four points. Senator Wallin would say that she never used more than a single point for a trip, and never exceeded the annual limit of sixty-four travel points, "otherwise I would have paid personally," without accounting for the fact she conflated some unconnected flights over a number of days into "a single trip" home to make everything fit her heavy workload and overbooked schedule. Notionally, she was right; administratively, not so much.

The reasons Pamela Wallin flew to other places in Canada related to both Senate work and private sector work alike, fulfilling the multiple dimensions of one workaholic person. In New York and Toronto, she engaged in remunerative private work, but did so in tandem with Senate roles that constantly engaged her too. Over lunches with officials at public events, her conversation could slip seamlessly back and forth between, say, government policy on civil aviation and trends she knew about as a director of Porter Airlines, and so on through various categories of her intense, many-faceted engagement with the world around her.

Like other senators doing the same thing, Pamela Wallin straddled several worlds simultaneously. It was not a conflict of interest but a confluence of interests. She was an integrator of her many roles: a star in business, the academic world, the creative arts, journalism, public office, and the Conservative Party of Canada. The biggest trick was to keep everything in its correct separate category when charging for the costs.

The private companies on whose boards Wallin sat were prepared to pay flight costs when she was travelling on their behalf, and sometimes did. The same was the case, more or less, with a number of the charitable and educational organizations for whom Senator Wallin performed services and added the star power they craved. But in the scramble of her unrefined record-keeping Wallin was always behind and, trying at intervals to catch up, hastily dumped costs onto the Senate for reimbursement from public funds.

The Senate's relic "honour system" kicked in. Reimbursements were made to Senator Wallin, despite the extraordinary rigours of scrutiny Senator Tkachuk had boasted every claim was subject to in detail. Rather than acting as a brake on improper invoicing, the Senate Budget Office smoothed a pattern for Wallin to maintain her troublesome habit.

Of the many flights with ticket stubs and proofs of payment, the easiest for Alison Stodin to sort and claim were the ones exclusively for Pamela Wallin's Senate work because they had been recorded by Senate staff while making the original booking. Yet mingled into the mishmash of materials she was sorting were receipts for other flights, trips with more than one leg, for instance to Manhattan and Toronto, and stopovers of several days' duration. Those required more than a single travel point, but that was tricky to determine. On top of this, those trips mixed Senate work with other activity, for which there were also receipts to be claimed for reimbursement, and which might have been at least partly paid by others.

Some of those costs, not just the flights but the use of limousines, the meals, accommodation, and incidentals, seemed more appropriately allocable to the companies Pamela Wallin worked for in a well-remunerated capacity, or to at least some of the charitable organizations she served. Yet, here were those expense records, too, tossed onto the accumulated pile of Wallin's pieces of paper. Credit card statements catalogued a swath of spending, but into which of the many categories, or for which of the particular trips, did each of the entries belong? The dates sometimes defied matchup. Stodin stared at the omelette and could not see how to turn it back into eggs.

After weeks of mounting exasperation, and with the senator not around to explain, Stodin called the finance people in Senate administration, "Can I meet with you to go over some files? I don't know what to do." She'd been trying to reconcile outstanding American Express accounts and travel expenses.

It was Friday, August 10, an extremely quiet day at the Senate. "Sure, come right over," was the response.

When Wallin asked Stodin by telephone where she'd been when she'd tried to reach her earlier, "she 'freaked' when I told her I'd been to the Senate Budget Office to get some clarity about processing some of these. 'Don't ever go there again, they are not to see anything!' she shouted."

When Senator Wallin returned to her parliamentary office on August 22, she fired Stodin.

There are a couple of ways to interpret Wallin's remark, "They are not to see anything!" One is that Pamela Wallin had something legally problematic to hide; the other that she was embarrassed by her inexcusable record keeping. You can be a radiant star in public and still not want fans to see the dust balls under your bed.

I tested the two possibilities with a senior lawyer who knows Wallin and a retired Deloitte partner who had himself previously conducted Senate audits. Both agreed the senator's reaction could have erupted from either of those possibilities — something to hide from the authorities, or instinctive human embarrassment. Even so, both felt that given the nature of the relationship between the two, they'd have expected Stodin to review matters with Wallin — if only to agree how serious the confusion was and that guidance was needed from the Senate's Budget Office — *before* the paperwork was seen by others outside her office in its raw and indigestible form.

Knowing both women, my sense is that Wallin wanted the mess cleaned up on her own terms, with any required corrections made with her knowledge, so she could present the finished product as a clean bundle with a bow ribbon to the Senate Budget Office and get on with larger matters. Stodin, I knew from the days she'd run my MP's office so professionally in the 1990s, took pride in sorting out back-office details so that a busy parliamentarian could focus instead on public issues. She would not want to admit she was stumped and, as self-starter, would seek tips from a Senate budget officer on how to allocate a senator's expenses in ways that legitimately complied with the rules.

In that heated moment when Wallin fired Stodin, the senator told the staffer she was incompetent and threatened to destroy her reputation. Over her decades in politics and on Parliament Hill, Stodin had "never been treated with more abuse," just as Wallin had never felt more betrayed.

Wallin believed, as she told me in October 2013, that hard-core right-wing elements in the Conservative caucus had it out for her because she didn't "have an 'R' branded on my forehead" — she was not Reform enough. Also, she stated that many were jealous of her "good personal access to the prime minister," which in part dated from the days Wallin served on the PM's advisory panel about the future of Canada's military mission in Afghanistan. Quite a few senators no doubt also sneered at her self-declared status as an "activist senator," which implied her colleagues were inactive do-nothings. Revealing her expense claim materials to the Budget Office was, Wallin feared, their plot to get her. She now saw Stodin as a plant, sent into her office to nail down incriminating evidence. Wallin believed that whatever mess she had with her accounts paled in comparison to her personal vulnerability and political isolation among back-stabbers on The Hill.

Stung, Stodin faced a dilemma. She, too, was now feeling isolated after being fired near the end of her career; she was vulnerable, engaged in a serious dispute with a senator who threatened to trash her reputation, and she was ill. She needed advice. She telephoned Carolyn Stewart-Olsen. The two had known and worked together for two decades after the Reform Party swept into the House of Commons in 1993, and Carolyn was now on the Senate's Internal Economy Committee. Stodin was more concerned than ever about the Senate of Canada's finances mess, a growing problem that had now claimed her as a victim.

Senator Stewart-Olsen told her to put the facts in a letter to the Internal Economy Committee. "So I just put down on paper my concerns," Stodin explained to me in December 2013, "and sent it confidentially to the Senate committee."

The Stodin letter crystallized for Internal Economy Committee members a number of concerns that had been floating around the Senate for years.

Her August 24 document highlighted shortcomings that several dedicated staff budget officers and auditors had, in intermittent campaigns, sought to address to no effect. The Stodin letter now forced them to face directly the still smouldering smudge arising from the auditor general's recent report about some senators' expense claims, though undocumented, having been reimbursed anyway.

Unrelated to the letter's actual contents, Alison Stodin's message also excited worries already on the minds of committee members about several senators living full-time near Ottawa but claiming distant "primary residences" to get extra money from the Senate for their secondary accommodation allowance, a practice that had occurred with Senate approbation for several years. It troubled some of them that this pattern of the Senate Budget Office paying these housing allowances had now become well established. A couple even entertained doubts about their own claims, now that such payments were being reframed by the developing Senate scandal, although they could reassure themselves by remembering that whatever they were doing complied with the foggy Senate rules for reimbursements.

Stodin's letter identified issues that ultimately were the Senate's problems, as an institution, far more than they were Pamela Wallin's headaches as an individual. Wallin's shoddy financial practices only showed them up for what they were.

If those running the upper house's administration had been stung by what Auditor General Ferguson revealed about their less than "rigorous" operation, they now were forced to realize it was no longer good enough just to look at any errant or sloppy or even criminally culpable acts of individual senators and their expense claims as if the fault belonged to those senators alone. The institution the Internal Economy Committee operated was the stage on which all this was playing out. Several budget officers had tried to upgrade Senate administration — a move that had also been a warning — only to be stonewalled by long-term senators protecting the status quo by deferring to the "honour system."

With the stories reporters were now digging out, and the increasing demand for certain senators to pay back expense money to the Senate, surely it would dawn on people that somebody in the Senate had approved the claims, after they'd passed through the Senate administration's "rigorous scrutiny" including, at least in theory, two sets of budget officer eyes. Only Franz Kafka could portray the Senate requiring reimbursement of reimbursements as normal, and he was, lamentably, dead.

Senate administrators needed to take responsibility for the Budget Office's tolerant practices and the elasticity of the Senate's "honour system," but their self-protective instinct drove them to duck so all blame would reach, unimpeded, the highest heads on the public horizon — Stephen Harper's readily identifiable celebrity scapegoats, the ones whose claims had all been paid.

The venerable "honour system" of the upper house had been in place since Confederation, a limp code in contrast to rigorous counterpart procedures governing Parliament's lower house, the Commons.

A Senate administrative rule stated, like scripture: "Senators act on their personal honour and senators are presumed to have acted honourably in carrying out their administrative functions unless and until the Senate or the Internal Economy Committee determines otherwise." It was a beautiful sentiment, ostensibly reflecting an idyllic earlier age, covering a practice that enabled Tory and Grit senators to do the honourable thing of working for their parties' electoral and partisan interests, in Ottawa and across the country, without scrutiny. As a cover for public consumption, the notion of "honour" about money rode alongside the Senate's two other well-publicized fictions, that it was a body offering "sober second thoughts" and that it was uniquely speaking for "regional" interests.

Under the honour system, senators would routinely claim an expense simply by noting the amount was for "Senate business." In practice, no receipt was required, nor was any explanation of the nature of the "Senate business." Nor was there even a requirement that the purpose of a Senate trip be stated. Most senators in the modern era, accustomed to submitting reimbursement claims over their adult careers, did so as second nature, and generally included receipts or proof of payment. Those who did not — contrary to what the Internal Economy Committee told the public was established practice to protect taxpayer dollars "more efficiently than any second-level sign-off" — still got reimbursed anyway, as Canada's auditor general had discovered and reported.

So-called "Senate business" sometimes included attending a daughter's ballet class or a film industry awards banquet, but often it entailed travelling the country for partisan work. Because the Senate was tacitly embraced by the Liberals and Conservatives as an adjunct operation of their parties, nothing was ever done to tighten up Senate budget administration. Foolish attempts to do so, by those who just didn't get what the Senate was really all about, were routinely ignored. The powers-that-be did not want stringent rules that would constrain Liberals or clamp down on Conservatives fund-raising and working for campaigns while on the taxpayers' tab.

The magic of the euphemism "honour system" by which Liberal and Conservative senators coded their approach to financial administration resided in the term's vagueness. "Honour" was the expected hallmark for members of Canada's most senior legislature, and "system" connoted order and efficiency of operation. The phrase served well to mist over partisan campaigning and reinforce the impression that senators were honourable people who could be trusted. The fact most could be, because of their personal ethical standards and trustworthiness, only reinforced the belief of incumbent senators that they truly were, as they were called, "Honourable." This blinded them to the fact that there was no part of honour in enacting a strict election finance reform law in the 1970s yet continuing the vigorous operation of a system to circumvent that statute's provisions for a level playing field in Canadian politics.

Canada's senators live across the country but work in the Parliament Buildings at Ottawa. They have no choice because the Constitution stipulates a person must reside in his or her home province or territory to qualify for Senate membership.

To ease the cost of needing two living places and commuting across the country to and from work, the Senate contributes to the cost of a place to stay while in the National Capital Region and pays for travel between a senator's home and Parliament.

The Senate's Internal Economy Committee made few rules about the allowance, just enough to cover several basics: a senator's *primary* residence had to be more that one hundred kilometres from Parliament; the *secondary* accommodation in the National Capital Region whose costs the senators could claim reimbursement for could be either a hotel suite or a private rental unit, provided they didn't lease from a family member; and the daily rate of $30 reaches its upper limit at $900 per month. An out-of-town senator would need to be in the National Capital full-time to exceed $10,000 a year, which of course would never happen since the Senate typically only sits about three months out of every twelve.

Nothing else was specified. That left it up to senators to figure things out for themselves. Although there was no uniform practice, the Internal Economy Committee was reviewing the thorny cases of certain senators who'd received the housing subsidy, in some instances for several years. Both Conservative and Liberal senators were involved, so the issue did not fall along partisan lines. The dubious allowance claims included at least a couple of senators who'd pre-cleared their arrangement with the Senate administration, so any "problem" that was starting to scandalize the public could not be blamed on those senators alone. The Senate itself was implicated.

For lawyers who pondered this problem, a stumbling block was the legal doctrine of *estoppel*. The Senate's own financial officers had approved the set-up, received the claims, approved them, and cut the cheques to reimburse these out-of-town senators. They had not done so once by inadvertent error, but repeatedly, over a number of years, establishing a clear pattern of acts that established Senate policy through official practice. The Senate was consequently prevented, or estopped, from now ordering those senators to repay the money. If this point had come to serious debate, lawyers might have found arguments for the other side of this case, too, invoking doctrines and precedents to countermand the interpretation that, for the Senate housing allowance, customary practice had created an accepted, even if unwritten, rule.

But no such debate resolved the issue. It wasn't the Senate's way. In a place where an easy-going approach was the administrative norm, there were no other rules about the accommodation allowance, beyond those just noted, to invoke.

Taxpayers with two or more living places know about designating one as their "primary residence" to qualify for the financial benefit of being exempt from capital gains tax when selling the place. In an analogous way, legally if not ethically, Mike Duffy or Mac Harb or Patrick Brazeau or others figured they could designate a place one hundred kilometres or more from Ottawa as their "primary residence" to get the accommodation allowance for out-of-town senators coming to Ottawa for parliamentary duties.

As far-fetched as this practice appeared once reporters published photos of Mike Duffy's "permanent residence" — a snowbound cottage in the P.E.I. village of Cavendish — and Mac Harb's undisturbed "permanent" home in a village up the Ottawa Valley, these arrangements had been acceptable to the Senate of Canada, which, as already noted several times, had approved and paid their Ottawa accommodation allowances for several years.

Yet other senators saw the accommodation benefit differently. They understood it to be a subsidy to make it financially easier only for "out-of-town" senators forced to maintain two residences, not those within driving distance of Parliament Hill. Such senators living in the Ottawa area as Marjory LeBreton, Jim Munson, Colin Kenny, and Vern White made no claim for the *secondary* accommodation subsidy, the way an Ottawa senator like Mac Harb did. At the same time, it was revealing — in the context of this ill-defined plan — how other senators living outside the one hundred–kilometre exclusion zone, and therefore eligible for the housing allowance, chose not to claim it. Senators Anne Cools, Marie Charette-Poulin, and Pierre De Bané felt they were already well enough paid, and respected public funds enough to not draw on them without need.

Overall, from 2010 to 2012, senators collectively claimed more than $2.5 million in National Capital Region living expenses. Uniform practice did not exist. Apart from those senators who had a moral compass about what was proper and claimed nothing, the Senate's vague criteria for determining one's "primary" residence produced conflicting interpretations by a number of their Senate colleagues.

Through the summer and early fall of 2012, the continuing Parliament Hill chat about Senator Patrick Brazeau included reports that he seemed to live full-time in Gatineau but claimed a "permanent residence" in Maniwaki, more than one hundred kilometres away, to get the accommodation allowance as an out-of-town senator. By mid-November 2012, the Internal Economy Committee asked a panel of three senators to review his housing claim, as Robert Fife had been reporting.

The committee also turned its attention to a similar practice by Senator Mike Duffy, who'd lived in Ottawa since coming to Parliament Hill as a reporter in the 1970s but who now claimed his "permanent residence" was a cottage in Prince Edward Island and was billing the Senate the out-of-towners' allowance for living in his Ottawa home next to the Kanata Golf and Country Club, which he and his wife Heather had bought in 2003. Some senators buy a place in Ottawa once appointed, but the Duffys had purchased and lived full-time in the Kanata house five years before his Senate appointment.

The committee's chairman, Senator Tkachuk, told Ottawa *Citizen* reporter Glen McGregor, on December 2, 2012, that Mike Duffy's expenses were "entirely within the rules" and stated that he believed there was no reason for Duffy not to claim the housing allowance in Ottawa. "Why wouldn't he?" asked Tkachuk, as if puzzled this was even an issue. "When you travel to Ottawa, you get expenses for living in Ottawa. In his case, he has a home here, so he would charge off whatever the daily rate is."

During the first week of December 2012, the committee looked at similar housing allowances paid to Senator Mac Harb, who had declared his "primary residence" to be more than one hundred kilometres up the Ottawa Valley, enabling him to be paid the allowance as an out-of-towner regularly for several years.

The Internal Economy Committee knew it had a problem. It decided to audit all such claims by senators for the "secondary residence" allowance. Announcing this internal audit, David Tkachuk answered a reporter who wondered what criteria the upper house would use to determine a senator's primary residence. "Your primary residence is what you say your primary residence is," he replied. "It's where you file your income taxes from, where you get your mail." The test was no higher than that — essentially, a personal declaration, the "honour system" in operation.

A lot of people, thinking honour an unreliable rail to carry ethical conduct in contemporary Canadian society, suggested to the chairman his minimal standard was insufficient. As a result, he wrote a letter to each senator a week later, in which the head of the committee running the Senate stated, "Residency is a very complicated issue. The Senate has never tested it."

To clarify matters, Senator Tkachuck added new criteria. To prove residency claims, senators would henceforth need a provincial health card, driver's licence, and income tax return to confirm residency information, and a signed letter stating where they vote. January 31, 2013 was the deadline to submit proof of one's primary residence.

Would these new criteria apply retroactively, to claims already reimbursed? That would depend on how much the Senate was committed to rule of law principles, one of which states that you don't apply new rules retroactively to behaviour that was lawfully compliant at the time.

Mike Duffy was not on the voters' list in Prince Edward Island in 2011, but he had voted in that year's Ontario provincial election. He immediately applied for a P.E.I. health card, requesting it be sent on an expedited basis, that he needed it before the end of January. As the year

2012 drew to a close, annoyed Conservative senators, feeling besmirched by Mike Duffy's performance, asked him at a closed-door caucus meeting to just repay the housing allowance. One asked him to resign his seat in the Senate. The anxious P.E.I. senator sought help from Ottawa's top political fixers, the men in the PMO, while asserting to reporters that he had done nothing wrong, was getting tired of their "BS" and was, as Canadians knew, a man of honour.

Patrick Brazeau pushed back combatively, stating that he had done nothing wrong and, moreover, his housing claim arrangements had been approved by Senate administration. Mac Harb sniffed that he'd done nothing wrong and complained that his lawyer had not been allowed to speak at the in camera session with the Internal Economy Committee.

Through December, the Internal Economy Committee members had also been reviewing records showing Senator Wallin had billed $142,190.26 for trips between March 1, 2011, and February 29, 2012, though only $10,551.99 of those expenses related to travel between Ottawa and Saskatchewan, with the balance of $131,638.27 described simply as "Other."

That "miscellaneous" category is the catch-all senators use when making a trip that is not to their home province or territory. Typically, such travel includes a bit of Senate business to justify the cost to the public, around which could be clustered additional events on behalf of the Conservative or Liberal Party, some private business, and personal diversions.

The Internal Economy Committee knew that the public, which was footing Senator Wallin's bills, would not find it acceptable for senators themselves to rule on the validity of her claims. After all, the Senate had already scrupulously scrutinized them before, and reimbursed them in full. For this reason alone, the issue was really as damaging to the Senate as it was to Pamela Wallin. The committee tried to keep the matter under wraps by holding in camera sessions on the subject of Wallin's expenses. Who really had the stomach to confront one of their own, or the political stupidity to take on one of the prime minister's Senate stars, in what would be an ugly confrontation over ethical conduct and, possibly, even criminal wrongdoing?

An arms-length entity was needed. Although the Senate did have an Ethics Office, it was acknowledged to be ineffective, and was inappropriate anyway because it was connected with the Senate's own operations even though characterized as being independent from them. The Internal Economy Committee decided the Deloitte firm, having done Senate audits in the past and having prestigious clout as one of Canada's Big Four accounting firms, would be suitable for an independent review of Senator Wallin's travel costs. On January 3, 2013, the Senate formally retained Deloitte. The audit would review her expenses from April 2011 to September 2012.

Alison Stodin was heading to the hospital when she heard radio news that the Senate's Internal Economy Committee had hired Deloitte. As she explained to me a year and a half later, "I knew it would now only be a matter of time before the mess would be made public and get dealt with."

As 2013 began, the Internal Economy Committee resumed pondering what to do about allowance claims for housing and meals the Senate had previously paid to a number of its members.

Through January, the committee again took stock of the claims by Mac Harb, Mike Duffy, and Patrick Brazeau. Each of these senators, they had already determined during their in camera sessions, occupied established residences in the National Capital Region so did not really qualify for the out-of-towner allowance. Still, it wasn't going to be painless dealing with them. The Senate had next to no rules governing the matter. The Senate had already been paying these claims for some time. Two of the senators were high-profile choices of the prime minister himself. The increasingly discredited Senate would find it hard to deal with such senators in any way the public or the press or Senate abolitionists like the Official Opposition NDP in the Commons would find acceptable. Their safest solution, these political veterans knew, was to pass the problem to someone else.

Having already hired Deloitte to audit Senator Wallin's expenses, on February 8 the committee extended the firm's contract to include a review of the housing allowance claims of senators Brazeau, Duffy, and Harb. The Senate committee once again manoeuvred its hot potato into the accountants' cool hands.

The issue was now fully alive in the country at large, however, and in the Commons, the NDP's Charlie Angus was very effective in channeling public outrage about the Senate in general and the developing Senate expenses scandal in particular into embarrassing questions to the government.

The Internal Economy Committee got urgent orders from on high. On February 11, 2013, Conservative Senate Leader Marjory LeBreton, acting in concert with the PMO, jointly requested with Liberal Senate Leader James Cowan that the committee "proceed to interview each senator who has claimed a secondary residential allowance to confirm the legitimacy of such claims."

Without acknowledging that the rules about such claims had never been properly clarified by the Senate, nor that the Senate Budget Office had reviewed and paid all such claims, the Senate leaders manoeuvred the Senate's own mess away from the institution and onto individual senators alone.

"Should any senator be unable to convince you that the claim is valid," the Government and Opposition Senate leaders asserted, invoking nothing but their own authority, "that senator should be required to pay immediately all monies so paid, with interest."

In an interview that same evening on CTV, Senator Cowan said he and Senator LeBreton "agree wholeheartedly" on the importance of getting to the bottom of the allegations. The interviewer did not ask Mr. Cowan if that meant the Senate would investigate its own Budget Office and procedures for validating expense claims. Let easily off the hook, lawyer Senator Cowan pressed his side of the case further, "We have zero tolerance for anyone who is abusing the rules, and we think as a first step that they should pay the money back," thus making sure the public knew who the culprits were. Any possible "second step" would not be one taken against the Senate, it now seemed clear, but would only involve individual senators — the "culprits" — who could face criminal prosecution.

Various senators were accordingly put through in camera hearings to vet whether some of them had improperly drawn on the $21,000 annual meal-and-housing allowance offered to those whose primary residence is more than one hundred kilometres from Ottawa, creating the need for accommodation when in the capital or, in Senate parlance, "on travel status."

On February 14, 2013, Senator Dennis Patterson, the former NWT premier who'd been named to the Senate as a representative for Nunavut by Prime Minister Harper in 2009, was one of those who responded to the committee's questions about his claims. At the same time, CTV Ottawa Bureau Chief Robert Fife broke an exclusive story, based on weeks of journalistic investigation, raising doubts about whether Senator Patterson actually lived in Nunavut.

Interest in his residency arose, both from Internal Economy Committee members and the Press Gallery, because Senator Patterson was collecting the housing allowance for out-of-town senators, but it was unclear where his "primary residence" was located, or if he even had one in the northern territory at all. British Columbia provincial land title records showed Mr. Patterson, who'd lived and worked as a private consultant in Vancouver before his Senate appointment, owned a home in Vancouver. In turn, municipal records showed him claiming a homeowner grant only available to those primarily living in the province, as evidenced by having most of their personal belongings in British Columbia, possessing or being eligible for a B.C. driver's licence, qualifying for provincial medical insurance, and filing a B.C. income tax return.

Senator Patterson responded to CTV News that he'd rented out his Vancouver home in 2012 and purchased a condo in Ottawa. The Nunavut senator, echoing Senator Tkachuk's earlier view, said residency was a "complex matter with many facets" and that he didn't "believe national television is the place to examine all the facets." He added, "I've had a residence in Nunavut since I was appointed to the Senate." He later emailed CTV News to explain he resided in a rented apartment in Iqaluit.

Meanwhile, Senator Patterson continued to provide relevant information to the Internal Economy Committee. "I look forward to the results of the review and I do believe that I have conducted my affairs in a way that is in compliance with the rules," he said. In due course, they found he had.

Manitoba Liberal Senator Rod Zimmer was also questioned in February 2013 by the committee's three-member steering committee about his claims for travel and living expenses. He was cleared by their in camera inquiry into his housing arrangements before month's end. The committee, chaired by Senator Tkachuk, announced it was satisfied with Senator Zimmer's explanations. Later, however, after senators voted in June on Conservative Senate Leader Marjory LeBreton's motion to request that Auditor General Michael Ferguson make a comprehensive audit of the Senate, including senators' expenses, Senator Zimmer would resign in August, citing health reasons, five years before reaching mandatory retirement age.

On February 28, the Senate approved the Internal Economy Committee's recommendation that out-of-town senators making their declaration of primary residence should now back it up with a driver's licence, a health card, and the relevant page of their income tax form — the first crack in the "honour system."

Québec Conservative senator Pierre-Hugues Boisvenu briefly provided titillating fuel to the Senate expenses scandal in March 2013 when it made news that he'd collected some $20,000 under the housing allowance even though the senator "on travel status" was living just a short drive across the Ottawa River in a Gatineau residence. Senator Boisvenu claimed his "primary residence" was in Sherbrooke, but tipsters told Montreal's *La Presse* he'd been staying in Gatineau full-time after separating in February the year before from his wife, who continued to occupy their Sherbrooke condominium. The Gatineau residence belonged to Isabelle Lapointe, who worked in the senator's office.

Senator Boisvenu defended his claims for the housing allowance, noting the payments were legitimately within Senate rules. When the Internal Economy Committee reviewed his file, they did not ask him, according to Senator Tkachuck, about his delicate personal situation. A few days later, on March 7, it was reported that Senator Boisvenu had repaid the Senate $907 for his housing expense claims while staying with his assistant, Isabelle Lapointe, with whom he'd been romantically linked at the time.

By the time the Internal Economy Committee completed its in-house audit, some ninety-five senators had "completely satisfied the residency questions," chairman Tkachuk happily reported. "We have no concern in this regard."

Among the senators who'd claimed the out-of-towner's allowance for housing and meals in Ottawa was Carolyn Stewart-Olsen, a key member of the Internal Economy Committee and its steering committee, which had cleared the ninety-five claimants and found, as with the rest, that she had complied with the existing rules.

Still, the Senate seemed determined to prove it was serious about cleaning things up and did not skip a beat in running the stricter new rules back in time, to challenge prior behaviour that now seemed fraudulent though those practices had once not just been winked at but had even been fostered by Senate administrators.

Despite all of this, Senator Tkachuk declined media requests for a telephone interview or follow-up questions by email. MP Charlie Angus, ethics critic for the NDP, claimed the internal review by the Senate did not go far enough. The Senate is in "full damage control" stated Mr. Angus, adding, "they'll say anything and do anything to get this scandal to go away."

Retaining an independent auditor proved to be the critical turning point.

The need for an arm's-length assessment by a reputed firm like Deloitte — an improvised version of the "Senate watch-dog" Peter Worthington had called for but had been told was unneeded — ignited the real conflagration of the Senate expenses scandal.

All three of Prime Minister Harper's celebrity senators, Pamela Wallin, Mike Duffy, and Patrick Brazeau, now found their financial affairs being combed through in dispassionate detail by Deloitte's team of accountants. If not for their star power lustre, the problems at the Senate would have been just as real, but would not have attracted media attention nor would they have ignited a national political scandal.

In the days to come, Deloitte's audit would trigger further events that also would never have happened if the expenses scandal had remained within Senate cloisters, and which would not have occurred had the independent review — as Deloitte itself recognized in its report on Senator Wallin's expenses — not been triggered by the wake-up bang of Alison Stodin's firecracker.

The consequences would consume the careers of many senators, backlight the daunting scandal of the Senate's very existence as a political institution, and scorch the prime minister and those working for him in the PMO.

CHAPTER 6

The Booster Rocket Kicks In

The scandal about a few senators' expense claims highlighted greed, sloppiness, and slipshod Senate administration. This mundane and tawdry testament to Parliament's upper house could never have soared into a full-blown government crisis, however, without a surging boost from the PMO.

The personal ability of strong long-term prime ministers Pierre Trudeau, Brian Mulroney, Jean Chrétien, and Stephen Harper to flex their muscles and wield power has been magnified by the formidable operation supporting them. After Mr. Trudeau remade the PMO in his own image as a focused, disciplined, and tough-as-steel operation, the Prime Minister's Office as a political institution has continued to expand its power, extend its control, and get its way.

In 1971 political scientist Thomas Hockin wrote the book *Apex of Power* to examine political leadership in Canada, documenting how Canada's traditional parliamentary system had morphed into all-controlling prime ministerial government. His study traced the intricate dance steps by which Canada is now governed as Ottawa moves in harmonized rhythm to musical strains emanating from the PMO.

In the mid-1980s, Hockin was elected a Progressive Conservative MP for London West and entered Prime Minister Mulroney's cabinet. After several months, I asked him if the concentration of power he'd described as an academic from the outside resembled what he was now experiencing as a minister on the inside. He looked at me straight on and, not missing a beat, answered, "It's even worse, much worse!" My suggestion that he should write an updated edition of *Apex of Power* brought an enthusiastic smile from the political scientist and academic in him. When we parted, Tom seemed fully primed to revise his book. A couple of months later, I asked how the revised edition was coming along. His smile vanished. He replied he'd been directed by the PMO not to write it.

When an issue affects a prime minister of Canada, our nation's leader does not deal with it alone. On the policy and administrative side, a PM is guided by top-rank public servants working in the Privy Council Office. On the political and governance side, a parallel role falls to party-minded staff in the Prime Minister's Office. The PCO and PMO are the twin screws driving the massive apparatus that is the Government of Canada, our "ship of state."

Seldom does the PMO put its engines in neutral, even less frequently, into reverse. If something in the waters ahead could cause damage to the prime minister, the instinct of those in the PMO charged with "issues management" and "strategic communications" is to take hold of the problem, not stand back from it.

At the helm of the PMO in 2012 was Nigel Wright. As the prime minister's chief of staff, Wright bore a solemn duty to oversee the political interests of Stephen Harper in governing our country.

Nigel Wright was known to friends, colleagues, and professional associates as ethical, industrious, and compassionate, devout in his spiritual being, athletic in his personal life, and wealthy in worldly means as a result of his opportunities and actions on Toronto's Bay Street while one of Onex Corporation's principal dealmakers.

At Onex, the Gerald Schwartz–run private equity fund that manages assets valued at roughly $36 billion, Mr. Wright had headed up the aerospace, defence, energy, and transportation groups. According to data compiled by Bloomberg News at the time he left Onex to join the prime minister, his shareholding interests were estimated at about $3.5 million. He used his personal funds to support needy people and aid worthy causes. Some associates called Nigel Wright one of "the best and brightest."

"Nigel is one the brightest Canadians I know, and he's incredibly focused on doing the right thing," Duncan Dee, chief operating officer for Air Canada, told the *Financial Post* in September 2010. "He'll bring a tremendous sense of the economy and of politics, which is very rare. There aren't many people who can synthesize both the economy and politics," said Dee, who knew Wright from prior dealings between Air Canada and Onex.

Nigel Wright and Stephen Harper shared a strong interest in both the future of the Canadian economy and the political fortunes of the Conservative Party of Canada. Both had been devoted to the interests of political conservatism for years. Earlier in his career Nigel had been drawn to Parliament Hill, working in the PMO's policy and speechwriting division for Prime Minister Brian Mulroney. That is where I first saw him in action — clean-cut, bright, friendly, and discreet.

Over the decade since Stephen Harper returned to national politics in 2002, the Conservative leader was in frequent contact with Nigel Wright and the two developed close rapport on economic issues and conservative values. This connection helped the PM persuade Wright to leave Onex and come back to Ottawa, too. At the end of September 2010, Nigel was sworn in as his chief of staff. While Prime Minister Harper's right-hand man in the PMO, he also served the Conservative Party of Canada as an officer, sitting on its board of directors and chairing the audit committee. He would be able to synthesize everything.

Nigel Wright was reputed to be "one of the few who could speak candidly with the PM," which should not have been remarkable because candour is a prerequisite at this level. However, it seems clear that open and honest communication has been something of a precious commodity in Stephen Harper's PMO. Certainly, serious questions have been raised about the degree of information sharing that took place in the Prime Minister's Office regarding the Senate scandal. Who knew what when, or, more specifically, how much did Nigel Wright share with Stephen Harper, is the question that has intrigued followers of the scandal for some time.

Being chief of staff also requires being a political fixer. Somebody must make the boss's problems go away, even if doing so entails sacrificing yourself. Norman Spector, a chief of staff to Prime Minister Mulroney as well as principal secretary to British Columbia premier Bill Bennett, explained to CBC *Newsworld* anchor Ian Hanomansing in the context of the Senate scandal, "The day I started, Bennett explained the rule, telling me, 'When we have to walk the gang-plank, I'm the last one to go, and you walk right ahead of me.'"

A good chief of staff cleans up messes and covers over problems without bothering the top man with the details. A ship's captain, preoccupied on the bridge, likely does not need to know a passenger just spilled coffee in a lower galley. Aboard the ship of state, a prime minister's chief of staff might avoid saying anything about a mess he's mopping up below decks, knowing that if the trouble should ever become public, the prime minister could truthfully say that he knew nothing about it. Such narrow and defensive reasoning is the ethically limp doctrine of "plausible deniability" much in vogue with professional political operators.

Translated, that means the guy in charge doesn't know what's going on. Apart from the truth of this in any particular case — nobody can know everything, after all — this idea that a leader's fate hangs on what he did not know is untenable, both politically in terms of credibility and constitutionally in terms of the responsible government doctrine holding those at the top responsible for what government does, regardless of their innocence, indifference, or ignorance.

Besides being a widely acknowledged master deal-maker, as the PM's chief of staff Nigel Wright was expected to tidy up awkward situations out of sight. Working in the rarefied precincts of the PMO, where political power is fully concentrated, it seemed natural for him to see it as his duty to control the agenda, direct political behaviours, and stomp out problems. A person working in the PMO had reason to believe he could accomplish anything he wanted.

Nigel Wright and his colleagues, highly motivated and zealously driven, accelerated the pace rather than slowing it down. Their governance ethic had little of the calming political wisdom seasoned veterans can impart. On the contrary, in contrast to the deliberate atmosphere that abided in earlier versions of the PMO when a measured pace accompanied the serious running of government, the high-octane PMO under Stephen Harper closely resembled a partisan "war room" of the type normally found at party headquarters during a general election campaign when the mode of thinking is intense, blinkered, and devoted to damage control.

* * *

In 2012, word began spreading around Parliament Hill of problems in Senate financial administration. As fragmentary tips about expenses first trickled and then flowed into the gossip sluiceway from backrooms into Parliament's corridors, around the Senate and into Press Gallery news reports, the PMO felt mild heat from a low-smouldering scandal over at the Senate.

By 2013, though, as more information about the contentious expenses of the PM's celebrity senators came to light, the PMO firefighters found themselves answering a three-alarm call, with rising temperatures stoked by the Official Opposition, the scorching curiosity of news reporters, and an inflamed base of the Conservative Party. If not addicted interventionists, Nigel Wright and his staff in the PMO were at least acclimatized to management norms that impelled them to take control of everything political that stirred in Ottawa. On cue, they propelled forward into the Senate scandal.

What was perverse about their after-the-fact attempt at damage control was the fact the PMO had not anticipated the problems Prime Minister Harper's celebrity senators would attract. Being so prominent in the public eye, spending public funds in the course of advancing party interests, how could senators Pamela Wallin, Mike Duffy, and Patrick Brazeau not have been provided special support services for their political high-wire role? Partisan activity on the public tab by senators was a practice of such long standing that many tolerated the shoddy routine as an accepted norm. But to have high-profile news magnets doing it was qualitatively different. With hindsight, the PMO no doubt rued its failure to provide management for Mr. Harper's stars, just some simple system consistent with the probity in public spending that Conservatives advocated, to see that the Conservative Party itself paid for the benefits it was receiving and to thereby reduce critical exposure for the celebrity senators' efforts. Mike Duffy even requested it.

The PMO tracked media accounts about the Conservative big names in the Senate. Nigel Wright was disquieted by reports from Conservative Senate Leader Marjory LeBreton. The PMO's point person on the Internal Economy Committee, Senator Carolyn Stewart-Olsen, indicated things were getting messy in complicated ways. Neither the PM nor those in his service at the PMO had put in place measures they should have, evidently, to avoid attacks on their vulnerable Senate flank. Wallin, Duffy, and Brazeau had been meant to attract new support, not bad press.

To the PMO's dismay, the Senate Internal Economy Committee had launched a rocket with no control system when it sent Mike Duffy's expense claims to Deloitte on February 8, 2013, along with those of senators Harb and Brazeau, for an arm's-length auditor's review.

Three days after the committee crossed that point of no return, Senate leaders Marjory LeBreton for the Conservatives and James Cowan for the Liberals did their best to establish that the designated villains in the piece would be the individual senators only, not the Senate itself. Anyone who wrongfully claimed housing allowance "should repay money with interest," they asserted. "We believe it is vital for the reputation of the Senate and those senators who are in full compliance with our rules and regulations that this determination be made as soon as possible and that the result be made public."

A couple of weeks later, when it was emerging that the Senate's lax administration and vague rules were also to blame, Marjory LeBreton gave a token nod to this deeper problem, saying, "Very clearly, this exercise has pointed out that we have considerable work to do to further strengthen and clarify the rules." Still, nobody running the Senate was seen coming forward to take any responsibility for how the expense claim problems could have gone on, with the Senate writing cheques, for years. Instead, they closed their office doors and hid behind their newspapers.

The public's wrath was being directed at the impugned senators. The tirade was well deserved. But the lightning of outrage, striking the obvious highest points and making them the sole newsworthy scapegoats for the general malaise in the Senate itself, only magnified the problems of damage control with the prime minister's celebrity senators.

The PMO was frustrated by its inability to control the senators, from their decision to retain Deloitte for an audit to some of the messages Conservative Senate leader LeBreton was conveying to the public. This was not how things worked. The PMO ran the show. There was unhappiness that the matter had been allowed to get so far beyond control. Nigel Wright would have to focus on this as a priority and clean it up.

The PM's chief of staff, though a philosophic conservative, perhaps had not yet meditated long enough on Alexander Hamilton's proverb, "That which is not necessary to do, it is necessary not to do." Nor, perhaps, had Nigel even pondered why Prime Minister John A. Macdonald's success as a politician and statesman was in part attributable to why he'd been nicknamed "Old Tomorrow." The ethos of the PMO, rather, was that pre-emptive action is superior to taking no action, that direct intervention is better than standing apart, and that passage of time will only make things worse rather than bring bland resolution to an apparent crisis.

The PM's chief of staff, mulling over his dilemma during a pre-dawn jog, resolved to diffuse the lapses of Mike Duffy, whose good efforts had contributed much to the improved fortunes of the Conservatives, to spare Stephen Harper distraction and free him to address the transcending economic challenges facing Canada. For Nigel Wright it was, quite simply, a matter of honour.

The legendary deal-maker would intervene, untie the twisted knot of ribbons, and refashion them into a decorative bow on a gift package for all concerned. A man with Nigel Wright's talents and resources could salvage the situation. As head of the PMO, after all, he had at his fingertips the formidable levers of the most powerful organization in Canadian politics.

Anchoring the southern corner of Ottawa's Parliament Hill landscape, just across Wellington Street and by the curve onto Elgin Street's opening into Confederation Square, squats a caramel-coloured sandstone fortress called the Langevin Block. It is seat of operations for the PMO.

At the security desk inside the entrance, Senator Mike Duffy signs his name, enters the date — February 11, 2013, the day senators LeBreton and Cowan have just declared that wrongfully claimed amounts should be fully repaid — and jots down the time as just past noon, then proceeds to Room 204 to meet with Nigel Wright. The two thrash things out in Wright's second-floor office for almost an hour.

The next day, the Internal Economy Committee's chair David Tkachuk comes to Room 204 to brief Wright, for a quarter of an hour, on the Duffy audit. As the Saskatchewan senator departs, Wright's call to

Senator Irving Gerstein brings him to the PMO about twenty minutes later, where he remains for a couple of hours while the two men talk over plans about what to do.

The following morning, February 13, after the Conservative caucus weekly meeting winds up, Senator Duffy and Prime Minister Harper meet, with Nigel Wright present, to speak about the expense claims. Members of the Conservative Party, especially those once baptised in Reform Party waters, have been animated by the scandal because they hate waste of public money and revile an unelected Senate. They've been registering strong complaint with their leader, giving the scandal sharper definition on Stephen Harper's political radar than would otherwise have been the case. Mike Duffy sticks to his story that he's done nothing wrong. The PM tells him that expenses he'd claimed have to be repaid.

The specific steps that then followed Nigel Wright's decision to become involved in the problems of one senator's expense claims still await explanation in detail.

Current versions of what took place conflict. The facts remain wrapped in a shroud of intrigue, clouded by partial accounts and revised explanations by some of the leading participants. But even an imperfect synopsis of how the inexplicable occurred is needed — not to make findings that only a law court might, but simply to let this strange saga impart its larger lessons about the limits of power and the low state of the Senate as a political institution.

In broad terms it is easy to see how wading into this morass simply reflected the prevailing PMO belief that its destiny was to direct political cause and consequence. In addition to that impulse, though, were inescapable personal pressures.

Mike Duffy had rendered stellar performance for the Conservatives. He'd headlined big events, hosted party conferences, inundated party donors with emails that generated cash because of his prestigious name, attacked the kind of journalists who attacked the Conservatives, posed for photos with candidates and supporters. His financial affairs had become a scandal, but the scoundrel deserved protection and help. Sure, Duffy was his own worst enemy, but so was the Senate. It had contributed to the mess. To be candid, the PMO and Conservative Party were also culpable for not having anticipated, from Mike Duffy's well-publicized issues over expenses in his prior career and Pamela Wallin's well-known spending rampages, the need for some safeguards. Everybody, as Nigel Wright could discern, deserved to eat a share of this pie.

Duffy was in trouble and knew it. If he repaid the money it would look like he was caught doing something wrong. "I did not do anything wrong," he repeatedly asserted, in these private meetings as well as to reporters in public. If he was going to be forced to repay the money, using funds he claimed he didn't have, it would need to be done in a way, he emphasized, that did not damage his reputation. Mike Duffy was certainly not going to resign.

The conundrum for the Conservatives and the PM was that the party was going to be stuck for eight more years with a well-known senator who had little remaining credibility and was now perceived almost universally as a pariah. What good was that?

Something had to be done to remove the sting. Perhaps a starting point would be for the Conservative Party to cut Duffy a cheque so he could repay the money, as the PM had insisted he do, to douse the main flames of his scandal.

Mike would go along with what might be proposed, provided he was "made whole" financially at the end of it all, and that his concern was somehow addressed about paying back the money without making it look like he'd been caught cheating, because that would be a blight on his good name and reputation. Just because something was impossible was no reason a person couldn't fantasize it.

But the fact an independent audit was now underway made it problematic, to say the least, for the PMO to contain the scandal. It would help with damage control, at least, if Mike Duffy did not co-operate with Deloitte.

Irving Gerstein was the ideal person for Nigel Wright to work with in sorting out how to structure a solution. One controlled the party's financial resources; the other, the levers of power.

Reaching this moment, Gerstein and Wright had already travelled many of the same paths: through the ranks of Toronto's business community, into charitable community work, and on to service to country through politics, including roles with the Conservative Fund which the senator chaired and on whose board the chief of staff sat.

If Wright was a skilled deal-maker, so was Gerstein. As president of Peoples Jewellers, he'd led major corporate takeovers in the 1980s and 1990s that made him head of the world's largest jewellery retail empire. Irving's other business experience included heading or serving as a director of Atlantic Power Corporation, Medical Facilities Corporation, Student Transportation of America, Economic Investment Trust, CTV Inc., Traders Group Limited, Guaranty Trust Company of Canada, Confederation Life Insurance, and Scott's Hospitality. In community service he'd been chair of Mount Sinai Hospital in Toronto, board member of the Canadian Institute for Advanced Research, and chair of the PC Canada Fund, then the Conservative Party Fund following the party mergers in 2003. For being a "respected businessman and a loyal and diligent volunteer and philanthropist," Irving was inducted into the Order of Canada in 1999, and three years later received the Order of Ontario.

Like Nigel Wright, Irving was seasoned in high-level politics. After being sworn into the Senate with Mike Duffy on January 2, 2009, he chaired the Senate's prestigious Banking, Trade, and Commerce Committee, which was just now studying the effectiveness of measures to combat money laundering and terrorist financing, and whose report, entitled *Follow the Money*, he would present in 2013. In the partisan arena, Irving had learned to absorb hits without yielding. In 2011, as head of the Conservative Fund, he'd been charged, along with Senator Doug Finley, who was Conservative campaign chairman, for violating the Canada Elections Act after Elections Canada alleged they were complicit in a scheme of false tax claims and exceeding spending limits for campaign advertisements, the so-called "In-and-Out" scheme, but charges were dropped when the Conservative party simply paid a $52,000 fine. Irving Gerstein's distinguished bearing, easy smile, and devotion to dignified roles gave him the air of a friendly man not to be tampered with.

It seemed fitting, given all the money Mike Duffy had helped raise for the party, and all he had done to improve what marketers called the party "brand," that Conservative Fund chair Gerstein should orchestrate a party cheque to cover his repayment amount. It would be a one-time payment rather than a recurring future charge. Irving Gerstein, as an out-of-town Senator himself, knew the Internal Economy Committee was mulling over revising the rules for the senators' housing allowance. Marjory LeBreton had spoken of it.

Duffy did not have resources of his own to pay back the expenses the way the PM had ordered. Although he could always go to the bank and borrow enough money, the way he might reasonably be expected to do, Duffy had been adamant that, if he was going to have to do this to save the party political embarrassment, he was sure as hell not going to end up in debt. He wanted to be "left whole" at the end of the exercise. Besides, Duffy was saying what he did was not wrong. That was his story and he was sticking to it.

Prudent Irving Gerstein decided to ascertain precisely how much money would have to be paid on Duffy's behalf from the Conservative Fund. It was thought to be in the $15,000 to $20,000 range. An unusual expenditure for an unbudgeted amount would, if above $30,000, need special board approval. While such approval could be obtained, Nigel talked about "circling the wagons," because the fewer people who knew about this back-channel payment to help the senator, the better. Wright wanted to keep everything quiet and out of the public eye.

When Gerstein got information from committee chair Tkachuk that the bill could run close to $100,000, the chair of the Conservative Fund swallowed hard. After thinking about how it would look for the Conservative Party to pay a senator such a substantial amount, Irving Gerstein knew he was in an impossible position.

While plans were being hammered out in private, reporters continued to press Mike Duffy in public whenever they could.

One reporter in Prince Edward Island inquired, on February 19, why it looked as if his "permanent home" in Cavendish had nobody living in it. The senator explained that he rented a second home in Charlottetown during the winter, making his Cavendish residence appear unoccupied. Previously, the Island's senator had explained he'd spent $100,000 on the Cavendish property to make it "a year-round home." Prior to that, at the time of his appointment in 2009, the PMO had explained on his behalf that Mike Duffy owned a Charlottetown home with his brother where he lived. He cemented this latest version by telling the newspaper, "Canadians know I'm an honest man and I wouldn't cheat on my expenses."

Not faring well on the public front, Mike Duffy pressed with greater insistence for some solution. The next day, on February 20, he wrote in an email that various scenarios had been worked out with Nigel Wright.

For their part, Gerstein and Wright grasped that many problems would ensue if the Conservative Party covered Duffy's expenses. A party payment to Duffy would add gasoline to the still-small flames of this expenses scandal. The adverse publicity would, in turn, discourage party donors from contributing money to the Conservative Fund. Indeed, feedback from the never-ending fundraising campaign by the party's "Members' Services" branch suggested chagrined contributors were closing their chequebooks, at least until they could see how this problem with the prominent senators got sorted out.

Senator Gerstein called Deloitte's managing partner, Michael Runia, whom he was on good terms with, to check if the amount really might be as high as $100,000 and explore whether, if it were paid, there'd still be any need to bother further with the Duffy audit. Michael Runia telephoned Gary Timm, Deloitte's lead auditor on the Duffy file, inquiring about how much money Mike Duffy would owe if his living expense claims were found to be invalid. When Mr. Timm reminded his partner Mr. Runia that it would be inappropriate professionally to discuss a confidential audit, the call ended.

The information Gerstein and Wright wanted could not be obtained because the confidentiality walls around Deloitte's chartered accountants who were conducting the audit precluded communication about their work. With no possibility of determining the exact liability, or of somehow getting the audit aborted, Gerstein and Wright would just have to await the Deloitte report, quietly pay off Duffy's debt to the Senate, and ensure that whatever report from the Senate got issued to the public about the audit would be sanitized to deflate the scandal as much as possible.

The PMO was not devoting this kind of attention to the Deloitte audits simultaneously underway of the expenses of senators Wallin and Brazeau, although their problems redounded equally upon the Conservatives and the prime minister who'd appointed them to the Senate. More than a few people began to speculate, "What does Mike Duffy have on Stephen Harper?"

The process the Internal Economy Committee had initiated with the auditors was not one over which the PMO had control or influence. Even if somehow such strings could be pulled, it would make for an even bigger scandal to have the audit of one senator's expenses suspended while other senators' expenses continued to be reviewed. The only way out was to get Duffy's debt paid off, so that the issue would swallow itself.

Nigel Wright probably agreed with Mike Duffy that he'd undertaken all his trips to speak to Conservative events at the behest of the prime minister or his political staff, so he would see that Duffy was reimbursed for the money he now was being called upon to repay to the Senate for travel expenses he'd previously submitted.

But when the amount turned out not to be around $15,000 to $20,000, but five times that much, chairman Gerstein balked. He recognized that Duffy had to have been padding the expenses. For the Conservative Fund to cut a cheque for $90,000 would implicate the party in his wrongdoing. In addition to the damaging legal implications of that, Conservative fortunes would be imperilled as party loyalists discovered what their donations to support Canadian conservatism were actually used for, and as voters turned their backs on it all.

Nigel Wright, being a person of integrity, probably felt he'd made a commitment to Senator Duffy about reimbursement and was honour-bound to follow through. As well, it was hard to see any other way to mop up this mess. If the Conservative Fund could not pay the debt, he would, from his own funds. As a man of personal wealth, he had money aplenty to support worthy causes and to cause worthwhile things to happen, which he routinely did through a number of charitable activities and his church work — Mike Duffy had to be a charity case.

Since the party's lawyers were incurring costs putting rules about the Duffy deal in place, perhaps the legal fees could, at least, be covered by the Conservative Fund. Because the party was paying his law firm for a number of matters over the course of the year, Arthur Hamilton's invoice covering services rendered in connection with a Conservative senator, ultimately for some $15,000, wouldn't look too much out of place.

On February 21, the P.E.I. senator publicly announced he would repay his living expenses, acknowledging he may have made a mistake declaring his primary residence was in Prince Edward Island. "The Senate rules on housing allowances aren't clear and the forms are confusing," he justified. "I filled out the Senate forms in good faith and believed I was in compliance with the rules. Now it turns out I may have been mistaken." That eroded his qualification as a senator.

In March, Nigel Wright sent an email saying Senator Duffy's repayment should be "the final chapter of the expenses issue." He clarified, "That is something to which senators LeBreton and Tkachuk and Stewart-Olsen already agreed once."

The fact Nigel Wright was independently wealthy made his desperate solution to the Duffy scandal possible. It appears his desire and ability to close the scandal down quickly was a case of a bright person doing a dumb thing — writing a personal cheque while chief of staff to the prime minister of Canada for the benefit of a senator being investigated over improper expense claims.

A payment of $90,302 for Senator Duffy appears to have been made in March 2013. But it was not mentioned until April 19, when, in an almost off-hand way, Mike Duffy acknowledged that he'd repaid the money the month before. "I have always said that I am a man of my word. In keeping with the commitment I made to Canadians, I can confirm that I repaid these expenses in March 2013."

Mystery still surrounds this. The saga would be rendered even more perplexing by Mike Duffy's subsequent assertion to the Senate, on October 28, 2013, "I have never seen a cheque from Nigel Wright." Giving this opaque sketch of the episode only provides a tentative outline of what happened, but it is the basis for stating conclusively that intervention by the PMO, intended to contain a scandal, made it indescribably worse. And that, in turn, helped reduced the future prospects for the Senate itself.

* * *

On May 9, 2013, the Senate released its report into housing claims, along with results of the Deloitte audit. The auditors confirmed that senators Harb, Brazeau, and Duffy resided permanently in the Ottawa area, but added that the rules and guidelines were unclear, which made it difficult to say categorically anyone broke the rules.

When the Senate Internal Economy Committee wrote its own report, based on Deloitte's findings, senators David Tkachuk and Carolyn Stewart-Olsen were light in criticizing their party colleague Senator Duffy. When asked by a reporter if this was a "whitewash" job, committee chair Tkachuk replied, "I wasn't interested in criticizing Senator Duffy at this point," because the money had been repaid to the Senate. "So, as far as I was concerned," he concluded, "his issue was over." In the Senate of Canada, fraudulent claims could be tolerated if the money was recouped. Criminal intent was soluble in "the honour system." Canadians became irate seeing Mike Duffy immune from the fate that would befall them in such a case.

As for the others, the Senate Internal Economy Committee ordered Mac Harb to repay $51,000 and Patrick Brazeau, $48,000. Senator Harb stated he would fight the decision. Senator Brazeau asserted that he'd broken no rules and would explore all options to overturn the Senate's repayment order.

On May 12, the RCMP announced it was conducting a criminal investigation into all the contested Senate expense claims, giving scandalized Canadians hope that, if the Senate was incapable of doing anything, at least the Mounties would get their men.

The Senate expenses scandal became a national political story in part thanks to CTV and the network's Ottawa bureau chief, Robert Fife.

He had an inside track on the dubious expense accounts being reviewed at the Senate, although the identity of his whistle-blower remained a secret. Then Robert Fife stunned everyone with his dramatic scoop that Nigel Wright, chief of staff to the prime minister, had been the one to pay Mike Duffy's $90,000 debt to the Senate for improperly claimed expenses. Not only had the top man in the PMO paid the money, Fife reported in his broadcast, but an agreement had been struck between the prime minister's chief of staff and Senator Duffy. The wagons may have been circled, but an informant was inside the security perimeter. On May 15, the PMO tersely confirmed that Wright had personally footed the bill for Mike Duffy, simply helping out because the senator could not himself make a timely payment.

If Nigel Wright wrote a cheque for the benefit of a senator under investigation and did so while chief of staff to the prime minister of Canada, he'd not only done something politically dumb but seemed to have also taken the role of political fixer into compromising territory by presumably violating section 16 of the Parliament of Canada Act, which makes that sort of thing a criminal offence.

At the same time and behind the scenes, the PMO proposed to Mike Duffy that he withdraw from the Conservative caucus until everything blew over. He protested and refused, resolving to fight for his status and reputation. Told that his choice, within the day, was to either resign from caucus on his own or be dismissed by the prime minister, he took the option that allowed greater face-saving. On May 16, 2013, Mike Duffy became an "Independent" senator for Prince Edward Island.

He joined Senator Patrick Brazeau, also an "Independent" since Prime Minister Harper had summarily dismissed him from the Conservative caucus the morning charges had been laid as a result of a domestic dispute, even though Mr. Brazeau had entered a plea of "not guilty" and had had no chance yet to defend himself in court.

Next, Pamela Wallin announced her departure from the Conservative caucus. She, too, had received a telephone call giving her the choice to resign or be fired, take her pick, but to do it that day. Her travel expenses, which totalled more than $321,000 since September 2010, were still the subject of Deloitte's ongoing audit. It was taking them a long time to dissect the omelette.

After that call from Ray Novak in the PMO, Wallin got another call, this time from Marjory LeBreton, House Leader for the Conservatives in the Senate and a cabinet minister, telling her to resign from caucus. The former journalist responded, "If you think this will take attention away from Nigel and his payment to Mike Duffy, you're wrong. The media can cover two stories at once." This was not a time for reasoning. Wallin was given one hour to resign from the Conservative caucus, and did.

On Sunday of the same long weekend, Nigel Wright resigned as chief of staff and left the PMO, a decision the prime minister accepted "with great regret."

Journalists had no trouble covering both stories. After all, they were just two parts of a single phenomenon, the fate of Stephen Harper's celebrity senators.

CHAPTER 7

Senate Scandal Liftoff

A shower of outrage poured through phone-in shows, letters to the editor, tweets, personal conversations, gossip, and online comments in response to the latest news.

After the basic elements for scandal had combined, they certainly had ignited. A number of impugned senators, taking advantage of ineffectual administration and loose reimbursement rules, had submitted ineligible claims to top up their $132,300 salaries. Not only were they seen as greedy, but worse, these privileged individuals who make our laws were now known to be breaking the rules. Canadians, resentful of anyone occupying a public office who takes personal advantage of it, were especially galled that no punishment seemed to befall these senators, who were getting away with something for which average Canadians would not only lose their jobs over but would also be charged by the police for doing.

Then the bungled attempt by powerful people close to the prime minister to intervene, while pretending they hadn't, boosted the spectacle high enough for everybody to notice. With the cover-up ploy exposed, people who were already incensed felt a further sense of betrayal.

When Parliament adjourned on June 18, 2013, the government counted on summer's doldrums and its pleasing distractions to ground the Senate controversies. Often passage of time can spare a government grief, as its mess gets upstaged by some dramatic new development and forgotten. The summer of 2013 generated lots of galvanizing news, from a deadly train explosion in Lac Mégantic to disastrous floods in Alberta, but the hoped-for fate of obscurity did not befall the Senate scandal. Intermittent revelations of new tidbits of information, in fact, only helped ensure that interest stayed at a fever pitch. So the prime minister, seeking more time to defuse the Senate crisis, persuaded Governor

General David Johnson to prorogue Parliament, delaying the new session to October. That did not work, either.

By October, the outpouring of letters, emails, and tweets from thousands of Canadians to media outlets reached a zenith. Each new turn or unexpected development in the scandal, and there were many, was not merely reported. Each became hyped as "breaking news." Journalists had much to relay, commentators plenty to analyze, and politicians something contentious to contend with. People in all walks of life remained mesmerized. The air was electric with outrage and condemnation. Canadians switched from reality TV shows to the parliamentary channel for a stronger jolt.

The morning of October 23 started for me with a radio interview about the Senate scandal by Matt Galloway on CBC Toronto's *Metro Morning* program. Following that came wider discussion about implications of the scandal with CBC's Wei Chen on *Ontario Morning*. That afternoon, Isabelle Routhier interviewed me about the Senate's fate for Ontario French-language listeners on Radio-Canada's *L'heure de pointe.* I'd already been Rex Murphy's guest on CBC's *Cross Country Checkup* for a pulse-taker on the same topic, and given more than thirty regional CBC Radio interviews right across Canada. I was just one in a small army of people being asked about the issue. Every open airwave needed a constant flow of Senate scandal content to fill it.

Six days later, I arrived at the CBC Broadcasting Centre in Toronto for a network television interview by *News Now* host Reshmi Nair about the issues discussed in this book, which by then I'd begun to write. Her producer told me, "In ten years, we've never had this strong a response to any other issue." Another producer joined in. She described the Senate expenses scandal as "the story that keeps on giving."

Few Canadians had trouble figuring out how they'd deal with self-bonusing well-paid public officials. Most seemed to identify three clearly ranked issues.

Recoupment of money, resignation from office, and punishment of offenders stood foremost. Next, the confusion caused by non-existent or ineffective Senate rules called for a day of reckoning. Somebody had to be in charge, and whoever it was needed to be held accountable for the mess. Third was the looming issue of Senate reform. Many people expressed concern that a "culture of entitlement" had overtaken senators, softening their ability to work effectively and frugally.

I was about to finish that sentence "on behalf of the Canadian people."

But senators do not represent people, so I checked myself. Then I was going to put "on behalf of the province or territory they are appointed to represent." But I know senators don't actually do that, and no Canadian really expects them to, so I really couldn't do anything more with that sentence than put a period after "work effectively and frugally." To say who senators work for, or what they do, is a big part of this national problem. That black void is another reason the Senate scandal quickly involved so much more than expense claims.

What incensed people generally was the fact nobody at the Senate seemed to understand these concerns, or even to care. Wasn't paying money back, as the Senate was now demanding, admission of wrongdoing? If there was wrongdoing, why did the senators not resign? Why was no penalty being imposed?

But the senators protested they had done nothing wrong, vowed to stay on, and desperately resolved to fight for their reputations — providing by their very resistance the force needed to further accelerate liftoff.

Scandal over people submitting improper expense claims gradually broadened when it also emerged that those running the Senate had fumbled their supervisory roles and that the place still operated, like a quaint club, on an "honour system." Honour?

Most Canadians wanted to see the backs of the scoundrels as they departed for good. It was black-and-white. Housing allowances for out-of-town senators had been claimed by three who already had permanent accommodation in the National Capital Region. Billings had been made for per diem disbursements on days the Senate was not even in session or the senator was not in town for Senate business. Air travel expenses had been claimed for non-public business or double-billed.

Yet a smaller group was now starting to see a shade of grey. After all, these claims had all been reviewed by the Senate, approved, and paid.

Only later, after the auditor general of Canada and reporters from the Parliamentary Press Gallery identified problems, did the claims get again reviewed by the Senate, this time rejected, and a demand issued for the money to be reimbursed. Had Senate administration been right the first time, or the second?

This minority, though in no way supportive of senators who'd scammed the public, felt the Senate had to address its own ethical conduct as manifested through ineffectual financial administration over an extended period. It might just clear the air if the scoundrels did not go quietly into the night, but stayed, challenged the powers-that-be, and nailed this harder truth about our scandalous Senate. Senator Mac Harb vowed to do so. One was almost tempted to applaud.

Following the Deloitte audit report on his expenses in May, the Internal Economy Committee ordered Senator Harb to repay more than $230,000 in living and travel expenses — some five times more than the $51,000 the Internal Economy Committee asked for when completing its internal audit — plus interest, dating back eight years. Senator Harb left the Liberal caucus, denied any wrongdoing, and launched legal action in an Ontario court to challenge the repayment order. He claimed the committee unfairly applied a test of residency retroactively, that all his expense claims had been approved by Senate finance officials, and specifically that Senate Clerk Paul Bélisle had cleared him to claim expenses in Ottawa.

Fighting back was not going to be an easy gambit, however, because the Senate scandal had become a morality play with a sold-out audience.

Conservatives in the Commons, trying to protect the PM's celebrity senators by scoring off an errant Liberal senator, seized on Mr. Harb's court challenge as an act of brazen defiance. Conservative Duffy, by this point saying he would repay the money as the Senate asked, provided their counterpoint. House Leader Peter Van Loan told the Commons that the P.E.I. senator "showed the kind of leadership that we would like to see from Liberal senator Mac Harb, who instead is taking up arms against the Senate, saying that he should not have to pay back inappropriate funds."

To argue that "our scoundrels are better than your scoundrel" hardly represented seizing high moral ground. Mr. Van Loan's interpretation proved to have limited shelf-life, in any case.

The morality play was just as tricky for its central characters. By fighting back, Mac Harb, Pamela Wallin, Mike Duffy, and Patrick Brazeau honed a sharp new edge to the scandal by re-positioning themselves as "victims." From this altered stance, they complained about "a flawed process" and argued strenuously that they were being "denied the rule of law." The fog of moral ambiguity, and doubt, that began to creep in and settle over the scandal only helped raise the issues higher and rendered them worthy of debate by ethicists and philosophers.

As a drama about ethical behaviour, the actors' roles really seemed jumbled. Their switch from villain to victim caused consternation in the public mind. Pamela Wallin argued a case that she'd been unfairly treated, having been subjected to retroactive application of newly made rules, which denied a fundamental principle of Canadian law. Mike Duffy, having negotiated a secret deal for others to repay his debt to the Senate in the spring, by autumn called the whole thing "a monstrous scheme" and castigated the PMO's Nigel Wright whose career had been ruined trying to help him.

Few had any sympathy at all for the P.E.I. senator at this stage, yet his chameleon-like conversion from Stephen Harper's best buddy to desperate battler against overbearing prime ministerial power made Mike Duffy an improbable champion for a cause many wanted fought.

The Senate expenses scandal entwined with the way a large number of Canadians felt about Prime Minister Harper's governing style and the steely institutional power wielded in his name by the PMO. A pre-existing sentiment about the PMO kicked in, both in Ottawa and across the country, for citizens who harboured negative feelings ranging from concern through apprehension to fear about the prime minister and the PMO as a powerhouse vehicle facilitating his role. By the end of October, 2013, a man whose kids wanted "something scary" for their Halloween jack-o'-lantern carved a pumpkin so that, shining out of the night's darkness, appeared three initials: PMO.

By late 2013, when information about Senator Gerstein's contact with Deloitte became public, Mr. Timm and other members of his audit team insisted their audit had not been influenced by Mr. Runia or anyone else.

Efforts by the Liberal senators to have Mr. Runia appear before them to testify were turned back by the Conservative Senate majority. Some emails that the RCMP obtained, however, indicate senior staff in the PMO appeared to have inside, advance knowledge that the audit would not be able to make any finding on Mike Duffy's primary residence because the senator had refused to meet with auditors.

Senator Gerstein told delegates at the Conservative convention in Calgary on November 2, 2013, "I made it absolutely clear to Nigel Wright that the Conservative Fund of Canada would not pay for Senator Mike Duffy's disputed expenses, and it never did." The technically correct assertion in Irving Gerstein's forceful address to the Conservative Party delegates must have seemed to those running "strategic communications" in the PMO as a good way to nail Mike Duffy while putting the Senate expenses scandal to rest.

It did nothing of the kind when it later came to light that about $15,000 of Conservative Party money had gone to pay Mike Duffy's legal bills in the matter.

If similar revelations of expense account scams had involved MPs, uproar in the House of Commons would have produced consequences, but could never have spiralled into the full-blown government crisis occurring with the Senate expenses. The reason lay in the core differences between Parliament's two houses.

The Senate for its own sake was, in principle, best forgotten. Humans look better out of intense light and Canada's senators especially have valid reason to prefer shuffling quietly in twilight, due to the very nature of the Senate itself.

Public focus on a scandal at the Senate could jeopardize far more than the individuals directly under investigation because Parliament's upper house never fares well with Canadians when its activities get into the news. The expenses scandal was stirring awake our festering annoyance about the undemocratic, costly, and hugely irrelevant second assembly still tacked onto our national parliament. The numb anger about the Senate's unwanted existence that dwells in our political subconscious resurfaced over this example of sloppiness and greed at the Senate. Yesteryear's questions began to be asked all over again.

Why, *really*, do we suffer the presence of this fully appointed law-making body while claiming to be one of the world's textbook democracies? What costs, *truly*, do we pay for a cozy legislature occupied by people who are individually fascinating but who collectively have no authentic role to play, leaving the best of them to "make work" for themselves by taking up personal causes and pursuing private interests? Yes, we lay out close to a hundred million dollars every year to maintain this private club as a public institution, but isn't the Senate imposing far greater costs on Canadian society than just its financial burden alone can measure?

Instinctive understanding of the answers made visceral our widespread antipathy to this colonial relic still present in our modern nation's capital.

People's conscious awareness of the Senate is generally little more than of something that is a vague mystery. While writing this book, I asked many people for their thoughts about the Senate, whose answers I pooled with what I remember clearly from my decade representing 100,000 people in the Commons. In a word, most Canadians know nothing about the Senate because it is a quaint irrelevance to their lives. When asked about Parliament's upper house, most people realize they cannot even say why it exists. Yet the same Canadians know the importance of schools, hospitals, arenas, theatres, libraries, courts, municipal councils, and the House of Commons.

Certainly a number of Canadians do follow public affairs closely, enough to be able to speak informatively about the Senate. Yet even a growing number of them, possibly because "familiarity breeds contempt," now find themselves struggling more than ever to make a case for why Parliament's upper house should still exist. Even some senators understand they are only in the place as a reward or convenience, not expected to do much except stay out of trouble. Theirs is not, as the joke goes, a "thankless task" but a "taskless thanks."

Taken together, these resentments formed an emotional receptor for news about money problems in the Senate, a synapse transferring high-voltage outrage from citizens into unanticipated responses from the PMO and compulsive engagement by Canada's news media. In all, the phenomenon became even more — a humiliating reminder of century-long impotence. Self-governing Canadians proved time and again unable to either rid ourselves of Parliament's upper house or even just to reform it.

Other factors, too, caused "the story that keeps on giving" to gain higher prominence with us, among them the police, news media, politicians, and contemporary communications.

The police deserve first mention.

When the RCMP asked CTV's Robert Fife to reveal the source for his scoop about the deal between Nigel Wright and Mike Duffy, he refused. "It is not a reporter's job to help the police do their work," said Carleton University's respected journalism professor Christopher Waddell, reinforcing journalistic integrity and freedom of the press. Protecting sources can be critical for a sensitive story, provided a reporter can substantiate the confidential information.

But as the Senate scandal proceeded, the idea got turned around: the RCMP was working for the news media.

Normally, police inform reporters about results only after they've achieved them: a major drug bust, a series of pre-dawn arrests coordinated across several jurisdictions to sweep up participants in a child pornography network, or details about the stunning arrest of a most-wanted criminal. Otherwise, police are closed-mouthed about matters under investigation. If they can't find enough evidence to press charges, they won't damage somebody's reputation if they don't make it known they were being investigated. It also helps police save face in the scenario where they do not ultimately substantiate an allegation against a citizen. Silence prevents tipping off suspects, too, denying them a chance to skip the jurisdiction or destroy evidence.

The Senate scandal, in contrast, found the police even keener to share information than a helpful reference librarian. Lengthy police affidavits brought a flood of incriminating allegations as the RCMP made public its in-progress detective work.

Corporal Greg Horton, a Mountie with over two decades of service, gained prominence when his explosive affidavits summarized the information he had so far and stated his belief about the facts, and about alleged relationships that were suspected but as yet unproven. Each affidavit was sworn to support an application for a court order to gain access to confidential information, such as emails and bank records, of various senators and officials.

Corporal Horton's untested allegations, summaries indicating the current status of the RCMP investigation into questionable Senate spending, and the police's working hypotheses in the case, were all neatly laid out and made clear to the public. The fact the police were operating within the framework of a process they had to follow did not change the larger reality that, rather than proceeding with charges and going to court with evidence to substantiate them, the RCMP initiated "trial by press" instead. The police were not yet ready to lay criminal charges, because doing so would require sufficient evidence to support and defend the charges in court. In the meantime, however, while still looking for enough such evidence, the RCMP made no effort to keep these records sealed from the public.

Like prospectors panning a Yukon stream for placer gold, Press Gallery journalists pored over the information embedded in the RCMP affidavits, teasing out the meanings and spotting the contradictions in messages between senior people in the Prime Minister's Office, the Senate, and the Conservative Party during the months of attempted damage control.

This record of highly confidential emails written with unguarded abandon by senior officials led political observer Chantal Hébert to suggest this was Canada's first political scandal where indiscreet emails laid out a clear path of incriminating evidence. She contrasted this to the primitive era when people, unable to communicate with the ease of email, instead had to meet more inconveniently face to face to settle a shady deal, in the process leaving no documentation to later damn them.

From the police, parliamentary reporters discovered more information than they otherwise could have obtained about the Senate expenses scandal. Many telephoned the Ottawa court administrator daily to see if the RCMP had filed anything new.

The ready-made stories sometimes impinged the civil rights of the individuals concerned because the incriminating revelations, or even just information about the kinds of records the police were seeking and from whom, fed another round of "breaking news," which fostered the trial of Senate scandal culprits in the court of public opinion. Media hosts and panels of commentators happily wading through all of this material acted like jurors discussing evidence in a criminal trial, pausing only once or twice to note in passing, "These are just allegations, of course. Nothing yet has yet been proven in court."

To some, this seemed a subversion of due legal process, an abrogation of the rule of law, an infringement on the right of an accused individual to have a timely chance to defend against a specific charge in court. To others it posed questions about the RCMP's ability to conduct a fair inquiry. "Unjustified criminal charges could give rise to questions not just of incompetence," wrote Tonda MacCharles from the *Toronto Star*'s Ottawa Bureau on November 24, 2013, "but whether political agendas are at play." It certainly seemed the Mounties were playing a high-risk game, throwing some bait in the water, putting out information that might spark informants to come forward and assist the police in their complex and sensitive investigation.

In November 2013, Corporal Horton swore before Ontario judge Hugh Fraser in an Ottawa court he had "reasonable grounds" to believe Prime Minister Harper's chief of staff, Nigel Wright, and Senator Mike Duffy had entered into a bribery scheme to buy Duffy's silence, produce an altered Deloitte audit, create a sanitized Senate committee report on his expense claims, and offer political cover to ride out the controversy. The affidavit before Judge Fraser was to persuade him to issue further "production orders" so the RCMP could gets its hands on even more records.

Because these allegations were not "sealed" by the court to keep them confidential while the investigation continued, they were available to reporters, who swiftly highlighted the most damning allegations and got them into the newspapers, onto the airwaves, and out through cyberspace.

Corporal Horton appeared in public as lead investigator, but was hardly on his own. Backing him up was a team of two dozen other RCMP detectives patiently combing through bank records, emails, and other information. They wove their documentary evidence together with clues and interpretations from principal players in the scandal, going to interview whistle-blower Alison Stodin for five hours at her Ontario home near Picton, quizzing Senator David Tkachuk in Saskatchewan while he was undergoing cancer treatment.

Releasing affidavits with premature information and openly laying out interim police conclusions presents a hard issue for Canada's justice system — how is it possible to balance openness in police investigations and due protection of a citizen's civil rights? A 2005 Supreme Court of Canada decision in the case of *Toronto Star Newspapers Ltd. v. Ontario* held that "Court proceedings are presumptively 'open' in Canada." In that case, the *Star* and other media companies objected to search warrant applications being "sealed" for a police investigation of an Aylmer meat-packing plant. Because the Supreme Court considers open access to court information basic to a free and democratic society, it ruled that to justify sealing a search warrant application, the police had to demonstrate that the integrity of their criminal investigation would be at risk.

In the Senate investigation, as Tonda MacCharles reported, Mounties received legal advice from a provincial Crown attorney on whether an application to seal the warrants was justified. On one of the first applications filed by the RCMP, a sealing order was in fact sought, and granted. But when media organizations challenged the order, the Crown and RCMP decided there were insufficient grounds to maintain sealing. From then on, no further effort would be made to keep information confidential during the Mounties' investigation of the Senate expenses scandal.

The RCMP did not require a court order to get documents from the PMO. Once the RCMP confirmed in May that it was investigating the Senate expenses, Prime Minister Harper personally ordered relevant emails be retained and turned over to the police, waived parliamentary privilege, and instructed Privy Council officials to release all its PMO-related documents in the matter to the RCMP, yielding in all some 260,000 electronic records.

Not everyone with potentially relevant evidence was that forthcoming, though. An RCMP affidavit in late November 2013 supported an application for a court order to produce Senate documents, which the Senate, as master of its own administration, would only release if authorized and required to do.

* * *

News media, starting with Parliamentary Press corps members who recognized a compelling story and kept digging, engaged the Senate scandal in ways that pushed it into the political stratosphere.

At the same time, the media juggernaut's insatiable twenty-four-hour appetite for fresh stories and new angles devoured all the content reporters could provide. The combined effect kept the spectacle refreshed, fed the public's sense of dismay, anger, and puzzlement, and gave the scandal ongoing presence in the minds of Ottawa's political class and citizens across the country.

CBC Television virtually institutionalized its coverage of the Senate scandal, establishing a built-in media drive to fulfill its own reporters' prophecy that "this story is not going away anytime soon." Live coverage of Question Period confrontations on the network's news channel meant Canadians tuned in to watch a daily round of confrontational action in the national political arena. Regular panels appeared Monday to Friday on Evan Solomon's well-timed 5 to 7 p.m. *Power & Politics* show, capturing each afternoon's hottest Senate scandal developments with current-event urgency that the host magnified by his intensity of tone and relentless questioning.

One panel, consisting typically of Conservative MP Paul Calandra, New Democrat MP Charlie Angus, and Liberal MP Ralph Goodale, elaborated their parties' respective takes on the latest action, like sports commentators assessing and trying to influence perception of a game during a break in play. To supplement that presentation, *Power & Politics* also featured a panel of four articulate individuals whose close attention to public affairs and general affiliation with different political parties generated a further close sorting of the daily catch.

Interspersed with panel segments were one-on-one interviews with players themselves. One day, for example, Senate Liberal Leader James Cowan arrived to give his reaction to the Conservatives' defeat, just moments earlier, of a Liberal motion to call Deloitte's senior partner before the Internal Economy Committee to explore the nature of Senator Gerstein's interaction with the firm at the time it was auditing Senator Mike Duffy's expense claims. Evan Solomon asked Senator Cowan what the Liberals would do in the next round to counter that outcome — perhaps raise a question of privilege in the Senate? It was like holding the microphone to a sweating player between periods of a game, asking how his team would overcome its bad outing so far.

While *Power & Politics* presented its primary interview segments, it simultaneously ran across the bottom of the same screen the latest news in single-phrase instalments. Above that appeared a frequently changing box of text, either a "headline" type summary of what was just being said by the person then speaking, or a question posed to viewers about the topic at hand. To the right appeared another panel of info, reporting on the "Question of the Day" poll of viewers, sometimes with questions so facile — "Do you think all emails from the PMO should be made public?" — that results were unsurprisingly lopsided: 98 percent for and 2 percent against.

Trying to cram the screen with maximum information in overwhelming fashion, another horizontal bar now and then appeared at the top, blocking out even more of the available space for the main presentation, to display a viewer's tweet — a truncated opinion with hashtag and sender's name. While filters screened which few of the many tweets got displayed in this jostling pastiche, they operated more to spare the CBC trouble over defamation or use of crude words than to provide any barrier to partisan, cynical, or factually incorrect potshots.

Generally, these hodgepodge components did not increase informative content of *Power & Politics* so much as detract from the program's serious attempt to give Canadians added value to basic news. However, the main contribution to the Senate scandal of this visual bombardment was to heighten viewers' sense of a national outrage erupting. The impact of such over-the-top production was impressionistic, giving viewers even as they were watching the show the sense their fellow citizens were getting even more agitated by the developments, wouldn't take it anymore, and were figuratively throwing open their windows and shouting out their protest by keying in twenty-six characters. It was little wonder the Senate scandal didn't "go away anytime soon."

At the weekend, Evan Solomon switched over to CBC Radio's Saturday morning airwaves for a "behind the scenes" recap of the week's national political developments on *The House*. Although radio is an easier medium than television, Solomon proved just as relentless in asking his hard questions, repeating as he did on TV the same question a second and even a third time, needling his on-air guest to deliver a desired response. In terms of the Senate expenses scandal, Evan Solomon became to CBC television and radio what Thomas Mulcair became to the House of Commons — Interrogator-in-Chief.

During the evening, CBC Television remained locked on the scandal, often opening *The National* with a full-frontal view of Thomas Mulcair launching yet another crisply damning question at the prime minister in the House of Commons. After Peter Mansbridge introduced separate political updates on the day's Senate front by Terry Milewski, Chris Hall, Susan Bonner, and others, he would often interview someone else from the CBC covering Parliamentary politics — Rosemary Barton, for example, for a more humanistic take on the same events — helping to further bond viewers with the personal dramas in this strange story.

With the panel formula also a format staple in *The National*, each week, Peter Mansbridge posed questions to "Canada's most-watched political panel," featuring *Toronto Star* columnist Chantal Hébert, *National Post* columnist Andrew Coyne, and Bruce Anderson of National Public Relations. With so much Senate scandal "breaking news" to comment on, sometimes this trio had to reconvene just days apart to interpret all the developments. If one panel is good, two are better. Every week *The National* also broadcast news anchor Mansbridge interacting with the members of "The Insiders" panel, usually Kathleen Monk, Jaime Watt, and David Herle, who stepped above their affiliations with the New Democratic, Conservative, and Liberal parties to proffer astutely non-partisan commentary and insight on political strategies.

Both panels commented on a number of developments, but overwhelmingly, for months, the leading topic was the Senate expenses scandal. If further punctuation on the Senate woes was needed, Rex Murphy — in his on-going lexicographer's contest with Conrad Black for most grand words used in the fewest sentences — provided it. The hour-long nightly CBC Television newscast was repeated throughout prime time and could be seen on both of the broadcaster's two national English-language networks.

On CBC's Newsworld, daily segments with Ian Hanomansing channelled continuous flow of informative interviews, while "Point of View" instalments by Sarah Galashan gave viewers breathless summaries of what was "trending," a public affairs imitation of updating medical report readings on the pulse of a critical-care patient. The POV info did not alter the substance of what was taking place in Ottawa, or increase anybody's understanding of it, but did amplify the scandal with outraged reactions of people across the country to news of Senate wrongdoing.

The other English-language television networks were likewise engaged by Senate issues to the full extent of their resources, while Radio-Canada's French-language broadcasts offered more concise but insightful coverage of the Senate problems. Nobody could follow them all, but across the country, whether a network or a local station, media outlets covering the Senate stories created a circular interaction by fostering broad public awareness of the scandal's dominating importance, in turn causing more Canadians to tune in frequently and avidly remain current on Senate-related news.

Throughout all this, digital communication and the Internet inflamed the scandal in ways not previously imaginable. They gave immediacy and intimacy to these Senate-related issues. The "social media" showed their anti-social potency often. Canadian Press reporter Jennifer Ditchburn, after submitting her story critical of Senator Brazeau's attendance record to the Canadian Press editor, contacted her wide circle of Facebook friends about the article's contents. In response, a steamed Patrick Brazeau tweeted that the "D" of Ditchburn should be changed to "B," and the rush of inflammatory exchanges that message provoked is a study in how, like a virus, electronic messaging can flare fast and spread far. This textbook example was only one of a million powering the Senate scandal's many details, innuendos, and condemnations through cyberspace and into political outer space.

Traditional mainstream media, fully adapted to the digital age, incorporated all possible strands of Internet action into the Senate scandal reportage. Telecasts, magazines, radio broadcasts, and newspapers all directed readers, viewers, and listeners to "more" on their websites. Real-time "polls" on a hot-button Senate question of the day were constantly updated, displaying shifting Yes/No/Undecided percentages during network television news programs. Tweets flying around space were monitored, not for content but mere mention of a key name, to tell the public what was "trending." Where opinion polls once got a bad rap for simplifying complex issues and grouping dissimilar views into meaningless categories, their methodology was applied science compared to the swamp of incomprehension offered by trends of tweets. No matter, the breathless urgency of such reporting gave an adrenalin rush to anyone desiring only a sense of "breaking news" rather than a grounded appreciation about what was actually going on.

The "Comments" section at the end of online articles published by news organizations sometimes included nuggets of new information, an insightful critique from an unorthodox perspective, a pithy phrase, useful hints about related developments, or links to online resources that further illuminated the topic under discussion. But not often. Despite this branch of Internet communication being "moderated," many comments are like letters-to-the-editor with the editor on vacation.

All this analysis, hype, information, and emotion was then turned back onto people's elected representatives when MPs returned home to their ridings on the weekends, causing Conservatives unease and opposition members to smell blood.

In the House of Commons, New Democrats and Liberals were drawn by the hypnotic lure of this unexpected way to defeat, or at least diminish, a Conservative prime minister who, at the head of a tightly controlled majority government and leading a well-organized and fully funded political party, had seemed close to invincible just months before. The role of elected representatives thus became a further escalating force giving the Senate scandal political lift.

A few members of Parliament's lower house felt protective traditionalist instincts toward "the other place" and the prime minister's celebrity senators, and so preferred not to speak with reporters about the scandal. Others had little tolerance, and some even abiding dislike, for the PMO and Senate and the powers and privileges of both. These MPs were ready, willing, and able to question and condemn. Many called out, but the voice of Thomas Mulcair, leader of the NDP and of the Official Opposition, was heard above all others as he effectively pummelled Prime Minister Harper with relentless questioning.

Mr. Mulcair realized Question Period's importance for "responsible government," with ministers of the Crown directly facing those who scrutinize their acts on behalf of the people and hold them to account. He succinctly asked precise questions and demanded the prime minister reply with "Yes" or "No." It was dramatic, a refreshing change as the NDP leader rescued the Commons from the wearisome theatrics which, ever since arrival of television cameras in 1977, saw MPs pump themselves up with feigned anger, deliver longwinded declamations, and end their allotted time with an up-speak inflection to turn their tirade into some semblance of a question. If nothing else, those lengthy "questions" gave plenty of time for a respondent to find a good answer. Not so with the Opposition Leader's potent brevity.

The politically rewarding nightly television play that Thomas Mulcair's afternoon inquisition of Prime Minister Harper got in national broadcasts reinforced and extended the communications loop of spiralling fascination. The NDP leader's role was less to bring new information to the show than it was to pick up on news in the media and directly confront the PM for answers about it the way reporters could not.

The answers Mr. Mulcair often got were scripted, narrow, and technical. The same replies were repeated time and again, or else a non sequitur was thrown back across the aisle. Either way, it was an effort to stonewall and weary the Opposition. Prime Minister Harper gave the impression he had no seasoned mentor available with sage advice about how to extricate himself from a scandal involving senators he'd appointed and staff he had hired, nor even much in the way of innate political skills to give him intuitive guidance in the matter, which was another surprise about the Senate affair.

Until the expenses scandal exposed this lack of astuteness, Stephen Harper had seemed a strong prime minister. After coming to office in 2006, he'd always seemed to get his way, whether closing down Parliament to prevent an opposition coalition ousting his minority government, proroguing Parliament to buy more time for the Senate expenses scandal to fade away, or ensuring that on parliamentary committees and in the Commons his will would be done by ministers who never strayed from their approved "talking points" and members who always toed the party line and voted as whipped.

The protracted hammering he'd been absorbing from the New

Democrat Official Opposition and in the news media began to diminish his political standing. The Conservatives held the party's two seats in the November 25, 2013, by-elections, but with great effort and much nervousness. In early December 2013, Conservative MP Gordon Chong gained wide interest and support for a bill to redress the imbalance in Parliament by curtailing prime ministerial control. The prime minister appeared vulnerable in ways not before discernible, unable to take full charge of his own circumstances.

Aggravating such perils was the backroom thinking that, if a leader could "plausibly deny" knowledge of or involvement in a matter that's become scandalous, he'd be able to safely bluff his way across thin ice to the far shore. People cannot blame him, runs this sophist's excuse for ducking responsibility of office, if he "did not know." The concept of plausible deniability suggests a leader is either incompetent, or controlled by others, neither possibility enhancing the renown of the person in question: the leader is either inept or a pawn, take your pick. This approach to "issues management" damages government itself by dissolving accountability and candour, like acid corroding the support wires of public trust that hold in place the structure of democratic government.

Due to his reluctance or inability to confront and surmount the Senate expenses scandal, mere effort at damage control turned the affair into a long-running nightmare for Stephen Harper. His success depended on what he did not know. All that his partisan opponents and the politicized media had to do was show up at work each day to be served another helping of the Conservative government's failure to master the Senate conundrum.

Day after day, Mr. Harper faced inquisitor Mulcair in the Commons. The government fended off attacks on the PM's fading star Conservative senators — whether it was Pamela Wallin's travel costs, a secret payment of $90,000 to benefit Mike Duffy, or Patrick Brazeau's expense claims and personal problems. The government defended itself, too, over the role of the PMO in helping Senator Duffy and its attempted cover-up of the arrangement.

Over the months, the PM maintained a direct and emphatic manner concerning the scandal. The problem was that as time passed his own positions turned inside out: defending his celebrity senators then later disdainfully excoriating them; accepting Nigel Wright's resignation with "deep regret" in May, then changing the story to say he'd been "dismissed," and by October accusing his former chief of staff of "deception."

Sometimes the prime minister signalled the line of defence by his own limited explanations, clearly playing down the issues and seeking to diminish the importance the opposition and news media were according them. More often the rejoinders came from his parliamentary secretary instead, in a further effort to diminish the issue by wearing down those asking questions about it. For the opening months, MP Dean Del Mastro, who was in his own battle with Elections Canada over alleged campaign finance violations, had this role. Then a shuffle of parliamentary secretaries early in September 2013 gave MP Paul Calandra the unenviable task.

Parliamentary Secretary Calandra crafted his role in the morality play not as a respondent but as a protagonist who sought to distract and annoy the opposition, deflecting their barbed arrows by refusing to join issue, offering them anything but direct answers. During one Question Period in early November 2013, rising to deflect questions aimed at the PM, the Ontario MP for Oak Ridges-Markham blithely turned his face into the storm and toughed it out with twenty-three consecutive responses.

The character Mr. Calandra developed integrated the decidedly mixed qualities of barroom bouncer and court jester. Sometimes he'd push an aggressor out the debating door or counter-attack the questioner, attempting to impugn NDP leader Thomas Mulcair and former Liberal leader Stéphane Dion. Or he'd simply drive off the opposition interrogators by frustrating them away from the scene, introducing unrelated references to sports events or cultural life in distant parts of the country.

Other times the PM's parliamentary secretary held attention with folksy stories. Members of Parliament heard about his Italian immigrant father's eighteen-hour days running a pizza shop, the man who delivered their pizzas, and his two young daughters working to earn their weekly allowance. Each time, the moral in the story entailed right conduct, which he then contrasted to the ethical standards of the morally deficient senators.

For a complete change-up, parliamentary secretary Calandra tried mystifying by allusion: "Kids in short pants to Mike Duffy apparently is like garlic to a vampire!"

Whatever tactic, by the time he'd finished, time was up. The question was dead in the centre aisle. Across the country, many saw it as just another way for the government to say, "No comment." And for those who'd been watching for months, what had seemed certain in the spring was revised during the summer and reversed by the fall.

Canada's House of Commons remained consumed with problems that arose from Parliament's other chamber. It was certainly not a productive use of parliamentary time and resources, but it helped to keep the Senate scandal aloft.

Electronic communications helped the Senate scandal reach new heights.

Once the RCMP investigators got as far as they could with the evidence they had, another affidavit would be sworn to get a court order for subpoenaing more documents. As noted, these progress reports about an on-going criminal investigation brought new revelations into the public domain. Although nothing alleged had yet been proven in court, Canadians got the impression that the individuals whose faces they were seeing on newscasts — a widening circle from one or two at the start who were said to have knowledge of the Wright-Duffy deal, to "a few" as the PM acknowledged in the Commons on October 24, to some thirteen a week later, to fifteen by mid-November 2013, in the running tally by the Press Gallery — were "guilty."

New allegations the media plucked from affidavits were quickly relayed to their ever-hungry news organizations to become part of the ongoing coverage of the RCMP's unfolding Senate investigation. The police documents were also posted online where they could be read in their entirety by anyone. That is where the Deloitte audit reports, minus some elements, were also to be found by anyone interested.

Today's websites that consolidate information on developing events combine traditional information gathering and high-tech components of communications. This integration brings Canadians news that not only scandalizes us, but also makes us part of the story. A viewer can watch the breaking news, tweet a comment about it, and see his or her capsule opinion appear, moments later, on the nation's television screens.

Each medium converges and every method leverages off the other.

Each reinforces the others, melding into a single flow, a news-making and information juggernaut that holds a power of fascination over us in equal parts of shocking revelation, political education, and dramatic entertainment. Big-name journalists are crowded by previously unknown bloggers and individuals who just happened to be holding their camera phone in the wrong place at the right time and have uploaded images that go viral.

This omnipresent machine trolls relentlessly, discovering what fits the story, vectoring public opinion onto an issue until it acquires critical mass in part measured by "hits" and "likes," capturing the mind of citizens and convulsing public affairs of the country. In the course of following the dynamic unfolding of Senate scandal events, Canadians became participant observers.

Finally, what holds fascination in the scandal for Canadians is paradox.

In our national makeup is a subtle attraction to double-meanings, even a sense of dark humour about the innate contradiction of things.

Yes, the hard reality is inescapable. The Senate scandal, still far from over, has already seen reputations go down in flames. Political positions, at first staked out so authoritatively, were later abandoned or even reversed. Ten times more money has been spent, so far, to recover funds from senators than they had wrongly claimed.

Even these rudimentary facts hold irony. So did the conundrum of Stephen Harper's government which, seeking to distance itself from the Senate mess, only became more ensnared by it.

Yet there is a higher level in politics from which Canadians take meaning. As with our country itself, where much is absurd but perhaps actually well founded, our political culture also embraces and expresses self-contradictions. When I was a member of Parliament, as a "Progressive Conservative" I could go in two opposite directions at the same time and still be consistent. I also embodied, as an elected representative of the people who was at the same time parliamentary secretary to a minister of the Crown, our contradictory reality that Canada has not one, but two, sovereigns. The mechanisms of governance through which I worked, from our Constitution with its rival juxtaposition of individual and group rights, to regional programs jointly sponsored by different levels of government, represented the institutionalization of ambiguity. Our unified country embraces divided loyalties, and public life teems with conflict over pre-conceived understandings about what is reasonable or possible. Canadians recognize paradox, and paradox was the very face of the Senate scandal.

A paradox of the news media being able to take such an active role in stirring up the Senate scandal that so damaged Prime Minister Harper was that reporters' time and talent had been freed up by the PM's and PMO's own restrictions on the flow of information about government matters. A relatively idle and hungry Ottawa press corps, starving for substantial fodder for news, devoured such mundane matters as a few expense accounts by senators. The Parliamentary Press Gallery helped make the story sensational until it overwhelmed Mr. Harper and pro-voked the PMO to intervene.

National political columnist Chantal Hébert suggests "a crowded policy agenda certainly makes it harder for scandal-related stories to sus-tain momentum." In the late 1980s and early 1990s, I witnessed as an MP on Parliament Hill how hard-working journalists were swamped keep-ing up with major stories about free trade, the Constitution, the end of the Cold War, Québec sovereignty, the GST, equality issues, Aboriginal questions, and abortion rights. That hectic Mulroney government era contrasts with Prime Minster Harper's time in office when "the news flow has trickled down to drops and information control has routinely defaulted to outright suppression."

From the Conservative perspective, though, many valuable ini-tiatives were being taken by the Harper government. So the perverse paradox from their partisan slant was that wall-to-wall news coverage of the Senate scandals, and the sustained public heat it generated, combined to prevent the PM and Conservatives from getting deserved attention for important work and credit for successful accomplishments.

Even on a personal level, the altered public perception of the PM flowing from the Senate scandal detracted from Stephen Harper's per-sonal satisfaction in getting his fine book on early professional hockey, *A Great Game*, published in September 2013. In a country where hockey is our national bonding agent, he'd expected and deserved a happier outing.

A truly poignant paradox was the fate of all three of Stephen Harper's celebrity senators. At the Conservative Party's 2011 biennial convention in Ottawa, Pamela Wallin and Mike Duffy had been happy co-hosts at centre stage. For the 2013 convention in Calgary, the duo was not only noticeably absent, but the two former Conservative darlings were now condemned by leader Stephen Harper. Politics is an unforgiving trade.

These well-known personalities, widely recognized non-partisans before they were appointed to the Senate, had been chosen to enhance the Conservative party's lustre by lending it some of their fame. But in the end, each star's fall from heaven inflicted far greater damage to the Conservatives than if the Tory trio of Wallin, Duffy, and Brazeau had just been grey unknowns sitting quietly at infrequent Senate meetings collecting their generous pay.

Canadians are renowned for saying "Sorry!" for the slightest blip, even when the other person is at fault, but the embarrassing expenses fiasco in the Senate did not follow this pattern — making it seem like a most un-Canadian event. Nobody was contrite, or said they were sorry, or apologized. Did anyone even admit to mistakes? Almost nobody retreated into obscurity by exiting down the avenue of shame. Instead, everyone under attack just fought back. The instinctive survival response of choice was a brazenly childish stance that something or someone else was to blame: "It was raining." "My sister made me do it." "The forms were confusing." From the prime minister on, everyone tried to pass the buck.

One person who did retreat without blaming anybody and who has remained silent about everything up to the time this book was going to press, Nigel Wright, personified the paradox of the whole scandal. A man who sought so hard to help did the greatest damage. "His decision to personally reimburse the housing allowance of a high-maintenance Conservative senator," observed Chantal Hébert, "has wreaked unprecedented havoc on a sitting prime minister and his palace guard."

Also paradoxical is what had become a general practice. A number of principal players in the Senate scandal treated email as a secure channel for secret and sensitive matters, although everybody knows an email is about as confidential as a postcard to the world. RCMP investigators reconstructed a trail of incriminating digital messages between people in high places, individuals who later wished they'd picked up the phone or talked face to face instead of efficiently hitting SEND. The trials at which such "paperless" communications may be tendered as documents in evidence of criminal intent could, in future, curb such facile use of digital communication and so reinforce Ottawa's dominant culture of secrecy.

A crowning paradox was that the all-powerful PMO found its match, and discovered the limits of its power, in the most ineffectual political institution in Canada.

Stepping back from these many features and details of the scandal, a larger reality comes into view.

The Senate, illuminated by the glare of its expenses debacle, is now fully visible for what it is: a time-trapped oasis of contentment, a body undeserving of a place in contemporary Canada, puzzling to us for even still existing, a hollow shell bereft of real purpose, a legislative assembly devoid of meaning, contributing nothing but costing us abundantly.

Stirred by this reality, agitated Canadians express in many ways, including opinion polls, intensifying resolve to push the Senate into its unwelcoming future, where either reform or abolition await.

Meanwhile, hollowing out of the Senate accelerates.

CHAPTER 8

Scandal Hollows Out Canada's Senate

Mac Harb resigned from the Senate of Canada in August 2013, igniting another round of media and public attention to the expenses scandal, keeping the issue hot in summer's doldrums.

He had first vehemently denied he'd done anything wrong when interviewed late in 2012 about his housing expense claims by the Senate Internal Economy Committee. He protested again when the committee sent his claims to Deloitte for audit. When that review was completed in May, Deloitte auditors reported "a lack of clarity" in Senate rules on housing expenses and concluded they were "not able to assess the status of the primary residence declared by Senator Harb." The Senate Internal Economy Committee, though, was in no mood to see any part of the problem laid at the feet of Senate administration, so it wrote a report saying the rules were clear and ordered Senator Harb to pay back the money.

Canadians were incensed, seeing the chance being given to Mr. Harb to simply repay money they understood he'd fraudulently claimed and still be able to carry on as a senator. If somebody stole from their employer but got caught, they reasoned, just returning the funds wouldn't be enough. There needed to be a penalty, too. Did senators operate according to some special code of ethics that placed them above laws applied to others?

Senator Harb, however, was just as incensed. Protesting he'd done nothing wrong, he initiated a court challenge against the Senate to quash its repayment order. He contended "most senators made similar claims" and said his were in keeping with common Senate practice. He'd resign from the Liberal caucus, but remain in the Senate as an Independent while fighting his court case. Liberal leader Justin Trudeau had said if Senator Harb cleared his name, he could return to the Liberal caucus.

So why was Mac Harb now reversing himself about the money, retiring, and abandoning his court challenge?

One reason of course was that Mike Duffy, who'd also protested he'd not done anything wrong in submitting similar expense claims, had now orchestrated repayment of his own $91,172 debt to the Senate. Duffy's reversal was tantamount to admitting he'd been wrong, which by extension undermined Mac Harb's position, making his court challenge an even greater uphill battle. Even so, as Mr. Harb departed the Senate, he still contended he'd done nothing wrong, that he'd been treated unfairly by a Conservative-dominated Internal Economy Committee, and predicted the auditor general's investigation, due to be completed by 2015, would vindicate him.

But apart from Senator Duffy's switch, there was more at play that caused Mac Harb to call it a day. Repaying a total of $231,649 as he quit the Senate, the veteran parliamentarian explained that his dispute with the Internal Economy Committee "made working effectively in the Senate unrealistic." His lawyer, Paul Champ, said his client just didn't want to be "the poster boy" for the Senate scandal anymore. Had he not walked away, Mac Harb might have remained a senator until 2028.

The Liberal leader in the Senate, James Cowan, greeted the news by reinforcing the broad line of Senate defence that the united front of Liberals and Conservatives had adopted: "I've always said this is not a problem of the Senate. This is a problem of some individual senators and their interpretation of the rules."

A significant point is that leaving seemed not to make much difference in income. In 2013, a senator earned $135,200 annually for doing relatively little work. For doing no work at all, Mac Harb would still get $122,989 each year for the rest of his life, if the parliamentary pension for his combined years as MP and senator, as calculated by the Canadian Taxpayers Federation, was correct.

Once Mr. Harb began collecting a pension almost as large as his Senate salary, this unexpected twist further scandalized Canadians. People resolved anew that something had to be done about Parliament's upper house.

In the Senate itself, other senators took note of this development. It wasn't the same around the place anymore. The comforting shroud of public indifference had been replaced by riveting attention. The Senate had become a more partisan, less collegial club. Inspired by Mac Harb's timely example, other senators who'd put in six years and thus qualified for a Senate pension realized that early retirement could be a personally satisfying option for them, too. With the Senate on its way down, why stick around to age seventy-five?

In August 2013, Mac Harb ended his court case against the Senate, saving himself a long and expensive legal battle, but that didn't mean he still mightn't be in court over his Senate expenses. The RCMP was on his case. After the Ottawa Centre MP was appointed to the Senate in September 2003, he claimed a "primary residence" just far enough away to qualify as an out-of-town senator eligible for the secondary accommodation allowance when staying in his Ottawa residence. At one time he claimed his "primary residence" was in Westmeath near Pembroke, at another juncture in Cobden, a small community up the Ottawa River Valley between Renfrew and Pembroke on Highway 17. The RCMP visited his "primary residence" up the Ottawa Valley, but found the place not much lived in, except for the accumulated thousands of flies who'd perished inside over time. On February 4, 2014, the RCMP charged former Senator Harb with breach of trust and fraud. The maximum penalties upon conviction for these Criminal Code offences are five years imprisonment for the former, and fourteen years for the latter.

Mac Harb was not the only person to resign from the Senate of Canada in August 2013.

Manitoban Rod Zimmer, an engaging Winnipeg businessman and philanthropist who'd been involved in dozens of sports organizations and cultural activities and raised a great of money for the Liberal Party, had difficulty getting serious recognition for his contributions in the Senate after arriving in 2005 as an appointee of Prime Minister Chrétien. Whatever Senator Zimmer did in the upper house seemed to get upstaged by his other news.

On August 27, 2011, the senator achieved wide publicity for his marriage to Maygan Sensenberger by artfully using Parliament Hill as a stage set. The happy newlyweds made a prominent procession past the trim green lawns and the Gothic revival stone buildings in bright sunshine, the long train of her white wedding gown held by two happy attendants, followed by a parade of well-wishing friends in dark sunglasses. The couple had kept their love secret until she, an aspiring actress, had turned twenty-one.

More routine publicity in the months that followed included posing with Burton Cummings of the Guess Who, posing in a big kiss while holding their pet dog, posing beside a private jet before winging down to Florida, and such. Sharing these memorable moments with the universe through the Internet did not do much to underscore Mr. Zimmer's work in the Senate either.

The next really big news came on August 27, their first wedding anniversary. This time the international spotlight was not publicity Senator Zimmer sought. An Air Canada morning flight from Ottawa to Saskatoon was forced to land so the crew and police could deal with a dramatic disturbance on board caused by Maygan acting up and making alarming threats, reported in court documents to include "I'll slit your throat!" and "I'll bring this plane down!" After she was held in jail that morning, the senator's wife appeared in provincial court and was ordered by judge Albert Lavoie in Saskatoon to keep distance from her husband until the case was heard. In September she entered a plea of guilty to causing a disturbance and the charge of threatening her husband was dropped. Senator Zimmer, embarrassed by the situation, appeared with his wife in court, and was supportive. What made this sensationalist news tabloid-worthy was not only the fact that the handsome Mr. Zimmer was a fit and energetic Canadian senator, but that at sixty-nine he was forty-six years older than his attractive aspiring actress wife.

Senator Zimmer's next appearance in the news was actually related to the Senate itself. In February 2013, the Internal Economy Committee held in camera meetings with him to review questions about his housing allowance claims. This drew TV cameras. The committee pronounced that there were no problems.

Two months after the Senate voted in June 2013, however, requesting a comprehensive audit of all senators' expenses by Canada's auditor general, Mr. Zimmer resigned, citing health reasons, five years ahead of reaching mandatory retirement age.

* * *

Every senator was annoyed by the expenses fiasco. Some felt they were being singled out for malfeasance, as Mac Harb alleged "most senators are doing." The rest rued how the scandal besmirched them.

As early as December 2012, at least one of his Senate Conservatives colleagues had told Mike Duffy to resign his seat. By spring 2013, a number were declaiming in public about the senators whose claims had started the scandal. Their general line was that nothing was wrong with the Senate, just a few of its bad characters. Seeking to restore their reputations by distancing themselves from the culprits, these worthy incumbents accomplished nothing more, however, than feeding the intensifying public mood that was making the Senate itself an even hollower place.

On May 21, 2013, one of the Senate's most active members, Colin Kenny, stated, "With respect to the housing allowances, three senators took advantage of a rule that allowed them to designate any abode as their principal residence. All three chose places outside Ottawa — places they visited from time to time but that weren't their homes. By anyone's definition of morality the three shouldn't have done this. But the rule said they could, so they did, and received generous housing allowances for doing so."

Starting from "the original finding of the Senate Committee for Internal Economy that the three had pulled a fast one when it came to claiming housing allowances," Senator Kenny went on to say that, beyond the Senate's order they pay back the money, "there has been no attempt on the part of the Senate to reprimand anyone for bad behaviour." He continued, "You can't just sweep things like this under the rug and pretend it is business as usual. Wrong is wrong, and without formal censure, the Senate becomes part of the wrong."

Senator Kenny, a Liberal, nailed perfectly a dimension that really bothered Canadians — the Senate idea that if you just repay, all is okay. His emphasis on the need for punishment eventually translated into the Conservative resolutions five months later by which the Senate voted to suspend senators Wallin, Duffy, and Brazeau.

However, Mr. Kenny's quest for "reprimands" only emphasized the larger issue at the core of the scandal. By omitting the Senate administration from any culpability, he was as determined as anyone to create a few high-profile scapegoats while avoiding any criticism of the structure that allowed the senators to operate as they had. Everything else, the deeper problems of a malfunctioning Senate, would be "swept under the rug" so senators could "pretend it is business as usual."

One of the few effective senators — he'd been especially active in leading the Senate National Security and Defence Committee, and he'd previously held high offices in the Liberal Party and worked closely with Prime Minister Trudeau — Senator Kenny was certainly someone to heed.

However, Senator Kenny's ability to address big issues became compromised in the public mind when complaints from one of his female staff members became highly publicized. In October 2013, Pascale Brisson told reporters she'd had to spend half her office time handling personal, non-Senate chores for Mr. Kenny — booking medical appointments, paying his credit card and utility bills, even finding him a personal trainer. Without the scandal spotlight already on the Senate, and without Senator Kenny having been outspoken about the behaviour of other senators earlier in the year, the story would not have gained traction. In November, Pascale Brisson also filed a formal complaint of sexual harassment against Mr. Kenny. This news was even hotter, in the context of how bad things were at the Senate, especially when it sparked other women to come forward and report earlier alleged episodes involving him. Mr. Kenny resigned from the Liberal caucus while the allegation was being investigated. He confidently stated his name would be cleared, and by April 2014, it was, by fellow senators.

But now his once clear voice was mostly just an echo.

Senator Mike Duffy, Senator Pamela Wallin, and Senator Patrick Brazeau were suspended from the Senate of Canada in October 2013.

Mr. Duffy's $91,172 in expense claims had been repaid, apparently by Nigel Wright, the prime minister's chief of staff, using his own money. Ms. Wallin's order to repay $138,969 to the Senate had been satisfied, seemingly using money from selling her New York condominium.

Mr. Brazeau had been unable to repay the $51,482 required by the Senate, so in July 2013 the Senate began garnishing 20 percent of his earnings to recover the amount over time.

The call for punishment that first sprang from the throats of Canadians upon learning of the Senate expenses scandal, then had been voiced by senators themselves, by autumn 2013 was taken up by Prime Minister Harper. He had changed. In April he'd told the Commons that he'd looked at Pamela Wallin's travel costs and found them in line with what a senator from Western Canada would incur over the number of months involved, but the PM now signalled to his troops in both houses of Parliament and to Canadians across the land that those who cheated had to be punished.

Weeks of procedural wrangling ensued in the Senate. The Conservatives initially tried to oust the designated scoundrels with separate motions, then a combined one, then further individual motions — requiring separate votes on the fate of each of the three senators.

"The Senate of Canada is the place where 'due process' comes to die," said Senator Patrick Brazeau when speaking in the upper house on October 22. He was addressing his fellow senators about the resolution before them to suspend him from the upper house. He, as well as senators Wallin and Duffy and several others on both sides of the aisle, condemned the proceedings as circumventing the rule of law and due process because they were being denied a proper hearing and timely presentation of all relevant evidence.

Each of Stephen Harper's celebrity senators mounted dramatic self-defences in the upper house, which included specific allegations and personal accusations, earning return fire from Marjory LeBreton, David Tkachuk, and Claude Carignan. Mr. Carignan had replaced Senator LeBreton as Government Leader in the Senate on August 30.

One of those criticizing the measures to remove the three senators' salaries and privileges and place their offices under the administration of the Internal Economy Committee was Conservative Senator Hugh Segal, who said the Senate was, "firing them without firing them."

Other Conservative parliamentarians critical of this rush to judge the impugned trio were Senator Donald Plett of Manitoba, a past president of the Conservative Party appointed to the Senate by Prime Minister

Harper, and Blake Goldring, Conservative MP for Edmonton Centre-East. Mr. Goldring, a lawyer with a quarter-century of experience in constitutional matters, took it upon himself to intercede on behalf of the three senators and make a case that the resolutions were unconstitutional. He suggested that, if the measures to suspend the senators passed, Governor General David Johnston ought to invoke his reserved powers under the Constitution to set them aside.

These critics saw the Senate acting as prosecutor, jury, judge, and executioner. Canadian law and practice requires "due process" and senators Wallin, Duffy, and Brazeau were entitled, they argued, to have clear charges against them; evidence adduced that would prove the charges laid against them; detached deliberation by a neutral tribunal, not an assembly of self-interested partisan peers who included many seeking to make them scapegoats; and objective determination of the appropriate sanction to be applied.

The resolutions were seen quite differently by others. Those scandalized by the way the three senators in question had received public money to which they were not entitled, and further scandalized by the fact repayment seemed to be the only thing required of the senators to set things right, saw kicking them out of the Senate of Canada was urgent, necessary, and just. "If I'd taken money from my employer like that, I'd not just have to pay it back," went the common refrain, "I'd lose my job, too."

A number of senators called for a proper hearing of their cases. Senator Segal castigated the Senate for acting like a "Star Chamber," a reference perhaps obscure to those unfamiliar with the secret court of the king of England in which individuals were tried, often on vague charges, and convicted, usually with no chance to offer a defence, and sentenced, normally to death, all without the trial ever being made public.

What was happening in the Senate of Canada in October 2013 fell far short of those standards for closed-circuit "justice." But the fact that such hyperbole and emotion prevailed in the Senate of Canada underscored why it was unsuited for its self-assumed role as a court, in addition to the fact that what it was doing had dubious constitutional authority. The inherent problem, in this as in other matters, is that Canada's Senate — although a public institution — is a universe unto itself, making its own rules, judging its own conduct, sealing its own fate.

* * *

During this phase, while the Conservatives tried to align procedural protocols and political support to oust senators Brazeau, Duffy, and Wallin, other controversies related to the expenses scandal seized Senate committees and ensured more top billing for the upper house.

The Internal Economy Committee was, naturally, one such committee. It was now being chaired by Senator Gerald Comeau, who had replaced Senator David Tkachuk after he had stepped down to concentrate on his cancer treatment. The committee was riven over whether to call representatives from Deloitte to testify about Senator Gerstein's role at the time of the firm's audit of senator's expense claims. Senator Comeau, in leading the Conservatives to defeat this Liberal initiative, observed that the RCMP — who were now already looking into the case — were better suited than a Senate committee to conduct a police investigation.

In the Banking, Trade, and Commerce Committee, yet another front of battle, Senator Céline Hervieux-Payette in early December 2013 sought, as the committee's Liberal deputy chair, to force the committee chair, Conservative Irving Gerstein, to step down.

Her move, which caught Mr. Gerstein by surprise, caused little astonishment to others who had been witnessing the Senate sink into a complete void. The reputed "bi-partisan" and "collegial bond" of Senate committees had always been a convenient myth to help justify the Senate to its well-wishers, but the reality of partisan politics now rose into full sight. On the grounds that Senator Gerstein's embroilment in the scandal with Nigel Wright and Mike Duffy was tarnishing the Senate's most prestigious committee, Senator Hervieux-Payette moved that he resign. She held up the esteem and credibility of the committee, but her partisan opponents saw an attempted Liberal putsch.

As the elected chair of the committee, Senator Gerstein ruled her motion out of order.

Donald Oliver retired from the Senate of Canada in November 2013.

Upon leaving the upper house, the twenty-three-year veteran of the Senate and its Deputy Speaker decided he just did not want to be in his seat for his last Senate session that week. The Conservative senator from Nova Scotia quietly told reporter Jane Taber of the *Globe and Mail* that, instead of basking in the glory of the traditional fond farewell, "I just want to sort of slip away." It was, Taber thought sadly, "hardly a fitting end to an illustrious career."

"I'm sort of going out in a cloud of ignominy," he said in Pleasant River, Nova Scotia, "which is not what all of the work I have done over the years should signify."

Donald Oliver was no stranger to public humiliation growing up in Nova Scotia, as I'd come to know over many years of friendship with him. He'd been punched, bullied, spat upon and, as Jane Taber added, once was sneered at by a waiter in Halifax, "You niggers can sit there as long as you want — we don't serve people like you!" after his family had been ignored for twenty minutes. Now, more than five decades later, Senator Oliver recalled those bleak years to observe that he was still subject to derision, but for a very different reason. "We all, since the summer, have been ridiculed. Many senators have been humiliated by comments and questions made by the general public arising from this scandal."

At the time Mr. Oliver spoke, the Conservative majority in the Senate had just forced by its unprecedented vote the suspension of three of its members — Mike Duffy, Pamela Wallin, and Patrick Brazeau — without pay for the duration of the Forty-First Parliament. Although proud of his years in Ottawa, listening to fellow senators squabble made him lament, "What a terrible way to have to leave an institution that I think so highly of."

Senator Carolyn Stewart-Olsen had been at the epicentre of the Senate's handling of the expenses issues as a member of the Internal Economy Committee and its steering committee.

Appointed by Prime Minister Harper to the upper house in August 2009 to represent her home province of New Brunswick, the long-time Ottawa resident who'd moved to the capital in the 1980s had worked as a nurse before converting to political activity with the Reform Party and becoming a confidant and strong supporter of Stephen Harper. She owned a condominium on Ottawa's Carling Avenue, where she continued living after becoming a senator until selling the property in May 2011.

As an out-of-town New Brunswick senator, Carolyn Stewart-Olsen claimed the home she and husband Terry Olsen had built at Cape Spear, where her family has roots, as her "primary residence." That made her Ottawa condominium a "secondary residence" and made her eligible to claim an $86.35 per diem for food and the housing allowance in Ottawa. This was consistent with Senate rules.

When the *Huffington Post* reviewed Senate records, it appeared Senator Stewart-Olsen had claimed $63,594 in travel and living allowances during her first nineteen months as a senator. Also, between September 2010 and May 2011, she had claimed per diems on days the Senate did not sit, no committee or caucus meetings took place, and she herself had no Senate-related business in Ottawa. Although that sort of practice would scandalize Canadians, it was accepted practice under Senate rules. Only in May 2013, in the crush of bad publicity the Senate was sustaining, did the senators decide it would be prudent to modify their rules and stipulate that per diems could only be charged on days senators had legitimate business in Ottawa.

Something else the *Huffington Post* noted was that Ms. Stewart-Olsen claimed $4,360.88 in living expenses during a three-month period, from December 1, 2010, to February 28, 2011, when the Senate sat for only seventeen days: eight in December, none in January, and nine in February. When asked about those reimbursements, the senator told *Huffington Post* she should not have made claims for days the Senate was not sitting. "I will absolutely repay immediately if my staff … if we, made an error in claiming per diems," she said.

Ms. Stewart-Olsen's Senate calendar showed no public business in Ottawa during this same period, although she was paid $2,520 for her home accommodations and $1,840.88 for meals on days the Senate did not sit. She told the *Huffington Post* the housing allocations were fairly claimed under the $22,000 annual budget senators have for living costs in Ottawa, but said her staff shouldn't have charged per diems for days the Senate was not sitting.

"It hasn't been easy for any of us, and I am extremely sorry that our own people kind of got caught up in the web of all of this. But you have to learn from mistakes. You have to learn that if you did something wrong, you have to own up to it," she said, the strangest of any apology.

Three weeks later, as the Senate prepared for its second day of contentious debate on motions to suspend senators Duffy, Brazeau, and Wallin without pay, Senator Stewart-Olsen announced she was resigning from the Senate subcommittee responsible for the series of controversial dealings with their expense claims.

Ms. Stewart-Olsen, as one of the three members on the steering committee of the Internal Economy Committee, had come under scrutiny earlier in 2013 for the steering committee's handling of a report on Senator Duffy's housing expenses. Both she and Senator David Tkachuk, who had chaired the subcommittee, said their report did not criticize Senator Duffy because he'd already repaid the money at the time its report on him was released.

In an email to the *Globe and Mail*, Senator Stewart-Olsen explained, "It has been a difficult time."

As the scandal deepened and swamped their lives, senators became distressed by the continuing demise of the institution they occupied. Some felt a possessive sense of protection, defenders of a place they alone seemed to understand.

Needing to clear things up and to show the public that senators were at least responsive to public outrage, the Senate initiated actions implicitly damning of its Internal Economy Committee and its own administrative operations.

First, the Senate asked the RCMP to investigate some of the expense claims, as if it did not know that in Canada the police never need an invitation to look into suspicious behaviour. However, the Mounties did acknowledge that they were conducting a criminal investigation. Meanwhile, the Senate's request to the RCMP caused the Senate ethics officer, Lyse Ricard, to suspend her own investigation. In early June 2013 she issued a terse statement that she'd have no further comment. Senator Raynell Andreychuk, chair of the Conflict of Interest for Senators

Committee, had to explain to the public that senators had not ordered Ms. Ricard to put her investigation on hold, and that the Senate ethics officer was not "walking away" from the issue.

Second, the Senate also voted to ask the auditor general to examine and report on financial compliance in all senators' records, something not previously requested by the Internal Economy Committee when it retained Deloitte at the start of 2013 to review claims for only four senators.

One of these initiatives addressed criminality at the Senate. The other confronted financial impropriety. Both focused on the same subject, the operating practices of the Senate of Canada. Each ensured there would be new dimensions and long life yet for the Senate scandal. Neither the work of the RCMP nor that of the auditor general would improve the feeling Canadians had for the Senate; rather, they would inflame it further.

Some senators, who had been passed over in the internal review conducted by their Senate colleagues in 2012 and 2013, had sombre premonitions about what an external, professional audit might expose in 2014. While some senators resigning before reaching age seventy-five were leaving because they no longer wanted guilt by association with Canada's Senate, cynical observers suspected others departing did not want to find themselves subject to the auditor general's scrutiny of their expenses.

Apart from the police and the auditors, there were the reporters. A number of senators found themselves in an unaccustomed spotlight for expense claim problems or for participating in damage control that compromised their ethical conduct and challenged the rule of law.

Puzzling to just about every Canadian, because of the PM's reputation for being all-controlling and because of the extensive powers of the PMO, was the Conservative government's glaring inability to respond intelligently to the Senate expenses scandal or successfully contain it.

The simpler truth, though, was that the institutional inertia of Parliament's upper house was merely claiming yet another crop of those who would interfere with the place. Anyone who actually thought they could engage with the Senate entered treacherous territory at their political peril.

The frustration the PMO experienced with the Senate was no product of deliberate check or intelligent counterbalancing of power by those in the upper house. It was simply the routine operation of the Senate's black-hole phenomenon, a death force in Canadian public affairs akin to the Bermuda Triangle's mysterious powers in civil aviation.

Senator Gerald Comeau resigned from the Senate of Canada in November 2013.

The Nova Scotia Conservative who'd been chairing the powerful Internal Economy Committee said his decision was not related to the expenses scandal. Even so, the all-consuming fiasco prompted questions from Parliament Hill reporters, requiring him to reply that his resignation had "nothing to do with the scandal, no. You can trust me on that." To be sure, he added, "I'm not leaving with any clouds over my head. I'm as clean as a whistle."

The sixty-seven-year-old senator from Meteghan Station had been appointed in 1990 by Prime Minister Mulroney and before that had served in the Commons as MP for West Nova between 1984 and 1988, which is when I got to know personable Gerald Comeau. He said he'd actually decided two years earlier that he would retire by the end of 2013, before the expenses scandal soured life for everyone in the upper house, but only told Prime Minister Harper about his decision in June 2013, when the Senate was under siege. It is hard to think the embattled mood of the place didn't create a tipping point to reinforce his thoughts that it might be time to depart.

But when Senator Tkachuk gave up chairing the Internal Economy Committee, Senate Government Leader Marjory LeBreton asked her reliable and steady colleague Gerald Comeau to take over the powerful position. He agreed to do so until the fall, and steered the committee through several more turbulent months. On his last day as a senator, Gerald was making the case that the committee did not need to hear senior Deloitte partners about their audit, which Liberal senators were pushing for, because, as he argued, any investigations were better handled by police trained for that purpose than by a committee of senators.

He stuck with his plan to leave on his own schedule, despite now chairing the most powerful Senate committee and having years ahead as a senator. Gerald Comeau's retirement at the end of November 2013 came seven years before the end of his term in office.

Senator David Braley resigned from the Senate of Canada at the end of November 2013.

An old-style Progressive Conservative who'd always worked hard at the constituency level in every campaign, even ones the party was not going to win, Dave had memorably helped in the 1984 election, which saw the PCs win a landslide, driving old ladies to the polls in his Cadillac. He raised money for the party, and was the single largest contributor to Stephen Harper's Conservative Party leadership campaign in 2004. At the time Prime Minister Harper named Mr. Braley to the Senate in May of 2010, records showed he'd donated a total of some $86,500.

As owner of the Toronto Argonauts and B.C. Lions, David Braley is the only person to own two CFL franchises. His engagement in sports has extended to chairing the CFL Board of Governors, owning the Vancouver Whitecaps Football Club, chairing the 2003 World Cycling Championships in Hamilton, and being a director of Ontario's successful bid to host the 2015 Pan Am Games. He is also owner and president of Orlick Industries Limited, a leading auto parts manufacturer. In the greater Hamilton community, he is an important employer and well-known philanthropist.

When first arriving in the Senate, Mr. Braley told Canadian Press his appointment was "a great, great honour," and that he looked forward to using the opportunity it provided to make his community "a better place." He was used to being someone who made a difference.

One party insider, who's known him for years, told me, "David Braley cannot be controlled by anybody. The PMO's effort to run the Senate rankled him."

When Senator Braley announced he was resigning November 30, 2013, Senate Government Leader Claude Carignan suggested that, while "every senator has had a bad experience" with the Senate scandal, he did not think it was part of the Hamilton senator's decision to resign. But when interviewed by CTV's Mercedes Stephenson, he indicated he'd chosen to retire early from the Senate because of frustrations and disappointment over the ongoing Senate expenses scandal.

Earlier, in September 2013, he'd also told the *Hamilton Community News*, articulating the prevailing Senate line that nothing was wrong with the Senate itself, "There are four people who are causing the problems for the other hundred senators." As a result, "We are being tarred and feathered." The senator added that his wife had asked if he'd consider retiring, understandably concerned how the ongoing Senate expenses scandal was hurting the reputation of anyone who was a senator.

When he departed, David Braley was leaving the Senate of Canada three years before the end of his term.

Senator Hugh Segal announced in December 2013 he was resigning from the Senate of Canada, effective June 2014.

Long a pillar of the Conservative Party, Mr. Segal was actually appointed to the Senate by Liberal Prime Minister Paul Martin, who at the time was trying a cosmetically less partisan approach by interspersing a couple of non-Liberals among his Liberal appointees. He also named a Saskatchewan senator who'd been affiliated with the NDP.

While in the Senate, Hugh Segal took issue with several bills that had the support of the Harper Conservative government. Having once been chief of staff to Prime Minister Mulroney, though, Hugh knew something about the PMO perspective so kept its senior people, as well as the PM, regularly appraised of his positions, which prevented the antagonism directed to other senators who seemed, as they put it, to "freelance."

Senator Segal was, as noted, outspoken on issues relating to the Senate expenses scandal and the process used to suspend the three senators. He told CBC's Rosemary Barton, "On these core principles — due process, rule of law, and presumption of innocence — it is when someone is unpopular that you have to stand up and fight as hard as you can. It's not hard for people to say we think those principles should apply to people who are popular. But when people end up not being popular, that's when you really have no choice but to make that stand."

On Senate reform, Mr. Segal had supported shortening terms to nine years in office, as the Harper government proposed. When he reached that milestone himself, even without it being made law, he decided to move on to a new position as Master of Massey College in Toronto, where he would succeed former journalist John Fraser.

Hugh Segal left the Senate twelve years before the end of his term.

Following their suspension from the Senate for the duration of the current Parliament, Mike Duffy remained the most sphinx-like of his entire life, Pamela Wallin retreated home to Wadena to give solace to her ailing parents while they sought as every parent does to console and make things right for their child, and Patrick Brazeau's plight provided an unflattering reflection on public life in contemporary society. His career portrays the nature of our country starkly.

Without money and without work, facing court dates and looking for accommodation, Patrick stood defensively and alone. Several senators who saw the torture of a courageous human being sought to help. Some felt a point of explosion was close. He could not go back to the Congress of Aboriginal Peoples, since the organization had forsaken its former national chief, whom it had so enthusiastically embraced earlier. He could not go back to the Senate, because moments after senators voted to suspend him without pay, his office door was locked, his phones and email barred, and he became *persona non grata*.

Looking for work and seeking a channel "to get some of the hard questions answered," Patrick Brazeau applied to join the Parliamentary Press Gallery, as a writer for *Frank* magazine. His application was rejected, on the grounds he was still a senator. His writing for *Frank* ended when he refused to pen sensational and salacious stories. For trying to maintain focus and personal dignity, he was trashed in the publication's next edition.

Some weeks later his job as day manager at Bare Fax, a central Ottawa restaurant, bar, and strip club, brought a media swarm to record a further low, as they saw it, for Patrick Brazeau. He was earning the money he needed for food and support payments, and quietly explained "a job is a job." All this fed the Internet commentators and critics who exceeded themselves in denigrating a person who was now both down and out. Smugness and smirks greeted any news about Patrick Brazeau from those living easy, comfortable lives.

Senator Patrick Brazeau's hard edge and sharp comments made him a target in many quarters. Whenever he stirred up a "social media" firestorm of commentary it was unequal battle. Senator Brazeau, to his detriment, remained an active combatant when he should better have retired from cyberspace battle. The effort to diminish and denounce the former national chief of the Congress of Aboriginal Peoples was not confined to Twitter exchanges and the like, but included also a sanitizing purge of the CAP website to remove Patrick Brazeau from history, and deft removal from Wikipedia of links to Senate proceedings in which he'd told his side of the story on expense claims.

Parliament Hill officials tell me Patrick Brazeau was "difficult to work with" and that "there were problems." Reporters did not shy away from sensationalizing to the public any personal information about missed child support payments, allegations of sexual abuse, or absence from Senate committee meetings. Chiefs from the Assembly of First Nations chided the national chief of their rival organization and wrote the minister of Indian affairs with a catechism of allegations about Brazeau. It had always been this way.

Patrick Brazeau's character and perspective put him at odds with many folk, so it was unsurprising he decided the best defence is a good offence. In high school he learned karate. Later, he went into military training. He learned to box. When the Twitterverse was invented, he struck out through it, too, becoming his own worst enemy because a lack of "netiquette" meant he inflamed rather than cooled those he interacted with. When Ron Garrett interviewed him at Maniwaki for the Ottawa *Citizen,* before he became a senator, he reported an ongoing rivalry between Brazeau and another young Aboriginal leader in the community. When it came to national politics and the future of First Nations, especially Aboriginals living off reserve, the stakes were higher and the recriminations greater. All his life he's had to fight.

On February 4, 2014, the RCMP laid charges against Patrick Brazeau for breach of trust and fraud, the same Criminal Code offences that Mac Harb faces. It's the same penalty, too, a possibility of five years imprisonment for breach of trust and fourteen for fraud.

Ten days later, the Conservative government, having turned on those it once lionized, left no detail unattended. Finance Minister Jim Flaherty announced, in his 2014 budget tabled on February 14, legislation to prohibit suspended senators accruing pensionable service. A senator must serve for six years before his or her pension vests, so a further way to punish those being punished is to shave this benefit as closely as possible. It makes sense, but is such fine grinding of a punitive measure as to seem vindictive.

Several senators are concerned, as am I, about the well-being of Senator Brazeau, a man tested like few others. He is not, as Senator Marjory LeBreton told a reporter interviewing her over a pleasant summer lunch, "a failed experiment."

Just being a senator was now enough to get someone into the news, since the press had declared open season on Canada's most protected species. Senator Roméo Dallaire made national news for falling asleep and driving into a lamppost on Parliament Hill, without injury to himself or anyone else. Previously, Senator Fabian Manning of Newfoundland and Labrador earned publicity being hospitalized after hitting a moose while driving in a rural area between St. John's and St. Brides.

As for the Senate itself, the year 2013 turned out very badly in the news department. It sustained a number of premature resignations. Vacancies accumulated, with the prime minister taking a pass on filling them. Public opinion shifted further in favour of abolition. The New Democratic Party got plenty of signatures on its petition to "Roll up the Red Carpet," a poetically energized term for Senate abolition. Resolutions in favour of abolition passed in several provincial legislatures.

All senators felt mounting unease about the quest to reform or abolish the body of which they were members. Only about 6 percent of the population did not favour one or the other. Even the Harper government seemed to be shifting from reformist to abolitionist.

Since 2006, the Harper government had bills in Parliament to shorten a senator's parliamentary life to a single term of eight or nine years. The government also introduced legislation to facilitate election of senators. Neither measure had yet been enacted. Strong opposition came from Liberal senators. Loud objection was heard from several provincial governments, protesting that such measures needed not just a federal statute as Mr. Harper proposed, but a constitutional amendment that would involve them. The Senate bills were not pushed ahead in Parliament by the Conservative government; it seemed like it was losing heart for tinkering over an institution that it was now learning for itself is impossible to change.

Who knew what would happen next? The six or seven years during which the Harper government had attempted to reform the Senate had, by now, contributed to a sense of misgiving among the senators themselves. Each of the many senators whom Prime Minister Harper had named to the upper house had been required to pledge his or her support for Senate reform as a condition of entry. But they came to like the old ship pretty much as they found her after starting upon the voyage.

The PM had repeatedly declared that the Senate had to be changed, and had received several electoral mandates to do so. Suspecting he needed confirmation about the course he'd set, he initiated a reference to the Supreme Court of Canada about how his plans to shorten senators' terms of office and provide for their election meshed with the Constitution — a ruling that, as this book went to press, was still awaited. Already, however, Québec's Court of Appeal had ruled that the PM's proposed changes to the Senate required amendment to the Constitution. In October 2013, the Harper government's Speech from the Throne said tersely that the Senate would either be reformed or would vanish.

Throughout the piece, all senators continued to exist in bittersweet limbo.

Those still occupying seats in the Senate of Canada realized they had deck chairs on a ghost ship.

CHAPTER 9

A Relic Lost in Orbit

"An appointed Senate," said Conservative Party leader Stephen Harper on December 14, 2005, "is a relic of the nineteenth century." He was being gentle.

The physical presence of Canada's only legislative upper house is still to be found in Ottawa, included for the sake of its visual appeal in guided tours of our country's Parliament Buildings. The institution itself, however, is lost in time, a relic from centuries past, only seeming to be modern because of a website giving it virtual presence in cyberspace.

In the east end of the main Parliament Building, atop the rocky promontory where the once-strategic Rideau Canal descends to join the mighty flow of the Ottawa River, the sedate Senate chamber is one of Canada's more striking rooms. Its carved stonework and high-vaulted ceilings with stained-glass windows and grand chandeliers exude the very atmosphere of history. The walls display eight massive oil paintings depicting scenes of the Great War. Desks and chairs in elevating ranges, three aside, face each other so that when partisan appointees are from time to time present, they can face each other as Government and Opposition supporters, in the adversarial structure of political life inherited from England. The slowly fluctuating membership of the Senate is itself often a record of prior levels of Liberal or Conservative electoral strength in the country, making even the Senate's representation outdated.

The floor is covered with thick red carpet, giving the chamber a cloak of silence by muffling sound and expressing the Senate's character as "the Red Chamber." Red is the colour of royalty. Seven hundred years ago in Britain, when the king and his subjects began battling over just who was going to run the country, their saw-off was to have two houses in Parliament, one for the monarch, a second for the people.

The name "parliament" was derived from the French verb "parler" meaning "to speak," and the upper house spoke for the king. The lower was where the people's voice would be heard. The houses were not called "upper" and "lower" because they were physically stacked, but because in the profoundly hierarchical society of feudal England, the king and the aristocracy supporting him were, in the view of those bequeathing names to institutions, seen as superior. By the same standard, the common people were "uneducated rabble" in the preponderant view of the upper class, a view that reinforced their resistance to any democratic or populist impulses in society and to their easy designation of the peoples' chamber as Parliament's "lower" house. After the French Revolution in the last decade of the 1700s toppled that country's king and transformed England's Gallic neighbour, Britain's social establishment was seized by revivified anti-democratic instincts, a big setback for the people trying to gain a greater say in their government.

The king, or intermittently queen, did not sit in the upper house, but came on certain occasions. Those in regular attendance at the upper house of Parliament were the nobility of the country, his lords of the realm. That is why the place got its name, the "House of Lords," and its red carpet designating regal lineages and status. The House of Lords remained a powerful body, being closely associated with the reigning monarch, who wielded great power, imposing taxes, raising armies, and expanding the fleet of ships in the Royal Navy to enable Britain to control the world's seas and expand its global empire to places like North America.

The lower house was likewise populated by stand-ins for the real source of its power, the people. They elected representatives to attend and speak in their name. As a result, the lower house for the common people's spokesmen came to be known as the "House of Commons." Colours were important to identity, so if the Lords had red as a symbolic extension of their regal status, representatives of the commoners adopted green for its association with the grass on the village or town "common," the open space of community where citizens could freely assemble, mix, and speak.

Today in Ottawa, centuries later, the Senate's red carpet is matched by the counterpart green carpet of the Commons. The security pins worn by senators incorporate red, those of MPs, green. Senate letterhead and business cards are printed with red ink, those of the Commons, green. Colonial heritage is retained even in the details.

With their separate chambers and chosen colours, the Lords and the Commons proceeded, over the next half-millennium, to work out their relationship, make laws, authorize taxes, approve spending, and balance the powers of government between Crown and people.

Such a parliament, with its two rooms to accommodate its separate assemblies is classified by those who make up categories as "two-roomed" or "bicameral" — *camera* being Latin for room. This distinguishes it from a "unicameral" legislature, which is what all Canadian provinces have today. Such legislatures are typical of societies free from a hierarchical social system, societies that do not need two separate legislative rooms to keep class warfare at bay, as was the case in Britain. Unicameral legislatures exist where any notion of "class" or privilege in politics is antithetical.

However, as mentioned, such was not the case in England. The lords and nobles who were proxies for Crown interests got their positions in Parliament simply by being born into Britain's hereditary class structure and held them for life. Members of the House of Commons got their temporary positions by being elected or re-elected by the people at regular elections. Those in the Commons who were elected to Parliament had to remain attentive to the needs and interests of the king's subjects who voted; those in the Lords who were unelected did not.

One of the basic rules was that the king was barred from entering the House of Commons. This not only symbolized the independence of the people's representatives, but helped preclude intimidation or coercion of them by their sovereign. Establishing a parliamentary "no-go zone" was reciprocal. Representatives of the people could not enter the House of Lords. What linked the two solitudes in this institutional standoff was a second rule. Any new law would have to be approved by a majority in each of Parliament's two houses.

Even though the king had a strong buffer zone in the House of Lords to protect his power, he needed to hedge his bets. So another rule was put in place, which stipulated that no new law passed by Parliament could become valid until the king himself had signed it. Thus the umbrella term "Parliament" in fact covers three elements — the House of Lords, the House of Commons, and the Reigning Monarch.

Over many centuries in Britain, further rules were added to this operation. One resulted from a major battle about how the king and his ministers in government were spending the money raised from taxing the people. At the end of this protracted struggle over "control of the public purse," this new rule stipulated the House of Lords could no longer initiate any measures that involved spending of money, nor could it create any new taxes or increase existing ones. Only the people's elected representatives in the Commons could do that. This victory was a milestone on the road to greater control by the king's subjects over his government. The transition would eventually be labelled "the rise of democracy" as convenient shorthand for many changes gradually accomplishing transfer of power from monarch to people.

As both cause and effect of this power-shift, the right to vote for elected representatives was expanded from a restrictive "franchise," held only by mature males who owned property, to a "universal franchise" that included everyone.

While all this was happening, Britain embarked on fashioning an empire with overseas colonies, its very first being the island of "New-found-land," whose fishery was the magnetic attraction. Later, other colonies were established, first on continental North America, and then elsewhere around the globe. Colonization entailed exporting British business, language, currency, naval and land military forces, religion, justices of the peace, laws, and legislatures. The overseas extension would replicate "the Mother Country," a reference by which colonials acknowledged their infancy status. Colonists would be governed to British standards and values.

By the time the northern North American colonies that would eventually become "Canada" received this cultural implant, these imported, centuries-old British institutions and practices had already been altered by history's slow-rising tide of democracy.

In the Canadian colonial provinces then came further changes. The right to vote was extended to wider circles of people far more easily than it had been in Britain. With so few settlers, the voters' lists were skimpy and elections would have seemed comical if only a handful of people could participate. Britain's political establishment resisted any drive to extend the franchise, because that would mean poor and uneducated people in class-riddled Britain voting; and besides, Britain's more populous electoral districts had a big enough electorate to give the existing arrangements the appearance of being acceptable.

In the British North American colonies that would later become provinces in Confederation, another change involved the melting away with time of the British prejudices that restricted the franchise. The ban against Roman Catholics holding public office was removed early. The vote would be extended over time to those who did not own property, women, younger people, minority groups, Aboriginal peoples, prisoners, individuals with mental disabilities, and, finally, judges.

As for the institution to which these voters were electing representatives, the "Legislative Assembly," or lower house in the transplanted British model for a parliament, it also evolved in its more egalitarian North American setting, as did the appointed upper house, whose appointed members were hand-picked by the colonial governor. Calling the upper house a "House of Lords" would have been just as easily mocked as the wearing of powdered wigs in rough-hewn log cabin settlements, so, instead, it was called the "Legislative Council." Its members were the most powerful and influential men in the colony. They maintained Establishment control over colonial life.

The governor himself, of course, was an all-powerful official dispatched by Britain to run the colony. Inevitably chosen from the upper class, and appointed by the monarch in concert with the prime minister and minister for colonial affairs, such governors were to a man well-bred and also well suited for the requirements of maintaining a hierarchical structure. The tradition of British-born aristocrats serving as head of state would linger interminably in colonial Canada until 1953 when the first Canadian was finally appointed governor general.

In this social and political hierarchy of Canada's colonial provinces, the people's elected representatives in the Legislative Assembly were voices unheeded. Real power remained vested in the Legislative Council, which fit like a glove around the governor's hand. It would take armed rebellions to achieve realignment of government to better balance power between Crown and the people. The first thirteen of the king's North American colonies to rebel went beyond seeking just a better balance. They succeeded in breaking from the control of King George III through all-out war that began in 1775 and ended when they formed an independent country, the United States of America.

Two more colonies, Upper Canada and Lower Canada, followed with armed rebellions in 1837. They were unsuccessful in achieving complete regime change, but did trigger a constitutional transformation. The British, having already lost their most populous and prosperous North American colonies, panicked at the prospect of others joining the rebellious thirteen. Lord Durham was dispatched to discover what was troubling the remaining British North American colonials. After his fact-finding tour to the forerunners of today's provinces of Québec, Ontario, and Nova Scotia, Durham recommended the fusion of the Legislative Assembly, where the people were represented, and the ministers of the Crown, who exercised the powers of government. This concept for "responsible government" came into existence with revamped constitutions for these colonies. As a result, from 1840 ministers met face to face with elected representatives in the same chamber.

Again some new rules were needed. The ministers who formed the colonial government, chosen now from among the elected representatives, could only govern if they retained the confidence of a majority of the people's representatives, "confidence" being expressed by their votes. If a premier and his ministers had majority support for their proposed measures, such as new laws or tax increases, they could continue to govern. If they did not, the governor could invite another member to form a government if it appeared he might garner majority support in the Assembly instead. Otherwise, the governor could dissolve the Assembly so the people could elect a refreshed one in a general election.

In this democratic transition to responsible government in Canada, a question arose: What are we supposed to do with the old Legislative Council?

Nobody was really sure. It was a leftover, a spare part.

In two colonies, the forerunners of today's provinces of Ontario and Prince Edward Island, it was decided that, at a minimum, if the legislature's upper house was to continue at all, it should be elected by the people. In both cases, though, it became clear that electing members of the upper house was as inappropriate a stopgap as fitting a sailing ship with a steam engine.

Even though Ontario proceeded to elect members of its Legislative Council for the next quarter-century, it was recognized as outdated. An institution to curb the democratic impulses of the people, it had no contemporary value to Ontarians. As long as the Legislative Council existed, it would continue costing inconvenience and money just for the sake of enacting the same laws twice instead of once. Monarchical restraint on the law-making system still existed in Ontario anyway because the Crown, as embodied in the lieutenant-governor, remained part of the law-making process. He still had to sign a bill that had been voted into law by a majority in the Legislative Assembly before it could take effect.

Because Confederation enabled Ontario to revise various aspects of its government, it used the opportunity to make one major overdue change. It jettisoned its upper house. In the years since, nobody has even noticed it's gone.

In Prince Edward Island, the Legislative Council was retained for a short while after Confederation, although Islanders were as able as Ontarians to see that their upper house was unnecessary. It only took longer because Islanders went down the road of changing an existing legislative body rather than simply abolishing it. It took decades of acrimony, back-pedalling, and damaged careers to push through the institutional consolidation. Eventually they managed to merge the Legislative Council into their Legislative Assembly. The result was one legislature for Prince Edward Island, with two categories of members — assemblymen and councillors — both elected by essentially the same voters. No real distinction remained between the two categories as time passed, and fewer and fewer remembered to refer to them by their slightly different titles. In the twentieth century, that distinction collapsed completely.

For other colonial provinces that came into Confederation with upper houses still part of their constitutions, only a few more decades of practical governing were needed to demonstrate that they, too, had been saddled with an inappropriate colonial vestige. Colonists had already shucked off other wildly unsuited institutions and practices Britain had exported that were doomed in the New World because they neither fit the values nor met the needs of our more egalitarian society.

The effort to establish "state religion" in colonies where freedom of religion was paramount had been one example. Setting apart "clergy reserves" of prime land for the Anglican and Presbyterian churches was anathema to the classless society gradually emerging in the territories that would become Canada. So was the law preventing Roman Catholics holding elected office, a relic from the days King Henry VIII couldn't get a divorce so overthrew the Church of Rome and its pontiff and made himself head of the replacement "Church of England," which promptly granted him a divorce. That ecclesiastical chess game, which included banning Catholics — anyone who took "the oath of transubstantiation" — from serving our country in public office, was deemed unworthy of lasting imprint here.

Slavery was abolished, too, starting with a statute in Upper Canada in 1793, and culminating with complete abolition in 1833. White owners had both Aboriginal and black slaves, and some First Nations individuals also had slaves, both Aboriginal and black. Chief Joseph Brant owned some forty black slaves.

The same spirit that helped Canadians shuck off these inappropriate traps and trappings from earlier eras would also come to bear, understandably, on the colonial version of the House of Lords, the Senate of Canada.

The whole thrust of history was to liberate Canada from its colonial harness.

We did not embrace bloody revolutionary war to do this, but rather deliberate and peaceful evolution. Milestones in the twentieth century started with Canada's contributions to the Royal Navy; followed with our insistence on being a sovereign signatory to the Treaty of Versailles ending World War I in which Canadians had sacrificed so much but which saw our country come of age among the nations of the world; then proceeded with the Statute of Westminster in 1930, which ended any further enactments by Britain's Parliament having force or effect in other countries such as Canada that were still part of the British Empire. In the 1930s came creation of the Bank of Canada to establish government control over monetary policy and money supply, and formation of the Canadian Broadcasting Corporation on the premise that the airwaves are a public resource belonging to the people of Canada.

In the 1940s, after another world war in which Canada became a significant military power, came the end of judicial appeals to Britain so that Canada's own Supreme Court really lived up to its name, serving as the highest and final court for determining justice in our country. This was followed by the phasing out the concept of Canadians being "British subjects" when the Canadian Citizenship Act created a new status of equality for all people across our land. In the 1960s, this democratic idea was extended when the right to vote was given to Aboriginal Canadians and the Bill of Rights enacted to secure the civil liberties of Canadian citizens. By the 1980s this principle was further advanced by entrenching a Charter of Rights and Freedoms in the Constitution of Canada. Another milestone was the provision that henceforth no amendments to our Constitution would need to be enacted by Britain's Parliament, but could instead be carried through here in our own country.

From abolition of the clergy land reserves for exclusive benefit of approved state religion, to the elimination of appointed second chambers from all our provinces after Confederation, these changes defined Canada's peaceful evolution into a modern, diversified nation.

Despite widespread progressive reform, an obvious vestigial remnant of medieval England lingered — the Senate of Canada.

Having two sovereigns, the Crown and the people, has institutionalized ambiguity and bequeathed to Canadian political life its perpetual foggy greyness. As a result, we operate in a constant cloud of confusion about who is really in charge, something compounded by a federal division of powers giving us two ministers separately in charge of such common realms as agriculture and transport, environment and commerce. Having two legislatures instead of one — a lower and an upper house — further cloaks comprehensive accountability in Canadian government.

The good in so much division of power is that it makes it hard for a tyrant to take charge. Muddling through is the cost we pay for our "Canadian way" of governing, which is highly frustrating both to citizens and those inside the process, but at least provides an innate check on power.

We've operated with these two solitudes of sovereign power — the Crown and the people — for so long that individuals accept as normal a government system based on rival sources of political legitimacy. Life becomes most complicated at the points where Crown and people connect and overlap, which they do in Parliament. So another rule was developed to address this, stipulating that no member of the Commons could "hold an office of profit or benefit from any emolument under the Crown." This meant nobody in the chamber of Parliament where the people were represented would be in service or obligation to the Crown, or getting pay from government funds. This rule was an extended application of the old rule keeping the House of Commons and House of Lords (in Canada, the Senate) separate from each other.

Prohibiting an elected representative of the people from holding any office under the Crown became a problem, however, when he or she was appointed a minister of the Crown, as the new face of "responsible government" required. Cabinet ministers in our country were chosen from among members of the legislature and, from 1867 onwards, from the House of Commons and Senate of Canada as well.

At first, the solution was for an elected representative, on being named to cabinet, to resign his seat so a by-election would have to take place. Then the individual would run for re-election in that by-election, giving the people in his electoral district a chance to consent for him to serve the Crown while still being their representative. In short, the sovereign people would, in each case, vote on whether to make an exception to the rule.

This was, however, a time-consuming and costly burden in forming a cabinet to run the government. It even made it hard just to shuffle cabinet ministers, because an elected representative would get a *different* office under the Crown if, say, moved from being minister of canals and railways to minister of finance or postmaster general. In 1857, after more than a decade and a half of this difficulty, the law was modified in

Canada to exempt ministers from fighting by-elections if the change to a different cabinet position came within thirty days of their last appointment as a minister of the Crown.

It was a technical provision to permit a minor adjustment, but the fertile mind of John A. Macdonald hit upon using this exemption to have ministers sworn in one day, sworn into a different portfolio the next day, then get reversed to their original position. Dubbed "the double shuffle," this expedient manoeuvre circumvented the vestigial rule from medieval England; it also drew criticism from Macdonald's political opponents and those who were enslaved by tradition, but greatly pleased an increasing number of people in this country.

An exception to this exception was the Senate of Canada. As many as three or four, and once even five, senators served as cabinet ministers in the Canadian government after Confederation, in days when the full cabinet had only ten or twelve ministers. Because these senators were not elected representatives of the people, the rule did not apply. It was hard to say just who the senators did represent.

They were lost in limbo in the evolution of Canada's constitutional governance. Members of the Commons clearly served the people who elected them and some of them also had also been authorized to serve the Crown as its ministers. By comparison, the role of senators was ambiguous — to the point of being unknowable.

In this interface between the people and the Crown, the place of Canada's senators faded away in the background. They lived into old age and died in office, to be replaced by other aging men, shuffling in the twilight of uncertainty for another century while the antiquated role of the institution they occupied evaporated entirely.

Pascal Poirier would occupy his habitual place in the Senate of Canada from March 9, 1885, to September 25, 1933, which added up to forty-eight years, six months, and sixteen days. That gave Pascal the Canadian record as the senator who served for the longest time. A more recent example is Lowell Murray, who was the longest serving senator when forced to retire at seventy-five. Appointed to the Senate on September 13, 1979, and departing September 26, 2011, Lowell spent more than thirty-two years and thirteen days in the place. Canadian senators become noteworthy for their longevity, not their legislation.

When senators could hold office for life, the records were more sensational. Georges-Casimir Dessaulles was still a senator when he died in 1930 at the age of 102 years, 6 and 1/2 months. On at least two occasions Canada held the dubious distinction of having the oldest legislator on the planet. First was Senator David Wark, who'd been in the upper house for nearly thirty-eight years when he died in 1905 in his 102nd year. The second was the aforementioned Senator Dessaulles, who was already eighty when appointed to the Senate but appeared ageless over time in his unchanging full white beard. He died, a Canadian senator, in his 103rd year.

A subcategory of senators with longevity consists of those who start in the Commons and finish in the Senate, like Mac Harb and Gerald Comeau, except the time of those two was short compared to that of Azellus Denis, a parliamentarian for fifty-five years and eleven months. Azellus was first elected to the Commons in the general election of October 14, 1935, and re-elected up to the time he was moved over to the Senate on February 3, 1964 — a year before the new mandatory retirement age of seventy-five, meaning he was "grandfathered" and could stay on. When Senator Denis died, Prime Minister Mulroney appointed as his Senate replacement long-serving Liberal MP Marcel Prud'homme, a parliamentarian for close to half a century. Marcel entered the Commons as a young man on February 10, 1964, and was re-elected up to his appointment to the Senate on May 25, 1993, remaining in the Senate until retiring at seventy-five in 2009.

The presence of so many old people in the posh upper house over the years provided rich material for jokes, but often the truth was funnier, if harsher — senators asleep in their seats row after row, senators with Alzheimer's commanding Senate pages to help rush them to important meetings with cabinet ministers that turned out had only been scheduled by some fragmentary trick of memory in a slipping mind.

In 1963, the Québec government changed the rule allowing the appointed members of the province's twenty-four-seat Legislative Council to hold their position for life, forcing them to retire instead at age seventy-five. In 1965, Prime Minister Lester Pearson's government also restricted senators to a term of office ending at age seventy-five, copying this reform already implemented in Québec as one detail in the far-reaching Quiet Revolution. Mr. Pearson's government is often hailed for its body of social legislation, but few remember to list as one of the kindest acts of Liberal welfare in that decade closing at least one wing of Canada's costliest old-age home.

Even though senators now only sat to age seventy-five, this small coterie of a hundred-odd Canadians continued to play out roles according to the old rules. The substance was gone. The shadow remained.

The rule about keeping the monarch out of the Commons, and commoners out of the Senate, still endures intact today through dutiful observance, most recently in October 2013 when Governor General Johnson, Canada's vice-regal personage, opened a new parliamentary session by reading the Speech from the Throne. Sometimes this function has even been performed by Her Majesty Queen Elizabeth II when in Canada, reading a script handed to her that outlines in anodyne terminology "My Government's" plans for the upcoming legislative program.

The deed is done in the regal Red Chamber. The prime minister is in attendance, as are other cabinet members, not in their capacity as MPs but allowed to enter because of their status as Ministers of the Crown. Former ministers of the Crown, who predominate "the Privy Council," which never meets except for ceremonial occasions such as this, are present, in such numbers as are able or interested to attend. Justices of the Supreme Court of Canada are seated comfortably on nine large cushioned chairs placed temporarily in the centre aisle. They, too, are at home in the Red Chamber, for Canada's courts are "Her Majesty's" courts, where justice is pursued by Crown prosecutors and rendered under the authority and in the name of the Crown.

Absent from this posh ceremony whose centrepiece is a Speech from the Throne outlining intentions of the democratically elected government of Canadians are the elected representatives of the people themselves.

The old British rule about mutually exclusive no-go zones is strictly adhered to in present-day Ottawa, although none of Canada's provinces experiences any problems when the lieutenant-governor, representing the same Crown, enters the chamber of elected representatives for counterpart ceremonies.

For the decade I was a member of the House of Commons, at first I attempted to fall into step with the hoary old practice Canada's national parliament perpetuates in honour of a colonial institution that time left behind and our provinces left in the trash bin of history. Maybe I just needed to overcome my bad attitude as a democrat. Despite believing the Senate and everything dragged along with it was foreign and an irrelevant nuisance to the proper, focused, democratic operation of institutions for contemporary governance, I tried.

I went to hear the Speech from the Throne. Because MPs cannot go into the Senate, we who'd paraded down the marble corridor from the Commons clustered at the Senate entrance to watch the ceremony and discover what the government had in mind for us to do. We could not wander in by mistake, or get pushed in by the crush of other MPs behind us hoping to glimpse the semi-regal spectacle, because a barrier kept us out. We could see some members of the Privy Council — cabinet ministers past and present, mostly past, who had returned to Parliament Hill for another dose of this tradition-laden state occasion. We could spot, between the rows of appointed senators, the appointed members of the Supreme Court in their splendid, colourful robes.

The Speech from the Throne proceedings are televised, unlike the actual Senate sessions themselves. The densely packed Red Chamber, despite its high ceiling, is claustrophobic. It's hard to breathe because all the oxygen is being consumed. The temperature rises steadily because the heat of the television lights bathes the scene from above. The intense brightness turns the densely packed place into an imposing stage set. This is theatre where the audience is part of the cast.

We elected representatives, having no part to play, are definite "outcasts." We cram the unlighted antechamber, stand on tiptoes, perch on carved stone ledges, hearing little and seeing less. Wearying of this most peripheral of roles as silent onlookers for a formalized pageant, we strike up conversations, some serious, a few flippant, among ourselves. Others just wander off, perhaps to watch the proceedings on television, getting the same view of Parliament's official opening as the people we represent.

* * *

For many years Québec lagged behind the rest of Canada — last to abolish its appointed upper house, last to give women the vote, last to establish a department of education, last to create a public utility for the supply of electric power, even last to permit drive-in movie theatres as the firm reach of the Catholic Church removed temptation by prohibiting such "passion pits." But the Quiet Revolution in the 1960s ushered in modernizing leadership resolved to make up for lost time, on all fronts.

Among the sudden swift changes, in 1968 the Union Nationale government of Premier Jean-Jacques Bertrand converted the province's bicameral legislature into an efficient unicameral Legislative Assembly. Efforts to eliminate the appointed twenty-four-member Legislative Council, which dated from 1791, had been attempted since the late 1800s. Effective December 31, 1968, the upper chamber vanished, and with the same reform came re-designation of the Legislative Assembly of Québec as the National Assembly.

The large chamber that housed the Legislative Council was known as *le salon rouge* or "the Red Room"; its traditional upper-house colour extended from its carpeting to a stylish predominance on its red walls. Today the impressive space is more productively used for meetings of standing committees and important state functions worthy of an imposing hall, such as solemn inductions into the National Order of Québec or animated receptions following the brief formal opening of a new session of the National Assembly.

In streamlining the provincial assembly into a modern institution, ceremonial bits derived from ancient Britain were eliminated. The presiding officers now appear in contemporary clothing instead of gowns, creating the context of a present-day atmosphere for the conduct of public business.

The staged theatrics of a Speech from the Throne ceremony, a throwback to antiquated heritage no part of the province's own history, was ended. The lieutenant-governor of Québec still officially opens a parliamentary session, but once quickly done, the proceeding adjourns and a lively reception takes place down the corridor in the Red Room for the elected members, cabinet ministers, and other invited guests. Instead of a Throne Speech read by the lieutenant-governor, a new session of the National Assembly begins, the following day, by the premier delivering an Opening Speech in the Assembly to outline the Québec government's legislative intentions for the coming session. The premier speaks in direct and plain language. Gone is the verbal gauze of vice-regal pronouncement that is still the stilted standard of other Speeches from the Throne in other Canadian legislatures, and in the Senate chamber at Ottawa.

In *la belle province*, the Crown's representative is no longer forced to pretend a role everyone present knows no longer exists. As for the province's appointed upper house, just like the Senate in Ottawa, everyone present also knew that these improbable second chambers never had, in our country, the historical or social setting of Britain's House of Lords to sustain them.

CHAPTER 10

An Improbable Institution

From the law-makers who occupy it to the myths and mistakes that sustain it, everything about the Canadian Senate makes it one of the world's most improbable institutions.

People create a political institution at a certain time in history to meet a particular need of the era. So, in trying to grasp why the Senate continues to exist today, it helps to recap what actually gave rise to the place in the 1860s.

Having the Senate was a political expedient. Establishing an appointed second chamber for Parliament, in addition to the elected House of Commons, was a temporary step, part of the compromise needed so that at least four provinces — more had been hoped for — were able to find enough agreement to unite politically in 1867. Canadians in recent decades have witnessed the frustrating difficulties of our political leaders trying to get agreement between different governments on health care programs, pension plans, securities regulation, and manpower training, so it doesn't take much effort to empathize with 1860s political leaders searching for enough common ground to do something infinitely harder — create a new country.

With so many issues keeping the colonial provinces apart, it was simplest to reach agreement that the proposed national parliament would have an upper house, only because that's what each of the colonies already had. The upper house had been in the original governance package exported from Britain to her colonies when giving them a local law-making franchise. For politicians trying to envisage a new country, to incorporate aspects they were already familiar with was reassuring to them as well as to members of the public generally.

Yet their direct experience of provincial upper houses also meant the delegates negotiating Confederation fully understood the problems inherent in a law-making system where two separate legislative assemblies take turns working on the same legislation. More rules would be needed for the separate yet joint operation of the House of Commons and Senate.

Working out provisions for Senate-Commons interaction and the kind of body the Senate itself would be preoccupied delegates from the colonial provinces. Their two main meetings to negotiate Canada's constitution took place in Québec City and Charlottetown, and fully half the days at one were consumed by debate about the Senate, and much of the time at the other as well. It was a sobering early glimpse of how the subject of Canada's Senate could consume time, talk, talent, and treasure.

The delegates also had to decide what to call the second chamber. True colonials, they remained mindful of the importance of adapting British institutions to New World conditions. Their dilemma in doing so was that Britain's upper house was called, for historic reasons, the House of Lords, but because Canada had escaped the feudal era, our country had no lords or other peers of the realm. Even the seigniorial system, which had earlier governed feudal New France, no longer offered a basis for a "House of Seigniors" since that nod to antiquity only pertained to a relatively small part of the new country anyway. The provincial upper houses were "Legislative Councils," but because the intended Parliament of Canada would not have a "Legislative Assembly" but a "House of Commons," some more prestigious designation was needed for the upper house, too.

To import political terminology from the United States was distasteful to these British North Americans urgently negotiating to form a unified northern country precisely so they could withstand American incursions. Yet it seemed the only choice. They reached south and borrowed the reviled republic's name of its upper house for ours. The "Senate" of Canada would certainly be distinctive. Not one of the provinces with upper houses called its that.

The importance of the Senate for Canada's French-speaking peoples, a minority in the larger English-speaking union being envisaged, was its institutionalized guarantee of both status and identity.

By creating two houses for Parliament, it was possible to persuade Quebecers to agree to "representation by population" in the Commons, where they knew they would be outnumbered, since they would be guaranteed the condition of equality in the Senate. Québec and Ontario got twenty-four senators each. "On no other condition," said George Brown, one of the Fathers of Confederation, "could we have advanced a step." This same pragmatic sense of "regional parity" reassured Maritimers, who believed that Senate representation would ensure their perspective would be heard in the national parliament. With their overrepresentation in the Senate on a population basis, the Maritime provinces would thus counterbalance, it was believed, domination of the Commons by MPs from Québec and Ontario. The regions would be represented through the Senate, said John A. Macdonald, "on the principle of equality ... for the purpose of defending such interests against the combinations of majorities in the Assembly." In 1867, Ontario was the most populous, fastest-growing province, but Québec and the Maritimes were more important to the national economy than their size of population suggested. They dared not leave matters such as tariffs, taxation, and railways to the mercy of an Ontario-dominated Commons, and they insisted on equal regional representation in the upper house, without which there would have been no Confederation.

The single greatest role of the Senate was this, enabling Confederation to take place at all. The day Confederation became reality on July 1, 1867, the Senate's principal function had already been fulfilled.

That hardly meant it could be scrapped right away, however.

Concern for due representation of all interests in the country remained real, whether they were the needs of French-speaking Canadians faced with the dominance of English-speaking ones, the interests of the Maritimes balanced against the centre of the country, or the concerns of Western Canadians in relationship to the East. Some decades would have to pass before there would be any possibility of changing the Senate.

A century in fact would still be needed to reassure Canadians how three other political institutions — the House of Commons, with its strong regional ministers and representatives; provincial governments, far more powerful than those that had first been envisaged by the Fathers of Confederation in 1867; and the Supreme Court of Canada, genuinely supreme after appeals to Britain's judiciary ended in 1949, and particularly vital once the constitutionally entrenched Charter of Rights and Freedoms in 1981 made the courts rather than Parliament the highest arbiter in the land — could each accommodate these imperatives much better than the Senate was fitted to do.

Although there is value in the plodding pace embraced by Canada's political culture, it does have drawbacks. Because the eclipse of the Senate was not immediate but took place gradually over a century, and because this happened through a number of separate developments rather than one dramatic event, there was never a single obvious moment in history for someone to declare "Mission complete!"

The further problem was behavioural. The longer the Senate lingered on the scene, the more people got acclimatized to its presence. It seemed to belong just because it was there. Inertia of the system overpowered zeal for reform.

This resistance to change grew stronger as the decades passed, but first became apparent even within a decade of Confederation. Serious concern was voiced early on about the need for "Senate reform," but the instinct to modernize could not be translated into action.

The most obvious challenge was that senators were appointed, not elected.

Even in 1867 this seemed inappropriate to many, especially those who had come north from the United States to live in Canada and who were familiar with a fully elected Congress. There were also the negative experiences of those who'd suffered through the high-handed abuses of appointed governing bodies in pre-Confederation days. As a result of those factors, two of Canada's colonial provinces converted to electing members for their upper houses, well before Confederation. This contributed a predisposition, on the part of some delegates negotiating Confederation, to choose members of the new Canadian Senate by direct vote of the people, but the preponderant view favoured appointment instead. Hand-picked senators would offer an unobtrusive way to ensure, over time, that established powers in society could retain control over enactment of new laws or proposed "reforms" in old ones. The Senate was to provide what Father of Confederation George-Étienne Cartier explicitly called a "power of resistance to oppose the democratic element." The genesis of the Senate was anti-democratic and it was structured in the Constitution to stay that way.

Prince Edward Island was one of the colonies that had created an elected upper house. When politicians from other colonial provinces reassembled in the P.E.I. capital of Charlottetown to continue negotiating Confederation, more discussion ensued about the Senate. Islanders decided to take a pass on political union in 1867 for a number of reasons, including the prospect that the proposed new country's national legislature would have an *appointed* second chamber. Islanders had come through a highly contentious period to convert the Island's upper house into an elected body in 1861 and had good reason to dislike any appointed second chamber.

Yet Ontario, the second colonial province to have also gone through a rough patch democratizing its legislature's second chamber, did join Confederation from the outset in 1867. The move involved a fascinating political trade-off with far-reaching impact.

Almost from the province's inception in 1791, settlers in what became Ontario had grown justifiably angry with the upper house. For its first four decades of operation, the privileged members of the "Family Compact" running the province, who'd been appointed to the Legislative Council by the governor, ignored elected representatives in the Legislative Assembly as readily as they turned aside people's petitions and lengthening lists of grievances. Colonists even had to get official permission to hold a public meeting, so controlled was "freedom of assembly." After the inevitable reaction of armed rebellion in 1837, the outcome was the gaining of "responsible government" in 1840, with its new concept of democratic accountability over government. The foundation of political life, henceforth, was that the Crown was sovereign, but *so were the people.* The seeds of "constitutional monarchy" were sprouting in the colony.

Integral to this change was provision for voters in the province to elect members to both the Legislative Assembly *and* the Legislative Council. Benefiting from this experience during the 1840s to mid-1860s, pragmatic people up and down the province came to see that a second legislative chamber was redundant. Why pay for two sets of legislators to pass a law when one alone could do the job?

By 1867, it was easy for political leaders in Ontario to see the next step required for evolution of provincial political institutions. They chose what a later premier of Ontario, John Robarts, would call "a made in Ontario solution for a made in Ontario problem." They had no precedent for what they decided to do, but seeing no redeeming value to the province's upper house, even as an elected body, they simply gave up the Legislative Council to history as the new province entered into Confederation.

The other side of the bargain was to allow for the creation of an appointed upper house for the new national parliament. Seasoned Ontario politicians like John A. Macdonald and George Brown needed a Senate for its practical use as a sweetener to achieve political union and a shock absorber to smooth Confederation's early ride. They knew, from political experience in the pre-Confederation province, that many Ontarians imbued with a confident and rising democratic instinct would welcome an elected upper house, but for reasons of pragmatic politics, they chose in their challenging circumstance to make the Senate of Canada a hand-picked body. Senatorships for resisters was the trade-off.

Ontario's bold act in changing its provincial constitution recommended itself to others. Rather than mucking about for decades, wasting time and money tinkering with reforms around the edges of an unnecessary institution, the clean solution was to just outright abolish a province's second chamber.

Ontario has progressed favourably with a single-chamber legislature ever since. Even those closely involved with politics in the province have never heard anyone complain, "We sure need a Senate in this province. Lawmaking would be more attentive to detail, deliberations less partisan, and holding government to account more effective, if only a second chamber could be added to our legislature. We're in dire need of sober second thought around here."

People recognized that the vestigial institution exported from Britain did not fit and was indeed counterproductive. Over ensuing decades each of the other colonial provinces that joined Confederation with second chambers as part of their constitutions abolished them, too.

Ontario, as mentioned, got rid of its upper house in 1867; it was followed by Manitoba in 1876, New Brunswick in 1892, Prince Edward Island in 1893, Nova Scotia in 1928, Newfoundland (upon joining Confederation) in 1949, and Québec in 1968. Although Québec was last to eliminate its Legislative Council, efforts had been made to do so since the late 1800s. The two separate Pacific colonies of Vancouver Island and British Columbia, which united in 1866, acquired an appointed Legislative Council in the 1860s, but it was abolished when the province entered Confederation in 1871.

New provinces created out of the sprawling Northwest Territories were saved that step, simply because their governements were created to reflect contemporary Canadian values not deal with antiquated British problems that had been institutionalized over the course of that country's history. Alberta and Saskatchewan were erected as new Canadian provinces in 1905 under constitutions enacted by Parliament in Ottawa. Even though the Alberta Act and the Saskatchewan Act had to be voted on by the Senate of Canada as part of this process, nobody in Ottawa — not even those senators — thought that creating a second legislative chamber made sense or was required for these new Canadian provinces.

Canada was now in the twentieth century. Prime Minister Wilfrid Laurier envisaged a bright and more democratic future for the growing nation. "The twentieth century will belong to Canada!" he declared. Within that bright image more than a century ago, nobody saw an upper chamber as part of the future, certainly not one filled with hand-picked appointees.

With fully democratic provincial government established through a single-chamber legislative assembly in their respective capitals of Edmonton and Regina, both provinces built impressive, contemporary legislative buildings, on a bold scale matching the grand edifice in Winnipeg housing Manitoba's legislative assembly. The majestic buildings of Canada's Prairie Provinces symbolized the cleaner, fresher era of open democratic politics and the modern Canadian nation that was rising.

* * *

The Laurier government, in constituting these two new Prairie provinces, not only reflected Canada's enhanced democratic pragmatism about legislative institutions. Ottawa's deliberate preference for unicameral legislatures also helped crystallize Canadian political consensus on the subject.

Canada's Senate had thus been relegated even further to the margin. As the century advanced, its reason for existing seemed to vanish altogether. The place was no longer supported by public belief in it. At best there was uncritical acceptance of an institution that, because it was there, must somehow be important. This fog of misunderstanding consigned the place to decades of quietude in a political backwater.

Open acknowledgment of this condition by Canadian political scientists was commonplace, as if the condition was so natural as to be unremarkable. In the University of Toronto's "Canadian Government Series" published at mid-twentieth century, Queen's University political science professor Hugh Thorburn described what had happened to the Senate with passive acceptance. "Actually," he wrote about New Brunswick's federal representatives, "appointment to the Senate has become a form of reward for loyal service to the party in power — service rendered either as a member of Parliament, as a defeated candidate, or as a financial supporter. Provincial service is also recognized by a summons to the Senate in the case of the more prominent supporters of the appropriate party."

So, that's just the way it was, with nothing to be done.

Not long after Canada's inaugural election in 1867 produced members for our first House of Commons, attention turned to what to do about the Senate.

Talk of Senate reform in the 1870s, however, was not yet about getting rid of the place. Having an upper house had been part of the political deal-making in creating the new country, and most provinces had not yet seen the value of abolishing theirs. So being stuck with a Senate in Ottawa, the only consideration was how to make it better.

In 1874 the House of Commons debated, and rejected, a proposal to allow each province to select its own senators — an early version of the

Conservative plan for Senate elections in Prime Minister Harper's current Senate Reform Act, Bill C-7, an idea already rejected 140 years ago.

Despite many further discussions about making the Senate more appropriate to Canada's political realities, nothing came of it. No change occurred — except for growth in size. The Senate's membership enlarged, as other provinces joined Confederation and as Ottawa created new ones, each getting an allocation of seats in the House of Commons and Senate.

As time passed, the option of simply getting rid of the Senate, the way provinces that still had upper houses had been steadily eliminating them, became a bold stroke beyond the ability of Canada's politicians. Their capacity to act was restrained by three main factors. Quebecers saw their contingent of twenty-four senators in the upper house as necessary to offset the growing representation of non-French-speaking constituencies in the Commons, and enough Maritimers and Westerners had similarly bought into the idea that the Senate was somehow protecting them, too. Second, the prime minister and party in power at any given time found the partisan advantage of naming senators too valuable to ditch, and because they were running the national political scene they had little difficulty sidelining proposals, which were frequent, for "Senate reform." Finally, the inertia of the institution itself had become a dead weight. The Senate of Canada, always in favour with its own members, resisted change by doing nothing except existing. All that had to happen for it to endure was for enough senators to get up in the morning and keep breathing for another day.

Since the Senate was still around as more colonial provinces joined Confederation — Manitoba in 1870, British Columbia in 1871, Prince Edward Island in 1873, and Newfoundland in 1949 — there was no choice but to give them Senate representation. The new Prairie provinces, Alberta and Saskatchewan, likewise got a share of Senate space in 1905, and by the end of the 1900s the self-governing territories of Yukon, Northwest Territories, and Nunavut each received a Senate seat.

Sections 21 and 22 of the Constitution, dealing with Senate representation, were amended to accommodate this expansion of the country's provinces and territories, allocating members into four "divisions" — Ontario, with twenty-four senators; Québec, with twenty-four; the three Maritime provinces with twenty-four (Nova Scotia, ten; New Brunswick, ten; and Prince Edward Island, four); and the four Western provinces, again twenty-four (six each for Manitoba, British Columbia, Alberta, and Saskatchewan). In addition to these ninety-six senators from the four regional divisions, Newfoundland has six, while each territory has one, bringing today's total to 105 Senate seats.

Unchanged over all these years are the qualifications necessary to become a senator. The Constitution requires senators to be subjects of the Queen; at least thirty years old; have real property worth $4,000 free of mortgage and a net worth of at least $4,000; and reside in the province or territory for which they are appointed (in Québec, which is divided into twenty-four senatorial districts, senators must also reside or have their real property in the division for which they are appointed).

The requirements that senators be thirty and own property worth $4,000 — which would be about $150,000 if that provision were being written today — reflect how the Fathers of Confederation sought to use the Senate to protect societal interests in a way that no longer corresponds with contemporary Canadian values and may even violate principles in the Charter of Rights and Freedoms. Yet patterns of anti-democratic thinking were not confined to that earlier Canadian era alone. Even in 2014, Liberal leader Justin Trudeau would propose that senators not only remain appointed to office, but that the entity appointing them should itself be an appointees body rather than a democratically elected prime minister, the envisaged result being a national assembly of lawmakers not once, but *twice removed* from democratic control of the sovereign people.

Another important stipulation in the Constitution, which figures prominently in the expenses scandal for senators Mike Duffy and Pamela Wallin, is that a senator "shall be resident in the Province for which he [or she] is appointed." In the case of Québec's senators, each of the twenty-four is appointed to represent a particular electoral division in the province according to boundaries that existed in 1859. In other provinces and in the territories senators can live anywhere in the jurisdiction they represent, provided they own property worth $4,000 somewhere in it.

When senators Wallin and Duffy were challenged about meeting residency qualifications, it was not the first scramble over complying with the Constitution's stipulated rules for being a senator. Someone picked by Prime Minister Chrétien showed how the need to own $4,000 worth of property could be finessed. This requirement proved a stumbling block when the PM selected Peggy Butts in 1997. A Roman Catholic nun, Butts had taken a vow of poverty and owned no property, so she failed to meet one of the qualifications. This impediment produced scurrying behind the scenes, orchestrated by the PMO, to ensure her appointment. The Sisters of Notre Dame, her religious order, transferred a small parcel of land into her name. Nobody was scandalized. Many people, including journalists, smiled to see how the Senate's rules could be complied with, given some accommodating winks. For her part, as a senator, social activist Peggy Butts remained true to her vow. She donated her entire salary to the poor.

Filling the Senate with members is fairly straightforward. When a vacancy occurs, the governor general is directed by section 32 of the Constitution, "by Summons to a fit and qualified Person" to fill it. Yet Canada's political system as a constitutional monarchy means our prime minister directs the exercise of many powers formally allocated to the governor general. So the most senior representative of the Crown in Canada does not fill a Senate vacancy, under that procedure laid down in the Constitution, unless and until the PM triggers it by naming a candidate for appointment.

In the same way, a vacancy in the Commons is not filled until a PM gives the green light for a by-election to be held. In a country living under the rule of law, elections to vacant Commons seats should automatically occur according to a provision needed in the Parliament of Canada Act; representation in the Commons is a right of citizens in an electoral district. By the same standard, a similar provision should apply to filling a vacant Senate seat. Neither should be subject to the whim of a prime minister's partisan calculations.

Getting into the Senate is one thing; leaving, another.

Vacancies in the Senate occur in four ways: a senator reaches age seventy-five, resigns from office, dies in office, or is disqualified. Dying or having a seventy-fifth birthday are easiest. For a resignation, which could be for any number of tortured reasons, the deed itself is simple.

Section 30 says, "A Senator may by Writing under his Hand addressed to the Governor General resign his Place in the Senate, and thereupon the same shall be vacant."

However, disqualification is more complex. The Constitution in section 31 stipulates that senators will lose their seats if they become aliens; become bankrupt, insolvent or public defaulters; are attainted or convicted of felony or any infamous crime; lose their residence or property qualification; or are absent for two consecutive sessions of Parliament. Leaving the Senate is not optional when a senator becomes disqualified, but as the case of Senator Andrew Thomson revealed, the point at which one is considered "disqualified" can be contentious to determine and problematic to enforce.

The duty falls to senators themselves, which exacerbates the problem because it contributes to the place being run more like a private club than a public institution. Section 33 stipulates that, should any question arise "respecting the Qualification of a Senator or a Vacancy in the Senate, the same shall be heard and determined by the Senate."

The Senate was deeply embroiled in autumn 2013 over its process for suspending three senators for the duration of the current Parliament. The procedures were debated, and different interpretations of constitutional authority offered. But even where there is a move to formally remove a senator for good, the process is not clear cut, as was shown by the strange case of Canada's senator from Mexico.

When Senator Andy Thompson failed to report for duty, the Senate simply mailed his paycheque to his new permanent residence in Mexico, only stopping the charade after several years when reporters, the public, and Reform Party MPs, scandalized by the freeloading former Ontario Liberal leader, pressured the Senate to act.

Thompson, a social worker, had shown initial promise at Queen's Park after the MPP became provincial Liberal leader in 1964, but a couple of years later he resigned for health reasons, never even leading his party into an election. In 1967 Prime Minister Pearson appointed him to the Senate.

For a decade starting in the late 1980s, realizing that his attendance made no difference, Mr. Thompson seldom bothered to show up at the Senate, behaviour his friends portrayed as "keeping a low profile" to mask the reality that Thompson had the worst attendance of any senator. The Senator nevertheless continued to draw his salary by the ploy of appearing on one or two days at the start of each session to stay in technical compliance of the rule that a senator cannot miss two complete consecutive sittings. Liberals and Conservatives did not make a fuss about it. The Grits had sympathy for him. The Tories felt it meant one less Liberal to contend with.

Thompson's paid absence and his Senate colleagues' tolerance of it was based on the fact that they all understood it really made no difference to the perfunctory role of the Senate anyway. A number secretly envied the senator from Mexico.

But the Reform Party was different. Zealous with intent to eradicate the slovenly waste tolerated by the old-line parties, Reform MPs gleefully hired a Mexican mariachi band to play in the Senate lobby while they handed out burritos, mocking the absentee Canadian senator for Mexico with a political circus the news media had keen fun televising. The clever send-up scandalized Canadians and pressured the senators to act.

They proceeded quickly, at least for senators. On November 19, 1997, the Liberals expelled Thompson from their caucus, a negligible change since he'd not been attending anyway. A month later, on December 12, Liberal Senator Colin Kenny, once executive director of the Liberal Party of Canada in Ontario and a politician who appreciated the damage Thompson was doing to the Liberals, moved that the senator be summoned from Mexico to appear before the Senate and explain his absence. After a full day's delay over procedural disagreements on the matter, senators voted on December 16 to approve Kenny's motion. The Senate order failed, however, to bring the truant senator north for a day of reckoning. It was, after all, winter in Canada.

A couple of months later, the senators returned to the subject, having decided to apply sober second thought to their own actions. What to do with Andy Thompson was thrashed out at length. Reconsidering the question, a subcommittee reported on February 19, 1998 to recommend that Senator Thompson be found in contempt and suspended for the rest of the current session of Parliament. It was also recommended that the issue of his expense allowance be acted on immediately by the Internal Economy Committee. These recommendations were adopted.

Still the senators did not let go of the matter, knowing that senators had never before suspended one of their own members and that whatever they did would become a precedent that could someday come back to be used detrimentally against the Senate — as in fact happened fifteen years later when senators Duffy, Wallin, and Brazeau were being dealt with.

Usually an arm's-length authority or independent tribunal hears evidence and makes a ruling on suspending or expelling a member. For the Senate to do so itself resembled a proceeding in a private club more than a national legislature, but this is what the Constitution provided. Legally trained senators, worried about overriding the fundamentals of due legal process, made the process as deliberate as possible. Another report on Senator Thompson was tabled in the Senate on February 25. It was debated the following month.

In the end, the senators closed Andy Thompson's Senate office, removed his parliamentary privileges and other perquisites of office, found him in contempt of the Senate for not returning to Canada as ordered to explain his attendance record, and suspended his $64,400 salary and $10,100 tax-free expense allowance. Some senators disagreed with mere suspension as too lenient, contending the senator living in Mexico should have been expelled from the chamber for good.

Having had time for some sober second thought of his own on how to outfox his Senate colleagues, Thompson promptly sent them his resignation so that, from March 23, 1998, onward, he began receiving his annual Senate pension of $48,000, instead of his $64,000 unearned and temporarily suspended salary, thereby ensuring a steady future supply of Canadian taxpayer money to pay for his margaritas in the sun.

Most of Canada's 105 senators report for duty, many with assiduous attention to matters at hand, several invariably promoting specific causes such as improving literacy rates or awareness of autism. The public record contains quotable statements attesting to the character and quality of senatorial performance. Senators are seasoned, interesting people. Drawing on rich and highly diverse experiences, they constitute a valuable source of information and insight about Canada, Canadians, and our country's public policies.

Over the years, for example, careful studies by Senate committees have dealt with land use, unemployment, science policy, poverty, aging, and Indian affairs. It cannot be said with certainty how many recommendations have eventually translated into government policy, for that is hard to trace with precision, but the committee reports are now cited, by Senate defenders, as one of the justifications for Parliament's upper house.

Reference is perhaps most often made to the work of the Senate committee chaired by Michael Kirby on the future of Canada's health care system. The senators on the committee held public hearings, met together at length to discuss their findings and formulate recommendations. Anyone connected to the report the senators eventually produced speaks highly of their work.

No greater indictment of this Senate study can be made, however, than the fact that its health care review was overridden by Liberal Prime Minister Chrétien naming the Romanow Royal Commission on Health Care in 2001 to do exactly the same work at precisely the same time. The prime minister and Senator Kirby were even members of the same political party, a further slap in the senatorial face.

Another example involves the deep concern about concentration of media ownership in Canada that MP John Munro raised in the 1960s at the national Liberal caucus, which is where Senator Keith Davey heard the message and quickly laid the groundwork for Mr. Pearson's government to establish a special Senate Committee on Media, chaired by Mr. Davey. It was a major undertaking, with a substantial report. I had meetings with Keith Davey during this period, and with John Munro years later. Munro was agitated that nothing had come of the royal commission's recommendations, saying that he wanted to revive a transcending national issue he felt had been removed from the political arena of Parliament by the years-long project to study ownership issues in Canadian mass media by Canada's senators. All the while, concentration in the ownership of news media, and new patterns of cross-ownership, accelerated.

The examples run on, but the point they all make is that investigation into major Canadian issues by senators is either redundant or serves to insulate a matter from needed action. Public policy evaluation is now undertaken by a wide range of public policy organizations whose efforts serve our country well. These bodies did not exist in the early years of Confederation, but today they are numerous, and many receive public funding. Canada's need is not for a committee of senators to replicate their work at high expense and cost of time. Parliament itself is already well served by the Research Branch of the Library of Parliament, which is adept at consolidating deep background and the complete menu of recommended solutions for its members, be they in the Commons or Senate, to utilize when making recommendations to government.

People can be dispatched on assignments that are improbable, impractical, even impossible. Our country's institutions — military, educational, religious, and political — have generated a wide variety of such assignments over the years. Because institutions control the lives of those operating within them, they can route individuals into improbable channels. The assignment of being a Canadian senator is a task nobody can fulfill, because the mission itself has become impossible.

The Senate's reason for existing was fulfilled more than a century ago, once Confederation had been cemented. Today, the Senate is entirely out of phase with the democratic impulse of Canadians. When taking an active role as a full-fledged legislative assembly, the upper house of Canada's Parliament is condemned for interfering with the work of the people's elected representatives. When being passive and simply passing legislation from the Commons, however, the Senate is criticized as "a mere rubber-stamp" and thus not worth the millions of dollars it costs every year. Senators must drive with one foot on the gas and the other on the brake. There has already been enough compromising and balancing in law-making without adding the complication of being half-hearted in going about the business.

If not dismantled, an entity keeps automatically running, costly but irrelevant to its time and place — just casting about for some new mandate, as we have seen with NATO since the end of the Cold War, or the Senate of Canada for more than a century. Failure to wind up an institution once it has completed its role can leave results of the kinds we have all been front-row witnesses to this past year. The Canadian Senate is an improbable institution, saddled with a role that is impossible to perform, left with the pretence that, somehow, its purpose is conducive to the workings of a democratic society.

It would seem that the only reason for keeping the Senate on life-support is that it functions as a partisan and administrative adjunct to prime ministerial government.

CHAPTER 11

A Prime Minister's Handmaid

The political fortunes of Canada's prime ministers are so closely entwined with the Senate that some might never have reached highest political office had they not promised so many of the faithful an appointment to the upper house on their way to the top.

Prime Minister Lester Pearson was certainly not alone in doing this, but my time of extensively circulating through political circles of fine and friendly Liberals allowed me to hear in personal testimony how many of them had received his solemn pledge of a Senate seat. It was offered in exchange for their support to put the diplomat politician in the prime minister's chair so he could make it happen. For many, though, the support given to help him become PM was not rewarded. They did not become senators.

Of course Prime Minister Pearson did make many appointments to the Senate, including thirty-nine-year-old Keith Davey, the principal architect of his election campaign victories. In his early years as PM, Mr. Pearson hoped to actually reform the Senate, accomplishing what others had failed to do despite talking about it for decades. He wanted "changes in the method of appointment and in the structure of the Senate." At least he managed in 1965, following an example two years earlier from Québec, to impose a retirement age of seventy-five on senators.

After making that change, he was content to let things be. His only other engagement with the Senate involved appointing "Liberals who had been active in one form or another of party work," including a few of those campaign organizers and fundraisers who kept reminding the PM of his prior pledges, "to give them a base in the Senate from which they could operate." By the time Mr. Pearson had retired and was penning his memoirs, he reflected, "I do not think I would make any drastic Senate reform, except perhaps to abolish it."

* * *

All those seeking highest political office have used the promise of a Senate seat to grease their way to power. Not dozens but hundreds, and probably thousands, of well-placed Canadians over the years have heard the promise of Senate seats that never materialized. None who became prime minister has been above brandishing this enticement even though, had they kept count, their pledges vastly exceeded the spaces available.

The magic in this prospect of a senatorship, as a ploy for getting somebody to do something for you politically, is that it only depends on their gullibility. Holding out the prospect of becoming a senator is in league with a seducer who promises matrimony but never follows through once the prize has been claimed.

In fact, so potent is the prospect of being in the Senate that the offer can even be successfully extended by political operators who have no intention of becoming PM. Back in 1907, when a Liberal nomination came open in Saskatchewan due to a constituency vacancy, four strong prospective candidates wanted it because whichever candidate was chosen would likely be elected MP.

The principal centre in the riding was Prince Albert, where Thomas Osborne Davis's political machine dominated the local scene. John Diefenbaker, who himself got to know this scene as an elected MP from Prince Albert, later chuckled to recall how Davis had "an attractive personality but in politics was thoroughly unreliable." Davis approached each of the four "in private and in strictest confidence" saying, in effect, "If you support me and I'm elected I'll put you in the Senate." The strong prospect of Davis getting elected made the deal seem certain. Each of the four knew that, whereas an MP would have to fight re-elections, a senator held office for life with secure pay and no real work. Having successfully removed his competition, Davis got the nomination and won election to the Commons. When the Senate seat for Saskatchewan became available, T.O. Davis took it for himself.

* * *

Some prime ministers have even needed the Senate's help for their own career after they reached the top office.

When Prime Minister Mackenzie King lost his North York seat in the 1925 general election, he was desperate to remain Liberal leader so needed another seat through which to re-enter the Commons. He persuaded freshly elected Liberal MP Charles McDonald from Saskatchewan's Prince Albert riding to step down. He did, creating a vacancy. The prime minister promptly called a by-election for Prince Albert, ran and won, an Ontarian returning to Parliament as a Prairie MP and PM of Canada.

How had King persuaded McDonald? He'd promised him a seat in the Senate. But it took a decade to materialize, since it was necessary to wait for a vacancy, something that required extra patience in an era where senators stayed in office for life. McDonald finally received his long-promised appointment in 1935. He died before taking his seat in the upper house, however, making him a contender for Ripley's *Believe It or Not*, as John Diefenbaker liked to quip, as "the only person in our history ever elected to the House of Commons and appointed to the Senate who was never to sit in either."

In addition to helping politicians advance their own careers, the Senate assists prime ministers, once in office, to run the government.

Prime ministers have routinely used the Senate to ease cabinet members into retirement, softening the hard blows of political reality as they shuffle their ministerial talent. Using this expedient to remove incompetent or scandal-plagued colleagues, prime ministers in effect buy them off while rendering their own task of firing them less wrenching.

Sending someone to the Senate in fact brings joy to a prime minister, not only because it spares the blow-back from an unpleasant firing, but because most who are destined for the Red Chamber cannot believe their luck. The power of the prize is so great that it led Senator Keith Davey to observe, "The Senate is the ultimate gift a prime minister can bestow."

As Jim Coyle notes in his ebook *Housebroken*, a Senate seat is "almost irresistible." Editor of the *Ottawa Journal* Grattan O'Leary had railed against the Senate in the late 1940s, denigrating the position of senator as only he could: "A senatorship isn't a job. It's a title. Also it's a blessing, a stroke of good fate; something like drawing to a royal straight flush in the biggest pot of the evening." Mr. O'Leary, whose Conservatism had early motivated him to run for Parliament in Gaspé and who thereafter steadfastly supported Conservative positions in his newspaper editorials, accepted his stroke of good fate in 1962 when Prime Minister Diefenbaker appointed him to the Senate.

Far more outspoken had been Liberal MP and agriculture minister Eugene Whalen, who'd criticized the Senate for years, trying to dissuade friends like Keith Davey from accepting a seat in the place, and campaigning for abolition of the upper house. Mr. Whalen was offered a senatorship by Prime Minister Trudeau, then on his way into retirement and busy compiling a lengthy list of patronage appointments for John Turner to make, as a form of penitence for prior slights, on his way into the prime minister's office. Making the appointments would become one of the factors contributing to the new Liberal prime minister's defeat by Brian Mulroney in 1984.

Mr. Trudeau's sense of humour led him to test his green-Stetsoned agriculture minister, when reviewing the patronage options with him and inquiring about what he would like to do next. "I don't suppose you want to go to the Senate."

"You guessed it right, Mr. Prime Minister," Whelan chuckled.

Even so, this ardent opponent of the Senate would succumb to the more persuasive Jean Chrétien's offer of the irresistible prize, a decade and a half later. Senator Eugene Whelan was sworn into office in 1996.

Because of its high value as a haven, if not indeed a heaven, for political wrecks and party operatives, a prime minister guards jealously his power to hand out passes to the plush-carpeted and exceedingly comfortable upper house.

Prime Minister King, who was painstakingly attentive to his own interests, safeguarded his prized Senate appointments for the political treasures they were, never squandering a space in the upper chamber to help someone else. When Ontario's provincial Liberal government was imploding in 1942, with two ministers contending to replace Premier Mitch Hepburn, the emissary for one, Gordon Conant, journeyed to

Ottawa and implored King to appoint the rival, Harry Nixon, to the Senate in order to remove him from play.

The prime minister thought the request "infernal cheek" and refused.

Being in the Senate, the way prime ministers Abbott and Bowell were, made it just that much easier to use the upper house, the way every PM has, as a vital instrument in the exercise of power.

Most prime ministers jump at the opportunity to fill every vacancy in the upper chamber. The only trick is to remain in office long enough. Kim Campbell is the one PM to never name anyone to the Senate. Another short-term prime minister, John Turner, managed to appoint three in his two and a half months on the job, using the list Pierre Trudeau left him, while Joe Clark appointed eleven senators during his nine months as PM. Paul Martin appointed seventeen senators in his two years in office. Arthur Meighen appointed fifteen during his total year and nine months as PM. Charles Tupper had the chance to appoint one senator during his sixty-nine days as prime minister.

Any PM able to settle into office and take charge, from Confederation to the present day, has discovered in the unique prerogative to appoint senators just how accommodating Parliament's upper house is to governing needs and partisan interests. Nothing in the Constitution makes the Senate of Canada a component of partisan statecraft, yet for more than 140 years, this has been its primary role in governing our country.

Strictly speaking, of course, the governor general "summons" a qualified person to the Senate under power conferred by the Constitution, but the only "qualified persons" are those who, in addition to meeting age, citizenship, property ownership, and residency requirements, have their names on a list handed to the governor general by the prime minister.

Prime Ministers exercise this power for a variety of purposes — to advance or perpetuate their own careers, or to take an easy way out of hard choices, such as where to put a veteran minister when shuffling the cabinet.

Another reason for such appointments, one that explains Mr. Pearson placing Keith Davey down the corridor in the Senate, is that they allow a PM a convenient and cost-free way to keep senior party organizers close at hand, where they are able to network in the nation's capital, participate in the partisan mix of governing, and bask in prestigious recognition as reward for often ignominious political work. What makes this even sweeter is that the PM knows his supporters can accomplish all their party fundraising and campaign organizing on the *public* payroll.

As this type of appointee became prevalent, more Canadians raised the fundamental objection that patronage appointees should not occupy a position of authority in a democracy. It was a century ago that the first modern prime minister of Canada, Robert Borden, came to office on a clear election platform that included creating a Public Service Commission and ending political patronage in our country's civil service. While that change was implemented, no similar reform touched the Senate. Canada retains the embarrassing tradition of having patronage appointees constitute the entire membership of our country's senior law-making assembly.

Thus, over the decades, the pattern of prime ministers exploiting the Senate for partisan goals became entrenched and accepted as normal, only coming under critical scrutiny if a scandal turned the spotlight on what was really taking place. In this way, the current Senate expenses scandal has reminded Canadians that a tacit understanding keeps the upper house in existence, when no other reason for it exists, like a prime minister's back garden.

Although inserting someone in the Senate's soil carries risk, this is not always recognized. Certainly Prime Minister Harper's selection of three celebrity senators makes this point, but he is hardly alone. One of Mr. Chrétien's replanting efforts failed to take root, too.

The case of Raymond Lavigne not only showed how the Senate patch is treated by prime ministers as convenient winter storage, but also what happens when a member of Parliament wilts when put into the Red Chamber rather than the cabinet. Lavigne found little to do except figure out how to take extra advantage of his new shaded location.

A Montreal businessman, Raymond Lavigne was the three-term MP for Verdun-St. Paul riding when Prime Minister Chrétien, wanting more female candidates and caucus members with greater prominence, appointed the backbench MP to the Senate on March 26, 2002, creating a by-election so former Québec minister of communications and Radio-Canada television host Liza Frulla could enter the House of Commons.

After four years in the upper house, Senator Lavigne was expelled from the Liberal caucus for allegedly misusing Senate funds for personal use — some $23,000 for work on his estate, including having his executive assistant cut down trees on the property. It seemed that Senator Lavigne had also deliberately falsified his Senate travel claims. He'd give a staff member $50 to drive him to or from Montreal, then claimed $217 from the Senate for the trip and pocketed the difference. The senator did not do that once, but fifty-four times. At one point, Senator Lavigne's lawyers said he would repay the $23,000, though he would do so without admitting he'd done anything wrong.

Meanwhile, the RCMP was investigating his estate improvement program, as well as other activities by Senator Lavigne, and in August the following year charged him with fraud over $5,000, breach of trust, and obstruction of justice. His 2007 criminal charges barred Lavigne from sitting in the Senate or taking part in its committee meetings, but his salary continued to be paid and he remained entitled to claim expenses.

The senator's trial was a drawn-out affair, beginning two years later on December 9, 2009, and stretched by the full menu of possible delays, until finally closing arguments took place on September 17, 2010.

Even on November 12, 2010, when Ontario Superior Court Judge Robert Smith announced he was ready to deliver his decision, a date could not be set to release his verdict because Mr. Lavigne's lawyers would not show up. At last the final ruling was scheduled to be issued on February 22, 2011. But when that date arrived, the court instead agreed to hear fresh argument, at the request of Mr. Lavigne's lawyers, on how much weight should be given to a Senate report on expenses spending, arising from the issues with senators Mac Harb, Patrick Brazeau, and Mike Duffy, with his lawyers arguing Senator Lavigne should not be found guilty because the rules were "unclear."

Despite his lawyer's last-minute attempts to further delay his case, on March 11, 2011, the senator was found guilty of both fraud and breach of trust, though he was acquitted of the charge of obstructing justice. He was sentenced to six months in prison and an additional six month to be served at home. In addition to serving time, Senator

Lavigne was ordered to give $10,000, the rounded amount he'd claimed from the Senate for non-existent expenses, to charity. It is unclear why Judge Smith did not simply order the money paid back to the public treasury, since it was the Senate and taxpayers who'd been defrauded of the $10,000, although after hearing the case, the judge probably had little confidence the Senate could supervise its administration of money any better a second time around.

Ten days later, Raymond Lavigne resigned from the Senate.

More than two years later, Senator Lavigne's appeal of both his convictions and his sentences was heard on June 5, 2013. Three Court of Appeal justices dismissed the appeal, saying Mr. Lavigne had knowingly defrauded the public treasury. They rejected his twisted argument, a product of the senator having had plenty of time for sober second thought, that the public purse was not harmed because the funds rightfully belonged to his former employees whom he had cheated out of money. Lavigne began serving his sentence that month, some seven years after the Liberals had first expelled him from their caucus.

When it came time for Raymond Lavigne's parole hearing, Michel Biron, a retired Liberal senator and Senator Lavigne's helpful friend, suggested a retread of the argument his lawyers had tried when stalling Judge Smith's decision, contending the Senate's recent attention to its policies for senators' travel claims helped the convicted senator. "If the rules aren't clear now," Biron explained, "then they weren't clear for him then." That's how senators connect the dots when trying to cushion their pals who cheat their own employees and the institution they serve.

Meanwhile, Liza Frulla's career in national politics had come and gone, with election to the Commons and service in the cabinets of prime ministers Chrétien and Martin, until her defeat in 2006 — years before Senator Lavigne's case even got to court.

Jean Chrétien's appointment of a number of noteworthy Canadians who had no prior connection with the politics of legislatures indicates he did not expect them to actually do much in the Senate in the way of being attentive legislators.

It was beneficence on his part, and a way of making a statement about some important aspect of Canadian life by recognizing an individual who'd dedicated his or her life to society's greater good, from hockey to education to social activism. He did not really expect his appointees from non-political and non-governmental backgrounds to become adept legislators; few Canadians expect this from senators, either.

Mr. Chrétien could not have counted on them picking up the arts of statecraft in a couple of years either, which was all the time some of them had to learn the parliamentary ropes before hitting the fixed quitting age. The first nun to become a Canadian senator, Peggy Butts, served only two years in Parliament's upper house before retiring. She hadn't left in despair, but because she'd reached mandatory retirement age of seventy-five, only twenty-four months after being appointed. Prime Minister Jean Chrétien had invented several new approaches to exercising his powers and prerogatives of office, and using the Senate as a brief reward for worthy Canadians was one.

He recognized that the Senate was largely an honorific place to recognize special people, so he named a number of notable individuals to the upper house just several years shy of their seventy-fifth birthday, the mandatory retirement age. In his program to spread goodwill and accord recognition, Prime Minister Chrétien named some seventy-five people to the Senate of Canada. A reason he could appoint so many was, of course, the frequency of turnover, since a number were only in the Senate for a relatively short period. Another was his advantage of having three consecutive terms in office to do this.

Certainly Prime Minister Chrétien also appointed senators who had enough time to make a contribution. Many of these were key campaign organizers and party officers, people who knew politics and parliamentary procedure. One of them was his steadfast supporter Mac Harb, who looked forward to many years in the upper house.

Only four prime ministers have appointed more senators than Mr. Chrétien. Pierre Trudeau and Wilfrid Laurier, each in office for fifteen years, named eighty-one people to the upper house during their respective tenures in office as prime minister. Prime Minister John A. Macdonald, who served nineteen years as prime minister, accounted for ninety-one men being called to the upper house. Prime Minister Mackenzie King set the appointment record with 103 senators to his credit during his twenty-one years as Canada's prime minister, which was also a record-setting tenure of office as PM — each record closely connected to the other.

Prime Minister Pearson might have jumped near the top of these ranks by creating a lot of vacancies to fill when he reduced the life-time Senate appointment to one ending at age seventy-five, had he not "grand-fathered" senators named prior to his 1965 change. Rather than forcing a massive retirement of senators that year, all incumbents, so many of them being Liberals anyway, were allowed to finish off their lives in the accommodating Red Chamber. It is a principle that new laws should not apply retroactively. Only senators appointed from 1965 on would be subject to the law requiring them, like judges, to leave office at the three-quarter-century mark.

Prime Minister Mulroney liked to include the names of younger people on his lists, to help the old Senate seem somehow more relevant to the times and, even more important, to ensure long-term Tory votes in the upper house. He wanted to build up, as he put it several times, "a Conservative dynasty." But he mixed in some non-Conservatives as appeasement to his steady roster of party fundraisers and campaign organizers and PC party officers, and also included highly distinguished Canadians such as Dr. Wilbur Keon, a leading heart surgeon.

Later, Prime Minister Paul Martin worked a variant on this theme. I was speaking at York University in late March 2005, at a session attended by Senator David Smith, past president of the Liberals, organizer of Liberal campaigns in Ontario, and a fellow law partner and friend from the days we were at the Toronto firm Fraser & Beatty. David was tapped on the shoulder and slipped out for a couple of moments, returning with names scrawled on the back of an envelope. He'd just been reached by the PMO informing him that, in an hour, announcement would be made of Mr. Martin's new senators. He showed me the list he'd jotted down standing at telephone in the corridor: nine names. We both looked with disbelief at the name of Hugh Segal.

Paul Martin was appointing a prominent Progressive Conservative who'd been part of the Big Blue Machine, chief of staff to Prime Minister Mulroney, senior adviser to Ontario premier Bill Davis, and a candidate for the leadership of the Progressive Conservative Party. Another

Progressive Conservative senator was outspoken feminist Nancy Ruth. There was also a New Democrat, Lillian Eva Dyck.

The six Liberal senators were former Toronto mayor and federal cabinet minister Art Eggleton, retired general Roméo Dallaire, Halifax lawyer James Cowan, who'd chaired the 2004 federal Liberal campaign in Nova Scotia, Robert Peterson who'd chaired the Liberal campaign in Saskatchewan, former Alberta Liberal party leader Grant Mitchell, and Claudette Tardif, an Alberta academic with a history of championing bilingualism.

At first it appeared Mr. Martin was adapting a constructive cross-party stance. His press release later that day, March 24, stated, "Liberal governments don't normally appoint members of the opposition. But these people are not going to sit as Liberals, they're going to sit as members of the opposition caucus and I think it's up to the leaders of the opposition parties to decide whether in fact they'll be welcomed in their caucus." That made clear he knew he was throwing firecrackers into the ranks of his political opponents.

Hugh Segal and Nancy Ruth were identified as "Progressive Conservatives," a party that no longer existed at the national level. It had been disbanded in 2004 upon the merger with the Canadian Alliance to form the Conservative Party, and only a rump of three PC holdouts still sat in the Senate, Lowell Murray, Norman Atkins, and William Doody. Geoff Norquay, an articulate long-time PC worker now media spokesperson for Conservative leader Stephen Harper, responded, saying the PM "hasn't appointed any Conservatives, he's appointed some fake Liberals." In time, both Nancy Ruth and Hugh Segal chose to sit as Conservatives and join the national caucus.

For Lillian Eva Dyck, the prime minister's clever ploy proved more problematic. She was an anomaly, a New Democrat who'd been nominated as a senator when her party believed in Senate abolition. Upon her appointment, Lillian Dyck sought to sit as a New Democratic Party senator, but NDP spokesperson Karl Bélanger stated the party would not recognize her as a member of its caucus. The NDP refused to confer legitimacy on the upper house by accepting Dyck. "If she was a real New Democrat," said Bélanger, "the first thing she'd do would be to put a motion forward to abolish the Senate."

Party officials drove in another spike by verifying that Professor Dyck's membership in the NDP had lapsed. "In my naiveté," she explained, "I decided to become a New Democratic Party senator." If the NDP had "bothered to contact me to inquire about my Senate appointment," she felt they would have found someone who seemed a perfect standard-bearer for the party. "I was a First Nations, first-generation Chinese, feminist, scientist, and senior university administrator." Although the NDP would not allow Senator Dyck to join their caucus, the NDP women invited her to their meetings. After a year or so, because Senate rules permit senators to designate themselves however they want, Senator Dyck changed her designation to *Independent New Democratic Party*. Then, in 2009, she joined the Liberal caucus. In 2014, Senator Dyck again found herself politically homeless, this time rejected by another party leader, Justin Trudeau, who refused Liberal senators further place in his party's national caucus.

The variations between Senate appointments by prime ministers Mulroney, Chrétien, and Martin illustrate how PMs always find valid reasons to justify appointing the people they do to the Senate. But for celebrity nominees the motivation is, like the chosen dynamos themselves, special to the point of being unique. In his choice of star senators, Stephen Harper was experimenting with a new way to use the power of Senate appointment.

One reason Prime Minister Harper wanted to attract notable luminaries to Parliament's upper house, as several of his predecessors had attempted with cross-party and apolitical appointees, was to camouflage the larger number of appointments simultaneously being made of lesser-known Canadians who also happened to be key party organizers and major fundraisers. A few dazzling celebrities might distract comment about the others whose primary work would be to conduct publicly funded party operations for the governing party; their primary task would be not lawmaking but campaign fundraising, not scrutinizing legislation but organizing the next election.

In the shadow of new Conservative senators Patrick Brazeau, Nancy Greene, Pamela Wallin, and Mike Duffy were fourteen others appointed in January 2009, including the chair of the Conservative Fund, Irving Gerstein. Each new senator in the group had his or her network of friends and followers, his or her own reputation built upon prior political, governmental, or public service experience. Each had a solid record that would enable him or her to do valuable work advancing the interests of the Conservative Party of Canada — just as the Liberal counterparts across the Senate aisle were past-masters of the same game.

A further reason for a prime minister to pluck individuals with prominent national reputations from *outside* the political and governmental arena is to have them perform a stage role as a Canadian senator, acting the part more than performing the duties. Celebrities do not get this gig so they can plug away at scrutinizing legislation as dutiful legislators, or as "regional" representatives speaking for the province from which they've been appointed. They've been summoned to the Senate to help justify the continued existence of an institution that, if not for their personal fame, would have no fame at all.

Still another reason for appointing stars to the Senate is that, as Canadians of stellar accomplishment outside the political arena, they help the party bridge to *non-partisan* activity across the land. This role has a party purpose too, however, because it seeks to use their magnetism to recruit new people into the political system and gradually gain their loyalty and support.

An equally appealing reason to turn stars into senators, from a prime minister's perspective, is the fact that their celebrity drawing power can help attract contributors to party fundraising events. This has grown more important during the last couple decades because federal cabinet ministers have lost the *gravitas* they once projected, many of them now being close to non-entities even among the country's political class. A celebrity senator can fill that void.

These entwined justifications for naming essentially non-political yet lustrous individuals to Parliament's upper chamber have more to do with benefiting the PM who appoints them than enhancing Senate operations. Indeed, as Alberta Senator Bert Brown realistically observed when defending Mr. Harper's 2009 appointments, "the only way the Senate's ever been filled is by having people who are loyal to the prime minister appointing them."

It probably seems odd that the Conservative Party didn't pay Senator Duffy's travel costs for party-related events from the start, since he was doing this full-time. An explanation is that this is how both Liberals and Conservatives, with their prime minister's blessings and collusion, had been using the Senate of Canada for decades — an extension of party operations, subsidized from the public treasury. The standard nature of the practice lulled those who should have taken precautions from doing so. They did not appreciate, in time, that Senator Duffy's celebrity status, which attracted attention, including from those with axes to grind, and his complete devotion to this party work rather than any Senate duties, had moved the game into a new sphere.

If prime ministers and the Liberal and Conservative parties so abused the Senate of Canada, it was inevitable that, over time and by extension, those whom they ensconced in the place would evince similar behaviour.

When it came to appointing "elected senators" from Alberta, a real divide between Conservatives and Liberals opened up. Liberals do not want to change the Senate, so any move in this direction is considered by them to be an error. Conservatives want the Senate elected, so the Alberta plan was a step toward that goal. Both prime ministers Mulroney and Harper made such appointments, whereas prime ministers Chrétien and Martin reverted to standard practice and ignored the Western province's effort to democratize the upper house.

Prime Minister Mulroney, during his three-year wait for the Meech Lake Accord to be ratified, made Senate appointments in consultation with the provinces in all cases. For Alberta, he named Stan Waters, who'd been elected a "senator-in-waiting" to the upper house, in 1990.

In March 2005, Prime Minister Martin ignored the results of the prior November's election in Alberta of Conservative candidates Bert Brown, Betty Unger, and Cliff Breitkreuz, and independent Link Byfield, by the province's voters. Instead, Mr. Martin named Elaine McCoy, who'd served in the cabinet of Premier Don Getty, to sit in the Senate as a Progressive Conservative, which she subsequently modified to Independent Progressive Conservative.

When Stephen Harper became prime minister, hoping to extend the Alberta system of electing senators to the entire country, he appointed Bert Brown in 2007. In 2012, he named Betty Unger to the Senate, and in 2013, Douglas Black and Scott Tannas. All four had been elected as Progressive Conservatives, but sit in the Senate as Conservatives.

Sir John A. Macdonald's first cabinet had five senators out of a total of thirteen ministers. The prominence of senators in government has been in steady decline since then, however, a downward spiral from the days when two prime ministers were themselves senators, to the present when not a single senator is even in cabinet.

John Abbott was a senator from Québec during the year and a half he served as Canada's third prime minister in 1891 and 1892, after Sir John A. Macdonald died in office. The pattern repeated after the death of Prime Minister John Thompson when, for fifteen months between December 1894 and April 1896, Ontario senator Mackenzie Bowell was Canada's prime minister. Both men had been members of the Commons, but were senators for their entire time as prime ministers and, indeed, for much of their time as cabinet ministers, too. Bowell continued in the Senate until 1906, dying in office in his ninety-fourth year.

Then the drop-off became noticeable. From 1911 to 1979, there were seldom more than two senators in cabinet, often only one.

A variation in how prime ministers used the Senate when choosing their cabinets came at the end of the 1970s. This phase owed everything to the ability of PMs to name people to the upper house or use existing senators for purposes of governing. In 1979, the Progressive Conservatives were so short of Québec and French-Canadian members in the Commons that Prime Minister Clark got the Québec and francophone representation he needed in his cabinet by naming three senators to portfolios. From 1980 to 1984, when the Liberals were without MPs from Western Canada, Prime Minister Trudeau did the same. The sole exception Prime Minister Harper made, when appointing someone unelected to the Senate during his first three years in office, was for Michael Fortier — to bring him into cabinet to provide a voice for Montreal and Québec.

These three prime ministers treated the Senate as an expedient call-up team for needed ministers, not because of any role they could play in the upper house rendering sober second thought but because they needed them for practical governing of the country around the cabinet table. The Progressive Conservative, Liberal, and Conservative senator-ministers in these three governments were not representing their regions in the Senate but speaking to all Canadians on behalf of their ministries.

Since Prime Minister Harper's cabinet shuffle in the summer of 2013, when Senator Marjory LeBreton ceased to be a minister, there has been no one from the upper house in the ministry, for the first time. Given the low state of the Senate, the PM's difficulty getting it reformed, and a political need to distance his government from it, complete severance of the national cabinet from the Senate was, for Stephen Harper, as understandable as it was precedent-setting.

Early in 2014, Justin Trudeau followed the same example, in his own way, by severing all senators from his national Liberal caucus. On January 29, referring to the Senate as "a public institution," he said, "It should not be run like the prime minister's private club." That day he turfed thirty-two Liberal senators, including Québec senator Charlie Watt, the last remaining Liberal caucus member appointed by his father, out of his national caucus.

As long as people are gullible, ambitious men will make empty promises to them.

This aspect of human nature has ensured that prime ministers, and many other players in the ranked echelons of Canada's Liberal and Conservative parties, work at preserving the Senate of Canada for its enticement value.

Many who criticize the extensive power of Canada's prime minister focus on the tight control exercised by the PMO, the intense party discipline imposed on MPs in the Commons, and the regimen of party organization from the leader's requisite signing of a candidate's official nomination papers to his power to oust members from caucus at will.

Fewer notice how the Senate is an essential part of this control system. Those who do look see how utterly Parliament's upper house is an instrument of power, used like a personal handmaid by our country's prime ministers.

CHAPTER 12

The End of Regional Representation

The idea spread following Confederation that the reason for having the Senate was to give representation to the new country's "regions." This role, performed in combination with the other purpose ascribed for it — offering "sober second thought" to check democratic impulses of the Commons — might have worked out, but didn't.

Even at the time of Confederation, this "regional" representation idea quickly morphed into a concept of "provincial" representation, perhaps not surprisingly, since senators were appointed from a particular province and identified specifically with it. Today, many senators, on their websites and in public statements, refer specifically to the work they are doing for Newfoundland or Manitoba as if they are direct representatives of those individual provinces, not a more general region beyond provincial borders, or indeed a more specific region within their province.

There were only four provinces in Canada at the time of Confederation. The so-called "Fathers of Confederation," the political delegates who made up the constituent assembly discussing, debating, and detailing the provisions of the inaugural version of our Constitution — the British North America Act, 1867 — certainly hoped there would be more than four eventually, but in 1867 there were only four. Ontario was the most populous and fastest-growing of the provinces, but Québec and the Maritimes were more important to the national economy than their population size suggested. As noted, they dared not leave matters such as tariffs, taxation, and railways to the mercy of an Ontario-dominated Commons, and so insisted on equal regional representation in the upper house, without which there would have been no Confederation.

Leaders in the Confederation debates may have argued the need for "regional representation," but they allocated seats in the Senate according to provincial boundaries, not on a regional basis, because that was the only way to do it. The reason for allocating twenty-four seats to each was that Québec's electoral map had, from 1856 to the time of Confederation, been divided into two dozen districts. Those subdivisions were adopted in the Constitution, and they remain today. For equality, Ontario was also given twenty-four, and so were the east and west divisions of the country, for the day they would, it was hoped, join Confederation. It was the only practical way to handle the concept in the context and circumstances of the 1860s.

Yet our central reality today cannot be camouflaged by the rhetoric of that era. The Senate set-up, despite eloquent explanations justifying it at the time of Confederation, was never truly aligned with the country's "regions." In two cases, the seat allotment was to provinces (Québec and Ontario, which then were much smaller than they would become with later territorial additions), and in the other cases, the seat allotments were to east and west "divisions," within which the twenty-four seats would be parcelled out to several provinces.

In 1867, the country consisted only of Ontario, Québec, New Brunswick, and Nova Scotia. The two provinces of New Brunswick and Nova Scotia had previously been a single political entity. Though both had freely agreed to join Confederation, the latter spent the next couple of decades trying to get out of the larger union. A widely popular Nova Scotia separatist movement fuelled the belief that its provincial interests, never mind regional interests, would be subverted in the new political union.

Nova Scotia, however, stayed in Confederation, and later, when Prince Edward Island joined, the two, along with New Brunswick, were conveniently grouped as "the Maritime provinces" — a concept of "region" that lasted until 1949 when Newfoundland was admitted as another province of Canada. Although most Canadians in Central Canada and the West then saw the four eastern provinces as a "region," the latest arrival was not viewed by those in Eastern Canada themselves as akin to the provinces already present in Confederation. Newfoundland was not one of the "Maritime" provinces originally planned for. As a result, Newfoundland and Labrador got six *new* Senate seats that were tallied separately from the twenty-four seats in the distinctive regional grouping for P.E.I., Nova Scotia, and New Brunswick.

The only politically acceptable way to include all four in a single phrase is to refer to "the Atlantic provinces" — a term that gives the word "region" greater accuracy all right — but that's not how Senate seats are regionally classified. Over the decades, one solution to strengthen the region itself intermittently flowed into favour and then went out again, like the tides. "Maritime Union" has had a number of reports outlining the case politically and economically. Several conferences have discussed implementing the idea constitutionally. All this has culminated, despite a number of most pleasant get-togethers, in no change. Despite all these flows and eddies, the Senate of Canada's members from the eastern provinces repeated the line, until it became accepted as revealed truth, that they "spoke for region."

Then there was the centre, which quickly complicates any notion of "region." What today is identified as "Central Canada" in 1867 had two very different parts. One was the "distinct society" of Ontario, with its essentially non-French, pro-British, and strongly anti-American complexion. The other was Québec, whose society was "distinct" from Ontario's with its across the board *different* language (French not English), legal system (civil law not common law), educational structure (church-run not public), and religion (Catholic not Protestant). Of course there was some overlap, but even Québec's cultural integrity was different from Ontario's, extending through cuisine and music to a sympathetic view of the United States. Both provinces would become larger in size, too. Québec's land mass was extended to incorporate more northern territory, and Ontario quadrupled in size as it expanded to its north and west in the years after Confederation. As a result of their massive growth, the concept of a "regional interest" *within* early Ontario and Québec was redefined out of recognition by 1920 and 1940 with northern mining and forestry.

Western Canada's inclusion in Confederation followed 1867, and added a totally new dimension, which again recast the notion of regional interests. As the twentieth century progressed, many Canadians became comfortable with the country being described by politicians and others as having *five* "regions" — British Columbia, the Prairies, Ontario, Québec, and Atlantic Canada.

This effort to conceptualize Canada only added more confusion to the meaning of "region," and, by extension, what it entailed for anybody

— such as senators — to speak for one or other of them. Three of these five coincided with provincial boundaries, the basis on which Senate seats were allocated, but two did not. Complicating this was the fact that where somebody was geographically in the country affected whether the division of Canada into these "regions" made any sense or not.

When I worked as a newspaper reporter in Saskatchewan in the mid-1960s, it opened my eyes to hear how Saskatchewanians considered themselves distinct and different from Albertans and Manitobans. Growing up as an Ontarian, I'd only seen the Prairies as a common wide sweep of landscape, with a couple of artificial straight lines drawn down the map to divide the vast area into three sections for the convenience of governing.

Another revelation was hearing folks refer to where I'd come from only as "the East," with little appreciable differentiation between Ontario and Québec, except perhaps for a joke about the French-speaking part. As for Atlantic Canada, it was not even on the radar screens of the people who lived where I was working, in North Battleford. The four eastern provinces were merely an extended part of "the East," a misty section obscured in the distance beyond much reviled "Central Canada," with its banks, railway owners, and costly manufactured goods.

When I worked in British Columbia a year later, I discovered how, from the western side of the Rockies, the country had only two regions, British Columbia and "the Rest of Canada." That had a counterpart, I knew, from living and working in Québec. Novelist Hugh McLennan had first identified the "two solitudes" within Québec society, but the term, by common usage, had come to mean French-speaking Quebecers and the rest of Canada, which of course left French-speaking Canadians *outside* Québec in an identity quandary. People say that Canada as a whole defies geography in being a national entity; within our borders, geography and everything else is defied in trying to conceptualize "region."

If ordinary Canadians had trouble agreeing on the meaning of the term "region" as it applied to Canada, not to mention the number and location of these regions, political scientists offered little help in clarifying things. From political science departments, the concept of "regionalism" emerged, a term so general that everybody nodded with understanding when they first heard it. Under analysis, it turned out this broad intellectualization of Canadian reality had no real meaning, and using it to describe the political situation in the country was no better than pushing an empty wheelbarrow — which is the problem with most "isms." Joe Clark offered his help, speaking of Canada as "a community of communities," but this phrase had more poetic charm than political salience in the realities of governing.

Clearly, the meaning of "region" in Canada has shifted, not only through time geographically, but through our eyes culturally across the huge land mass that constitutes our country.

Despite all of this confusion, senators and others who still seek to find some justification for the Senate like to quote Sir John A. Macdonald or George Brown, each of whom left behind fine words about "regional representation" in relation to Parliament's upper house.

Macdonald and Brown were desperately trying to make a deal. They used all their chips to make the Confederation plan look like a winning pot to other colonial politicians, and talked a great line. Today, when people are suspiciously skeptical about everything contemporary political leaders say, is it surprising how justifications given by even wilier politicians from yesteryear are taken at face value. Indeed, not even at face value — since we cannot see or hear Sir John or the *Globe*'s editor Brown trying their persuasive best, but only in their printed words, and then only the ones they deemed expedient to record and perpetuate as a justification for the Senate.

Both these Fathers of Confederation came from Ontario, a province resolved to create a new day in its governance: changing its name (the "Upper Canada" of 1791 became "Canada West" in 1840 then finally "Ontario" by 1867); getting rid of its upper house in the provincial legislature; and, in the case of Macdonald, creating a new political party that eschewed the province's Tory heritage and would instead be home to all who were, as he called them, "*progressive* Conservatives." Macdonald, who would become first prime minister and fashion reality out of nothing but his dream, sought a new country with a modern complexion, just as steam and steel replaced wind and wood.

Having the Senate was only needed to make the Confederation deal saleable, and stable, and the line about "regional representation" was needed to give the appointed chamber an honourable creation story, even though the realities were more tawdry or commonplace. Many public officials who'd held appointed positions before Confederation — from Prince Edward Island to British Columbia — were opposed to the union, unless they were guaranteed that the changes would provide them with jobs or pensions. The creation of the Senate allowed this. The payoff of a seat in the Senate was enough to melt opposition, as men changed principles to embrace political union and secure a personal future consisting of interesting politics, prestige, and good income — for life.

The idea that the Senate of Canada represented the voice of "regional interests" was stillborn.

Because the concept of region itself was constantly changing, any identifiable regional interests were just as much in flux. The Constitution, both in 1867 and since, has tried to paper over the fact that Senate seats are apportioned on a provincial basis. It does this by lumping them into "divisions" that are notional stand-ins for "regions."

Yet when Mike Duffy emerged as a senator, he did not speak of how he was now going to be a strong voice for the "regional interests" of Atlantic Canada or the Maritimes. "I intend to work hard on the issues of Prince Edward Island," he said. A statement like that sounded, to my ears, more like the main mission of an elected Prince Edward Islander in the House of Commons, or a premier of the Island province — and we already have both of those.

Are we to think that, if each senator "works on projects" for his or her province, the cumulative result will provide "regional representation"? This neither fits with what Macdonald or Brown suggested in the 1800s nor today's reality that Canada has powerful premiers and provincial cabinet ministers speaking for each province's interests. Senators are bystanders, and if they have projects in their provinces or territories, they are make-work programs to fill their unused and unneeded capacity.

For a member of the Senate to say, as Mike Duffy did, that he'd work for Prince Edward Island is rhetoric. Whatever he said about who or what he represented, the reality is that he represented the Conservative Party. The expectation with Patrick Brazeau was that he would, if he represented anything or anybody, represent not the "regional interests" of Québec or his Repentigny district, but Aboriginal peoples, especially those living off-reserve, and, of course, the Conservative Party. Senator Pamela Wallin's connections to Saskatchewan are authentic and deeply felt by her, but her work in the Senate is not memorable for any special interest of the province or the Prairie region she gave voice to, but for her impact on trade issues, military matters, women's rights, and the Conservative Party.

The initial justification for the Senate to serve as a national forum for the voices and votes of Canada's various regions, most particularly those that would stand up to powerhouse Ontario, was important in the early years of Confederation. It served as a persuasive inducement for hesitant colonial provinces to enter the federal union. But this idea that the Canadian Senate represents the country's regions has been vaporized by changes since those early days.

Now provincial premiers speak for the regions; the House of Commons effectively expresses regional differences through MPs who are more directly in contact with the places and people across Canada; and laws, institutions, travel, and communications have ended the isolation of geographic regions and replaced them with an integrated Canadian community.

The reason Canadian senators can no longer act as regional representatives is that there is no such role to play.

The idea that the Senate gave voice to regional interests had worn thin even by the middle of the twentieth century. The story of the Senate and Canadian banks is as good an illustration as any.

When our first Parliament convened in 1867, among the first committees senators formed was a Standing Committee on Banking, Trade, and Commerce. Ever since, its membership has drawn heavily on senators appointed from senior ranks of our country's banking and financial community.

Each decade, as a result of a provision in the Bank Act that requires Parliament to review the statute every ten years, a triggering mechanism meant to ensure the law remains in phase with the society it governs, the banks have had a chance to completely update and refine Canadian banking law. Over the years, the original Canadian banks that received their operating charters through a special private act of Parliament have found themselves in the driver's seat and the Senate Banking Committee has become, in effect, an extension of the boardrooms of the chartered Canadian banks, helping to ensure that they would stay strong.

Few other sectors of the economy received such openly protective treatment, although the bond between the Senate Committee on Railways and Canals came in second, thanks to its cross-links with the owners of the many companies building and operating railways across Canada's sprawling terrain.

Senators, who were unbothered by elections and accountability to the people, owed their appointment to their party and the PM and remained in office for life. Their work was part-time and Parliament was only in session several months of the year. Senators with senior positions in banks and railway companies would more often be found in Montreal and Toronto, absorbing lessons about changes they'd need to make in the Bank Act, the Railway Act, and other statutes governing commerce and finance, when returning to Ottawa and the Senate chamber.

By the 1950s Canada's political establishment was well defined and sociologist John Porter and economist C.A. Ashley separately took stock of the concentration of corporate power.

Professor Porter documented, even then, how 907 individuals residing in the country (not all were Canadian citizens) shared between them 81 percent of directorships in the dominant corporations, 58 percent of the directorships in the nine chartered banks, and 58 percent of those in the life insurance companies. Porter added to this group of the economic elite seventy-eight bank directors "because of the importance of the banks in the economy" to show in total that 985 men held directorships in Canada's 170 dominant corporations, banks, and insurance companies.

Professor Ashley's work focused more specifically on the banks and their directors "because in this group is concentrated enormous economic power." For the four largest banks in 1955, the professor found the Bank of Montreal's thirty directors held 220 or more directorships in other companies. The twenty-five directors of the Royal

Bank of Canada held 240 other directorships. The Canadian Bank of Commerce's twenty-two directors, 225 other directorships. The twenty directors of the Bank of Nova Scotia, 220. In total, these ninety-seven men held between them 930 directorships "in corporations operating in every sector of the economy."

Since those days, other major updates on the concentration of economic power, with cross-directorships and company takeovers, have continued to be documented, revealing an even greater concentration of wealth and corporate power in Canada.

The position of Canada's banks, celebrated for their stability and a pillar of the Canadian economy, is well protected by their guardians on the Senate Banking Committee. The banks have taken over the trust companies, insurance business, financial services industry, and legal services pertaining to these activities. Monetary policy, unlike fiscal policy, is the dimension of Canada's economy unmentioned and undebated in our national Parliament and between our political parties. Canada's banking system is a child of the Senate or, more precisely, the Senate Banking Committee.

When Western Canadian protest movements arose — because their regional interests were manifestly not being effectively represented in the Senate — the Progressives, members of the Co-operative Commonwealth Federation, and Social Crediters in particular were propelled by deep hostility to the banks and railways. It was no quirk of our history that the strongest movement for Senate reform, and now abolition, emerged in Western Canada. Despite claims by senators that they speak for regional interests, this example shows that assertion is hollow.

Interests of labour, and even of agriculture, were seldom heard in the Senate, and when they were voiced, at best got a polite hearing from the representatives of banks, railways, and other major Canadian corporations.

No rules addressed conflict of interest in Canada at the national level until 1927, and even then only in the civil service at a minor level — an agricultural representative could not sell binder twine from the back of his truck when making official calls on farmers — and into the late 1950s it was still the norm for those in public office to use insider information for personal benefit or the advancement of their corporate interests.

If a single word summed up the relationship between Senate committees and the sector they regulated, it would be "cozy." One term that did not apply to their work was "representative of region."

Senators came from Canada's regions, but did not represent them. But because the Senate continued to exist, some reformers in the 1960s and 1970s thought it was time to take another run at fixing the place and achieve real regional representation at long last.

The push came on two fronts. One was from Quebecers of the "Quiet Revolution" who, emboldened by a new sense of cultural identity, wanted to regain control over governing powers that had temporarily been shopped to Ottawa during World War II but not relinquished when the war ended. Western Canadians likewise became vigorous in seeking to counteract federal institutions more oriented to the interests of Québec and Ontario than the unique needs of Western Canada. These social and political pressures from two of Canada's most dynamic regions fuelled, in turn, the more technical impetus of provincial governments seeking clarification of constitutional powers and acquisition of larger roles within Canada's federal system. It was odd that this potent new energy should strike Parliament's upper house, but lightning will sometimes hit the highest tree even if it is dead.

The upper house was criticized, rightly, for not providing effective regional representation in the federal legislative process. Rather than removing the Senate, however, some dreamed of revivifying the place. In the phrase of Professor Peter McCormack, there was "unused institutional space" in the Constitution's provisions for the Senate.

The first proposal on how to better use this space came from British Columbia in 1976. The government of Social Credit premier Bill Bennett proposed replacing the Senate with a "Council of the Provinces," an upper house that would in many ways resemble West Germany's *Bundesrat,* or federal chamber. The goal was to upgrade discussion of regional interests in the federal legislative process.

In 1978, the Liberal government of Prime Minister Pierre Trudeau replied by introducing a constitutional reform package that would transform the Senate into a new upper legislature that the federal government wanted to call the "House of the Federation." Revamping Parliament's upper house was intended to promote the expression of regional interests in Ottawa's legislative process while, just as important to Mr. Trudeau, also allowing him to hold firm and not actually give any new powers to provincial governments.

Under the proposal, both Ottawa and the provincial governments would select members for the House of the Federation. The federal government would appoint half, and individual provinces, the rest, as apportioned between them to ensure regional balance. Provincial representatives would be selected by legislatures, while the House of Commons would choose the federal members. In neither case would members of the House of the Federation — Parliament's second law-making chamber — be elected by citizens.

Representation in the House of the Federation would still be based on the four traditional Senate regions: Ontario, Québec, Western Canada, and Atlantic Canada (the Maritimes plus Newfoundland), but with some seat redistribution to overcome regional (in fact, provincial) imbalance. Ontario and Québec would still have twenty-four seats each. The Atlantic region would be increased from thirty to thirty-two (with Newfoundland getting both new seats). Western Canada would have twelve more seats (thirty-six in total), with British Columbia and Alberta taking four more each, and Saskatchewan and Manitoba, two more apiece. Each northern territory would continue to have one seat in the upper house.

Greater regional balance in the number of representatives was one thing, but the powers they'd wield is what really counted for Western Canadians "wanting in." For ordinary bills, the House of the Federation would only be able to delay passage of legislation, but for legislation of "special linguistic significance," a double majority of English-speaking and French-speaking members would be needed. The House of the Federation would also approve appointments to the Supreme Court of Canada, Crown Corporations, and major regulatory bodies. As with the Senate it would replace, the House of the Federation could not introduce bills to collect or disburse public funds.

The scramble to finally find a satisfactory role for Canada's antiquated Senate was reflected in the high number of alternative proposals that began winging through Canadian skies, all taking flight after British

Columbia sent its "Council of the Provinces" plan aloft. The same year the Trudeau government presented Bill C-60 for a new House of the Federation, four other Senate reform suggestions were also launched. They tended to take inspiration from the German model, but worked significant variations that tended to make none of them compatible.

The proposals came from the Québec wing of the Liberal Party of Canada, the Canada West Foundation, the Canadian Bar Association's Constitutional Committee, and Ontario's Advisory Committee on Confederation. Still in development under Ottawa's sponsorship was another plan from the Pépin-Roberts Task Force on Canadian Unity, which became public the following year. Five years later, in 1982, reflecting deepening Western Canadian frustration that none of these plans had resulted in change to the Senate, the Government of Alberta issued yet another proposal for Parliament's upper house.

The failure to implement any of these Senate proposals stemmed from the fact there were so many ideas that consensus among the supporters of them all was impossible.

Agreement would not be possible, either, because Prime Minister Trudeau took exception to how they would, to varying degrees, accord the revamped upper house of Parliament a channel for provincial government involvement in federal activity, from making laws to appointing officials, broadly pertaining to regional interests. Once he saw how hard the provinces pushed, the PM backtracked on some of his own earlier suggestions for how the House of the Federation might operate.

During this period, provincial governments had grown heady — establishing their own representative offices abroad rather than working in harmony with External Affairs for a single Canadian interest, borrowing directly on the international money market (something individual states in the American Union cannot, by contrast), and pushing for a role in areas of exclusive federal jurisdiction, from communications to immigration. Under some of these proposals, which Mr. Trudeau opposed, members in the upper house would have been provincial delegates, appointed by their respective premiers and provincial cabinets and following orders from them.

The Confederation idea that a national parliament would represent *regional* interests had, under this pressure, morphed into the idea that it would be a body where *provinces* took a hand in the national government. Yet regions and provinces are not the same, and, as Canadian history attests, their varying interests can sometimes result in major confrontations between provincial governments in the same region.

Members in the new House of the Federations would not represent geographic constituencies, such as local districts or even their provinces at large, but their respective provincial governments instead. Members would not vote as individuals in the new House, but as a provincial delegation empowered to cast a single bloc vote to reflect the position of the provincial government they served.

Some proposals, starting with the B.C. government's 1976 plan for a Council of the Provinces, envisaged far more legislative power for the revamped upper house than proposed by Mr. Trudeau for his House of the Federation. For example, British Columbia wanted to give an absolute veto over federal legislation affecting provincial jurisdictions, but the House of the Federation would merely have a temporary veto in most cases, and could be bypassed by the House of Commons after a certain delay time.

The deeper reason none of these ideas translated into action is that they could not. They were blueprints for a new institution, but there was already an existing structure that had been erected and was still standing on foundations laid according to an altogether different plan more than a century earlier. Professor McCormack could elegantly intellectualize about "institutional space" in the Constitution. His notion did nothing to remove the institutional reality of the Senate that was physically in place on Parliament Hill.

Upper house members appointed from the Maritimes, or the West, or Québec, do not primarily caucus as Maritimers, Western Canadians, or Quebecers, but as Liberals or Conservatives. Whenever push comes to shove, they line up with their party, not their region.

Of course they give voice to concerns and interests arising from their part of the country, when occasion permits or pressures demands, but they are not the only voices doing so. Amid the chorus of others — MPs from the region, public commentators, special interest groups, and provincial premiers — they are the last-heard and least-heeded. So many alternative, better channels convey to decision-makers and the Canadian public the grievances and goals of our country's various regions.

Far more than senators, it is the premiers who best express the views of their regions, in ways not imagined when the Senate was created in the mid-1860s. The powers that have accrued to provincial governments over the past 140 years, both as a result of constitutional interpretations that empowered provinces more than the Fathers of Confederation ever wanted, and of the growth in importance of major new fields of activity, such as education and health care, that have burgeoned beyond anything known in 1867, make provincial premiers powerhouse spokespersons for their regions. In addition, a new structure was invented to give them a forum for doing so, the federal-provincial conference, which is a complete bypass of the Senate. So prestigious did this Senate-replacement mechanism become, at least before it was largely abandoned by prime ministers Chrétien and Harper, that attending premiers were accorded the more impactful designation of "first ministers" to put them on a par with Canada's prime minister.

This change in status was already underway when Jean Chrétien arrived on Parliament Hill in 1963 as a young MP. Lester Pearson was prime minister and he was trying to usher in his new era of "co-operative federalism," which meant lots of conferences between the PM and provincial premiers, as well as almost continuous rounds of federal-provincial conferences between cabinet ministers and senior civil servants. Chrétien had become a cabinet minister when Mr. Pearson's successor, Prime Minister Pierre Trudeau, ditched the "co-operative" concept. Trudeau still persisted with federal-provincial conferences because he wanted to revamp the Constitution in order to make it amendable in Canada and to include a Charter of Rights and Freedoms.

Chrétien continued to witness the incessant parade of conferences during the decade Brian Mulroney was prime minister, trying to overcome the problems left by Mr. Trudeau's approach, such as excluding Québec from the new constitutional deal he'd negotiated for Canada. By the time the whole shebang ended on the night of October 26, 1992, when

Canadians voting on a major restructuring of constitutional government turned the idea down in a national referendum, Mr. Chrétien had been direct witness to thirty years of federal-provincial meetings that to some had become an alternative forum for governance but to most Canadians was just a costly and stagy sideshow that produced limited results for the effort expended.

To his credit, the astute Mr. Chrétien, upon becoming prime minister, did not stray any further down this road himself. Instead, he bundled Canada's premiers onto airplanes and flew them overseas with him on trade missions, his public agenda being to improve our country's economic prospects. His unpublicized agenda was to work out whatever issues needed resolution between Canada's governments and regions. Chatting informally while high above the clouds over the Atlantic or Pacific, taking another drink or eating a meal together, the premiers and prime minister bonded and bargained. With no TV cameras recording public-consumption generalities crafted by speechwriters, with no face-saving stances required, the first ministers of our country got the job done, out of sight.

Jean Chrétien has yet to receive credit, or even recognition, for this alternative approach to making the split powers of a federal state mesh better. Nor, for that matter, have Liberals — especially in the Senate — according him any gratitude for crafting this politically efficient and highly economic alternative to consulting *them* about "regional interests." Did Jean Chrétien, when a regional issue bubbled up, go into a huddle with his senators from that part of the country, or get on the telephone to the premiers directly concerned? The fact that the answer to that question is so obvious, that he did the latter, shows clearly how imaginary is the claim that the Senate serves as any kind of meaningful voice for the regions.

The voice of the regions is now also expressed by advocacy groups whose existence is built upon a specific regional interest and whose focus is highly targeted within government and among legislators. These groups have become very effective in news media and popular communications networks. Such entities did not exist in Canada's formative era, when it was felt the task of speaking up for regional needs should be entrusted to the Senate of Canada, because back then there were no other entities to do the job.

The House of Commons is itself an effective forum for ventilating regional concerns and interests. Its televised proceedings and the direct popular election of its members combine to make MPs more relevant and current exponents of the needs and aspirations of Canada's far-flung peoples. Not only do MPs speak for their localities, but they get more attention when doing so than do their Senate counterparts. Even if those unelected and unaccountable parliamentarians were echoing similar views, those views would probably be ignored, coming from a chamber to which little heed is paid.

When the voice of regions is not loud enough in the Commons, perhaps because MPs affiliated with a particular political party are constrained in what they can say, the response has not been to turn to the regional representatives in the Senate, but to form a new political party. The Progressives brought a Prairie perspective into national politics in the 1920s, the Co-operative Commonwealth Federation and Social Credit likewise, in the 1930s. The Bloc Populaire and the Bloc Québécois have, in two different eras, sent members to the House of Commons to speak clearly for Québec's sectional interests, finding their urgent concerns unrepresented by the province's senators in Ottawa. The CCF has become the NDP, which has advocated for a half-century for abolition of the Senate. The Bloc Québécois policy on the Senate is that it should be abolished. The long view of Canadian history is trying to teach us something.

Canada is not the regional country it once was.

In 1867, travel across the country was slower, employing horse-drawn vehicles, water-borne vessels, and railways where they ran. Getting from east to west, from Nova Scotia to British Columbia, meant sailing south, all the way down North and South America to the bottom of the South Atlantic, then around the treacherous Cape of Horn, and back up the west coasts of South and North America. The Panama Canal had not yet been built. After 1914, that journey was cut in half, and railways existed, but the trip from one part of Canada to another was still long.

Communication in 1867 was by telegraph (again, mostly only where railways ran) and the Post Office's delivery of letters and newspapers. The several regions that made up the remaining parts of British North America (after thirteen of Britain's colonies had broken away to form the United States) did indeed display great differences, from French-speaking Québec, to the two British-minded Pacific colonies of Vancouver Island and British Columbia, to the regions settled by Americans who had lost their colonial civil war and fled north into Nova Scotia, New Brunswick, and what would become Ontario.

If Prime Minister Macdonald or his contemporaries were to visit Canada today, their experience would be not only of another time but also of a vastly different place. Travel from coast to coast can now be completed in a few hours. Communications across the land is instantaneous. They would discover how the common laws that have been enacted for all Canadians — from the Criminal Code, which is uniform throughout the entire nation, to federal tax laws, monetary policy, the Canada Health Act, and Employment Insurance — as well as such things as the Canadian Armed Forces, the various trans-Canada pipelines, power lines, and highways, to mention only a partial list, have all worked to remove regional differences and replace them with a common experience and shared outlook.

The people of Canada are more united, and less regionally divided, than the electoral system suggests by its distortions. A few elections ago, *Maclean's*, billing itself as Canada's national magazine, oddly presented the outcome of a general election on its front cover as "Canada: A Nation Divided." The image, across a map of Canada, showed separate strengths of each party in different regions — NDP in British Columbia, Reform on the Prairies, the Bloc in Québec, PCs in Atlantic Canada, Liberals in Ontario — based on the seats each party had won in each region. But the first-past-the-post system's acknowledged inability to reflect the popular vote in seat allocation in the Commons was totally ignored in order to spook Canadians into thinking we inhabit a highly regional and deeply divided country.

Had the *Maclean's* editors looked instead at the deeper reality of how Canadian citizens had just voted, they could have run a banner headline proclaiming "Canada: A Nation United." Their story would have shown that, in every region across the land, Liberals, Progressive Conservatives, and New Democrats had solid support, and that in some ridings the difference between capturing or losing a Commons seat was only a small percentage of the votes cast. The story would also have recorded how the Reform Party of Canada had consistent support across all of Western Canada, and into Ontario, and even a serious presence, despite lighter levels of voting, in Atlantic Canada. And in Québec, which the magazine portrayed as being a regional fortress of the separatist Bloc Québécois, a more honest reflection would have shown that the Bloc and Liberals were closely matched combatants, and that both Progressive Conservative and New Democrat voters were present and accounted for in some ridings enough to tip the balance to one of the other parties.

Even more important than the fact that regional differences which required defence and advocacy in the 1800s have largely been supplanted by the regional similarities and national commonality that now exist, is the emergence of a single global culture that has undermined just about anything left of Canadian regionalism.

In today's world, Canadians in all parts of the country bond with twenty-four-hour news from around the world, global satellite broadcasts, even live reports by Canadian astronaut Chris Hadfield from outer space. Diseases and viral medical conditions can spread quickly without much heed to our boundaries. All world religions have adherents in Canada. The world financial market of which we are a part never sleeps, opening in Tokyo when it closes in Toronto or Vancouver, opening in London when Tokyo signs off. Civil aviation transports Canada's people and products to every continent and country and also brings humans and goods to our airports so that very little can any longer be called "foreign."

The Senate no longer is capable or competent to represent regional interests, nor does it need to. Acting as "regional representatives" is impossible for Canadian senators because no such role remains.

History has written it out of the script.

CHAPTER 13

Thinking Twice About Sober Second Thought

B ecause the ongoing Senate expenses scandal stirred Canadians to ask why the place even still exists, those hoping to justify the upper house needed a more credible reason than that Parliament's second chamber represents "regional interests."

So they said its real role is to provide "sober second thought." With increasing frequency and heightened defensiveness, they repeated *sober second thought* like a mantra, even making this claim with a straight face.

If taken literally, this role of being sober second thinkers would require Canada's senators to be moderate, well-balanced, and tranquil. They would be self-controlled and sedate. The "sober" nature of second-ary thinkers would require them to never be vehement or passionate or excited or wayward or fanciful or exaggerated. A senator would appear "sober as a judge."

If not so constituted as individuals, and on the face of it many Canadian senators fail to meet this self-described standard, at least those dispassionate and objective qualities should be the hallmark of anything emanating from an institution that purveys "sober second thought."

At Confederation in 1867, the Senate's intended role in providing "sober second thought" on legislation was a way of curbing democratic excesses. As noted earlier, the Senate would provide what Georges-Étienne Cartier called a "power of resistance to oppose the democratic element." It was not meant to be independent or objective or dispassionate, but a bulwark to thwart any challenges to the established social order.

It is essential to keep in mind today that this doctrine of "sober sec-ond thinking" was grounded in patterns of anti-democratic thought, because that element was baked into the institution that remains with us today. In addition to being fearful of herd thinking and suspicious of unintelligent responses by poorly educated, self-interested common people, this bias against democracy meshed with a reactionary desire to protect established interests. A number of those first appointed, for life, to the Senate had earlier been the appointed members of provincial upper houses where vested interest in the status quo was protected.

As things turned out, protection against revolutionary tendencies was not much needed. Canada's House of Commons infrequently enacted bills senators could consider radical, in terms of social and economic conditions anyway. One of the rare cases involved the Senate's blocking of a bill for pensions in the 1920s. At several other times in the twentieth century, senatorial challenges to significant legislation about the navy, sales tax reform, and trade with the United States also occurred, based on policy and partisan differences. But in the main, the Senate did not need to block radical measures trying to achieve social equality or to share the wealth of the nation more equitably, simply because Canadian governments and their majorities in the Commons seldom attempted it.

Many people hearing that much-favoured expression "sober second thought" roll off the tongues of senators and their defenders probably imagine a process or that is somehow higher than mere "second guessing."

Yet when I arrived in Parliament in the 1980s, second guessing and policy reversal was the order of the day, and the senators of Canada did not stand dispassionately apart offering sober deliberation, but, instead, passionately played the partisan game as ardently as anybody.

One act in this saga began when the Liberals were still in office under Prime Minister Pierre Trudeau, whose government had appointed the Honourable Donald S. Macdonald, a Toronto MP and bright star of Liberalism as well as Mr. Trudeau's former minister of finance, to lead a royal commission examining Canada's future economic prospects. While the Macdonald Commission was hard at work examining the fundamental framework and essential operations of our economy, Brian Mulroney was working just as hard to overcome his prior failed attempt to lead the Progressive Conservative Party.

His effort included building support by campaigning on traditional Conservative policy of protecting Canadians in our trade relations with the United States. Prime Minister John A. Macdonald had defined the Conservatives' "National Policy" of high tariffs to shield Canadian manufacturers from large U.S. competitors, and prime ministers Borden, Bennett, and Diefenbaker had each upheld this Canadian line of defence against American economic incursion during their turns in office over more than a century. Leadership candidate Mulroney compared Canada's trade relationship with the United States to the position of a mouse in bed with an elephant, with everything fine until the elephant rolled over. Mr. Mulroney, accordingly, pledged himself opposed to "continentalism" and became national leader of the Progressive Conservative Party.

After he won office in 1984 with a large popular vote and the biggest Commons majority in history, which could be taken as a mandate to keep Canada protected from the Americans, the Macdonald Royal Commission reported its recommendation that Canada should enter into a wall-to-wall trade treaty with the U.S.A. Liberal Donald Macdonald, a true liberal believing in the importance of trade between nations, sought to ensure Canada's economic future by opening access to the richest and most dynamic market on earth, that of our closely connected and convenient neighbour. Without any change in core economic policy ever being endorsed by the party, without even a debate in the Progressive Conservative national caucus about reversing a defining principle of the party, without any effort to square a contradiction in his electoral mandate, Prime Minister Mulroney announced his government would negotiate with the United States for "freer trade."

With the PC Party standing on its head, adopting the traditional policy of Canadian Liberals and embracing economic liberalism as recommended by leading Liberal Macdonald in a report originally intended for a Liberal government, the Liberals in turn reversed their own fundamental policy. From inception, the Liberal Party of Canada had sought freer trade — when Prime Minister Mackenzie first fought John A. Macdonald's protective tariffs, when Prime Minister Laurier negotiated a Reciprocity Treaty for trade with the U.S.A., when Prime Minister Pearson entered into a free-trade Auto Pact with the United States.

In the Commons, Liberal Opposition Leader John Turner condemned the Mulroney government's new trade treaty with the United States with all the energy he would have used to support it had the deal, instead, been negotiated by a Liberal government, such as the one he'd still be heading if Mr. Mulroney had not beaten him in the 1984 general election.

Unable to defeat the Canada-U.S. trade treaty in the Commons, Mr. Turner's Liberal caucus in the Senate quickly second-guessed themselves, instantly becoming "Conservatives" opposed to a treaty like the one Wilfrid Laurier had championed, now voicing alarm in the way Sir John A. Macdonald had when he rallied people for "neither truck nor trade with the Yankees!" Just as quickly as Progressive Conservatives under Prime Minister Mulroney had morphed into "Liberals" wanting reciprocity in trade with the Americans, in 1988 the Liberal majority in the Senate galvanized to refuse passage of the bill to implement the Canada-U.S. Free Trade Agreement.

It would be an impossible case for anyone to make that in this cross-dressing moment of Canadian history any "sober second thought" was coming from the Senate. Political Ottawa, and by extension the entire country, was consumed in economic debate where antagonists and protagonists reversed roles and partisanship mixed up a potent cocktail of economics, pro-American and anti-American sentiment, and Canadian relations with the United States. The Senate was totally involved. Sober second thinking was not.

A quarter of a century later, those hoping to persuade Canadians that the Senate really is home to "sober second thought" might fault me for picking that extreme example of the Free Trade Agreement as a dramatic one-off episode.

Such Senate defenders, seeking to promote belief that Senate deliberation is only offered to improve legislation, hope contemporary Canadians who did not live through those heady days of debate and confrontation might not think the free trade Senate battles typical of calm and detached senatorial thinking. They might even want to point out that, after the Senate refused to pass the Canada-U.S. trade treaty and an election was held and the Mulroney government was again elected with a majority of Commons seats, the bill was speedily passed by the Senate in the new Parliament's first session — to show how senators could indeed take a cue from the people in our democratic country.

But was bloody-minded blocking of the Free Trade Act in the Senate really just an exception?

After we'd passed the Goods and Services Tax bill in the House of Commons in 1990, I decided to stroll down the polished marble corridor to the Senate to see sober thinking in action. Even if I'd never before been to the east end of the Parliament Buildings, I'd have had little difficulty finding the Red Chamber in which senators do their thinking. I only had to head toward the noise.

Back in my early years at Bracebridge Public School, a cavernous old place with oversized rooms and wild kids, our teacher sometimes had to absent herself. Left on our own, we'd swing from upper-door ledges, start chalk fights, pull all the coats off the cloakroom hooks, toss boots, shout and war-whoop, throw the books of teacher's pets against the walls or dump them on the floor. If Miss Scovell was away long, we'd stop playing around and erupt into full scale pandemonium. Our little fuss was child's play compared to the raucous riot I witnessed as I reached the Senate door.

Members of the Senate of Canada were singing army songs. Many of them on the Opposition side, where the Liberal majority sat, were twirling wooden noisemakers usually heard only on New Year's Eve or at children's birthday parties. Others were blowing loud, harsh "music" through kazoos. Somebody ostensibly was speaking, in debate about the GST, but he could not be heard. The Senate Speaker was beyond controlling these sober thinkers. He'd given up even trying. I opened the door slightly, but the sound of thought taking place was so deafening I quickly closed it again.

The Senate had fifty-two Liberals, forty-six Progressive Conservatives, one Reform Party member, and five Independents. While the general custom was for the appointed Senate to support legislation passed by the elected Commons, or perhaps send it back with some amendments, the Liberal senators were bucking custom and doing everything imaginable to hold up the new tax law's passage. I could see that the very best senatorial thinking was not being applied to improving legislation; rather, it seemed to be directed to inventing obstreperous ways to thwart it.

Then I spotted a homeless person sleeping at the side of the corridor, wrapped in a sleeping-bag with a few clustered possessions and a thermos. I ventured over. To my amazement, it was not an unshaven hobo but Senator Jacques Hébert. He was on a "hunger strike" to protest the GST. I knew Jacques well through his leadership of Katimavik for young Canadians and had supported keeping his program's funding intact when our government cut it back. I knew him as an adventuresome intellectual who'd gone with Pierre Trudeau to Communist China, having, as a university student, read their revealing account in *Two Innocents Abroad*. I'd especially become attracted to the thinking of postwar France's "personalists" and valued how Hébert and Trudeau brought this more contemporary philosophy to Québec and Canada through writings in the periodical *Cité Libre*. Now I was a direct witness of how sober thinking could be manifested, not by mere words, but concrete personalist action — a hunger strike on the doorstep of Canada's Senate itself. Brilliant!

The noise of sobriety grew suddenly louder. The door had just swung open and several senators were emerging into the corridor, perhaps heading toward the toilets, maybe just wanting to extend the reach of their thoughtful deliberations to places the news media could take greater note. Two of them were long-time acquaintances I'd first met in Saskatchewan years before when I was a reporter for the North Battleford *News-Optimist*, Senator Herb Sparrow and Senator Davie Steuart. Sparrow had been president of the Saskatchewan Liberals and in the 1950s had opened the local Colonel Sanders fried chicken franchise — one of the first in all Canada; and Steuart had been minister of health and deputy premier in the Liberal government of Premier Ross Thatcher.

As my two Saskatchewan senator pals came past, the look in their glassy red eyes was unlike any I'd ever seen there before. Not only was it unfriendly, denying any existence of long-standing relationships that continued after we'd all found ourselves as parliamentarians in the 1980s, but it betrayed a state of altered consciousness. I instinctively stepped out of their path to safety. As they passed, I glimpsed what sober second thinking could do to grown men. Being heavily stoned was the closest condition it resembled.

The Liberal majority in the Senate continued to filibuster passage of the Goods and Services Tax to replace Canada's outdated mash of sales taxes that applied to some items but not others, applied in a dozen different rates to items that were taxable, was a nightmare for manufacturers and suppliers, and which Liberal-appointed royal commissions and committees had five separate times recommended changing, all without result. Prime Minister Mulroney was resolved to modernize and reform where others had failed. The tax measure had been included in the platform proposals PCs campaigned on in the 1988 general election, from which we'd returned with another majority government. A number of aspects of the GST, especially as Finance Minister Michael Wilson framed it, were objectionable and I raised a couple of criticisms myself. But the Liberals discovered that bloody-minded fighting against the GST made them popular.

Nothing could then make them relent. "Sober second thinking" was a euphemistic cover for hard-core partisan battle.

This deadlock over the GST between the Commons and Senate, a result of partisan differences between a freshly elected majority of Progressive Conservative MPs with a mandate for sales tax reform and an appointed cadre of appointed Liberal senators with no accountability except to advance the interests of their party by opposing a contentious public issue, paralyzed Parliament and dominated news from Parliament Hill. The GST's unpopularity made Liberal senators realize that they could sink the Mulroney government's popularity in the country by kicking up an extended fuss and delay in the Senate, which they did with stunning enthusiasm and skill.

How to break the impasse? How to wind down this intoxicating current round of sober thinking?

The Constitution of Canada authorizes creating additional senators in extraordinary circumstances. "If at any Time on the Recommendation of the Governor General the Queen thinks fit to direct that Four or Eight Members be added to the Senate," reads section 26, "the Governor General may by Summons to Four or Eight qualified Persons (as the Case may be), representing equally the Four Divisions of Canada, add to the Senate accordingly." This top-up provision for extra senators had never been used since Confederation.

In 1874, Liberal prime minister Alexander Mackenzie sought to use it to appoint extra senators, but the British government would not advise Queen Victoria to approve the appointments and his effort failed. A second attempt, by Conservative prime minister Robert Borden, hoping extra Conservative senators could overcome the Senate's Liberal filibuster of his Navy Bill, had been refused in 1913. So, after more than a century, according to the thinking of most constitutionalists, section 26 was considered to have lapsed for non-use, or become "*functus*" in legal terminology.

However, Prime Minister Mulroney was determined to prevail where others had floundered in modernizing Canada's taxes on sales of services and goods. Driven to inventive despair by the Liberal senators, the PM surprised them, and astonished everybody else too, by using the Constitution's provision for the first time in history, once the Queen herself consented. He added eight Progressive Conservative senators, giving the PCs an instant majority with fifty-four members, enough to pass the controversial legislation by out-voting the intransigent Liberals in the upper house.

In further protest against this new move in the parliamentary chess game, the Liberal senators then launched a long filibuster to halt the bill and its progress, inventing new tactics and filling the days with mind-numbing and time-consuming talk, designed to maximize Liberal popularity by adopting the role of fighters against the vile GST and preventing the vote from taking place. Their delaying second thoughts dragged out over two months. Ultimately, their thinking petered out and the GST came into effect January 1, 1991.

Only later did I discover that estimable Jacques Hébert performed a yearly ritual of fasting to cleanse himself of bodily impurities and rejuvenate his spirit. Why not multi-task?

On January 29, 2014, Liberal Leader Justin Trudeau registered a widely held conclusion Canadians had reached that we need to think twice about Canada's Senate as a fulcrum of sober second thinking.

"The Senate was once referred to as a place of sober second thought," he told members of the Parliamentary Press Gallery, "a place that allows for reflective deliberation on legislation, in-depth studies into issues of import to the country, and, to a certain extent, provides a check and balance on the politically driven House of Commons." That was not the reality, however. To Justin Trudeau, it had "become obvious how the party structure within the Senate interferes with these responsibilities. Instead of being separate from political or electoral concerns, senators now must consider not just what's best for their country, or their regions, but what's best for their party."

"At best," he said, "this renders the Senate redundant." At worst, "it amplifies the prime minister's power."

That is true, yet partisan politics is only one factor undercutting the Senate as home of sober second thinking.

Bench strength is another. There are only 105 senators, and while that is five more than the most powerful legislative assembly on earth, the United States Senate, Canada's senators work part-time. Most have a variety of other jobs. On top of that, the Canadian Senate is not open for work on the same demanding schedule known to others, mostly sitting three days a week, part of the year, about a total of seventy days every 365.

Compounding this is the fact the Senate is not some arm's-length, dispassionate, apolitical assembly. Senators occupy the same building on Parliament Hill as MPs. They dine in the same parliamentary dining room. They have two standing committees on which MPs sit with senators as members, being joint committees of both houses of Parliament. Those of religious bent hold common communion in weekly "prayer breakfasts" attended by parliamentarians from both houses. Senators caucus together with MPs of their same party affiliation, a practice that for the Liberals only ended this year.

In such circumstances of regular interaction, Canadians are entitled to a reasonable doubt about just how clear and dispassionate their view can be when evaluating the work of the House of Commons.

Senators claim they achieve a spirit of bipartisanship in committee work, but this selective interpretation draws on examples from good times of harmonious co-operation. MPs experience the same. But when the shoving starts, this thin veneer of non-partisan spirit evaporates quickly, as I experienced directly many times in the Commons and witnessed in the Senate. The current Senate expenses scandal, and its handling by the Senate's Internal Economy Committee over the past two years, is not an illustration of bi-partisan co-operation, and in a number of aspects it is just the opposite.

Something else that should preclude senators from trying to stake out ground as "sober second thinkers" is that not all bills from the Commons are scrutinized.

In truth, only a relatively small number gets the detailed review in Senate committees that would justify claiming the upper house provides sober second thought to legislation enacted by Parliament, a claim intended to give Canadians the impression the Senate operates like a quality-control inspector at the end of an assembly line, ensuring high standards are maintained before approving the product for shipment to consumers.

A number of senators make this claim to sobriety and thoughtfulness, but few are better exponents of the doctrine than Newfoundland's articulate George Baker. A former member of the Commons, and before that legislative clerk for the Legislative Assembly in St. John's, he is colourful yet clear in elaborating why Canada could not exist without the Senate. Walter Baker can hold forth in front of television cameras with panache, offering a particular example of an ineptly phrased provision or some egregious clause in a bill enacted by the Commons that would have screwed up public administration horrendously, except the Senate spotted it in time.

Had it not been for diligent Mr. Baker's alert eye, sober thought, and years of seasoning as a Liberal cabinet minister and opposition critic when himself a member of the Commons, the whole country would have gone the way of the cod fishery. Under his forceful charm, the pretense that the Senate does valuable work is maintained. Yet the Senate actually makes few changes in bills from the House of Commons, because on most of them it does not do the work he describes.

Walter is the most forceful spokesperson for sober second Senate thinking, by far. But Canadians should not fail to note the twinkle in his eye as he preaches.

Another big inhibitor of thoughtful action by senators is the fact they are unelected legislators in a democratic society.

If senators actually rethought in a dispassionate way the laws as enacted by the Commons, and if, upon deliberation, they recast them in ways they truly believed to be better, they would crash. They lack political legitimacy for rewriting laws. They would be condemned for "interfering with an elected government's mandate."

So they draw back and just do a partial job. But this is dangerous, too, because if they neglect too much being thinkers, they are damned for being merely "rubber stamps."

It takes artistry to look like you are on the job and working hard when you are not. In precarious balance, hoping to convince Canadians that they and the body of which they are members should continue, senators muddle through in mid-ground, tinkering a bit with some bills, tackling several in a substantive way, and letting most flow straight out the sluice gate without even a peek.

Tinkering by senators takes many forms, some almost mischievous. One example came with a bill to use the thousands of dollars tossed into the Centennial Flame fountain in front of the Parliament Buildings for the advancement of Canadians with disabilities. About 6 a.m. one morning, as I walked to Parliament Hill, I spotted men in orange jackets removing coins from the fountain. Wherever there's a fountain, people hoping for luck will throw money into it. Curiosity pulled me toward them. I discovered these maintenance men from Public Works scooped many thousands of coins and turned them over to a supervisor, but they were not sure what happened to the money after that. By the end of the day I'd pieced together that it ended up in the Consolidated Revenue Fund.

I thought something more appropriate could be done, and because I was chairing the new Parliamentary Committee on the Status of Disabled Persons, I drafted a private member's bill to redirect the money into a project where a Canadian with disabilities would be paid, with the money from the fountain, to research and report on contributions made to Canada by individuals with disabilities. The Committee on the

Status of Disabled Persons would oversee the plan and publicize the new information about how our fellow citizens overcame hurdles to make our country better.

Getting a private member's bill passed is not that easy, but it can happen. That's how Jean Chrétien, when he was a young MP, got "Trans-Canada Airways" renamed "Air Canada," and how Sean O'Sullivan got the beaver designated Canada's national animal, and how I got the Centennial Flame Research Award approved by my fellow MPs. When the senators glanced at the bill, they noted it did not mention the Senate. The fountain had coins tossed into it by people coming by Parliament, and the Senate is part of Parliament. So they tinkered with the bill to somehow incorporate themselves into the project, which was enough to get the bill sent back to the Commons as an amended piece of legislation. Getting a private member's bill through the House once is hard, twice is even harder.

I wondered if a few senators didn't want to teach me a lesson. Perhaps some knew how I'd gradually formed the idea, since first working as a political science student on Parliament Hill, that the only way to reform the Senate would be to abolish it. They likely figured their tinkering amendment would seal the fate of my bill.

But I am determined, and got the bill passed, as amended, a second time. Today there is a bronze plaque embedded in the stone pavement at the foot of the Centennial Flame Fountain that I'd first watched Prime Minister Pearson light at midnight on January 1, 1967, to launch our country's celebration of Confederation's first century. It explains the purpose of the Centennial Flame Research Award to recognize Canadians with disabilities, in French, English, and Braille.

It is rare that senators engage in substantive study of a bill. But the very limited value of the exercise, when they do, was illustrated after Prime Minister Stephen Harper formed a government in 2006 and his ministry opened the show with its cornerstone legislation, the Federal Accountability Act.

Intended to fulfill the Conservatives' campaign promise to clean up government after the Liberals' political and administrative scandals, and drawing on recommendations from Mr. Justice John Gomery's two-year public inquiry into the corruption involved in the Sponsorship Scandal, the Federal Accountability Act provided conflict-of-interest rules, restrictions on election financing, measures respecting administrative transparency, oversight, and accountability.

After intense review and debate in the Commons, the legislation reached the Senate in June 2006 and was placed under close study by the Senate's Standing Committee on Legal and Constitutional Affairs. The Liberals enjoyed a majority in the Senate, but as is custom, to reflect the fact that a different party controlled the government and House of Commons, the committee was chaired by a Conservative, Donald Oliver of Nova Scotia. The committee heard some 160 witnesses, made significant amendments to the bill, and returned it to the full Senate by the end of October.

Of special note, given the "honour system" and other problems of financial administration and ethical conduct in the Senate that would come to light with the expenses scandal in 2012, 2013, and 2014, the senators in 2006 were adamant about keeping control over their own conduct. The senators' amendments to the Federal Accountability Act were not so much the result of sober second thinking as a reflex response for self-protection. One might have expected them to realize that times were changing and the Senate of Canada, too, needed to be in step with new standards for ethical conduct and financial administration. Not so. The senators simply did not want the more stringent regime that the Harper government, drawing on recommendations in the Liberal-appointed Gomery Commission report, sought to impose.

In particular, the senators were deeply anxious about the plan to merge the Senate ethics officer's functions into those of a combined new conflict of interest and ethics commissioner, responsible for both houses of Parliament and the public sector. So the Senate amended the Federal Accountability Act to keep unchanged the role of the Senate ethics officer, and to ensure that the toughened-up Conflict of Interest Act and the new ethics commissioner's mandate would *not* cover senators or their code of ethics, only public office holders and MPs. To get the bill passed back in the Commons, MPs voted to allow the upper house to retain its own Senate ethics officer and its unique rules for ethical conduct.

Among another batch of the Senate's numerous amendments to the Federal Accountability Act appeared the wee ghost of my little bill about the Centennial Flame Research Award, where I'd omitted to mention the Senate. Once again, the senators sniffed at being overlooked or taken for granted — few of them wanting to acknowledge that, in the Commons, they are not held in high regard and would not, in a perfect world for many MPs, even need to be thought about or seen at all. The Senate amended several provisions in the Federal Accountability Act, which had recognized only the House of Commons, by adding an equivalent role or reference for the Senate in each case. However, the Commons, when the bill came back from the Senate, did not retain these amendments. The senators had wanted to be included for some purposes, excluded for others, and the common thread was to remain an oasis of tranquility, apart and unto itself.

Nor did the Commons keep changes proposed by the sober second thinkers dealing with contribution limits under the Canada Elections Act, the appointment processes for two new parliamentary officers called the director of public prosecutions and the parliamentary budget officer, a number of statutory limitation periods, or a series of upgrades to the Access to Information Act.

The senators had inserted new exclusions to the Access to Information Act for records held by the Canada Foundation for Sustainable Development Technology and by the National Arts Centre. They added a public interest test to permit heads of institutions to release information when "the public interest in the disclosure clearly outweighs in importance any loss, prejudice or harm that may result from the disclosure," unless the information relates to national security. In the midst of these somewhat defensible measures, however, the senators, once again trying to preserve their own operations free from inquiry by others, also snuck in new clauses to the Access to Information Act to exclude release of information held by officers of Parliament before the Conservatives' new rules came into effect — in short, all Senate records prior to 2006. Many other amendments at a technical level of tinkering were sprinkled throughout the bill by the senators, as were cosmetic changes. For instance, the sober senators wanted to change the name "Procurement Auditor" to "Procurement Ombudsman."

Then came a few more rounds of parliamentary ping-pong. The bill was returned to the House of Commons, where, as I noted, most amendments were rejected, some were revised, and a few adopted as they were. Then, because it had been altered in these ways, the legislation had to go back to the Senate again. Following some debate in the Senate, the bill was once more referred to the Senate Committee on Legal and Constitutional Affairs. The committee held several more meetings to hear witnesses and to discuss their response to how their earlier work had been received in the Commons.

By year end, the committee recommended that the Senate concur in the amendments the House of Commons had made to its prior work, that the Senate not insist on most of its original amendments to the Federal Accountability Act, and that the Senate insist only on retaining its own Senate ethics officer and excluding Parliament from the definition of "public sector entity" in the Conflict of Interest Act. To get the bill into law, the House of Commons accepted the Senate's final very limited position — in the process helping plant seeds that would sprout in 2012 as the Senate expenses scandal.

"Sober second thinking" had not improved the bill in the eyes of the democratically elected government and its supporters, but complicated it, tinkered needlessly with it, and in some ways even sabotaged it. Politically, the Senate's work amounted to a self-interested exercise, one that in time would even prove to be self-defeating.

The biggest problem Canada's senators face in holding themselves out as a forum for "sober second thought" is the competition. Others provide far more sober review of laws, do it much better, view statutes comprehensively, and judge them according to a standard that is uniform throughout all jurisdictions of our country.

The Supreme Court of Canada is our country's most authoritative source for sober second thought. It is constituted to be such by the selection of the nine justices who compose it and by the rules and practices by which it conducts itself. When it comes to evaluating laws, the Supreme Court lacks neither legitimacy nor credibility, factors that now so greatly hamper the Senate.

Long gone are the days when Parliament was "the highest court in the land," and on some fifteen occasions acted as an adjudicative tribunal with parties called to appear "before the bar" — the brass rail at the entrance to the House of Commons beyond which only elected representatives and those who serve them may go — to give evidence to the members and to undergo cross-examination by MPs. That practice ended decades ago, though the brass rail still remains.

By 1981, the Charter of Rights and Freedoms as entrenched in our Constitution became part of "the supreme law of Canada" and the Supreme Court was our country's unchallenged ultimate arbiter of whether "any law" was inconsistent with the rights and freedoms guaranteed to each Canadian. A law emanating from Parliament, or a provincial or territorial assembly, or even a municipal council's bylaw, that contravened the rights or freedoms of Canadians would be ruled "of no force or effect." That is much greater power than the Senate ever had.

Canada acquired a Charter of Rights that the Fathers of Confederation never proposed. Such charters were viewed by them to be anathema to the British parliamentary way of a constitutional monarchy, something only found in the constitutions of republican countries like France and the United States. Instead, those founders of early Canada suggested the Senate might justify its existence by providing some sober second thought on laws passed by the Commons. It made some sense in that era. Entrenchment of the Charter in our Constitution more than thirty years ago, however, drove yet another big nail into the Senate's coffin, although some people have still not realized it.

Even at the time, though, Prime Minister Trudeau's government, so immersed in the Charter's development that it could see the far-reaching impact it would have, envisaged that more was needed besides Senate review and court validation of federal statutes. So the Government of Canada set up a "Charter Challenge Fund," which provided money to citizens challenging prior enactments on the basis they were no longer constitutional in light of new provisions in the Charter. The senators became victims of yet another measure by which other players and different processes gained the role of providing sober second thought.

This is not just a matter of choosing alternatives, or taking account of how history has worked out. Sober review of Parliament's enactments is actually better conducted by judges than senators. Because while both are appointed, the difference is that Canada's judiciary is independent of government, the senators not.

Moreover, the courts, when called upon, provide detached evaluation of the laws enacted in this country, not only by Parliament in Ottawa, but, also, as noted, by the legislatures of Canada's ten provinces and three self-governing territories, and by the councils of Canada's several thousand municipalities, again something the Senate does not do. The courts across the land, not the Senate in Ottawa, are enhancing a common Canadian standard, because it is not only the Supreme Court of Canada, but lower courts as well, that address the validity of legislative enactments. The entire judicial system of our country provides a comprehensive net for catching laws that need to be qualified or quashed. And because it does so for all laws in the country, not just statutes enacted in Ottawa, the courts taken as a whole are the best system. The judiciary provides complete coverage that the Senate lacks, is already in place, fully staffed, and paid for.

The upper house's defenders who claim that a once-plausible role of "sober second thinking" is still valid today only perpetuate a myth.

Sober second thinking may be a theory, but it is not the practice. Touted by the upper house's defenders as a rationale for the Senate's existence, the concept is undermined by accumulated evidence. The record not only contradicts claims that the Senate is a place of sober second thinking, but discloses the high cost Canadians pay for second thoughts, and how instances of failing to provide such thought are legion.

The Senate of Canada has proven itself ineffectual in taking up this role — a result of its lack of legitimacy as a Canadian political institution, its track record of providing strident opposition to government measures to a degree that offsets any sober second thoughts it does provide, and the plain inefficiency of relying on an upper chamber of a legislature to provided focused and relevant judgment on highly contentious issues. On top of all that, better alternatives have emerged.

The Senate, in being bypassed in this sober thinking role just as in its function of speaking for regional interests, became even less relevant. By the late twentieth century, providing detached appraisal of federal laws had been fully assumed by judicial review under the Charter. The judges did not usurp a role being played by senators. They moved in to fill a void.

CHAPTER 14

Conflicting Mandates and Partisan Deadlock

Casting about for another self-justification, Canadian senators have sometimes portrayed their place of work as "a check on the House of Commons." Senator Mike Duffy lifted this notion of Senate as defence-man to a new plateau in October 2013, during debate on the resolution to oust him, by arguing the Senate was about the only place left in Ottawa "to restrain the unaccountable power of the PMO."

Despite institutional realities and operational practice that make this an improbable match-up — *unaccountable Senate* versus *unaccountable PMO* — the senator touched a nerve with many Canadians, who consider the PMO too powerful for their good, and even for its own. And Canada does have a history of conflict and deadlock with the Senate that has certainly been a "restraint" on the system.

A senatorial "check" is apparently something more rigorous than what is offered with mere "sober second thought." Yet we can't be sure because it: (a) happens haphazardly; (b) is not part of our Constitution; and (c) is another confusing application of an American term in a Canadian context. While I was writing this book, several educated people told me, "I like the *checks and balances.*"

They were importing, as if it applied to Canada's Parliament, a fundamental concept upon which all government in the United States is built. Believing it vital to prevent consolidation of political power in order to safeguard citizens, the American Constitution first divides the powers of state by separating the legislative, executive, and judicial operations of government, then tops that off with a formal set of procedures between these three branches that check and balance how the American republic can be governed. For example, the American president (the executive branch) may sign an international treaty, but the United States Senate (the legislative branch) must ratify it; Congress (the legislative branch) may enact a law, but the United States Supreme Court (the judicial branch) will rule on its own constitutional validity.

Between the three branches, there are many permutations or combinations to further counterbalance the exercise of power. The idea that Canada's Senate fits into this U.S. "checks and balances" template conflates incompatible concepts, is not supported by fact, and is at odds with our constitutional reality.

While it is true that over the past century several head-to-head standoffs have occurred between Parliament's two houses in Ottawa — over navy funding in 1912, regarding Bank of Canada governor James Coyne in 1961, and over the GST in 1989 — it's been nothing like the partisan deadlock of Washington. In October 2013, the entire U.S. government was shut down for more than two weeks after Congress (legislative, Republican) failed to appropriate money for the government departments (executive, Democrat) to keep operating. Americans lacked their benefits and government services as 800,000 federal employees stayed home while another 1,300,000 employees had to work without knowing when they'd get paid.

That sixteen-day government shutdown was the third-longest in U.S. history, following an eighteen-day shutdown that occurred in 1978 and another running twenty-one days in 1995–96, which involved the entire U.S. government. Some fifteen other shutdowns have stopped the world's most democratic country in its tracks intermittently — mostly for single days or weekends — after this precedent became established for the first time in 1976.

By contrast, under our Constitution, if the Government of Canada has not been voted funds by Parliament to keep operating, it requests the governor general to authorize "spending warrants," which keep money flowing and government operating until the Commons passes the budget for the coming year.

Cases of partisan standoffs creating deadlock are actually an unintended anomaly in our parliamentary system of government.

At Confederation, the Senate's absolute veto over a bill was not expected to amount to more than a delay, for the simple reason that up to 1867 governments were mostly short-lived, so none was thought able to build up a big enough majority in the Senate to block a successor government of the opposing party. The Fathers of Confederation never contemplated that one political party would be in office for extended periods, appointing senators of its own partisan affiliation in such numbers as to create an impasse between Parliament's two houses. When they were making provision for the Senate of Canada in the mid-1860s, political parties were still loose formations, not the disciplined cadres we know today. History played a trick on that idea.

As it turned out, Sir John A. Macdonald himself managed to develop a strong party, stay in office for nineteen years, and name some ninety-one men to the Senate. The by-product, a Canadian reality by the end of the nineteenth century when the Liberals came to power, was a pattern of one party dominating the Senate while another controlled the Commons.

Because such a problem had not been anticipated, no solution for it had been provided.

Worse, because the institutional relationship between Parliament's two houses had been embedded in our Constitution, Canada was stuck with an unintended brake that *could* be applied at any time to the parliamentary process by a legislative body whose members were not elected by the people. The longer this condition was perpetuated, while the people of Canada and our other political institutions became more democratic, the further the Senate slipped out of phase with Canadian reality.

Unlike the Americans, who intentionally designed a government structure to check and counterbalance itself, we just stumbled into an arrangement not anticipated by our Constitution, with no clear procedures to resolve deadlock when it happens. When we make it work, it is by "muddling through" more than by good planning or because of the proper functioning of Parliament.

Confusion about the Senate's role has been abetted by a misunderstanding of democratic principles that govern its relationship with the House of Commons.

Under the United States Constitution, to again make that contrast, the term "checks and balances" refers principally to the *separation* of powers. The executive, legislative, and judicial "branches" of government are segregated and distanced from each other, and each has overrides and counter-balancing powers against the other two. In Canada, the executive and legislative are not separated, but *combined.*

Rather than restraining the cabinet's exercise of power, we draw cabinet ministers from the legislature itself, require that they be in the legislature to face the people's representatives directly, and insist they can only govern so long as they keep winning majority votes from the people's representatives in the Commons. We jam both parts of government together for direct, visceral accountability, rather than separating them for an indirect balance or institutional check.

It is worth remembering that in the American system, the two-house or bicameral legislature is *not* fundamental to their structural division of powers. Two houses just provide an additional element within the far more fundamental separation of the executive branch of government (the president and cabinet, with the government departments and agencies they run) from the legislative branch (Congress's House of Representatives and its upper house, the Senate), both of them separate from the judicial branch, at the apex of which is the United States Supreme Court. This U.S. system of checks and balances, based on separation of powers, could still function if the legislature in Washington had only a single house.

The American theory of government, supporting a republic not a monarchy, embraces a single sovereign. The very first words of the U.S. Constitution make unmistakably clear who that "sovereign" is: "We the People ..."

Canada has not one but *two* sovereigns — the People and the Crown. Under our Constitution, the division of power is not between "branches" of government but between these two sovereigns. In our system, it is the balancing and interaction of these two sources of legitimacy that provide the primary checks on power in government. Since 1981 they have been accompanied by a third balancing element — the Charter of Rights and Freedoms interpreted by our country's independent judiciary.

So, as in the United States, our courts stand apart from government and, for over three decades now, have provided an independent check on it — not only interpreting the constitutionality of laws in light of the Charter, but, as in the case of the Harper government's reference to the

Supreme Court of Canada on plans for Senate reform, what may be done in changing democratic institutions according to the Constitution as interpreted by the Supreme Court justices.

The way we Canadians are governed by two sovereigns — the Crown and the People — is the product of a long history that not only incorporates our colonial past but all subsequent democratic evolution. Our dual or *divided sovereignty* results in the fact that government is conducted in the name of the Crown, but nobody can exercise those considerable powers until they are first elected to office by the People or appointed to office by individuals who themselves have been elected.

During its early years, the Harper Conservative government was confounded by a Liberal majority in the Senate that produced partisan conflict, not *within* a legislature, which is where we expect and need it, but *between* two legislatures, which is something essentially alien to Canadian political culture. The fact one house is democratically elected and accountable, but the other is not, further exacerbated this conundrum created by fundamental clash between Parliament's two houses in terms of political legitimacy.

This recent standoff was not an exception, but a recurring pattern.

Two decades earlier, the Senate had spawned incessant turmoil when the Liberal-dominated upper house, led by Nova Scotia Senator Allan MacEachen, threw up a blockade across the path of legislation proceeding from the duly elected majority Progressive Conservative government of Prime Minister Mulroney in the Commons.

It was no different four decades before that, when a majority Progressive Conservative government led by Prime Minister John Diefenbaker faced a solid Liberal majority in the Senate. In 1958, Diefenbaker's forces won the largest majority in the Commons to that date of any party since Confederation. But the Liberals had been in office for twenty-two consecutive years before Mr. Diefenbaker first came to power (he was elected with a minority government the previous year, in 1957). Such a large number of senators had been appointed by prime ministers King and St. Laurent that the Liberal party had the biggest majority in the upper house since Confederation.

Not only was there an overwhelming partisan mismatch between the two houses, but by the late 1950s there was also a big difference between, on one hand, the electorate's view of who they wanted governing them and, on the other hand, the situation that existed in Parliament. The PCs who passed legislation in the Commons had all just been elected by Canada's voters, whereas the Liberals who thwarted that legislation in the Senate had been appointed many years earlier. Never had the Senate-Commons war zone seen more rival troops massed for combat. Never had the time lag between the people's will of yesterday and today been more pronounced.

The imbalance was most dramatic in 1958, but it was still just one more example in the recurring pattern of Canada's parliamentary deadlocks. In 1912 and 1913, the majority Liberal-Conservative government of Prime Minister Robert Borden had a number of its measures, most memorably its Naval Aid Bill, turned back by an unyielding Liberal majority in the Senate.

Does the extent and validity of a majority Conservative mandate from the people trump any responsibility of the Liberal majority in the Senate to prevent and obstruct measures it takes exception to? When the tables are reversed and Liberals control the government and Commons but Conservatives the Senate, do the same principles apply? It seems they do, since both parties are so similar in these respects, but it is harder to say simply because history holds fewer examples. The Liberals were in power for such long runs — "Canada's natural governing party" — that they tended to control both houses of Parliament for most of the twentieth century.

On good days, in such situations, Canadian senators have temporized. They want to appear reasonable because they know they have an impossible role: damned if they become active; damned if they lay off too much. They try to modulate Senate action, generating enough motion to keep their antique boat moving, but not so much as to make it capsize.

On bad days, the show is more dramatic. To again recap some highlights, a Liberal-dominated Senate defeated the Borden Conservative government's Naval Aid Bill in 1912. In 1914, the same senators turned back the Commons legislation for redistribution of seats in Parliament. Fast forward three-quarters of a century, and a

Liberal-dominated Senate was just as active in opposing legislation of Mr. Mulroney's Progressive Conservative majority in the Commons dealing with the Canada-U.S. trade treaty, the goods and service tax, Unemployment Insurance Act reforms, patent drug laws, and borrowing bills. A Conservative government under Prime Minister Stephen Harper during this past decade again faced the same challenge in its initial years because a large Liberal majority, primed for active partisan war, had been banked in the Senate by a dozen years of Prime Minister Chrétien's appointments.

This real war of partisan politics between the two chambers causes consternation in the popularly elected government and also upsets, to some degree, members of the Canadian public, mostly because the Senate majority begins to act like the Official Opposition in the Commons. In the House, however, opposition MPs have been elected by the people, not appointed by a prime minister whose party is no longer in power but who continues to rule the country from his political grave. Although real estate law has a doctrine to prohibit the "dead hand" of someone governing property uses from the grave by provisions in a will or title deed, the Parliament of Canada has no such *mort main* protection from former prime ministers guiding the conduct of our law-making process.

Thwarted prime ministers have, from time to time, responded to the partisan provocation of a Senate filled with members from the Opposition. Prime Minister Borden was preparing a national referendum on Senate reform when election-timing and World War I intervened. Prime Minister Mulroney negotiated provisions for an elected Senate into the 1992 Charlottetown Accord constitutional amendments, but they were defeated in a national referendum, along with other fundamental constitutional changes that would have transformed Canada. In both those cases, as well as in other stabs at Senate reform over time, hopes rose that something would finally be done about the upper house. Yet circumstances changed, thanks to a foreign war or the defeat of constitutional amendments or some other overriding factor, sidelining once again the project to deal with our relic institution, which in the process could have resolved this core issue of the incompatible roles of Parliament's two houses in making our laws.

The struggle between the House of Commons and Senate boils down to conflicting mandates. It arises due to incompatibility in the constitutional theory of the upper house and has been embodied in our Constitution from the day it was written.

The Senate's parliamentary mandate has two different premises. One is the plebiscitary theory of democracy, under which a public body — the government, a legislature — receives its authority *directly from the people.* The other is the older theory of parliamentary government, which is grounded in the idea that a government derives its authority from Parliament, so that its mandate is *only indirectly from the people.* Parliamentary government was established before democracy took hold, so is the older of the two concepts that underpins the Senate of Canada. Robert Mackay succinctly explained in his book *The Unreformed Senate of Canada* how the "democratic theory has in effect been grafted onto the older and still legally correct theory of the sovereignty of parliament."

As an institution, the Senate thus embodies incompatible theories about the source of its authority as a law-making body. Having two different foundations makes life tricky for those occupying the single structure erected atop them. The unelected Senate must deal with legislation emanating from the elected House of Commons, which enacts laws on the basis of a mandate from the people. For this reason, it is in the Senate chamber where the legitimacy of a popular mandate from the Canadian electorate is most directly challenged. That challenge is expressed every time senators delay a Commons bill for an inordinate time, amend it in fundamental ways, refuse to pass it, or defeat it.

In 1957, for example, when Liberals dominated the Senate and Progressive Conservatives formed the government in the Commons, Senator Ross Macdonald, leading the Liberals in the Senate, endeavoured to explain how senators needed to act in the circumstances. "The overriding responsibility of the Senate is to make the Constitution work," he postulated, without elaborating very much.

By those words alone, however, Mr. Macdonald underscored how he and his Senate colleagues did not fit any model of democratic parliamentary government that Canadians, by the middle of the twentieth century, would accept. He proposed that senators should not "assert their legal rights and prerogatives to the prejudice of common sense or reason, or to the sacrifice of the proper functioning of our constitutional machinery." Nor did he think senators should "automatically resist every government measure which comes before us," because "to do so purely out of party considerations would hamper effective government of our nation." In short, he felt that "it wouldn't work if we exercise the powers we have."

Senator Macdonald reiterated this interpretation after Mr. Diefenbaker's Progressive Conservatives won another election in 1958, and again in 1962. His was not a solo interpretation, but an approach generally taken over the decades by Senate opposition leaders who had majorities in the upper house. He was articulating the hard truth that, should the Senate of Canada do what the Canadian constitution legally empowered it to do, the upper house would defeat the Constitution's more fundamental purpose of providing citizens with "responsible government" and allowing Canada "peace, order, and good government." This leading Canadian senator, who went on to become a warmly respected lieutenant-governor of Ontario, himself acknowledged that the Senate's mission, as constitutionally prescribed, is impossible to fulfill.

Only a diluted and temporized version of what the Constitution empowers senators to do, he asserted, would be acceptable. That meant senators themselves, rather than either the Supreme Court of Canada or citizens of our country, would decide when, where, and how to bend the Constitution. Put starkly, the senatorial dilemma is that to exercise any power at all, senators must subjectively interpret the law.

What makes subjective application of the Constitution by senators especially problematic is that sometimes, in identical circumstances, a different interpretation has been made. When this has happened, and senators have decided they wanted to stand up to government measures, no longer did Canada witness a phoney war between Parliament's two legislative assemblies, but a real one.

Echoing Liberal senator Ross Macdonald, in 2004, Progressive Conservative senator Lowell Murray noted that, since he and his colleagues were *appointed* legislators, it was necessary "to exercise the restraint … in the exercise of our legislative veto and other powers." Like a thief tip-toeing through an occupied house at night, senators try to pull off their assignment without disturbing the sleep of others. In addition to having an impossible role, they also have an unenviable one.

The Senate's role as a rubber stamp for legislation coming from the Commons appears easier when the same party that is in government has a majority in the upper house. During the Liberal Party's long governing hegemony through the twentieth century, as noted, this was a prevailing condition. But because being a Canadian senator is an impossible assignment, even this backfired. The quiescent Senate, routinely passing measures with little fuss and no bother, provoked an understandable response from journalists, political scientists, and citizens. Why are we paying for an unnecessary legislative assembly?

Enduring throughout all the years since Confederation, in these alternating cycles of restraint and real conflict between the Senate and the Commons, is the still unresolved issue of how far the Senate can really go in exercising its constitutional role.

To somehow keep operating, senators have had to make their own contentious interpretations of how much of the constitutional and statutory framework that creates and empowers them really needs to be heeded. Senators not only have a role in making our laws, but arrogate unto themselves deciding how Canada's laws apply to them. The imperative urge by senators to exempt themselves from the public sector regime for ethical conduct, to remove their records from public reach under the Access to Information Act, and to defiantly cling to an outdated system of financial control and budget administration, was no aberration. These were all clear expressions of the Senate of Canada's rogue role in contemporary democratic society. The greatest taunt to democratic accountability comes from Canada's most senior law-making body itself.

Following the 1962 general election, when the Diefenbaker government was re-elected with only minority support in the House of Commons, Liberal Senate leader Macdonald returned once more to the question of the popular mandate, in light of these changed circumstances. He wondered whether they now added any further or special responsibilities on the Senate.

The Diefenbaker government has "no clear mandate from the people, either as to general policy or as to specific measures," he declared. From this he concluded that the Senate must accordingly take the general attitude that no governmental legislation coming before the upper house had behind it a clear popular mandate. Under these circumstances, as Robert Mackay suggested decades earlier in *The Unreformed Senate of Canada*, it would be necessary for the Senate "to give all legislation more searching investigation than had been the custom following a conclusive popular verdict."

Progressive Conservative senators, who supported the Diefenbaker government, took a different view. They did not think senators should be either sloppy in their work if a government had a majority in the House of Commons, or stringently attentive only if a bill came from a House where a minority government was in office. "It makes no difference by whom a bill is introduced in the other place," asserted Senator Alfred Brooks, the government leader in the Senate, "if it receives a majority there it comes to us as a measure endorsed by the elected representatives of the people of Canada. The fact that it was sponsored by a minority government gives no cause to consider it differently than we would a measure introduced by the strongest of governments." Similarly, Senator Wallace McCutcheon asserted that the obligation of the Senate "at all times" was "to speak to the question and not to the electorate."

At this point the two different premises about a legislature's mandate identified by Mackay — the plebiscitary mandate directly from the people, and the parliamentary mandate derived internally from the Commons — converge.

A government receives its authority directly from the people when one party or another is returned to the House of Commons with a clear majority, but minority governments commonly result too, as they have eleven times in Canadian general elections from 1921 to 2008. If one believes governments should, constitutionally, have a clear majority, noted Mackay, "the implication is that any minority government is necessarily in the position of a caretaker government, with limited authority derived from, or assented to by, the House of Commons. Such authority would not extend to the introduction of unusual legislation which would constitutionally require a popular mandate."

But if one adopts the theory of parliamentary government advanced by Senator A.J. Brooks that the government's mandate was parliamentary and only indirectly a popular one, then, according to Mackay, the minority status of the government ought to be a matter of indifference to senators. From a strictly constitutional point of view, he'd reason, Senator Brooks's argument was no doubt sound, and thus "any bill coming up from the House of Commons was of equal validity with any other precisely because it had behind it the parliamentary mandate."

All this reasoning, while historically important and constitutionally relevant, must be viewed in the larger context that for ninety years Canada has operated a multi-party political system through a two-party electoral process that fails to proportion popular vote with seats in the House of Commons, an inconvenient truth that, more deeply, erodes any notion of an electoral mandate and the legitimacy of Parliament itself.

These problems of conflicting mandates and parliamentary deadlock are bound to continue in the future too, particularly if a New Democratic Party government is elected.

Parliament's upper house stands as an insurmountable barrier to any NDP government taking office in Canada. Some may think the prospect of a national New Democratic government unrealistic, but looking back into history, many Canadians were surprised every time a democratic socialist government came to power in a province, starting in 1944 with Saskatchewan — the first socialist government elected in North America — then on through British Columbia, Manitoba, Ontario, and Nova Scotia. Canada has decades ahead to witness the political conundrum that would result from a prolonged institutional standoff should an NDP government, able to get its legislation passed in the House of Commons, find itself stalled or defeated in the Senate.

Even battle lines drawn between Liberals and Conservatives, two parties of much common interest and shared outlook, have produced filibusters, created stalemate, and placed senators and MPs in prolonged and sometimes desperate legislative war. How would it be if those two parties combined to face off against New Democrats in a contest between Parliament's upper and lower houses?

Because the Senate's members have reached the upper house only through the personal choice of Liberal and Conservative prime ministers, they overwhelmingly are instinctive Grits and Tories, or at least sympathetic to and supportive of the party that appointed them. Most would refuse to give approval to NDP measures. Many would be keen to create political turmoil for an NDP government. In fairly short order, the standoff would become a constitutional crisis.

Anticipating this dystopia, New Democrats have long seen why their pathway into a happier Canadian future needs to have the Senate barrier blasted away. Abolition of the upper house is necessary NDP policy.

That, in turn, is why some would argue the Senate should continue: to prevent the socialist hordes from overriding traditional values and established relationships. Anti-democratic patterns of thought run deep in Canada still, with the Senate their strongest last bastion and best refuge.

A subtext in this struggle between Senate and Commons is the degree of "partisanship" involved. Senators often contend, speaking in their favour and knowing most Canadians find partisanship distasteful, that they are less partisan than members of the House of Commons.

This assertion, however, is as glib as it is ill-founded. When push comes to shove, senators have shown themselves every bit as cunning and brutal as parliamentarians in the Commons. Most senators are more seasoned players than MPs, because where our House of Commons has the highest turnover rate of members of any of the world's democracies, Canada's Senate has the greatest longevity in office. Senators have over time acquired the subtler arts of political battle. A majority of them are also seasoned veterans of political wars, so they know when to fight and when it helps to wear a pleasant pacifist's smile.

Another factor that contributes to the Senate appearing "less partisan" than the Commons is the diversity of MPs compared to upper house membership. Currently five different political parties have members in the Commons with significant differences in ideology, social strata, cultural backgrounds, and economic interests. MPs are bound to take strong and principled exception to the views and policies of each other. By contrast, senators in the main reflect Canada's political and economic establishment. When bills dealing with tax reform come to the Senate, for instance, the Senate's heavy representation of lawyers and business-people with positions in private companies becomes smoothly reflected in their fairly uniform reactions.

What really draws out their partisanship is not the stance senators take against one another, but against the House of Commons. The core issue has always been which of the two bodies had greater legitimacy in dealing with government measures.

A final dimension to this unhappy pairing of Parliament's two houses is its fundamental challenge to "responsible government" and our constitutional foundation.

In terms of holding "ministers of the Crown" to account, the role belongs to the Commons, not the Senate. Being itself a vestige of Crown authority, it was never credible that the Senate could perform this role, since under our Constitution such democratic accountability could only be extracted by elected representative of the sovereign People.

Members of cabinet are ministers of the Crown. In Parliament and in each provincial legislature, the Crown is an intrinsic part of lawmaking: any bill having gone through three readings and passed by the legislative assembly is only finally enacted into law when it receives "Royal Assent," as evidenced by the signature of the governor general or the provincial vice-regal counterpart, the lieutenant-governor.

As a constitutional monarchy, Canada retains these and other aspects of life as formerly developed under a monarch in feudal England, where the king or queen's absolute sovereignty was cut down and held in check by new measures imposed by people resolved to free themselves from arbitrary rule. Unlike Britain's thirteen Atlantic-seaboard colonies, where the colonists overthrew the king and established a republic, Canada is still made up of colonial remnants. The monarch continues as sovereign and still retains power in name, though in practice that power has become subjected to increasing constitutional restraints imposed, or extracted, by the sovereign people's elected representatives. The resulting complex set of governing arrangements is neatly summed up by describing our form of government as a "constitutional monarchy." The sovereign People are as much a component of this as is the Crown.

The result of this history and of the developing democratization of our institutions has confirmed for Canadians that a workable system of government could embrace a dual sovereignty shared by the People and the Crown. Its most important expression was through a legislative assembly where ministers of the Crown directly face the people's elected representatives. The "checks and balances" of our parliamentary government are found in the *same* chamber rather than between two chambers.

It is true that in the early years of Confederation, a greater practical need existed for this accountability to operate in *both* houses of parliament because as many as five cabinet ministers at a time were senators. Those were also times when most provinces still had appointed upper houses, and there was just more jumble about the way people got into office and greater blurring about the lines of democratic accountability as part of responsible government.

In modern times, however, the number of senator ministers has dwindled until just a token senator was lately found in cabinet. In July 2013, Prime Minister Harper finally cut this link entirely; with her retirement, the Honourable Marjory LeBreton became, as of now, the last Senate member of a federal cabinet. Now all cabinet ministers face democratically elected critics across the aisle in the Commons — one of the easiest Senate reforms, made by Prime Minister Harper with hardly any notice and certainly no adverse comment. It further served to sever the Senate from any remaining role it had, which was an inappropriate one at that.

The miasma of confusion in the relationship between the Senate and the House of Commons, as seen from all the doctrinal, constitutional, electoral, partisan, and historical conflicts it has spawned, cannot be cleared up. Still, this reality did not deter a number of Canadians from trying.

CHAPTER 15

Getting Serious About Senate Reform

If asked during his ascent to power within Québec's circles of influence, Brian Mulroney would likely have expressed a view that the Senate of Canada was a harmless entity but a useful adjunct to those wielding power and exercising statecraft.

To most Quebecers, the Senate was little more than a retirement gymnasium, a refined debating society, a golden handshake for public or party service, an elegant nursing home for venerable political warriors who still had the skills, but no longer the passion, for public issues.

The concept of "Senate reform" was so unimportant in Québec as to be non-existent. The province had its place ensured with twenty-four Senate seats, balanced against Ontario's twenty-four and corresponding numbers from the West and Maritimes. The succession of long-tenured and powerful Canadian prime ministers from Québec — Wilfrid Laurier, Louis St. Laurent, Pierre Trudeau, and Jean Chrétien — never sought office intending to change Parliament's upper house.

Brian Mulroney, though in a different party, was a product of the same political culture. The Senate was an auxiliary institution, worth cultivating only for the political supporters he could find among its limited number of Progressive Conservative members to advance his own ascent to power, certainly not worth heeding for advice on public issues or worrying about because of its truncated and obscure powers in governing the country.

When running for his party's leadership, Brian Mulroney spelled out his policy positions in cross-country speeches and the 1983 book, *Where I Stand*. The future prime minister said nothing about where he stood on the Senate, and neither he nor his audiences noticed anything crucial missing from his platform. He was preoccupied with economic, cultural, and social issues. Even when specifically addressing federalism and constitutional change, the upper house still eluded his field of vision.

Yet politics is the universe of surprise. Brian Mulroney would become the one national leader to try more than any other to change the Senate of Canada.

Six factors combined to create this improbable role for Canada's eighteenth prime minister. Together they forged a chain of linked events, each coupling inexorably with the next until Senate reform nearly broke the country apart. This sequence of events would transform the empty vessel of Canada's Senate into the improbable receptacle of aspirations for Canadian unity. These developments even now illuminate the path ahead for Canada's perpetually "unreformed" Senate.

The first event in this chain was the political upheaval flowing from Québec's "Quiet Revolution" in the 1960s.

Québec had long been a place unto itself. After being abandoned by France, its king no longer interested in more wars with England over this North American snow patch, the colonial province carried on with its transplanted version of the French language, its feudal system of seigniorial land-holding and the hierarchical structure of local government which that provided, its civil laws derived from the Napoleonic Code, and Roman Catholicism, which the Church parcelled out as faith, social control, and a bulwark of stability against the tides of change. To hold fast to what they had, as their best way of ensuring their survival, Quebecers became essentially conservative in culture, turning inward to survive cold winters and resist Britain's policies of assimilation.

As the province expanded, settlement extended further up the St. Lawrence River valley. To overcome the challenge of distance and to accommodate the presence of English-speaking settlers around the edges of lakes Ontario and Erie and in the Niagara Peninsula — loyalists to the Crown who'd fled during the war of rebellion by thirteen of Britain's American colonies — the province was divided in two. The part further up the river valley was aptly named Upper Canada, while the original settlements along the lower St. Lawrence River were designated Lower Canada. Changes in government helped consolidate this arrangement, with a new 1840 constitution that put both Upper and Lower Canada together as "Canada" and renamed the two sections Canada West and Canada East.

Within this constitutional and social arrangement, the basic institutions of French Canadians — language, religion, law, and education — as well as cultural attributes, from cuisine to music, remained intact. By 1867, a new constitution added two more colonial provinces, Nova Scotia and New Brunswick. "Canada" was a federal state now with four, not just two, provinces. Québec's status remained secure under the new arrangements.

For the next century, as more provinces were added to the Canadian federation, care was taken to ensure they did not swamp or override the existing protections, including representation in Parliament, for Québec's distinct nature. Throughout all these years, the Roman Catholic Church dominated Québec life and governance. Priests ensured that women brought forth as many children as possible so the French-speaking population would continue to hold its own, and large families, with fifteen to twenty children or more, were expected, demanded, and facilitated by the Church's edicts about birth control and abortion. Women did not get the right to vote in Québec elections until 1942. It would be decades more before a mother could take her injured or ailing child to a hospital on her own, without the father's consent, for medical care. The clergy's firm hand moved the performances of most politicians, teachers, lawyers, judges, newspaper editors, and small entrepreneurs.

But the 1960s opened the door of change. In 1960, a department of education was established as part of the Québec government, bringing in a new regime over schools and colleges until then operated by the Catholic Church.

The Quiet Revolution soon swept up far more than these cultural dimensions of life as it also spread into the economic realm. Neighbouring Ontario had created a public utility for hydroelectricity in 1906, and most other provinces had also done something similar, but Québec's electricity still flowed from private power companies. The skills needed for a modern workforce were not being imparted at the small classical colleges of Québec. The roads that served a tranquil province were no longer adequate for the burgeoning new Québec that was taking shape. Modernity took hold. Hydro Québec was created. New community colleges opened across the province to train young Quebecers in professions and trades. Fast modern *autoroutes* began linking the province's different regions. Exhilaration filled the air.

Quebecers' long twilight of docility and compliance was being replaced by the rising empowerment of being "masters in our own house." The grip of the Church slipped. As the pendulum swung toward a new era, women used birth control and families had but one, two, or three children. With a diminishing population and increased immigration from other countries, and the growing onslaught of English-language culture from English-speaking parts of Canada and even more from the United States, Quebecers' traditional struggle for "survival" was forced into new dimensions.

These included regaining control over the social and cultural powers the 1867 Constitution had given exclusively to provincial governments, but which, since the mid-1940s, the government in Ottawa had used its "spending power" to occupy, generally with the consent of Canada's other provinces. Québec's provincial politicians, expressing the new urgency of French-Canadian business leaders, professionals, educators, social scientists, and cultural leaders, presented a highly conservative view to Canada's national government: respect the constitution. To most English-speaking Canadians, the conservative stances of Liberal premier Jean Lesage, Union Nationale premier Daniel Johnson and his successor, Jean-Jacques Bertrand, and particularly that of Lesage's minister of energy, René Lévesque, who led the formation of Hydro-Québec then broke away to form a separatist political party, seemed "revolutionary." For those outside Québec, it appeared these leaders wanted to overthrow the existing order, rather than return it to what had been. There was no recognition that what was being demanded for Québec were powers that had been originally given to it — and the rest of the provinces — in the Constitution of 1867, but which Ottawa encroached on and occupied.

Québec's Quiet Revolution in the 1960s inexorably spread change beyond the province's geographic borders.

Where Québec nationalists were seeking to be modern, to make their province a contemporary and progressive state in step with other mid-twentieth-century jurisdictions, in what Premier Jean-Jacques Bertrand in 1969 called Québec's "logical last stage in a step-by-step definition of her identity," many elsewhere in Canada saw the province's leaders as disturbing radicals. Outside Québec, many citizens were perplexed. They had never received clear explanation or proper schooling about Canadian history; few had even learned to speak the language of a very large segment of Canadian society.

Increasingly, in a tone of perplexed exasperation, such Canadians asked, "What does Quebec want?"

The second link in the chain was the launch of an interminable series of gatherings initiated to answer that question.

The Canadian political system being what it is, a response to "Québec's demands" seemed necessary, though what followed was more a dialectic than dialogue. The governance tool box only contained two instruments for seeking a new synthesis — the royal commission, and the first ministers' conference. These devices had been reliable in the past for handling problematic issues, but were ill-suited to Quebecers' quest to recreate themselves within the framework of existing arrangements.

From Ottawa, the Liberal government of Prime Minister Lester Pearson would respond with a royal commission. From Toronto, the Progressive Conservative government of Premier John Robarts would proffer a constitutional conference.

The Royal Commission on Bilingualism and Biculturalism was launched in 1963 on the simple premise that issues arising from newly awakened Québec were, at their core, about language and culture. The Ontario "Confederation of Tomorrow" conference, convened in 1967, was inspired by the belief that, rather than a royal commission studying the discontents of Quebecers — the "Bi and Bi" Commission would still be mired in its labours four years later — it was more pragmatic to get the premier of Québec talking with his provincial counterparts who, after all, exercised the same provincial powers under the Constitution as Premier Daniel Johnson did and faced the same central government in Ottawa as he did too, just from different angles.

The royal commission, co-chaired by André Laurendeau and Davidson Dunton, made an initial report in 1965, stating that never before in history had Canada found itself on the brink of such a crisis. That dramatic hyperbole got serious attention at the highest levels in Ottawa and ensured plenty more resources for the long-running and costly commission. By the time it presented its final report, six years after starting the assignment, two significant changes would result. First, bilingualism became a policy of the Government of Canada, as the Official Languages Act put English and French on parity. Second, "multiculturalism," rather than "biculturalism," was established, seen as a better way to frame the nature and contributions of Canada's pluralistic society. The long-standing concept of "two founding peoples," a concept that ignored Aboriginal Canadians and all non-French and non-British citizens of our country, was deservedly killed off in the process.

The conference in Toronto, touted as "the first conference on national unity since the country's founding in 1867," was also sparked by the demands and complaints from Québec, but it, too, became a phenomenon dramatically different from its originating concept. Premier Robarts expected his summit meeting of premiers could look into the future, discern what a more ideal Confederation would look like in years to come, then use lateral thinking to work back from that ideal to the present reality and identify the steps required to get from here to there.

But the prime minister of Canada was not invited to help envisage tomorrow's Confederation. Some saw this as a partisan snub, others as a short-sighted error. It seemed wrong because the Government of Canada would need to be party to any changes in the Constitution. Excluding the PM reflected the heightened powers of provincial governments and the smugness this was engendering. Yet from the perspective of John Robarts and the talented senior civil servants helping him organize the conference, it was none of these things. They simply sought plain talk among pragmatic premiers who, despite the cultural and economic differences of their provinces, faced many issues in common. If they could sort out a clearer understanding of how the country was working, in relation to how the Constitution said it should operate, they'd have a cleaner set of proposals for any changes that, working later with the Government of Canada and Parliament, could pave the way toward a more harmonious and prosperous Canadian future. It could be, they mistakenly believed, a logical journey.

Although Ontario's "Confederation of Tomorrow" conference seemed a plausible "first step" in sorting out Québec's needs and provincial powers, leading to subsequent negotiations with Ottawa, it had unintended consequences. The first was that it kick-started an unending succession of conferences. You could not get everything sorted out in one sitting, so another meeting, then another, and even another, would be needed. Like an amoeba continuously subdividing through binary fission into multiple copies of itself, this replication of constitutional gatherings would stretch ahead for a quarter-century, creating what Brian Mulroney would call by 1983 Canada's peculiar self-analysis "cottage industry — highly paid and unproductive — in the field of constitutional reform."

Even by that date in the 1980s, another decade of such gatherings still lay ahead, with Mr. Mulroney chairing most of them.

A second unintended consequence of the Ontario premier's 1967 initiative was the launching of a new dimension of governance politics within our federal state — not between Ottawa and the provinces, but exclusively at the provincial level. Rather than being a one-off premiers' event, the Confederation of Tomorrow gathering became the precedent for ritual repeating conferences that have since continued as provincial premiers gather twice a year to decide, in the absence of the prime minister who wields the powers of the Government of Canada, how they think Ottawa should be running the country.

The third link in this chain of historic consequences was the traumatic national shock in 1976 of a separatist government being elected in Québec.

Pierre Trudeau had won the Liberal Party's leadership and then the 1968 general election, eight years earlier, by promising to "put Québec in its place." That concept turned on a clever bit of sophistry, since it allowed Quebecers to believe, as he sometimes said, "Québec's place is in Canada," while it also allowed voters across the rest of the country, either anti-French or just tired of Québec's demands, to infer the subtext that by "putting Québec in its place," he was going to swat down the separatists. Exhilarated at the time by "Trudeaumania," few had any way of grasping that the exciting new leader did not mean what he obviously intended them to think he meant. After all, had he not courageously stood firm, on the eve of the 1968 election, against the separatist demonstrators who'd thrown bottles at the reviewing stand where he sat during Montreal's Saint Jean Baptiste parade? He would stand strong for Canada.

But in 1976, a political party dedicated to Québec's separation from Canada occupied the seats of power in Canada's largest and most historic province. The country perched on a tipping point. This happened on guardian Pierre Trudeau's watch. The prime minister had already proclaimed by this date, "Separatism is dead!" Canadians were stunned.

Within three years, Quebecers were heading to the polls in a province-wide referendum initiated by the Parti Québcois government of Premier René Lévesque to answer a ballot question about separating from Canada. Just days before the May 20, 1980 vote, Prime Minister Trudeau addressed a boisterous assembly of federalist forces in Montreal's Paul Sauvé Arena, many dozens of Liberal MPs from across the province on stage with him. That night he gave "a most solemn commitment" that if Quebecers voted "*Non*" to the separatist option, he and his Québec Liberal MPs "will immediately take action to renew the Constitution, and we will not stop until we have done that." In the excitement, few had reason to believe the prime minister did not mean what he obviously intended them to think he meant. He conveyed the message that his Liberal government, in changing the Constitution, would accommodate the aspirations of Québec's people. Across Canada, citizens prayed his message was received by Québec voters and held their breath.

The federalist side won the referendum, so for now Québec would remain in Confederation. But the government of Mr. Trudeau was defeated in the next federal general election, bringing a minority Progressive Conservative government led by Joe Clark to office. Mr. Trudeau announced his retirement, and bleakly noted that reviews of his accomplishments as prime minister were generally unfavourable. Much had been promised, little accomplished.

The defeat of Joe Clark's government in the Commons, and the need for a Liberal leader in the ensuing general election, brought Pierre Trudeau out of retirement and then back to office as his party won again. He proclaimed "the universe is unfolding" as intended and promptly set about creating a better legacy than he'd seemingly left to posterity when leaving office just months earlier.

Two of his major initiatives were to deal with his abandoned pledge to Quebecers made in the Paul Sauvé Arena, and to move dramatically into the energy field with the National Energy Policy. The former would lead to patriation of the Constitution with a Charter of Rights and Freedoms and an amending formula so we could henceforth change the Constitution ourselves; the latter would lead to an intense negative response in Western Canada that turned prior alienation into virulent negativity about centralizing Ottawa and Eastern Canada interests.

Pent-up political anger in Western Canada roamed free, seeking ways to strike back. Defeating Liberal candidates who sought election to the House of Commons was one: no Liberals got elected. Turning the Senate of Canada into an effective legislative body that could restrain Ottawa from the centre was another: that became a major political project.

For constitutional renewal, Prime Minister Trudeau took another turn at the helm in chairing Canada's unending series of top-level conferences to change the Constitution. Entrenching a Charter of Rights and Freedoms was a goal he'd unveiled at Québec City, when minister of justice in the Pearson government addressing the annual meeting of the Canadian Bar Association. He envisaged a stronger and more comprehensive version of the Canadian Charter of Rights that had been pioneered by the strongest civil libertarian ever to occupy the prime minister's office, John Diefenbaker.

In addition to the Charter, as noted, there would be an "amending formula" so that in future the Canadian Constitution could be changed within our own country rather than by the parliament of another country. In the mid-1860s, since the future provinces of Canada were then still separate British North American colonies, the Constitution creating Confederation took the form of a statute passed by the Parliament of Great Britain. Ever since, the British North America Act, 1867, had been amended, whenever a change was needed — for instance, to let the Government of Canada create an unemployment insurance program,which was in provincial rather than federal jurisdiction — by the British Parliament. By the 1920s, Canadian political leaders wanted to change this, in keeping with our evolution into more independent nationhood, but could not agree on what sort of agreement would be required in this country — the "amending forumula" — before asking Parliament over in Britain to put through the change.

Almost everybody was embarrassed by the Canadian incapacity to resolve this dilemma of vestigial colonialism from the 1800s. In 1981, I spent a week in London as guest of Canada's high commissioner to the United Kingdom, Jean Casselman Wadds. Jean was working all diplomatic channels to ensure passage of the new constitutional package crafted under Prime Minister Trudeau's leadership. Over a dinner she hosted at the official residence, I listened as the minister for Commonwealth affairs told me he'd come down the stairs bright on New Year's Day morning, saying with a sigh of relief, "This is the year I can be rid of dealing with the internal affairs of ABC — Antigua, Belize, and Canada."

He wondered why, for more than a half century, Canadians had been unable to find an amending formula that would have allowed the British North America Act to become transformed into a document that could be changed in Canada by Canadians. The absence of such agreement had kept our charter document as a statute of Britain, needing the Parliament of the United Kingdom to change any of its 1860s provisions, even into the 1980s. In sheepish defence of Canada, I could only tell the minister that our political culture embraced study and discussion more than decision and action.

In addition to a Charter of Rights and Freedoms, which was a landmark change for Canada, Prime Minister Trudeau found that elusive amending formula. It emerged from his negotiations with the premiers once he offered two sweeteners. The first was a high threshold of agreement needed to make any future constitutional changes, so high that future amendments would be hard, if not impossible, to achieve. This satisfied several smaller and mid-sized provinces whose premiers feared their voices might no longer count. Senate "regional representation" wasn't real, as everybody knew.

The formula they agreed to in 1981 covers three categories of amendments to the Constitution. First, some changes need unanimous consent of all federal and provincial governments. These are changes to the offices of the monarchy and governor general, the composition of the Supreme Court of Canada, and the constitutional amending formula itself. "Unanimous" means consent by the House of Commons, the Senate, the governor general, and all provincial legislatures. A second category requires unanimous consent at the federal level but only majority consent at the provincial level. These include changes in the method of electing MPs, the powers of the Senate and the method of selecting senators, provincial representation in the Senate, extending existing provincial borders into the territories, and creation of new provinces. Approval of these requires consent nationally of the governor general, the House of Commons, and Senate, and provincially of at least two-thirds of the provinces representing more than 50 percent of the Canadian population. The third and final category of changes does not require approval from provinces but only consent of the governor general, the House of Commons, and the Senate. These would be changes to the executive government of Canada, Senate, and House of Commons — excluding, of course, amendments in the more significant categories of change covered by the other two amending formulas.

Had the package of constitutional amendments developed in 1981 by Prime Minister Trudeau and the premiers itself been subject to the threshold of support they required by their new amending formula, it would not have passed. The good in making it hard to amend the Constitution is that it broke the thirty-year addiction to trying to solve political problems through negotiated constitutional measures rather than in our democratic legislatures. Difficulty became a deterrent. The bad in it is that, as Prime Minister Mulroney would discover when trying to operate under this new dispensation, getting changes to the Constitution to deal with such matters as Québec's status in Confederation or Senate reform would, unless astutely handled in terms of ratification, elude our grasp.

The other sweetener added by Prime Minister Trudeau, to get support from the difficult premiers, was a clause in the Constitution allowing a province to remove itself from operation of the new regime — a strange provision for a constitution, providing for its provisions to be escaped. This section says that, "notwithstanding other provisions of the Charter," a legislature could enact a law that would operate for a limited time, until renewed, that avoided the requirements of the country's constitution. Known as "the notwithstanding clause," this provision would be invoked to a very limited degree, except in Québec's National Assembly where it became an automatic part of every bill enacted into law, a response to the new constitutional package negotiated by Mr. Trudeau having been imposed on Québec — despite the reality of its formal rejection by the people's representatives.

The reason Québec's legislature took this stance was the astounding fact that the revamped 1981 Canadian Constitution did not legitimately apply to Québec, the province for whom the whole exercise had been conducted in the first place. Prime Minister Trudeau, unable to get full agreement, imposed the constitutional deal despite both the Liberal Party of Québec and the Parti Québécois voting in the National Assembly against it. The measure was forced through the British Parliament in London, over strenuous objections from Québec's representatives as well as Canada's Aboriginal leaders. Québec was not a signatory to the agreement.

During the constitutional conferences that finally culminated in the 1981 changes to our Constitution, two subjects moved from the political periphery onto the core agenda, where they remain today — reform of the Senate and use of a referendum to ratify proposed constitutional changes.

The fourth link in this chain of events leading to where we now find ourselves was the channelling of Western Canadian political alienation into the cause of Senate reform.

By the 1980s, Western Canadians sought to reconcile their ramped-up grievances about the Canadian government working like a government for Central Canada with their dismay that so much effort to reform the Senate into a stronger voice of regions had failed to change a single thing.

Albertans assumed leadership of what, to most folks, seemed a truly lost cause: trying to make this hoary vestige of colonial Canada into a contemporary instrument of democratic governance. They discussed various proposals until everything crystallized into an idea of a Senate that was elected, more effective in its powers, and equal in representation from each province. The result was a new, wider, ever stronger push for overhauling the Senate. "The West Wants In!" summed up the message — a counterpoint to "Quebec Wants Out!" separatism — and a "triple-E" Senate was its vehicle.

Instead of only being a voice for regional interests — as attempted in the 1970s reform proposals for a House of the Federation — the Senate would now be completely redesigned by adding, as well as regional voice, provincial equality of seats and democratic legitimacy through election of the Senate's members by the people.

The first "E," standing for elected, was an easy sell. Canadians would elect senators. Members of the upper house would no longer be patronage appointees of the prime minister. To replace the fully appointed body with a legislature whose members were voted into office was an idea Central Canadians and citizens in Atlantic Canada generally had no difficulty accepting. Senators would also have a fixed number of years in office before having to retire or seek re-election, unlike the existing appointed senators who lingered in office until age seventy-five. This idea for elections and term limits harmonized with the fundamental Canadian value of democratic accountability between political institutions and citizens. Senators who had to be elected would keep in touch with citizens.

The equality "E" required that every province would have the same numeric representation in Parliament's upper house. This would make Canada's Senate like the American one, in which each state of the Union has two senators regardless of population or geographic size. Everyone could do the math for "equal." Changing the long-established regional representation in the Senate, unbalanced as it was for Alberta and British Columbia as provinces, if not as parts of a larger "Western District" region, showed just how bold, even brazen, proponents of the triple-E Senate were. Ontario, an economic juggernaut with twelve million people and a dynamic, pluralistic society, would be represented by the same number of law-makers as Prince Edward Island, with 280,000 people, a traditional society, and an economy rooted essentially in the fishery, agriculture, and tourism. Equality of provinces would not make the task of their senators equal.

It was one thing to conceptualize "equality" in the conference rooms of the Canada West Foundation, the rising wellspring of new zeal for Canada's old Senate, quite another to face real people and try to persuade them you weren't crazy. To have any hope of getting this equality of provinces idea accepted, the Albertans had to do two things. First, they postulated a concept never before heard in Canadian public affairs — "the sovereign equality of provinces" — as if it were part of natural law. Second, they linked the provincial equality idea with a couple of other ideas that were more palatable, so they could dress up the package and attempt to sell its name rather than its content. Those additional ideas, elections and effectiveness, produced the mantra-like tag "triple-E" that

Albertans could repeat over and over, until people absorbed its importance through osmosis without ever comprehending its true implications for Canadian politics.

That "effectiveness" component provided the third "E," and in broad terms this, too, like electing senators, was easier to sell. Everybody in Canada already knew the Senate was ineffectual. Canadians readily grasped the proposition that, if there was going to be a Senate at all, it should be effective in what it was supposed to do, given that we were paying for it to do something. Beyond such generalities, however, this "E" was the hardest to clarify. To be effective the way Albertans envisaged, it would be necessary for normally quiescent senators to do more than simply register a temporary veto over legislation or correct drafting slip-ups in bills from the Commons; instead, they would become activist legislators, taking an assertive role in the federal legislative process.

Doubters quickly grasped that the triple-E proposal for an *effective* reformed Senate was problematic. It required giving the Senate more powers and creating stronger interactions with the House of Commons, changing the balance of power, pitting the Senate against a body that was fully elected and already giving full voice to regional interests with MPs from every bay and bluff across the country. What power could be taken from the House and given to the Senate? Why would this be an improvement? This puzzle became a subject of many studies and conferences.

The third "E" threw an even greater and more destabilizing component into efforts to revamp the Senate. To have representation that was equal for each province would upset the *regional equality* already existing in Senate seats. It would create such disparities that huge increases would be needed in House of Commons representation to offset the imbalance. It seemed that making all provinces equal in the Senate would merely solve one problem by creating another.

And when thinking more deeply about the first "E," *elected* senators, skeptics realized this would give democratic legitimacy to an institution the country would actually be better off without. Why give a blood transfusion to a corpse?

Although the triple-E concept seemed a non-starter to many in Central Canada, that only made Albertans the keener for it. It was time, they felt, to pay back the East, whose own interests were being served at Albertans' expense by the Trudeau government's reviled National Energy Policy. Senate reform, on Alberta's terms, would start to redress the imbalance.

The Albertans' bullish approach to a triple-E Senate also stood in stark contrast to the Senate reform proposals of the 1970s, back when the tinkering envisaged with the "House of the Federation" or "Council of the Provinces" proposals seemed substantial. The triple-E Senate plan, as developed and launched by the Canada West Foundation in 1981, threw down the gauntlet for a national political battle.

In Alberta, Premier Peter Lougheed's Progressive Conservative government moved triple-E into the political arena by naming a select special committee of the legislature to study "Upper House Reform." When the committee reported in 1985, recommending implementation of a triple-E Senate, it spelled out an even more detailed plan, expanding and embellishing the Canada West Foundation's version.

On "Elected," for example, the committee of MLAs recommended senators be directly chosen by the people through a system of plurality voting in multiple-member, province-wide constituencies. Each province would have a specific number of Senate seats and voters would select representatives from a list of candidates, having as many votes as there were seats to be filled. Candidates getting the most votes would win, so if six Senate seats were to be filled, the top six would each get a seat. A senator's term in office would coincide with provincial elections, resulting in a variable terms in office since senatorial elections would be held with each province's general elections, which occurred at random times.

As for "Equal," the Alberta select committee advocated numeric equality between provinces in the rejigged Senate, each province getting six seats, and the territories two apiece. In terms of being "Effective," the committee of Alberta legislators suggested that, when dealing with ordinary legislation, constitutional amendments, spending bills, or taxation bills, senators would have a "suspensive" veto of ninety days duration for money bills and 120 days for other types of legislation. The House of Commons could override the Senate's delay of a piece of legislation, once the ninety or 120 days had lapsed — in effect giving the Commons time for its own "sober second thought." The Senate would also ratify non-military international treaties. The government of the day would not require support of a majority of senators, the way it had to enjoy the confidence of MPs, as expressed by their votes, to hold power. The triple-E Senate could not initiate taxes or spending measures.

The select committee's recommendations were then embraced by the Government of Alberta as its official position. The cause was taken up in earnest by Premier Don Getty, who'd replaced Mr. Lougheed in leading the province's Progressive Conservative government. (In 2003, after Premier Ralph Klein had in turn replaced Mr. Getty, the Alberta Progressive Conservatives would again endorse the plan for a triple-E Senate.)

The Alberta legislature, under Mr. Getty's leadership, even gave the "Elected" element of triple-E a further boost by enacting a statute under which provincial voters elected a senator whom the premier would then recommend to the prime minister for appointment to the Senate. Even within the existing Constitution, before getting triple-E changes made, the Albertans were pushing as hard and as cleverly as they could to change the nature of the Senate's membership.

Despite fundamental problems with the triple-E Senate, the articulate advocacy for it gradually gave credence to the concept in a widening circle of opinion. Especially for those who did not examine its implications deeply, triple-E seemed like a coherent plan to deal with an unreconstructed and unloved political institution. It would now be championed whenever federal-provincial conferences were held to decide what next to do about the Constitution. The political animus driving Western Canadians and democratic-minded Canadians across the country was increasingly channelled onto the strangest of all places, the long-lost cause of Senate reform. Rather than just advocating scrapping it, as all the provinces with an upper house had done, the triple-E concept for resurrecting the Senate emerged as the constitutionalists' new Holy Grail.

While all this was unfolding, the fifth link in these historic turning points emerged in the form of the Senate itself.

Here a more visceral challenge was stirring Brian Mulroney to stronger personal resolve for Senate reform. The deliberate and assertive role of Liberal senators during the 1980s, using their large majority in the upper house, was seen by the prime minister as a partisan campaign to block and break his Progressive Conservative government.

In a notable escalation above prior levels of Senate filibusters and blockades of legislation already approved by the elected House of Commons, the Liberals in the appointed upper house obstructed the work of Mr. Mulroney's popularly elected majority. One did not have to be a blind loyalist of the Progressive Conservatives to feel the PM's surging impulse to change the Senate. The record itself spoke with eloquent objectivity.

In late 1984, when he became prime minister with the largest majority of seats in the House of Commons in Canadian history, seventy-three Liberal senators faced down twenty-three Conservative and four Independent senators in the upper house. Breaking from prior practice, the Senate began to deliberately choose, each year, a major bill enacted by the Commons with which to create a parliamentary roadblock. The Liberal senators could wear down the government under the guise of providing "sober second thought."

In 1985, the Senate started off with Bill C-11, the Borrowing Authority Bill, by which the Government of Canada would get the money it needed to operate the public programs of the country. Without authority to borrow, the government would be in a crisis and have to close down operations, or run for a while on spending authorized by governor general's warrants. The general idea was to see the government hit the spending wall, as had just begun happening in the United States. It seemed absurd, but it was the intent of the Liberal senators' actions in the opening parliamentary session of Prime Minister Mulroney's newly mandated government.

In 1986, the Liberal senators threw up their barrier against Bill C-67, which included modernizing amendments to the Penitentiary Act addressing such practices as "gating," thereby challenging the Progressive Conservatives' mandate to deal with the criminal justice system. In 1987, upping the ante, the Liberal senators picked out two Mulroney government bills that had passed in the Commons: Bill C-22, dealing with patent drugs, and Bill C-84, dealing with unemployment insurance reforms. In 1988, now on a roll, the Liberal majority in the Senate blocked three — Bill C-60, dealing with the long-overdue changes to Canadian copyright law that had been essentially unchanged since the

1920s; Bill C-103, creating the Atlantic Canada Opportunities Agency to make federal subsidies more effective for economic development of the country's four eastern provinces; and, Bill C-130, which had likewise already passed the Commons, ratifying Canada's new trade treaty with the United States.

In 1989, with another general election victory giving the re-elected Progressive Conservatives under Prime Minister Mulroney a renewed majority in the Commons, the Liberals in the Senate remained programmed to formally oppose and amend bills from the lower house. That year, when the government's bill to again deal with the Unemployment Insurance Act based on a fresh mandate from the people reached the Senate as Bill C-21, it was picked out for special focus and formal opposition.

The following year, 1990, the senators opposed both Bill C-28, dealing with Income Tax Act amendments to recoup a modest percentage of entitlement money from middle and upper income taxpayers, and Bill C-62 to implement the goods and services tax. The next year, senators defeated the Abortion Bill on third reading, after an unprecedented effort in the House of Commons to find a balanced compromise on this divisive issue. By now the Senate seemed an especially perverse place to the beleaguered prime minister, since Liberals voting against the abortion bill were joined by several PC senators he had himself appointed.

It would be hard for any prime minister, subjected to that sustained and willful parliamentary blocking by appointed and unaccountable senators, to remain indifferent to the upper house. In addition to the higher purposes of statesmanship, Brian Mulroney, the battle-hardened politician, had justifiable cause to overhaul the Senate of Canada.

The last of the six links in this chain was the necessity of a referendum to ratify constitutional change.

In addition to being a "representative" democracy where our elected representatives deal with issues and enact laws on our behalf, Canadian law and political values also provide for "direct" democracy so that we citizens ourselves can vote on issues that are highly divisive or of transcending importance. We've had an on-again, off-again history of direct democracy. As proposals for constitutional change began to dominate public affairs, the referendum device once more took its rightful place among the working mechanisms of our democratic society.

In Québec, separatist governments began to ask citizens ballot questions on whether the province should separate from Confederation — about the most profound constitutional change possible. Whatever the vague wording on the ballot paper, when the separatists fogged the hard issue by wrapping it in obtuse wording about "sovereignty-association" and about "negotiating" such a relationship with Canada, voters knew that *"Non"* and *"Oui"* were choices between staying in Confederation or leaving.

With Quebecers having referendums on such a fundamental matter, the role of direct democracy understandably resurfaced in the rest of the country, too. Prime Minister Trudeau contemplated the use of a ballot question, and to prepare for the possibility, enabling legislation for Canada-wide referendums was introduced in Parliament by Marc Lalonde, his minister of intergovernmental affairs. After Prime Minister Mulroney came to office in the mid-1980s, the premiers of Newfoundland and British Columbia stated, and the premier of Manitoba mused, that they might ask citizens in their provinces to vote in a referendum prior to having a resolution on the Constitution decided in their legislatures.

By the early 1990s, three provinces — British Columbia, Alberta, and Québec — each had referendum laws that required submitting constitutional changes to their electorates for ratification. I had, repeatedly at each new session of Parliament, introduced the Canada Referendum and Plebiscite Act in the Commons, as a private member's bill, to create a national statutory framework for the same purpose. Just as the Canada Elections Act establishes the rules for elections, we likewise needed a permanent act to conduct voting on a ballot question. The Trudeau government's bill, sponsored by Mr. Lalonde, had never made it into the statute books. My point was that constitutions belong to the people, not governments, and that Canada's sovereign people needed to ratify any fundamental change in the constitutional framework within which we are governed. By 1991, this idea, fundamental to the legitimacy of governing structures, had been embraced by Prime Minister Mulroney, though not by his cabinet ministers Senator Lowell Murray or Constitutional Affairs Minister Joe Clark, who also were both involved in negotiating constitutional amendments and attempting to get them ratified with the unanimity required by the new amending formula.

Each of these events in Canadian affairs was linked and, like the chain they formed, pulled the issue of Senate reform onto the agenda where it dominated negotiations until it nearly broke the country apart.

CHAPTER 16

Backward Turned Backward

Prime Minister Trudeau brought change to Canada with a Charter of Rights and Freedoms and a method for making future constitutional changes here rather than in Britain. But Québec had not agreed to the arrangements, a perverse outcome since the task had specifically been undertaken to adjust Québec's position within Canada and implement the prime minister's pledge given in the Paul Sauvé Arena.

Both Québec's federalist Liberals and its separatist Parti Québécois had voted in the National Assembly against ratifying the 1981 constitutional package. The reality was that the constitutional deal, with Québec excluded, had been imposed.

Rather than leave Quebecers "abandoned on the snowbank," as Prime Minister Mulroney put it, he wanted them "willingly restored to the Canadian family." This statesmanlike impulse produced, in return, a concise proposal from Québec's reinstated federalist Liberal premier, Robert Bourassa. Without altering the substance of the 1981 amendments, he had five points that required clarification for the Government of Québec to "sign on."

Brian Mulroney's deep desire, as a Quebecer immersed in his province's politics and now his country's prime minister, was to have Québec reintegrated into the Constitution as amended during the Trudeau years. Although he'd earlier criticized Canada's "cottage industry" of endlessly negotiating over the Constitution, in 1987 he now called all provincial leaders to the cottage himself to deal with this unfinished national business.

The English-speaking premiers arrived with baskets of their own and began to put extra potluck items on the table, thinking they could be mixed in with Mr. Bourassa's neatly prepared meal. Their years of earlier constitutional work, supplemented by proposals from their legion of intergovernmental experts, generated many leftovers that never made it into Mr. Trudeau's final banquet, so here was a chance to try serving them again.

Several premiers from Western Canada saw an opening for long-desired Senate reform. In exchange for agreeing to Robert Bourassa's points, they would bargain for some of their own constitutional goals. The PM, however, did not want another full round of renegotiating the Constitution. He did not want this historic moment of willingness by Québec's federalist leader dissipated, or the uniqueness of this specific act of national reconciliation diluted.

To address reform of the Senate could only draw the government leaders into interminable discussion. This perpetual issue had reared up in 1864 to consume fully half the conference time at Québec City that the "Fathers of Confederation" had available to discuss plans for a new country and its constitution. In the 1970s, when more negotiations took place under Prime Minister Trudeau, debate over Senate reform had again consumed everyone's available time, resources, and patience, but with nothing new to show for it.

Brian Mulroney wanted Québec to sign the Constitution, as amended by that recent Trudeau round in 1981. He did not want Robert Bourassa humiliated, either around this meeting table or back home in Québec. The premier's failure to get five clarifications would inflame support for separatism. Many Québec federalists would finally give up, and even fan those flames higher themselves.

The prime minister explained to the national PC caucus how he would reopen the issue of constitutional reform in order to reintegrate Québec into "the Canadian constitutional family." Québec had officially rejected the constitutional changes engineered by Prime Minister Trudeau and the other premiers in the early 1980s, because its separatist premier, René Lévesque, had felt betrayed by the late-night compromises negotiated in Ottawa behind his back. He broke off discussions and, with his intergovernmental affairs minister, Claude Morin, returned home to Québec.

What now gave Mr. Mulroney hope, he said, was that Québec was governed by the federalist Liberals led by Premier Bourassa. The two men co-operated well. The PM was also bolstered by a strong contingent of Progressive Conservative MPs from Québec, part of his government which had the largest majority in Canadian history. If not now, when?

At first, neither Premier Bourassa nor any other Quebecer saw Senate reform anywhere on their radar. But Western Canadians did, especially Alberta's premier Don Getty. So too did the strong contingent of Alberta ministers in the federal cabinet and Alberta Tory MPs in the caucus. To get concessions for what Québec needed, something would have to be granted to Western Canada as well.

So that was the plan. The process would take two stages. Canada's negotiator-in-chief wanted to first get agreement of all concerned on Robert Bourassa's five points. Then, after that agreement had been ratified by Parliament and every province, as now required by the new formula for amending the Constitution, and once Québec had ceremonially signed the Constitution, the PM would call everyone together again to settle Senate reform and the other basket of items the various premiers had brought with them.

Negotiations for the Meech Lake Accord got underway in closed-door talks between Canada's first ministers.

Discussion focused, as announced, primarily on Québec's place in Canada. But proposals about the Senate began to encroach. To address this interest and get it off the table, the first ministers unanimously agreed to the idea that nobody could be appointed to the Senate unless he or she was acceptable to both levels of government. The Meech Lake Accord would maintain the prime minister's power to appoint senators, but it would secure more provincial involvement by requiring the PM to choose new members for the upper house from lists of nominees submitted by the provincial and territorial governments.

This limited stab at Senate reform reflected, from the PM's perspective, the enduring concern, earlier articulated by Prime Minister Trudeau, about not giving provinces and territories any greater voice in the upper house. Certainly Robert Bourassa did not want more, so that settled it as far as Mr. Mulroney was concerned.

Even so, to underscore the sense of victory several premiers felt upon winning this gain, and needing something specific to show people back home that represented progress on the Senate front, it was agreed that the proposed Constitution Amendment Act, 1987, to implement the Meech Lake Accord, would include a specific commitment that this new Senate nomination procedure would take effect "forthwith upon signature of the Accord and prior to the proclamation of the amendments." The provisional procedure would apply "until there are constitutional amendments regarding the Senate generally or until the Accord fails to be ratified."

Prime Minister Mulroney duly followed this protocol in appointing six new senators to fill vacancies between 1987 and 1990.

In 1990, the three-year limit for ratifying the Meech Lake Accord was about to expire without full ratification.

It would not gain approval from Manitoba's legislature, due to the single holdout by a member of the provincial assembly, Elijah Harper, a New Democrat MLA who was later elected to the Commons as a Liberal. Mr. Harper cited the lack of adequate participation and recognition of Aboriginal people in the Meech Lake process as his reason for withholding unanimous consent. Later, however, when the Charlottetown Accord included significant advances for First Nations as a result of considerable Aboriginal participation in those negotiations, Mr. Harper opposed it, too.

Yet Mr. Harper would not have been in a position to deny the unanimous consent the legislature needed to bring back the Meech Lake resolution to a vote, if the new PC premier, Gary Filmon, hadn't earlier sabotaged it by shunting the Accord onto a siding.

Howard Pawley's New Democrats had been in power when the Meech Lake Accord was negotiated and signed. Then Mr. Filmon and the Progressive Conservatives were elected with a minority government during the thirty-six-month ratification period. He was not interested in endorsing this important act of the previous government. On election night in Winnipeg, jubilant despite her own party's lack of success, Liberal leader Sharon Carstairs, who would later find her efforts as a spoiler rewarded with a seat in the Senate, declared, well ahead of the deadline for ratification, "Meech Lake is dead!"

With Liberal support, Premier Filmon withdrew the Accord from the legislature. The PC leader's knowledge of what had created the Accord was as shallow as his understanding of Québec history and the transformative pressures caused by the Quiet Revolution. He resolutely set about proving how dangerous it could be having such a man at the levers of power.

A similar thing happened in New Brunswick. Premier Richard Hatfield, who'd participated in the Meech Lake negotiations, deeply understood the larger imperatives. He was an Anglo who'd celebrated the Acadian presence in his province by making New Brunswick officially bilingual. But New Brunswick's legislature had not yet voted on Meech Lake, despite his own belief in it. There was lots of time, so what was the rush? Smoke more pot. In the summer of 1987, the prime minister, beginning to feel concern, urged a very relaxed Richard Hatfield to get on with ratification.

Instead, a provincial election brought Liberal leader Frank McKenna, who'd campaigned against the Meech Lake Accord, into office, claiming every last seat in the legislature. Premier McKenna postponed a vote in the legislature for a couple of years, giving time for the motivating spirit behind the Accord to grow stale and Quebecers to see the hollowness of the invitation "to return to the Canadian constitutional family."

The New Brunswick premier fielded calls from national media at his kitchen table, his early bullishness about not accommodating Québec now seeming just dull, oxen stubbornness. The New Brunswick legislature still withheld its vote to ratify the Meech Lake Accord. Robert Bourassa filled with enduring dismay. He would even remind Brian Mulroney a decade later, in their last conversation in 1996 before the Québec premier died, how Frank McKenna "started the obstructionism that allowed the time to flow that eventually brought Clyde Wells to power."

The parochialism evinced by Manitoba's political leaders, including Mr. Pawley's successor as NDP leader, Gary Doer, and especially anti-Meech Liberal leader Sharon Carstairs, when added to the dissipating role of Frank McKenna, New Brunswick's obstinate premier, gave time for Newfoundland's new premier Clyde Wells, as Mr. Bourassa had alluded, to "beam" himself into a visionary saviour of Confederation.

The lawyer from Buchans Junction had no more grasp of Québec's position in Canada and far less appreciation of the surging forces unleashed by the Quiet Revolution than the newly elected Mr. Filmon in Manitoba. But unlike both Manitoba and New Brunswick, Newfoundland and Labrador's MLAs had already ratified the Meech Lake Accord in 1988. When Mr. Wells came to power the following year, he became an outspoken critic of the Meech Lake Accord, encouraged by his constitutional advisor, Deborah Coyne, channelling the antagonism of Pierre Trudeau to the Accord. Premier Wells insisted on putting the Meech Lake resolution to an unprecedented second vote in his legislature, since the earlier ratification was now rescinded. Or, perhaps he might put the Accord to a provincial referendum, he sometimes mentioned. But he did neither.

Parliament had to approve the Accord, too. In the Commons, it passed it with all-party support. By April 1988, the Senate returned the Accord with a series of sweeping amendments made by the Liberal majority, many appointed to the upper house by Mr. Trudeau, to gut the Meech Lake Accord. "Sober second thought" had taken the form of killer amendments by senators who'd been players in the 1981 constitutional negotiations, the principal defect of which — Québec's exclusion — the Meech Lake Accord now sought to remedy.

It was hard to know which of premiers Filmon, McKenna, or Wells exasperated the others most.

"What the hell is the prize when we end up with a broken country?" demanded Saskatchewan premier Grant Devine, with raw emotion in his voice.

He was speaking at a dinner meeting the prime minister had convened in the nation's capital, at the Museum of Civilization in Hull, on June 3, 1990, "for one last try at saving Meech Lake." It would be, said Mr. Mulroney when later looking back at his entire time as prime minister, "the most challenging week of my public life."

Premier Devine was dismayed to see the Accord being killed off. One reason Clyde Wells gave for refusing to ratify it in Newfoundland was an esoteric consideration about a Senate clause that raised a question in his mind.

"Who gives a shit about the Senate then? Why should you wreck a country for something like that?" insisted the highly agitated Saskatchewan premier of his Atlantic counterpart. "The future of our economy is linked to Western diversification. I'm a Ph.D. in economics. I'm a farmer. I'm a politician. But all our efforts are not worth a damn if some Reform guy on horseback or in a Jeep takes control. And for what, the Senate?

"They have an equal Senate in the United States," continued the Prairie premier, "but it's not the prize some Canadians make it out to be. Has the triple-E Senate made North Dakota relatively more prosperous than Saskatchewan? No."

Other premiers waded in, trying to persuade the first ministers of Manitoba, New Brunswick, and Newfoundland. "We have to look at the realm of the possible rather than seek perfection," said one of the calmest voices that long summer night. Alberta's premier, Don Getty, himself ardent for Senate change, laid things out in plain terms for the trio: "Without Meech Lake, globally we look like jerks. Our economy will be in trouble. There will be no Senate reform. With Meech Lake, we save the country, we reinforce economic stability and prosperity, and we'll reform the Senate."

Prince Edward Island's premier, Joe Ghiz, explained that he knew back in 1987, when signing the Meech Lake Accord, that he "wasn't articulating the popular mood in Prince Edward Island or Atlantic Canada." But Meech Lake "was right for the future of our country." He and the others had made Senate reform "subject to the unanimity formula at Meech Lake because other provinces would not accept a veto for Québec alone."

The Island's Liberal premier told his fellow Eastern Canadian Liberal premier, "We are looking principally to you, Clyde Wells, for compromise. The prospect of failure makes me weep. I will feel that I have let my small province down, and my country, if I pay heed to polls in English Canada saying that we should let Québec go."

No amount of logic or true patriot love seemed to move the freshman premiers.

Gary Filmon contended that the Accord "is a body blow to aspirations for Senate reform," as well as women's rights and Aboriginal constitutional reform, and held out for "a companion resolution with some certainty of passage."

Clyde Wells delivered a generally condemnatory analysis of broad national conditions, and culminated by stating, "There is no balance in the exercise of national legislative power in this country. This is normally the role of the Senate. We must balance the principle of the majority of the population with the principle of the majority of the constituent parts of the federation. Senate reform will allow smaller provinces to fully participate in national legislative powers. This is the *magic* of a federal system exemplified by a triple-E Senate! I support the concept of Québec as a distinct society but cannot allow it to impair fundamental principles of a federal system."

Another Liberal premier, David Peterson, who spoke for Canada's most populous province, looked at the other men around the table, then focused on the three who seemed frozen by inability to recognize the historic turning point in this present moment and how it was quickly vanishing. "I believe that we are facing the possible breakup of this country. If Meech Lake goes down, this country will be transfixed on constitutional issues for the indefinite future. Aboriginal reform is put off. Senate reform becomes impossible. Without Meech Lake, we'll be considering how to negotiate, instead, the breakup of the country."

For four more pummelling days, Prime Minister Mulroney and the ten premiers pushed themselves to the outer edge of exhaustion negotiating in the same windowless room of Ottawa's central railway station, since converted to the Government Conference Centre, where earlier Prime Minister Trudeau and nine premiers had concluded the constitutional deal that excluded Québec, trying desperately to complete their unfinished task.

Brian Mulroney would later describe how their exhausting debate blurred through alternating turns of "eloquence, idealism, raised voices, anger, and despair." Matching the dramatics of this scene behind closed doors was the mounting public spectacle surrounding the Conference Centre. Events were being televised to watchful Canadians in heightening suspense, "the crowds of media seeming to grow with every passing hour as the entire nation speculated on what was happening in these sessions," noted the PM.

The cloistered first ministers inched toward Senate reform, reaching agreement on several ideas that pointed to future possibilities. Ontario Premier Peterson broke a stalemate at one point by agreeing to give up some of Ontario's Senate seats to help redress the representation deficit in Western Canada and Newfoundland. They agreed to set up a national commission to examine the triple-E Senate.

* * *

In the final hours of the three-year span, New Brunswick voted approval. In years to come, Frank McKenna's eyes would tear up in private expressing deep regret over his role in killing Meech. "What a mess I made. I thought I was doing the right thing, but it turned out I made a great mistake by acting the way I did."

Newfoundland's legislature did not proceed with its vote on the Accord, despite Premier Wells's commitment to the other first ministers that it would. He cancelled it on the last remaining day upon learning three of his Liberal MLAs intended to vote approval.

Manitoba's Elijah Harper held up his eagle feather, said "No," and took satisfaction in all the credit heaped upon him for killing the Meech Lake Accord.

The Meech Lake Accord had been approved by Parliament, and by the legislative assemblies of British Columbia, Alberta, Saskatchewan, Ontario, Québec, New Brunswick, Nova Scotia, and Prince Edward Island.

After such intensity of effort and so torturous a time, Meech Lake slipped out of reach by the narrowest margin of loss possible.

At the end of it all, Québec was still on the snowbank, excluded.

Failure by the Mulroney government to submit the Meech Lake Accord to a national referendum soon after it had been unanimously agreed to by all first ministers representing four different political parties was a fatal strategic failure to engage the legitimizing role of Canadian citizens consenting to changes in the Constitution under which we live.

Opinion polls showed the Accord to be popular with a majority of Canadians when it was unveiled in 1987, reflecting relief that Québec could return to Canada's constitutional fold and an expectation that this would cool down separatist antipathy toward the rest of Canada.

Rather than letting the people participate in the final act of the drama to which we had so long been an attentive audience, however, Canadian citizens caring deeply about our country had been left, for three agonizing years, as snubbed onlookers. We observed helplessly the slow demise of a worthy plan for a more unified Canada and, within it, measures for Senate reform.

With a referendum, Parliament and the legislatures would still have had to ratify the Accord, of course. But all elected representatives would have no doubt been guided by the direct verdict of the people who elected them, and the process would have been greatly accelerated, easily completed within a single year.

Over the ensuing three years, however, during the slow pace of Accord ratification in provincial legislatures, critics began to savage the agreement, encouraged by Pierre Trudeau. He came out of retirement to lead a splenetic attack on the Accord, accusing Brian Mulroney of having "sold out" to the provinces. The former prime minister's attacks on the Meech Lake Accord seemed inexplicable given that he'd have been able to make a similar agreement if he'd not been dealing with a separatist Québec government in 1981. During the same three year waiting game, Reform Party leader Preston Manning joined Mr. Trudeau's anti-Meech campaign, sticking his own needles in wherever he could.

Besides that strategic error on timing and not holding a referendum, Prime Minister Mulroney also made a tactical mistake to entrust responsibility for ensuring that provincial legislatures would pass resolutions approving the Accord over the drawn out period of thirty-six months into the hands of Senator Lowell Murray. The New Brunswicker had never held elected office and his political instincts were far more perfunctory than believed by his small network of inner-sanctum Tory confidants.

The process, ostensibly being shepherded to successful conclusion by Senator Murray, left the Mulroney government watching as its cherished prize — an agreement by which Québec would come back into "the family" — vanished into darkness.

"For me," said the prime minister, "the end of Meech was like a death in the family. I carry with me to this day a throbbing sense of loss for one of the greatest might-have-beens in Canada's 140-year history."

As it was becoming apparent the Meech Lake Accord would be defeated, taking down with it the plan for provincial co-operation with the prime minister in naming senators, Alberta's premier Don Getty introduced the Senatorial Selection Act.

This innovative electoral framework provided a process by which Albertans could vote for senators-in-waiting, the winners standing by to be appointed by the prime minister whenever a vacancy arose in an Alberta Senate seat. In the first election, Premier Getty's favoured candidate, Progressive Conservative Bert Brown, was defeated by Stan Waters of the fledgling Reform Party, which had opposed Meech Lake and called for more dramatic Senate reform.

Knowing he'd still need the support of all provinces to proceed with anything going forward, the PM maintained co-operative relations with his provincial allies. To please Mr. Getty, who'd urged him to name Mr. Waters to Parliament's upper house, the PM forced a smile and in 1990 announced Canada's first "elected" senator.

As a Progressive Conservative premier, holding most of the seats in the legislative assembly, Don Getty stood astride Alberta politics, since, more than any other Canadian jurisdiction, Alberta is a one-party province. He and Albertans all wanted Senate reform. Using his well-developed skills as a former quarterback with the Edmonton Eskimos, the Alberta premier threw a long perfect pass downfield to his best receiver, Brian Mulroney, who reluctantly caught the spiralling triple-E, but, for the sake of national unity, would gamely try to make some yardage with it.

After all, when negotiating Meech, he'd already agreed with the premiers on a commission to study the concept.

After the demise of the Meech Lake Accord, a deeply stung Premier Robert Bourassa created a Commission on the Political and Constitutional Future of Québec. Widely known as the Bélanger-Campeau Commission, it was to examine the political and constitutional status of Québec and make recommendations for changes.

On March 27, 1991, Bélanger-Campeau threw down the gauntlet.

The commission issued an unequivocal call for a Québec referendum on sovereignty, to be held in October 1992 at the latest — a year and a half away, unless before then the province had received acceptable terms from the rest of Canada to end the constitutional impasse.

As for Brian Mulroney, the grinding ache of loss over the Accord might have meant abandoning his effort to bring about Québec's ratification of the Constitution as changed in 1981, but it didn't. The heartbreaking setback doubled his resolve. More than that, Bélanger-Campeau's challenge set a deadline. Everything shifted to a new level of intensity.

Because essential change had come so close, a number of leaders, including the prime minister, reasoned that perhaps a more inclusive deal — incorporating everything from transferring certain federal powers to provincial governments to enhancing Aboriginal self-government, including recognition of Québec as a distinct society within Canada, far deeper reform of the Senate, better clarification of overlapping federal-provincial jurisdictions, more provisions respecting the status of women and the position of minorities, an inspirational clause to interpret what being Canadian means, and other substantive areas requiring changes to the Constitution — could be negotiated and adopted. The intense negotiations that had produced the Meech Lake Accord would now be re-channelled into fashioning what would eventually become known as "the Charlottetown Accord."

Western Canadians had responded to the failure in the 1970s to get a stronger voice in a rejigged Senate called the House of Regions by roaring back with an even bolder plan for a triple-E Senate. In a parallel way, now after the Meech Lake Accord's torturing defeat, Canadians from across the country would return with a greatly enlarged project for breathtaking national renewal.

As Meech died, the prime minister saw it was not the content of the agreement but the process to approve it that had been the killer.

From the time Canada's eleven first ministers signed it in unanimous agreement, three years elapsed. In politics, a week can be a lifetime. Certainly 156 weeks gave ample time for new premiers to want to change the Accord by adding new items, and for mischief-makers, bigots, resentful partisans, and worried citizens to pick away support and undermine a well-honed national compromise. Mr. Mulroney wrote in his *Memoirs*, "The process proved to be its undoing."

Now, heading into a second round, it seemed that searing experience had imparted a crucial lesson. As early as April 27, 1991, Mr. Mulroney was referring in his personal journal to a national referendum as part of the process this time.

> I hope that by October-November 1992 we will have: 1) Prepared a constitutional position that is generally okay for Québec and the other provinces, thereby obviating the need for the Québec referendum on sovereignty; and/or 2) Agreed with the other premiers on the general thrust of a constitutional package of sufficient attractiveness and clarity to also achieve the above result; 3) Agreed with other parliamentarians in the House on the principles and thrust of a new deal to be negotiated with the provinces if the province's consent/approval is granted to the govt. by way of a national referendum.

The prime minister's blueprint for the coming months had a national ballot question as a key feature embedded in its overall design. The Canadian people would not be left as bystanders this time, but would be made participants in remaking the country in which we live, whose costs we bear, under whose constitutional framework we operate, and in which we have direct interest as citizens.

How different Canada would be today, if only this had occurred to Mr. Mulroney the first time around.

To take charge of preparing "a constitutional position that is generally okay for Québec and the other provinces," the PM shuffled his cabinet, moving Joe Clark from External Affairs "to take over the new Constitutional Affairs department" and handing him a vast mandate.

The fact Mr. Clark had been mostly absent from the country for six and a half years working on behalf of Canada around the globe recommended itself to Mr. Mulroney, who interpreted this fact to mean Joe Clark would offer a fresh face for a new process, unbesmirched by association with Meech, the GST, the Free Trade Agreement, armed forces base closings, UIC reforms, and other contentious accomplishments of his government. To boot, he was a former prime minister, a Western Canadian, and bilingual.

A different view of the same facts was that Joe Clark was less familiar than anyone else in his cabinet about the current reality on the ground in Canada, and that he was mostly remembered by Canadians as the man whose misjudgment caused early defeat of his own minority Progressive Conservative government and brought Pierre Trudeau back as prime minister.

Perhaps it was nemesis that he should, in consequence, be handed what Brian Mulroney called "Canada's most sensitive file."

The prime minister and Joe Clark revived the national bargaining process once more, launching broad consultations between government leaders, interest groups, and the general public.

Getting participation in talks about the Constitution at this stage was as easy as getting Canadians to flock together in mid-winter for a pick-up game of street hockey. There were public hearings, new committee reports, and recast recommendations from the Charest Committee, the Beaudoin-Dobbie Committee, the Bélanger-Campeau Committee, and others. There were deadlines because, without them, Canadians would talk the St. Lawrence all the way to the sea.

Negotiations were interspersed with adjournment intervals when committees studied the ever-expanding list of constitutional proposals to reconfirm Québec's place in Canada, usher in a new day for First Nations' self-governance, transfer and clarify powers between national and provincial governments, craft ennobling words about being Canadian for a "Canada clause," and replace Parliament's relic upper house with a vital new Senate whose elected members would exercise enhanced powers.

Because this political journey from Meech to a further shore would be a daring if desperate mission to refashion Canada, all eyes again became fixed on those negotiating the fundamental reordering of our Constitution.

Back in 1983, leadership aspirant Brian Mulroney asserted that constitutional debate "would be entirely open to the public at all times. *There would be no sessions behind closed doors."* That was his own emphasis, in his book *Where I Stand.* But as prime minister he'd discovered that negotiating the Meech Lake constitutional agreement fell subject to the same constraints he'd known earlier hammering out labour agreements and, indeed, many greater pressures as well. He and the premiers cloistered themselves, just as they had for Meech.

Of course there were public hearings, a steady flow of reports, political analysis widely broadcast on television and radio, commentary in the press, and countless community meetings and campus colloquiums. This collectively gave a broad sense of the journey progressing. But because the negotiations themselves were behind closed doors, few really knew how grave the situation had become.

As the stakes increased, media stakeouts grew larger. Canadians in all parts of the land watched, waited, and wondered. An intermittent communiqué would be issued, a press conference held, a scrum conducted — each crumb of new information refuelling reporters and public commentators for the next hours of telecasting live from just outside the conference centre. Most every Canadian was expectant for the new constitutional deal apparently being born, while Québec's separatists were as nervously keen for it to miscarry.

In the perilous course of negotiating these changes over two years, the journey that started out to bring Québec back into the Constitution would almost break Canada and the Mulroney government apart — over, of all things, the Senate.

In Québec, the mood after Meech remained sour. The Allaire Commission made recommendations that, in Ottawa, seemed preposterous. Separatists led by Lucien Bouchard, whose own betrayal of his close friend Brian Mulroney and federalism alike, torqued the emotions of conflict in Parliament. In Québec's National Assembly, and across the province, the separatist Parti Québécois felt rising support. Public hearings in the extensive consultations for the Bélanger-Campeau Commission downplayed past advantages of Québec as part of Canada and highlighted Quebecers' future promise in a separate nation.

Elsewhere in Canada, the mood had become impatient. If Quebecers could not be satisfied, ran a common sentiment, then let them go! The backlash was fanned by Preston Manning and his Reform forces, and by Pierre Trudeau and his many allies, who'd earlier partnered to denigrate the Meech agreement and accuse Brian Mulroney of "giving in to Québec." Nothing had changed in their political orientations. The two "federalists" seemed almost bloody-minded about their perverse accomplishment of advancing Québec separatism. "Trudeau made anti-French bigotry respectable," commented Bob Rae icily.

Such feelings were understandably being absorbed by elected representatives across the land. This translated into nervous uncertainty about the constitutional sessions underway, making it harder for provincial premiers to find common ground. Since repatriation, the Constitution required unanimous consent for an important change. That was why the Meech Lake Accord had died, when just two provinces with a small fraction of the total population of Canada failed to give consent, despite eight provinces representing some 95 percent of the people in our country having approved. Getting a far more complex agreement, as was now the goal, would demand deft precision navigating Canada's cluttered political landscape, itself a heavily charged minefield.

Joe Clark's vast and extensive consultations for the next year drew in the northern territories, Aboriginal groups, and many others who'd felt themselves at the margins of Meech. His machinery of consultation became an effective operation that supported his unrelenting effort to assemble a grand plan of constitutional change that all provinces could support, that aligned with the requirements of the government of Canada, and that would be agreeable to the Canadian people.

Although Joe Clark talked little about his own past as prime minister or how Brian Mulroney had seized the leadership of the PC party from him, one sensed this historic initiative for remaking Canada through constitutional change had become his mission for personal vindication.

Early in July 1992, with the October 26 deadline looming in Québec, basic elements of the package were coming together as Prime Minister Mulroney left for the G7 Summit in Munich, Germany.

Before departing, the PM, Joe Clark as constitutional affairs minister, and the rest of cabinet had met and agreed that the government's position on Senate reform was "double-E," meaning elected and effective. Making it "equal" as well would require taking Senate seats from Québec. In the current climate, that would be like placing a stick of dynamite amidst candles on a birthday cake.

"We were resolved that if we failed to get this at the negotiating table," the PM recorded about the double-E Senate, "the government would walk away and put together a complete package of reforms, which we would submit to Parliament for a debate and then place on the ballot — either for a national referendum and/or the Québec referendum in October 1992 — as an alternative to sovereignty."

That is how strongly resolved the Mulroney government had now become to achieve Senate reform. It was an essential part of the national unity package, and Western Canada was an essential part of the Conservative party's base.

In Munich, Canada's prime minister took an urgent telephone call in the middle of the G7 Summit. Joe Clark, he heard in stunned disbelief, had agreed with the premiers of the nine English-speaking provinces on a triple-E Senate — elected, effective, and "equitable." The constitutional affairs minister had done this on his own. There'd been no consultation with the PM or other ministers. It was a breathtaking violation of the cabinet's agreement, of Joe Clark's word to the PM, and of the government's carefully laid plan.

"This news sent shock waves through the telephone lines between Ottawa and Munich," the PM later recalled, discussing how his government came close to disintegrating over that third "E" for the Senate, "and ignited perhaps the most explosive challenge of my nine-year term as prime minister. Joe had placed the government in a no-win situation."

Québec had made clear it did not accept a triple-E Senate. But some Western provinces, following Joe Clark's July 7 deal with them to extend equal representation in the upper house to all provinces, now viewed this as a *fait accompli*. And all nine non-Québec premiers, including Bob Rae of Ontario, had signed this July 7 agreement. To not proceed would lead

Western Canadians to protest that Brian Mulroney had backed down on real Senate reform in order to placate Québec.

In a moment of hubris, Joe Clark had boasted to the media that his nine-province deal on the Senate was the greatest constitutional agreement since 1867. But the truth of it was he'd created the worst possible conditions for the government and eliminated virtually all of its political options.

Breaking the Senate deadlock had been crucial to everything else. The nine premiers, before Joe Clark had pushed them to a consensus on "equitable" Senate representation, had been divided — six agreed with the less rigid equitable model that would redress regional imbalances in the West but not necessarily mean numeric equality of Senate seats for each individual province, three favoured triple-E, and Saskatchewan's Roy Romanow wavered between the choices. Joe Ghiz of Prince Edward Island actually wanted the Senate abolished, and especially did not like triple-E, but had agreed to it only to break the logjam and save the country. That's why the government's plan, before Joe Clark took it upon himself to freelance, was to forego "equality" and fight for what appeared within reach, an elected and effective Senate.

First Nations leaders were deeply troubled. The developing package included extensive constitutional changes to enable Aboriginal self-government in ways never before contemplated since the first arrival of the Europeans. Unless there was agreement on the Senate that included Québec, they'd risk losing all these negotiated gains.

Through hot July, positions oscillated like the whirring fans on office desks as premiers and the prime minister, and the circle of senior officials around each, interacted with one another in limitless permutations and combinations of long distance phone calls and face-to-face meetings. One saw movement on some aspect of Senate reform, then tested it with others, only to later find, say, Robert Bourassa's mention on Sunday night that *"Le concept d'un sénat égale, c'est okay"* could be modified as the week progressed and time continued to run out. Subsequently, at another point, the Québec premier was again more reassuring that a third E might be possible, because who really cared anyway? His view was that the Senate was nothing more an ineffectual debating society.

Robert Bourassa did have an oblique negotiating style. Years before, in 1971, he'd approved the Victoria Charter at a constitutional conference in British Columbia, only to reverse his position after getting back to Québec. Perhaps, at some point, his musing about the Senate had been misread by Joe Clark, personally desperate to make a deal, as a definite signal that triple-E might fly in Québec.

The Mulroney government wanted to close down this endless chasing after notions and put concrete proposals for constitutional change onto paper in order to present them a specially recalled session of Parliament, leading to a referendum.

But the PM also wanted consensus. As he told his cabinet, when it began to appear some version of triple-E Senate reform could be a possibility, "Let's remember, we are seeking a negotiated deal, not an imposed agreement like the 1981 Constitution. That means we are in the world of what's possible, the world of the good, not the perfect." The way forward lay through compromise, the honourable art of statecraft.

Prime Minister Mulroney never canvassed his entire cabinet on issues, except this once. Given the extraordinary importance of the Senate issue, he said later, "I had to ensure that each member of cabinet was consulted and had every opportunity to express himself or herself." It was tense, and difficult. With Joe Clark sitting to the PM's left at the oval cabinet table, each minister was being asked, one by one, to pass judgment on what he'd done. Mr. Mulroney made notes as each of his ministers weighed in.

"While we can't isolate Québec," said Manitoba's Jake Epp, "the triple-E Senate is seen as just as important, symbolically, in the West as the 'distinct society' is in Québec."

"This will never pass in Québec," concluded Jean Corbeil flatly.

Marcel Danis, who'd been Joe Clark's Québec campaign manager in the 1983 leadership campaign and who remained loyal to the former leader, though he had offered stalwart service to Brian Mulroney as well, did not let his personal feelings cloud his judgement. He had spoken with some thirty-five members of Parliament about the triple-E deal crafted by Joe Clark. "It is completely unacceptable for them, and for me."

Albertan Harvie Andre reported the deal was greeted "as a huge victory in Alberta," but added, "a triple-E Senate was not worth sacrificing the country for." He proposed a ten-year trial, a referendum with regional majorities, and if that failed, the best thing would be to "simply abolish the Senate or make it into a permanent constituent assembly."

Tom Siddon from British Columbia noted "most of our twenty-eight-point package has been achieved," leaving only "the enormous challenge of the triple-E Senate." The tension in the room eased slightly when Siddon added, "Prime Minister, I admired your defence of this crazy triple-E proposal in Munich — you almost had me believing in it!"

John Crosbie from Newfoundland called the triple-E Senate barbaric and ludicrous. "Walt Disney couldn't have dreamt up anything better than what we have on the table as a result of all these meetings."

Joe Clark intervened, hearing how his plan would be rejected in Québec, to rapidly escalate tensions. He demanded of his colleagues, "Who cares about the rest of Canada?"

"We do," replied Benoît Bouchard. A true Québécois, Benoît had grown into a proud Canadian patriot and sincere federalist after getting to Ottawa as an MP and being entrusted by Brian Mulroney with key positions in his cabinet.

"Bullshit!" snapped back the minister of constitutional affairs.

Everyone stared at him.

Gilles Loiselle stated firmly, "This agreement has absolutely no chance of being accepted as is. Even the principles are not acceptable. Prime Minister, you personally must now assume the leadership and make a final exploration of the file, to see if it can be salvaged without squeezing Bourassa anymore, because he is already in serious difficulty in Québec."

By early August, Brian Mulroney welcomed all premiers to Harrington Lake. It was the first meeting with Robert Bourassa since the death of the Meech Lake Accord.

Although the discussion touched on the various issues still before the first ministers, the central imperative was to find common ground on the Senate. "I am worried by the impact of this on the country in ten or fifteen years," said Premier Bourassa, "with such a reform adding a new Tower of Babel."

"We're trying to close a gap on Senate reform," responded Premier

Getty, "but we've been arguing something more fundamental — the equality of provinces." The Canada West Foundation's invented notion of "the sovereign equality of provinces" had reared its head. "I don't understand why Robert Bourassa doesn't view the triple-E as saleable," stated the Alberta premier, who'd grown up unilingual in Montreal's prosperous Anglo enclave of Westmount. "This is not about more senators for Alberta. This is about a new basis for Canada."

Premiers McKenna, Ghiz, and Rae each jumped in to defend Bourassa, pleading not to gang up on him, not to hand separatists an issue to clobber him to death with.

The meeting was on track to failure. The PM intervened to sum up the broad areas of agreement. Major disagreement existed on the Senate, but no one wanted to stop discussion and "see Canada fracture." Québec needed an offer from the rest of Canada to consider in October. All Canadians wanted a say in the matter. There would be one final meeting, in mid-August, to finalize the deal if agreeing on the Senate.

Roy Romanow agreed with the prime minister on ratification by Canadians, stating, "A referendum is required to consult all Canadians."

After the meeting concluded, the premiers headed home. The PM paused to assess the state of affairs. "I think the decision to proceed with referendum legislation has proved to be important," he noted.

Ontario Premier Bob Rae phoned from Toronto. He commended Brian Mulroney on achieving a likely agreement that, to all the other seasoned political leaders present, had seemed impossible. Just the Senate remained. "Without your special skills there would have been no deal."

Then he added, "I think you should have a national referendum. Do it quickly."

On August 18, the first ministers, territorial leaders, and national chiefs of the First Nations convened in Charlottetown to finish their work on the Senate and extract from the locale a name by which their comprehensive package of constitutional changes would be known.

The "Charlottetown Accord" contained substantial changes, and these were negotiated as an integrated system, which was no more divisible into separate parts — as some hoped to do by cherry-picking parts they liked when voting in the national referendum — than could a person handed a piece of cake ask to just have the milk, raisins, and eggs, but not the flour, spice, or baking powder.

The Charlottetown Accord placed before Canadians a masterful compromise of true statesmanship. It drew critics, including the now reliable duo of Pierre Trudeau and Preston Manning, but it was unmistakably an all-Canadian product. Agreeing on the parts dealing with the Senate had been the biggest hurdle.

Gone was the minor provision in the Meech Lake Accord about consulting provinces on Senate appointments. Now a bolder Senate plan spoke volumes about how ambitious the Charlottetown Accord vision had become.

Because the much larger package of amendments gave more scope to compromise, some premiers agreed to senators having increased powers in exchange for making concessions on Aboriginal self-government. A "distinct society" clause for Québec could offset loss of relative strength in the number of Québec Senate seats. And so it went, in seeking agreement on redesigning Parliament's upper house.

For the election of senators, the Charlottetown Accord offered provinces two options: either direct elections by provincial voters, or voting by the provincial or territorial legislatures. If a province decided that its citizens would directly elect its senators, the Accord did not specify a particular electoral system for the vote but left selection between the many possibilities to each province. Another optional provision gave provinces and territories the power to create rules for achieving gender equality in their Senate representation. Still another option allowed designating seats for specific purposes, such as the representation of minorities. Senators would be elected at the same time as general elections held to elect members to the House of Commons.

Provincial "equality" was provided by equal distribution of Senate seats, each province receiving six seats and each territory one. Additional seats would be created in the Senate for Aboriginal peoples' representatives.

As a means of making it more "effective," the redesigned Senate was given new powers. Senators could initiate legislation — except for money bills, continuing that key rule from antiquity — but now the House of Commons would have to deal with Senate bills in reasonable time. If the Senate were to defeat, amend, or veto ordinary legislation, a joint sitting of members from each house would decide the matter by simple majority. The Senate would have a "suspensive veto" over money bills, which meant the Commons could override upper house opposition after thirty days.

Increased clout for the elected senators involved their new power to veto bills changing fundamental tax policy directly related to natural resources. The new Senate could also, if it acted within thirty days of getting a "supply" bill authorizing the spending of money, force the Commons to re-enact the legislation. The Senate had an "absolute veto" — meaning no House of Commons override — on legislation materially affecting the French language or French culture. Passage in the Senate of such bills required approval by a double majority — both a majority of all senators voting, and a majority of all Francophone senators voting. These provisions on natural resources and French culture embodied the prime interests of Albertans and Quebecers.

Senators would ratify the government's proposed appointments to important regulatory agencies and cultural institutions. Or, put negatively, the Senate could block such appointments.

A significant stipulation was that senators were no longer eligible for cabinet positions. Since Confederation, virtually all cabinet posts in the government of Canada have been held at one time or another by a senator. In some early cabinets, with little more than a dozen portfolios to go around, as many as a quarter or a third were held by senators. Two Canadian governments, as earlier noted, were even led by senators. In more recent times, there have routinely been a couple of cabinet ministers from the Senate.

The provision in the Charlottetown Accord that senators would be barred from sitting in cabinet seemed a radical departure, especially since Parliament's upper house would now be elected, but it further signified how different Canada's new Senate would be from the old one.

In the national referendum on the constitutional amendments held October 26, 1992, the heavily negotiated packaged was defeated by 54 percent of Canadian voters.

In all four Western provinces, where the quest for Senate reform had been strongest, this chance to convert Parliament's appointed upper house, which was ineffectual and which underrepresented Western Canada, into one that was elected, effective, and equal, was rejected. Manitobans voted 61.7 percent to 37.9 percent against. Saskatchewanians cast 55.1 percent of their ballots against and 45.5 percent in favour. Albertans voiced "No" with 60.2 percent of the votes to 39.6 percent for "Yes." British Columbians registered the highest "No" vote in the country, with 67.8 percent opposed and only 31.9 percent supporting the Charlottetown Accord.

As for Québec, whose needs got all this started, the package of amendments, grown large in order to embrace the demands of Western Canadians for a different Senate, proved to be an equally toxic match up. The Charlottetown Accord went down to defeat in Québec, 55.4 percent to 42.4 percent.

Late that night, when the results from British Columbia were known, Prime Minister Brian Mulroney went over to the Parliament Buildings in Ottawa, faced the Canadian people through a row of national network television cameras, and brought down the curtain on Canada's longest running cycle of constitutional negotiations with a simple, unequivocal statement. "The Charlottetown Accord is history."

A valiant effort had been made to give importance, meaning, and legitimacy to Parliament's upper house.

Yet Herculean endeavour had accomplished no change. The Senate's maddening existence drove our politics into a void of unproductive activity, involved expenditure of many millions of dollars in researching and preparing proposals, entailed years of prime-time negotiating, and incurred an incalculable but vast "opportunity cost" for what might have been accomplished if all the effort had been spent on something else instead.

All of this might have been avoided, if only the upper house had long ago ceased to exist.

Between that first November 27, 1967 meeting in Toronto of Canada's ten premiers for a "Confederation of Tomorrow" conference, and this 1992 referendum a quarter of a century later that defeated the most extensive blueprint ever for restructuring primary components of Canadian governance, nothing about Canada's Senate had changed.

Contributing to the referendum result was the fact many Canadians were angry. So many years had been devoted to unending conferences about constitutional clauses — conferences that absorbed the attention and consumed the energy of our country's politicians — rather than tackling real problems: why some First Nations communities prospered while most did not; why the poverty of children did not end despite pledges that it would; why survival of the French language and culture required innovation instead of reaction; why the Canadian armed forces were expected to perform roles they no longer were equipped to do; why the national debt had climbed beyond emergency wartime levels throughout a long era of peacetime spending on ourselves; why productivity in factories had slipped; and why fertile fields were being covered in asphalt.

After October 26, 1992, a Canadian politician, like a reformed addict, would now stay away from the Constitution. Prime Minister Harper, in 2006, would try to make the Senate an elected body by choosing a plan he believed could spare returning to the tar pit of trying to amend it. Liberal leader Justin Trudeau, likewise, would choose a plan in 2014 to make the Senate into a body of worthy appointees because he'd sought a path to upgrade the Senate without, as he put it, "reopening the Constitution."

It had taken the defeat of the Charlottetown Accord through the referendum process in which all Canadians participated to finally break what had become a Canadian habit of dealing with our political issues by trying to remake our Constitution.

With the end of the Charlottetown Accord disappeared the most extensive plan that it was humanly possible to devise in the real world of Canadian politics for revamping the Senate.

Reforming the upper house required too many broad trade-offs on other significant aspects of governance, too many specific concessions in narrowing the choices for Senate reform. It was only possible to frame such Senate features in the widened scope of bargaining over many substantive goals at once. Yet the comprehensive package grew too big for many individuals to swallow, too complex for the country as a whole to digest at one time. That was our Canadian conundrum.

The deeply entrenched nature of the Senate made it impossible to change. Delusion had come to an end. We knew by late October 1992 that, after existing unaltered for 125 years, the Senate of Canada would never be reformed because it simply could not be changed.

CHAPTER 17

An Elected Senate, Even Worse

From the 1870s to the present, despite repeated major efforts to change the Senate, only three measurable changes have come about.

One has been the expansion of the upper chamber's size by adding more senators for Confederation's new provinces and self-governing territories, something already anticipated in 1867. The second was replacement of senators' original life-time appointments with the requirement to retire at age seventy-five, an accomplishment of a prime minister who'd initially hoped to end decades of talk by making significant Senate reforms. The third has been a partial adoption of the plan to appoint individuals who are elected as senators-in-waiting — to date occurring in a single province only.

Yet this near-total failure to improve the Senate did not prevent, over the past forty years, a mounting pile of proposals about how to reform Parliament's second chamber. They were a barometer measuring Canadians' darkening dissatisfaction with the Senate. The worse the upper house became, the more ideas people generated for fixing it.

A decade ago, Senator Serge Joyal, who brings sincere and intelligent interest to the subject, counted twenty-eight government and political party proposals for Senate reform, just in the current generation alone. Their variety is mind-numbing. They come from diverse sources. The only common thread across all is the recommendation that the Senate be converted to an elected body. Each proposal glows with this same shining belief that an elected Senate would be better than what we have now.

Yet worse than no change would be the wrong change.

In 1984, the Molgate-Cosgrove Report on Senate Reform called for an elected Senate. Senate seats would be adjusted to reflect population distribution between the provinces. Single-member constituencies would counter the party focus Molgate-Cosgrove feared would result if senators were elected by proportional representation. Elections would be in single-member Senate constituencies established on the basis of geographic, community, linguistic, and cultural factors. Elections would be held on fixed dates every three years, renewing one-third of the Senate's membership each time.

In 1985, Alberta's Select Committee on Senate Reform advocated an elected Senate of Canada, with each province having an equal number of senators. A "first-past-the-post" or simple plurality system would be used for voting in multi-member, province-wide constituencies. The elections would take place in conjunction with general elections for a province's legislature.

That same year, the Macdonald Royal Commission initiated by Prime Minister Trudeau's Liberal government, but whose report was received by Prime Minister Brian Mulroney's Progressive Conservative one, recommended that Senate reform should involve electing senators. The royal commission proposed that Senate seats be adjusted to reflect population distribution between provinces. Elections should employ proportional representation in tallying ballots and allocating seats. Senators would be elected in six-member constituencies, with elections taking place at the same time as general elections for the House of Commons.

By 1992 a joint Senate and Commons select committee joined this growing chorus to also sing praise for an elected upper house. The Beaudoin-Dobbie Report wanted Senate seats adjusted to reflect population distribution between provinces. Voting would use a system of proportional representation. Voters could choose from a slate of candidates nominated by the political parties, but independent candidates could also get themselves onto the ballot, somehow. The parliamentarians called for multi-member constituencies electing at least four senators, with voting to occur at fixed times but separate from elections to either the Commons or provincial legislatures.

That same year, Prime Minister Mulroney and the provincial premiers negotiated a package of constitutional amendments. Their Charlottetown Accord, in step with what Canada's political class was uniformly embracing for the unfinished business of Senate reform, envisaged an elected Senate. As detailed in the prior chapter, each province would have an equal number of senators. Elections to the Senate of Canada would occur simultaneously with election of MPs to the House of Commons. A province could opt for a system of selecting its senators by the provincial legislature, or choose a system of direct election by citizens residing in the province.

The cost of generating these recommendations ranged, all in, to somewhere between $1.5 and $2.8 billion. None of the measures was implemented.

The inarticulate major premise of these plans was that an elected Senate, like a miraculous religious conversion, would improve Canadian public life, unite the country, uplift senators, and remove difficulties between Parliament's two legislative chambers.

The shadow cast over this shining promise comes from all the stormy differences between the conflicting suggestions. Beyond the narrow common idea that it would be good to elect senators, the depth and range of disagreement is chilling.

- ▶ There is disagreement on the number of senators per province.
- ▶ There is disagreement over whether they should be elected province-wide, in several multi-member constituencies, or in a larger number of single-member constituencies.
- ▶ There is disagreement about using proportional representation or simple plurality electoral systems for counting up the ballots and deciding who's been elected.
- ▶ There is disagreement over whether voters should elect senators directly, or whether provincial legislatures should vote them into Parliament's upper house.
- ▶ For this latter possibility, there is further disagreement over whether the provincial legislature should vote on candidates already endorsed at the polls by the provincial electorate at large, or vote on candidates who are proposed in a manner similar to the way nominees are, according to one plan, for the Order of Canada. On this point, which is more salient

since Liberal leader Justin Trudeau's 2014 proposal to appoint senators the way people are chosen for the Order of Canada, it is worth noting that in naming six thousand people to the Order of Canada since the honour began in 1967, there's been controversy on who has been named — indeed, a number of past recipients have returned their medals in protest over subsequent nominees, such as Dr. Henry Morgentaler — some medals have been rescinded, and now there is disagreement over proposals to reform that selection process itself.

► Some proposals for Senate elections suggest that each province should be allowed to decide which method to use. The result would see senators in the same legislative chamber exercising the same powers as others but elected on the basis of a variety of criteria and voting methods.

That is just the start of it.

► There is also disagreement over how many years a senator would hold office, once elected.
► There are differences over whether an elected senator would face a fixed term, or could stand for re-election as often as he or she wanted and remained qualified.
► There is wide disagreement over the timing of senatorial elections. Some proposals insist they take place at the same time as provincial elections. Others stipulate they occur contemporaneously with the election of MPs to the House of Commons. Still others are adamant that senators not be elected when any other elections are underway.
► There is disagreement about whether all senators should be elected at the same time, or only a portion of them in order to provide rotation of incumbents. Some proposals want a portion of the senators, without stipulating how many, to be elected at a given time. Some specifically advocate that one-half the Senate's members be up for re-election at the same time. Others recommend only one-third of the senators face the electorate in the same round of voting.

> ▸ There is deep disagreement between proposals for an elected Canadian Senate when it comes to the role of political parties. Some proposals say the parties should institute a nominating process and produce lists of candidates. Others want the entire process of electing senators free from the dominance of political parties, arguing they already control the candidacy of those seeking election to the Commons. A few plans envisage a hybrid arrangement, combining both party lists and independent candidates.

These and other suggestions are all on the public record. Such a diverse jumble of ideas on what an elected Senate should look like is a built-in guarantee nothing will result from all the talk, innumerable studies, and endless conferences. There is no consensus, not even close.

There is not even agreement about whether an elected Senate would have more powers in law-making than it currently does, fewer, or the same as at present.

Nor is there concurrence about who should take the lead in forging a common plan. Usually Canadians look to our prime minister in such cases.

Prime Minister Mulroney used up a great deal of his dwindling political capital to drive through the plan in the Charlottetown Accord, with its proposal for an elected Senate. The result was rejected by Canadians in a national referendum.

Prime Minister Jean Chrétien, his successor, offered no such leadership. An astute man, he could see this roadway was a *cul de sac*. Even more germane, Liberal Party policy is to keep the Senate unchanged, the better to make appointments to it.

Prime Minister Paul Martin, his successor, made a broad statement coming into office about "changing the way Ottawa works," but had no interest in changing his party's stance on the Senate. What Mr. Martin did say was that "piecemeal" Senate reform would create an unworkable combination of appointed and elected senators. Given the chance to fill Senate vacancies from Alberta, he thus took a pass, as had Mr. Chrétien, on naming any elected "senators-in-waiting."

Prime Minister Stephen Harper, next man up, was an opponent of the Charlottetown Accord with its triple-E Senate reform. Yet the PM from Alberta remained imbued with a belief that the Senate had to become elected. He was just as resolved to avoid constitutional negotiations to bring that about. He meshed both goals into his 2006 plan to extend the pilot project begun in 1987 with the Alberta Senatorial Selection Act to the country as a whole, so every province could vote on its senators but he would still appoint them using the unchanged provisions in the Constitution. Mr. Harper's plan is a half-E Senate — not equal, not effective, but semi-elected — doing indirectly what he can't directly.

The Harper government's legislation to do even this little was stalled by Liberal senators in the upper house, and successfully challenged by the Liberal government of Premier Jean Charest in Québec. In 2013 it obtained from the province's Court of Appeal a ruling that the Alberta model for electing senators could only by implemented notionally by constitutional amendment.

Full circle, and back where we started: an unelected Senate. Things *could* be worse.

If a magician could distill a single plan for a revamped Senate from the many daunting permutations available, and if a miracle worker could achieve unanimous agreement to amend the Constitution so that we found ourselves electing members to Parliament's second chamber, we'd only face new problems.

Two fundamental issues would become quickly apparent.

Conflicting electoral mandates is the first. The question of whether the Commons or Senate had the stronger popular mandate from the country's electors would arise whenever disagreement arose between the two houses. It would not matter whether the disagreement had been caused by partisanship or policy differences, it would turn into conflict, then become a stalemate, and end in deadlock.

Just how ugly and unproductive this can be is now routinely showcased, for our benefit, by the American Congress and state legislatures (all but one of which are bicameral). The current era of antagonistic gridlock between upper and lower houses in the United States demonstrates how a warring Congress in Washington can shut down the government in one of the world's strongest democracies, resulting in an inability to proceed on a wide range of legislative initiatives.

When I mentioned this concern to Donald Wright, a highly respected Toronto lawyer who closely follows public affairs, he instinctively responded, "If the Senate is elected, you're going to have people who want a more active role and will exercise greater power than they do now, so we'd end up like the U.S., with the mess they have between their two houses in Congress. I know it's a different system, congressional rather than parliamentary, but we'd see a big change here, and get some kind of stalemate."

That is the first issue, in a nutshell: two legislative assemblies battling each other over *partisan or policy differences* as each claims a stronger electoral mandate from the same voters.

The second issue would arise from an elected Senate's *institutional* role to check or balance the Commons.

In those more than two dozen Senate reform proposals, apart from dealing with elections, the focus is on the power an elected Senate would wield. All plans spell out new powers, from approving of appointees to exercising vetoes. Under triple-E, an "effective" Senate would have real control in the legislative process at Ottawa, the way the present Senate does not, and other proposals likewise envisage increasing the institutional power of the Senate. After all, why go through the effort of democratizing the place unless those elected to it have clout in law-making?

If that same alchemy that could magically convert the existing Canadian Senate into an elected body worked to produce enhanced legislative powers for the upper house, the result would be to place the Senate and Commons on the same track like onrushing trains heading toward each other.

We can see how this institutional locking of horns in the U.S.A. is working out, but some may think that comparison to our parliamentary system inapt.

A better way for Canadians to see just how this would work out here might be for a couple of influential policy organizations — such as the Canada West Foundation, which is now promoting a new model for an effective Senate, and the Manning Centre for Building Democracy, which is promoting a decade-long schedule for doing something similar — to persuade the Alberta government to create an upper chamber for the Legislative Assembly in Edmonton. The Alberta Senate should not only be elected, but have significant legislative powers — pretty much like those being proposed now by the Canada West Foundation for the Senate in Ottawa, just translated into the provincial context. Canadians elsewhere, and in Alberta, could then watch how it works out when Alberta's elected MLAs and Alberta's elected senators grapple with provincial measures.

A benefit of Canada's federal system is that, with a dozen or so different governments, a pilot project by one can help us all ascertain how effective a theory turns out to be in practice. Alberta is the province of choice for this, being the most advanced of those pushing for Senate change, and being the only province today represented in the Senate of Canada by senators whom the people themselves selected by their votes. Alberta is also principal repository of a Canadian obsession with hypothetical senates that could resolve our country's political problems by some magic of restructuring.

I'd propose the experiment in Ontario, where I'm living, except we already ran it for a quarter century, back in the 1800s, and decided we did not want an elected and effective upper house after all. Cost-benefit analysis showed it was unwarranted, so it was abolished. The people had not liked the Legislative Council as an appointed extension of powerful and privileged elements in the province, but the reform of making it elected only proved that some "reforms" could, indeed, be even worse.

CHAPTER 18

Crazy Senate Scrambles

On December 2, 2013, Senate Speaker Noël Kinsella held an hour-long press conference on the floor of the Senate, the first time such a thing had ever occurred in this improbable setting.

In contrast to the House of Commons, where television coverage began three and a half decades ago in 1977, Senate proceedings are not televised. This helps maintain the obscurity desired and deserved by the senators.

On this inexplicable occasion, however, TV cameramen lugged their gear onto the plush red carpet, watched the legs of their camera tripods sink into its deep pile, and panned the hushed scene from a unique angle. Speaker Kinsella stood a little awkwardly at the end of the Senate Clerk's table, its highly polished wood surface uncluttered by a single thing, and reported to the invited reporters that the Senate of Canada does important work.

Mr. Kinsella had no announcement to make, the normal reason for calling the nation's news media into assembly. He simply wanted to counterbalance the Niagara-like flow of bad news that for more than a year had been swamping the Senate in scandal. Soon it became apparent his goodwill offensive on behalf of Parliament's upper chamber was faltering.

As members of the Parliamentary Press Gallery began to recover their journalistic instincts, only temporarily suppressed with awe at discovering themselves in Parliament's Red Chamber, they bombarded the Senate Speaker with hard questions about that day's urgent issues.

Should Senator Marjory LeBreton, a participant in the effort to deal with Senator Duffy's expenses, be on the committee now deciding which witnesses to call? Should the Deloitte auditors be summoned before the Senate committee to discuss any breached confidentiality of their work? What did Speaker Kinsella himself think about calling Senator Irving

Gerstein before the committee to explain his telephone call to Deloitte at a time the accounting firm was carrying out an arm's-length financial review for the Senate?

Because Speaker Kinsella avoided answering such questions, understandable in a press conference where he wanted only to talk about the *good things* the Senate did, not how it bungled its own financial administration and the senators' expenses, the reporters became perplexed. They did not see their role in this historic moment of grave developments enveloping the Senate of Canada to provide public relations for the institution over which Mr. Kinsella presided. The press conference would not yield anything their editors or producers might want. They left empty-handed, with no real "news," just a colour story that the first-ever Red Chamber press conference had been a perplexing bust. As the Senate, so a Senate press conference.

Their hour in the exquisite Senate chamber had simply underscored, again, the institution's ineffectual nature. But Speaker Kinsella was hardly alone in scrambling to do something, *anything,* to respond to the crazy mess that had become Canada's Senate scandal.

In May 2011, Premier Dalton McGuinty announced one morning via his Twitter feed: "Ontario's position on Senate reform: abolish the Senate."

A Canadian Press reporter, asking for elaboration at the end of the Ontario premier's Chrysler factory tour in Brampton later that morning, was told by Mr. McGuinty that he'd been speaking with other premiers and had come to believe "the simplest thing to do is abolish it. I think, frankly, to reform it in any substantive way is just not possible."

He continued, "Based on my discussions with other premiers, based on the formula that's now in place in order to make a reform, it's not going to happen. We have one elected, accountable body that sits in Ottawa for us in the House of Commons," he stated. "I just don't think we need a second, unelected, unaccountable body." With that, the power of another province, and a major one, was added to the drive for Senate abolition.

But two years later, Ontario's new premier, Kathleen Wynne, a Liberal like Mr. McGuinty, astonished the province's elected representatives. "I actually believe there is a role for a chamber of sober second thought," she told the legislature. "I believe that it is possible to reform the Senate."

Provincial New Democrats were caught off guard by the premier's decision to reverse Ontario's position. "I am quite surprised that the premier is so out of touch that she thinks the people of this country, and of this province, want to see the Senate continue to function," shot back Andrea Horwath, leader of the NDP. Ontario's Progressive Conservatives, favouring reform of the Senate, criticized Wynne, even though she'd moved to their camp. "It will be interesting to see as time goes on," responded deputy PC leader Christine Elliott in the Queen's Park Senate scramble, "whether her position changes again." The NDP gave a standing ovation to Mr. McGuinty, who'd returned to the legislature for only the second time since retiring, causing consternation in Liberal ranks — two leaders in the same session, two different policy positions on the Senate.

In Saskatchewan, meanwhile, things were also shifting around rapidly. Premier Brad Wall, formerly a Progressive Conservative, now heading the governing Saskatchewan Party, had for years been a strong proponent of Senate reform. In 2009 he and the provincial legislature had even created a voting system for Saskatchewanians to elect senators-in-waiting, whom the prime minister could then appoint to the Senate, following the model of neighbouring Alberta and the blueprint Mr. Harper's government was hoping to implement with its Senate Reform Act.

Before any Senate elections took place in Saskatchewan, however, Premier Wall led the legislature in repealing his own Senate election enabling law. He had moved on. By 2013, Mr. Wall no longer believed meaningful Senate reform possible. The premier now asserted "most people in Saskatchewan agree that the Senate no longer serves any useful purpose and is not worth the $100 million in taxpayer money spent on it each year."

Saying the Senate had "failed the test of being effective," Premier Wall then introduced a motion calling for abolition of Parliament's upper house. Acknowledging that many senators have done good work, the premier argued that the problems are with the nature of the institution itself. The motion to abolish the Senate passed with all-party support.

In supporting repeal of the Senate Election Act and a follow-on motion to abolish the Senate, Saskatchewan New Democrat leader Cameron Broten hoped this would be "part of a bigger discussion that we'll have in the country about the right steps to take on abolishing the Senate." He added, "I think Canadians agree, and it's not simply because we're outraged by current scandals."

As revelation often does to a convert, Saskatchewan's premier had become zealous for the cause, although he quipped he was "not going to hire a campaign bus" to hit the road in advocacy for his new belief. Yet Mr. Wall's worthy mission to liberate Canada from the Senate had already seen him proselytizing other premiers at their July 2013 annual summer gathering in Ontario, where he made little headway. In late February 2014, he was keynote speaker on Senate abolition at the Manning Centre's annual "networking conference" of conservatives interested in Canada's democratic condition, where he faced a more welcoming yet still tough audience.

In Manitoba, the scramble of provincial political leaders to respond to the abysmal state of the Senate played out at the same time. Many in the province were ashamed that their legislature had failed, in a fumbling way, to approve the Meech Lake Accord, which, among other things, would have cleared the path to an elected Senate. By 2009, Manitoba public consultations on the Senate led the New Democrat, Progressive Conservative, and Liberal provincial political parties to unanimously agree the Senate should be either elected or abolished. By November 2013, Manitoba's New Democrat premier Greg Selinger said, "We don't see the need to retain the Senate in its present form. We think it should be abolished and all the political parties in Manitoba support that."

As it turned out, the Manitoba Official Opposition Progressive Conservatives balked at supporting the Selinger government's November 2013 resolution, despite PC support for Senate reform if not outright abolition. Scrambling about the same way that Ontario PCs did when finding another party shared their policy on the Senate, the Manitoba Progressive Conservative MLAs protested that the Senate motion was merely an attempt by the NDP to distract attention from its proposal to increase the provincial sales tax without a referendum.

The provincial government responded by saying that the Senate serves partisan objectives rather than the public interest, and that any confidence Manitobans had in the upper house was shaken by the current expenses scandal. The motion, asking the federal government to begin consultations with the provinces to abolish the Senate, passed twenty-nine to eighteen.

During this period, the provincial governments or legislatures of Nova Scotia and British Columbia also spoke in favour of Senate abolition.

The cross-Canada provincial positions on what to do about the Senate shifts, as concern about the Senate scandal spreads and as leadership or parties in power changes. For example, Bob Rae's position about the Senate when Ontario's NDP premier between 1990 and 1995 was overtaken both by his return to the federal Liberal fold, with its Senate-retentionist stance, and by different parties coming to power at Queen's Park since those days. There could also be a switch on Senate abolition within the same party under different leaders, as the reversal of positions by Ontario's successive Liberal premiers, McGuinty and Wynne, showed. The same leader may even change his mind, as Premier Wall of Saskatchewan illustrated.

Staying abreast of policy positions of provincial governments and legislatures on the Senate is germane to the rising prospect of constitutional amendments for either Senate abolition or major Senate reform, because approval by each province will be needed to make the change.

Back in Ottawa, meanwhile, there was also some scrambling in the twilight zone of Senate administration.

The dysfunctional administrative operation of Parliament's second house became apparent once the expenses scandal started stripping away the imposing parliamentary cover of the Senate's august stage-set, revealing backstage financial practices as unusual as the institutional relic itself.

The senior administrative officer is the Senate clerk. The dozen men who've occupied this position since Confederation have been important to the functioning of Parliament's upper house, and the character it displays, largely because their familiarity with parliamentary procedure tends to rank above their knowledge of the skills necessary for the disciplined administration of a multi-million dollar operation.

Over the past couple decades there have been two Senate clerks, from 1994 to 2009, Paul C. Bélisle, and, currently, Gary O'Brien, who succeeded Mr. Bélisle in 2009. The qualifications of each underscore how emphasis on parliamentary procedure trumps administrative prowess. Mr. Bélisle graduated with a Bachelor of Social Sciences degree in political science, a certificate in Public Administration, and a law degree from University of Ottawa. He began as a procedural clerk with Senate committees. He was appointed associate director of committees in 1984, and served as a table officer for several years. Mr. Bélisle's interest in parliamentary procedure he shared with his spouse, Danielle Parent-Bélisle, a law graduate, who was herself serving as a procedural clerk nearby at the House of Commons. Gary O'Brien, started working at the Library of Parliament after receiving his MA in political science from Carleton University. Then he became a procedural analyst, and, in 1984, was appointed chief of journals in the Senate, completing his Ph.D. at Carleton while in this post. In 1999 he became deputy clerk of the Senate. Like his predecessor, Clerk O'Brien was not versed in administration or financial management, principally having interest in procedure of the Senate and its committees.

The Senate clerk in recent times has had a dozen or more "direct reports" — officials with some specific area of responsibility or other in Senate operations who interact directly with him and take instructions from him. Parliament Hill insiders pointedly suggest that, for an operation with a budget and personnel the size of the Senate's, a tighter administrative hierarchy is necessary.

Senate administration is run at two levels — the Committee on Internal Economy, Budgets, and Financial Administration whose members are senators, and the hired staff and Senate officers. Members of the Internal Economy Committee might view themselves as akin to those who sit on a corporate board, dealing with the big picture, developing broad policies, and giving general direction for the Senate. But instead they tend to take on the role of hands-on operators. Senators on the Internal Economy Committee, for many years, have embroiled themselves personally in the minutiae of individual cases and particular projects.

The Senate's administrative officers and senior staff include few with professional administrative training and some who have acquired administrative experience from what they could pick up working in the Senate. For anybody who acquires on-the-job administrative training, this would not normally be a problem, but the place in which they are learning administration is the Senate of Canada, where outdated procedures, lax standards, and ineffectual methods make the problem circular because newly emerging Senate administrators are schooled in inappropriate ways.

Relations between senators and Senate staff epitomize another aspect of this scene. Most senators remain in the upper house for at least a couple decades. During their long tenure, they acquire detailed information about every nook and cranny of Senate life. Staff approach senators on even the smallest matter — a security guard who feels upset because he's been badly treated, a researcher who's not clear about the reporting process — because they know the senator will deal with it. Senators have been immersed in the place's smallest details for so long it is they who run the place, for better and for worse, regardless of what organizational charts of neat boxes with connecting lines or dots may show. Even senior administrators tend to kowtow to the wishes and expectations of senators.

The potential for senatorial influence over administrative detail not only increases as time goes by, but is exaggerated because of the intrinsic nature of the Senate. The institution is small. It has an inward-looking busyness. It has a big budget. It does not institute proper contracting authority, such as to delegate power to officers dealing with even the smallest of matters. A senior administrative person must go all the way to the Senate clerk, the most senior official who should be engaged with the larger view, for approval on minor contracts. This is akin to the acquisitions officer in the Library of Parliament needing to get permission from the parliamentary librarian to buy a book.

The Senate provides reimbursement for expenses incurred by senators in the course of their work. In keeping with its club-like nature, the Senate has long operated on "an honour system" for such matters, grounded in the belief that honourable members would only submit claims that were justified. It is, truly, a beautiful thought.

Consistent with this approach, when the Senate introduced an entitlement for reimbursement of housing costs, it made no attempt to set out criteria for distinguishing between a senator's primary and secondary residence. There were just three broad rules. First, a senator's primary residence had to be more than one hundred kilometres from the National Capital Region. Second, the maximum accommodation claim a senator could bill for a month was $1,000, with another $10,000 a year for meals and such (the daily or "per diem" allowance that did not require any details and was always billed at the maximum permitted per day), resulting in a total allowable claim of $22,000 for "living expenses" annually. Third, if the senator was renting secondary accommodation in the National Capital Region, it could not be from family.

Several senators, including Patrick Brazeau and Mac Harb, made clear that they asked the Senate administration if their respective residences in Maniwaki and Westmeath (later relocated to Cobden), each more than one hundred kilometres distant, qualified as their primary residences, entitling them to claim the housing allowance. They were told they did. The clerk at the time, Paul Bélisle, when asked recently, told those questioning him that he could not recall the conversation. In any event, the senators submitted their housing allowance claims. The Senate administration reviewed them, according to what the chair of the Internal Economy Committee stated publicly was a stringent process, approved them, and paid the money to the senators.

Regarding the ethical conduct of senators, the upper house jealously guards control over who advises them on such matters and who has power to review any questionable transactions. Even creating a Senate Ethics Office in the first place showed what dysfunctional looks like when Canada's senior legislators take charge of something. Normally, the need for an office would be determined first; if it was justified, the office would be formally created, its powers delineated, its budget established, and a job description drawn up for the attributes considered most desirable when interviewing applicants. With the Senate of Canada, it was the opposite.

The senators started by hiring an ethics officer, then looked for a place to put him, then started discussing what role he should have, and debated whether they even really needed an ethics officer after all. When they finally agreed he should stay, Jean Fournier became a courageous pioneer in his work as first ethics officer for the Canadian Senate. On April 5, 2012, Lyse Ricard, a chartered accountant with a degree in business administration who'd worked for the auditor general of Canada and Revenue Canada, became Mr. Fournier's successor as Senate ethics officer.

In the interim, the Senate had made a great effort to ensure its ethical conduct would not come under the consolidated operation of Parliament's conflict of interest and ethics commissioner, as provided by the incoming Harper government's 2006 Accountability Act. In the seesaw battle between the Commons and Senate over provisions in the act, when the vast majority of the Senate amendments were rejected by the Commons, the "deal breaker" was the senators' insistence on keeping their own Ethics Office. They sought to guarantee that activities pertaining to conflict of interest issues and questions of proper conduct would not be reviewed by anybody except the upper house's "independent" Senate ethics officer, who operates within the Senate's own bailiwick. In 2013, as backstage scrambles at the Senate were taking place, Senate Ethics Officer Lyse Ricard stopped her investigation of the contested expense claims when the Senate asked the RCMP to investigate instead.

From retirement, Jean Fournier told the *Globe and Mail* at the end of 2013 that a major overhaul of the Senate's rules on conflict of interest was needed.

The Internal Economy Committee had been trying, with varying degrees of interest and commitment, to get some handle on the matter of the Senate's sloppy financial administration. The backstage reality belied the public impression committee chair Senator Tkachuck had been conveying about stringent standards and tight controls.

The Senate's finance department had complained to the committee for several years over its concerns about particular senators. For two years before the Senate scandal erupted in public, a couple staff members of the Senate's budget department, which has a functioning connection to the Internal Economy Committee if not a direct reporting relationship, had specifically been urging tightening procedures and revising rules to accommodate the Senate's new reality, people's changing values, altered public expectations, and a different generation of senators. But the administrator's zeal was cooled by savvy Liberals and Conservatives, who knew that too much accountability would put a damper on their practice of working, at public expense, for their respective parties in election preparedness.

The unravelling of everything at the Senate, however, with exposure of its ineptness in handling simple matters like expense claims — not to mention procurement of new technology systems and such big-dollar items — accelerated the scramble to respond. A sense dawned in the Senate that providing proof of payment to justify cutting a cheque from public funds might not be entirely out of line. But the "honour system" still guided senators.

The honour system had been a good fit for someone like Senator Eugene Forsey, who rode the public bus from his home in the Glebe to the Parliament Buildings and back. But what about Pamela Wallin commuting to Wadena via Halifax and Toronto with layovers of several days along the way? Not all senators were the same. Not all senators saw rules the same way. Ms. Wallin herself criticized the Senate rules for being antiquated, developed "back in the days when the only way senators could get to Ottawa was by train." She implied that in the age of civil aviation senators do things differently and the rules should embrace that, should be modified so that they were, well, more along the lines of her own practices.

Transportation expenses were not the only problem causing the Senate clerk and others to scramble. The easy-going "honour system," long a pillar of Senate financial administration, was also being eroded by the reports scandalizing Canadians that several senators claimed an accommodation allowance when they shouldn't have.

On May 9, 2013, Senator Tkachuk presented the Internal Economy Committee's recommendation to terminate the venerable "honour system" by deleting the Senate administrative rule that stated: "Senators act on their personal honour and senators are presumed to have acted honourably in carrying out their administrative functions unless and until the Senate or the Internal Economy Committee determines otherwise."

In this urge to respond — provoked *only* by public pressure over the scandal, never by the requests from their own financial administrators — the committee recommended further tweaking of rules. The changes were not radical, except in the context of the Senate of Canada. Travelling senators would now be required to state the purpose of a trip — although the names of those participating in a meeting or event to which the senator was flying would still not have to be disclosed.

Senators would now have to provide receipts if wanting reimbursement for taxi or limousine expenses; previously, the money was paid by the Senate for whatever amount the senator claimed, without any receipt.

Per diem allowances for out-of-town senators staying within the National Capital Region would now be paid only for days when the Senate was actually sitting, when members attended Senate committee meetings, or were in town for Senate and National Caucus meetings. Before this, senators were robustly claiming the daily tariff wherever they were (Mike Duffy billed some when in Florida), even when the Senate was not in session, even when Parliament itself had been dissolved for a general election. Routinely, a number of senators billed per diems to the maximum of days in a month. Yet to make this stringent new rule palatable, an extra twenty days of per diems would still be allowed a senator working on "Senate-related business," however he or she defined it. The sixty-four-point travel system was tweaked to specify that fifty-two points were for regular Senate business travel and twelve points for regional and national travel on Senate business.

As 2013 progressed, most senators, scrambling for cover from the scandals, became even more conspicuously unseen and unheard than normal.

The daring few who ventured to offer public defences of the Senate repeatedly sounded a couple of notes, first for "sober second thought." They publicized the idea that senators invest painstaking effort scrutinizing bills passed by the Commons and offer detached reflection on public policy embraced by such legislation. In fact, the Senate actually studies an embarrassingly small number of bills.

Their second argument of defence was the note that senators are valuable because they voice regional needs, an important role because of the size and diversity of Canada. This suggestion was however greeted skeptically by Canadians, who know the many channels and different organizations through which this is already done effectively by others on a daily basis.

Senate defenders put into circulation quotes from Sir John A.

Macdonald in the mid-1860s about senators speaking for regions to counterbalance the Commons. These carried no weight when placed alongside contemporary realities: senators are appointed on a provincial not a regional basis and identify themselves as much if not more with their province than a nebulous "region"; most senators are appointed as partisans and represent their party more than any "region"; elected representatives in the Commons come from every region of Canada and speak for the country's diverse interests and wide-ranging needs; and, provincial premiers and their cabinet ministers have supplanted senators as strong, legitimate, and informed spokespersons with more effective direct impact on national policy and programs than members of the appointed second chamber.

Perhaps the most dramatic scramble, at least so far, in response to the Senate scandal came early in 2014.

As the new leader of the Liberal Party, Justin Trudeau initially responded to the Senate scandal by levelling condemnation where he felt it was due, at the individual senators who stood accused, but as for what to about the institution itself, he simply replied, "We don't need to change the Senate. We need to appoint better senators."

But as 2013 unfolded and the Senate scandal soared into still greater prominence, Mr. Trudeau found it problematic to be a relative bystander in the Commons watching Stephen Harper and Thomas Mulcair duke it out over the issue. On top of that, the Liberal status quo stance itself was not popular. A June 2013 Nanos poll showed only 6 percent of Canadians still wanted to leave the Senate untouched. Without doing something major soon, Liberals would forfeit ground to their rivals.

Six months later, however, the Liberals had yet to respond in any imaginative way. No one really expected anything more, because Mr. Trudeau had said party policy would not be unveiled until the 2015 general election. Even at daybreak on January 29, 2014, the Liberal party's website dealt with "Democratic Reform" only in the broadest terms: "The Liberal Party of Canada believes that Parliament should belong to the people instead of the Prime Minister. Liberals are committed to exploring Parliamentary and Electoral reform in order to realign our institutions with democratic principles and to ensure more meaningful and effective representation."

January 29, being a Wednesday, typically meant Parliament would crest at its mid-week busiest. With most MPs and senators in Ottawa and each party holding its weekly caucus, the Press Gallery reporters were primed to scrum parliamentarians on the hottest issues of the week.

At 9 a.m., Liberal senators, summoned by Justin Trudeau, gathered on short notice for a meeting. No one knew what to expect, not even Liberal Senate Leader James Cowan. Waiting, they puzzled over what on earth their leader might need to say that he could not tell them an hour later at national caucus.

Mr. Trudeau entered the room alone. He explained the senators would no longer be members of the Liberal Parliamentary caucus. They would henceforth sit in the Senate as Independents, not Liberals. He'd be making political hay with this news. As seasoned Liberals, they would understand he had to take a bold initiative. He had to get their third-place party into competition with the Conservatives and New Democrats on what to do about Canada's Senate. He read them a prepared statement he'd already rehearsed several times and would deliver again to reporters in just a few moments.

The venerable Liberal senators, most of them instinctively devoted to the Liberal Party because it was in their DNA, sat in stunned silence, learning of their immediate and undeserved firing. They would be painted as political pariahs, representatives of the odious "patronage" Senate appointments Justin Trudeau now condemned — despite the fact that many were his friends and loyal supporters, and one, Québec senator Charlie Watt, was the last-remaining caucus member appointed by his father.

In this hushed Senate meeting room, Justin Trudeau's dramatic dismissal of his senators, for which there was no authority except that which he now established, seemed a Canadian equivalent to the party purges in the Soviet Union under Joseph Stalin. The newly "Independent" senators were shocked. As their leader departed for his press conference in the foyer of the House of Commons, the disowned senators remained limp.

Members of the Parliamentary Press Gallery had been no more prepared for a major news story from the Liberal leader than were his senators. He delivered to the press corps his explosive Senate news. "As of this morning," he announced, "only elected members of the House of Commons will serve as members of the Liberal caucus. The thirty-two formerly Liberal senators are now independent of the national Liberal caucus. They are no longer part of our parliamentary team. The only way to be a part of the Liberal caucus is to be put there by the voters of Canada."

This bold move thrust the Liberals back into the Senate battle that, for a year, had seen the New Democrat Official Opposition and the governing Conservatives square off, leaving Justin Trudeau mostly outside the ring as a front-seat spectator. Seeking to replace Thomas Mulcair in defying Stephen Harper's approach to Senate reform, the Liberal leader then challenged the prime minster to match his action. "I'm calling on the prime minister to do the right thing, to join us in making senators independent of political parties and end partisanship in the Senate."

Next, Justin Trudeau headed off to the weekly 10 a.m. meeting with his national Liberal caucus, its size now halved with only thirty-six elected MPs, to tell them about his morning so far.

While the unexpected drama caught news organizations and political Ottawa by surprise, leaving everyone in the media scrambling for a day of intense comment and widely different assessments of the new Liberal plan for Senate reform, the Liberal senators themselves huddled and promptly decided to form their own caucus.

Newfoundland senator George Baker said the Liberal senators were now free from the control of the party leader and could choose their own leader. They promptly re-elected Senator Cowan, who started the day as Liberal leader in the Senate and, after the morning purge, was still leading the Liberals in the Senate that afternoon.

Senate Speaker Noël Kinsella recognized the Liberals as the Official Opposition, and the senators remain identified as Liberals on the Senate website. British Columbia senator Mobina Jaffer told CBC's Carol Off, "An independent senator may want to do something, a good project or such, but if you are on your own you are weak. If you're a member of a group of thirty-two others, you are stronger."

When this response to the surprise attack on them by their own leader became public by early afternoon, the news undercut the Liberal leader's initiative to make senators "independent from any particular political brand." The irrepressible Liberal senators caused confusion and consternation, providing Prime Minister Harper with Question Period ammunition when challenged by Justin Trudeau to declare Conservative senators independent, too. "I gather the change announced by the Liberal leader today," came the PM's repost, "is that unelected Liberal senators will become unelected senators who happen to be Liberal."

One commentator on CBC Radio observed that "the contents of a jar do not change just because you change the label on the outside." That evening, Senator Cowan was on national CBC Television, showing *Power & Politics* host Evan Solomon his Liberal Party membership card and saying he was still, as he'd always been, a proud Liberal.

Across Canada, the Senate scandal, now reaching its third year and far from over, had lost none of its capacity to produce remarkable news and unexpected behaviour.

For even longer, the Senate had caused puzzling responses from the man who now, more than any other Canadian, had the fate of Parliament's relic upper house in his own hands.

CHAPTER 19

The Puzzle of Stephen Harper

"It has become a rite of passage for aspiring leaders and prime ministers to promise Senate reform," he said, pausing before delivering the punch — "on their way to the top!"

"The promises are usually made in Western Canada, and these statements of intent are usually warmly received by party activists, editorial writers, and ordinary people," he continued. Again, he then added a critique: "But once they are elected, Senate reform quickly falls to the bottom of the government's agenda. Nothing ever gets done. And the status quo goes on."

It sounded like a cynic speaking, but Stephen Harper was addressing senators as a realist on September 7, 2006, intent on galvanizing action. "This has got to stop," he declared, "for the Senate must change."

In support of his case, Canada's new prime minister quoted the author of a book who'd said, "Probably on no other public question in Canada has there been such unanimity of opinion as on that of the necessity for Senate reform." The author was Robert Mackay. The book, *The Unreformed Senate of Canada*. The year of publication, 1926.

Now eighty years later, Mr. Harper had replaced Prime Minister Paul Martin and his Liberal government with a Conservative ministry pledged, among other causes, to Senate reform. He'd started into his project on May 30 with a straightforward measure to shorten senators' terms to eight years in office. Appointing senators for terms of fifteen, thirty, even forty-five years, explained the PM, "is just not acceptable to the broad Canadian community of the twenty-first century." It seemed such an obvious point.

Indeed, it was the only point of Senate Bill S-4, and four months after it had been introduced, the senators were still giving it sober first thought.

The PM and others had felt that initiating the legislation as a Senate bill might be friendlier and somehow show that senators themselves could take a lead in reforming the upper house. But in September 2006 the unwelcoming senators were still playing hardball. They included a handful of holdout Progressive Conservatives whose sense of historic purity caused them to sniff at the PM and his "new" Conservative Party which they judged to be too "right wing." Many more were Liberal senators, occupying a majority of the seats and wanting neither to change the upper house nor help a Conservative minority government in the Commons that might fall if they just pushed it the right way. So they studied Bill S-4, but would not pass it.

Mr. Harper told the senators that Bill S-4 constituted "a first step" in the process of reforming the Senate, "a modest reform," as indeed it was. He explained that his government was "committed to pushing ahead" and would do so by introducing another bill that would create a process to choose elected senators.

A crucial point for Stephen Harper was the fact that shortening the term of office did not require constitutional amendment. "The government believes that S-4 is achievable through the action of Parliament itself." As for the length of time a senator could hold office, Mr. Harper noted that in 1984 Parliament's Joint Committee on Senate Reform, co-chaired by Liberal Senator Gildas Molgat and Liberal MP Paul Cosgrove, "not only made a similar recommendation regarding term length ... but argued that such a change was achievable without using the general constitutional amending formula."

All it took was for one senator to raise a doubt on that score, however, and more debate and questions would ensure that passage of S-4 could be further delayed.

The PM could not prevent senators speculating about whether shortening their term of office could be done by an act of Parliament or needed an amendment to the Constitution, but at least he made clear he was open to their changes about how long a senator could hold office. The Molgat-Cosgrove Report he'd mentioned called for a nine-year term. A later joint committee, co-chaired by Progressive Conservative senator Gerald Beaudoin and Progressive Conservative MP Dorothy Dobbie, had recommended six years. The PM said his government was flexible about accepting change to such details, so long as the result was "limited, fixed terms of office, not decades based on the antiquated criteria of age."

Bill S-4 was not passed by the Senate. Despite Mr. Harper's urgings, the measure was going nowhere.

One part of Stephen Harper's puzzle was what to do with the Senate. A second was how to go about doing it.

Jean Chrétien once instructed Canadians that to get a car out of a snow-drift, the trick is to back up and then go forward, then back, then forward, a little more each time, until enough rocking momentum is built up to break free and get back onto the road. Stephen Harper applied the lesson.

He took his term-limiting legislation back with him to the House of Commons, where it was introduced as Bill C-19 in the next session of Parliament, debated and passed, and sent flying back to the senators with the endorsement of the democratically elected House, hoping such momentum would help. But as with Bill S-4 before it, the same, straight-forward, term-limiting measure contained in Bill C-19 was studied in depth by another Senate committee. Liberal senators found many objections and, again, just kept the bill stuck in the snowbank.

Meanwhile, as he'd promised voters and told senators in September, Mr. Harper's government introduced legislation in December 2006 to provide a full electoral system applicable to the selection of senators. There would be non-binding elections in each province and territory, after which the prime minister of the day would recommend to the governor general appointment of the winners to vacancies in the Senate. The provisions of the Constitution governing appointment to the Senate would still be followed, unaltered in any respect. The difference would be that, instead of his personal and partisan choices, the PM would submit the people's democratic choices, a Canadian electoral college.

This time the PM made no effort at courtesy with a recalcitrant Senate. That December the measure was introduced in the House of Commons, as Bill C-43. It did not get passed there, either. The Conservative minority government faced opposition questions about the constitutionality of the measure. If both term limits and elections could be handled by simple legislation rather than constitutional amendment, why had the two related Senate reforms been split into separate bills? Why was one bill introduced in the Senate, another in the Commons? Did the PM have some doubts about his plan? Was this part of Harper's secret agenda? There were too many questions, it seemed, to press ahead with this now, especially as urgent economic issues crushed in upon Canadians.

In the following parliamentary session, the same legislation was reintroduced as Bill C-20. When Parliament was dissolved in September 2008 for a general election, Bill C-20 was still under study by the House of Commons Legislative Committee, and Bill C- 19 had not yet passed the Senate.

After winning re-election with another minority government on October 14, 2008, the Conservatives' Speech from the Throne in November reaffirmed their commitment to an elected Senate and limiting senators to eight years in office. For a second time, the pledge had been made to voters by Prime Minister Harper in an election. His victory in that election gave him a renewed mandate to act.

The Conservatives' measures on Senate "reform" seemed small change when contrasted to the full-scale institutional make-over proposed in the Charlottetown Accord. That was because the prime minister had a plan, of sorts.

Stephen Harper had witnessed the effort of negotiating the Meech Lake Accord, and, after its defeat, the even greater endeavour required to produce the Charlottetown Accord. He had seen both initiatives, led by Brian Mulroney, fail to change the Constitution or result in any reform to the Senate. Stephen Harper had opposed the Charlottetown Accord, which provided for election of senators, a more equal number of Senate seats for Western Canada, and more effective powers for the Senate. The perversity of opposing what he wanted seemed puzzling, though apparently could be explained on "ideological" grounds.

From that constitutional experience, however, Mr. Harper's take-away lesson was to avoid the strain of constitutional negotiations. A similar lesson had been deeply absorbed at an early age by Justin Trudeau from his father's years of frustrating effort negotiating constitutional amendments and, in the process, failing in his attempt to reinvent the

Senate as the House of the Federation. If history imparts lessons that can guide those advancing into the future, Stephen Harper and Justin Trudeau would both instinctively avoid revisiting the Constitution to deal with the Senate.

Stephen Harper, having learned that it was best to avoid the constitutional quagmire in trying to reform the Senate, decided that the best way forward was to only make incremental upper house reforms. He would not set himself up for the spectacular failures of earlier prime ministers attempting a big change all at once. Especially when tackling a body like Canada's Senate, an institution of deeply patterned resistance to change, just taking small nibbles seemed like the best plan.

Better than the records of prime ministers Borden, Trudeau, or Mulroney when dealing with the Senate was Prime Minister Lester Pearson's tidy little accomplishment. The Liberal leader who'd earlier shown enough diplomatic smarts to be awarded a Nobel Peace Prize managed the only Senate reform from Confederation to the present — a simple measure that changed just one attribute of senatorship, fixing a retirement age.

A third part of Prime Minister Harper's plan was to not appoint any senators himself. On March 14, 2004, he had pledged he would not. Leading the Official Opposition, he had criticized Prime Minister Martin for doing so. Refusing to fill vacancies in the Senate would distance him from practices he'd opposed. It would make the Senate even less functional than before and create additional pressures from the institution itself for change. If it wasn't for the fact the Senate had to pass bills before they could become laws, as required by the Constitution, you could just stop appointing anybody until, like other ghost towns, the place disappeared after the last person departed.

As perfunctory and dubious as this plan was, Stephen Harper had come to the prime minister's office more prepared to deal with Senate reform than any of his predecessors. He'd taken a perplexing route to get here.

As a youth Stephen started into politics as a Liberal. He joined the Liberal Club at his west-end Toronto high school, Richview Collegiate Institute, and likely would have remained a Liberal had the party under Mr.

Trudeau not brought in the National Energy Program and had his father not worked as an accountant for Imperial Oil. Dinner table conversation ventilated the oil company version of why the NEP was an egregious development and biased against Alberta oil producers. The Liberals' major governmental intervention into Canada's energy markets regulated prices, resulted in economic losses to Alberta, and created benefits for Central Canada. Stephen Harper parted company with Liberalism.

Graduating in 1978, he enrolled at University of Toronto, but found the experience at the big institution even less appealing than high school, where he'd been something of a nerdy loner. After two months he withdrew and headed to Edmonton for a job in Imperial Oil's mailroom. Talent rises and Stephen next was working on an Imperial Oil computer, a welcome placement for a young man most comfortable on his own.

When ready to resume studies, he enrolled in the Economics program at University of Calgary and completed a bachelor's degree. The Calgary West riding, the constituency once represented by Conservative prime minister R.B. Bennett, had elected Jim Hawkes, a psychologist on faculty at the university, as Progressive Conservative MP in 1979, re-elected him in 1980, then again in 1984, when he won 75 percent of all votes cast. The next year Stephen Harper joined the Calgary MP in Ottawa as his chief aide on Parliament Hill.

That is where Stephen Harper and I first got to know one another, in the cloistered government lobby when the House was in session. He was quiet, observant, and shyly unenthusiastic. Although raised in Etobicoke, one of whose electoral districts I represented, he had no interest in times past. I could discern that Stephen had emerged a strong Albertan, like other relocated Ontarians I knew who'd become zealous champions of Western Canada's causes.

He continued working as Jim Hawkes's protégé until 1986, with decreasing enthusiasm. It was not governing Canada that caused him despair, but the fiscal policies of Finance Minister Michael Wilson and his deficit budgets, the 1986 decision by the Mulroney government to award construction of CF-18 fighter jets to an unprepared contractor in Québec rather than a fully prepared contractor in Winnipeg who'd submitted a better bid, and the Mulroney government's inability to fully rescind the NEP until 1986. All were evidence to him that Progressive

Conservatives, like the now-reviled Liberals, favoured Central Canada at the expense of Western Canada. He would describe this time in Ottawa as "deeply disillusioning." Stephen Harper parted company with Progressive Conservatism.

When he came to the attention of Preston Manning, who was preparing to carve a new Western political protest party out of the Progressive Conservatives' flank and his father Premier Ernest Manning's political base that for decades nourished his Alberta Social Credit provincial government, the talent-scouting leader invited disgruntled Stephen Harper to participate. As one of the founders of the Reform Party, the willing recruit addressed the 1987 founding convention in Winnipeg.

For a political party whose *raison d'être* was policy, Stephen's importance quickly became apparent when he was designated the Reform Party's chief policy officer. For the general election in 1988, he popularized Reform's campaign slogan, "The West Wants In!" and played a central role in crafting the party's election platform. He even faced off against his prior political mentor and employer, MP Jim Hawke, in Calgary West. Reformer Harper was trounced, garnering just nine thousand votes to the Progressive Conservative incumbent's thirty-two thousand.

Preston Manning's fledgling political party did not in fact win any seats in that outing. But just five days after the November 21, 1988, general election, Tory MP John Dahmer, elected in northeast Alberta riding of Beaver River, died. Reform's candidate, Deborah Grey, a teacher and a single foster mother to native children, who'd come a distant fourth in the safe Progressive Conservative seat, was again nominated for the by-election. Grey soared ahead of new PC candidate, Dave Broda, with 18 percent more votes, and became Reform's first MP. Down to earth, the right-wing conservative with an easy smile, folksy ways, and iron will soon caught special attention by arriving for work on Parliament Hill in black leather riding gear astride her Honda Goldwing motorcycle. Keen to reinforce this Reform beachhead in Parliament, Stephen Harper joined Deborah Grey as her executive assistant, chief adviser, and speechwriter.

Meanwhile, he also remained prominent in Reform's national organization as policy chief. His interest was primarily in economic policy, secondarily in governing institutions and democracy, and lastly, despite his own evangelic religious faith, in the "social conservatism" of many Reformers who had no time for gay and lesbian rights and took an unyielding stance against abortion. He did not personally disagree with these views, but because his emphasis was so strongly on economic priorities, he played them down, believing they distracted the party from issues of far greater significance for Canada. He'd also begun to see that for some Reformers the only litmus test of acceptability was one's hard-line views on these issues, which Stephen felt were more the preserve of personal life than public discussion. If allowed to continue, he believed, this tendency would contract rather than expand support for Reform.

To shore up this primary focus on economic policies and institutional issues such as Senate reform that could give Western Canada more clout in Ottawa, Stephen encouraged Preston Manning to push party expansion beyond Reform's Western base. He knew that growth not only required election of MPs country-wide, but that the inclusion of the generally more moderate views of Central and Atlantic Canadians on the "social conservative" issues would counterbalance the Western extremists, whom he feared would take Reform down a dead-end road. He argued that a regional party risked take-over by radical elements. In 1991, he addressed the Reform Party national convention to condemn "extremist" views.

Although Stephen Harper was less devoted to democratic revival than Preston Manning, he nevertheless saw the potential of a revamped Senate as a new doorway through which marginalized Western Canadians could enter Ottawa's councils of decision-making. Reform leader Manning, in a 1992 book entitled *The New Canada*, called for "a new Senate to address the problem of regional alienation" and spoke about the "equality" of all provinces. The party's platform specifically advocated a triple-E Senate. As Reform's policy chief, Stephen Harper helped outline and advocate party policy on Senate reform.

By 1992, however, Stephen Harper had begun to disagree with Preston Manning. Prime Minister Mulroney and the premiers had reached agreement on another package of constitutional amendments, the Charlottetown Accord. The plan incorporated a version of the triple-E Senate and devolution of powers to the provinces, also a Reform goal. Preston Manning's initial instinct was to be accommodating of the constitutional package.

But Stephen Harper opposed the entire plan for ideological reasons. He influenced Mr. Manning to come out against the Charlottetown Accord.

Strains also arose between the two men over party development, especially after the leader hired Rick Anderson, a long-standing Liberal and member of the "Grindstone" group of devoted Grits who gathered each summer's end at Grindstone Island to swap political stories, drink well, and plot convivially for a couple of days. Where some suspected Mr. Anderson as being a Trojan Horse within Reform's fortress gates on a top-level mission of Liberal plotters, Stephen Harper believed Anderson was just not truly dedicated to Reform's economic and governance principles. Preston Manning, for his part, simply saw Rick as a talented individual prepared to help build the Reform Party in Central Canada, something Stephen Harper himself had advocated.

Stephen Harper resigned as the head of policy for the Reform Party in October 1992. He continued with Deborah Grey until 1993, the year he also completed a Master's degree in economics at the University of Calgary. When the 1993 general election took place on October 25, Reform candidate Stephen Harper defeated Jim Hawkes by doubling the Progressive Conservative's vote in Calgary West, thirty thousand to fifteen thousand — part of the national debacle under new PC leader Kim Campbell when Progressive Conservatives were not just taken off the playing field but escorted right out of the stadium, setting a world record by going from a majority government to just two seats and, the ultimate humiliation for Canada's oldest political party, losing party standing in Parliament.

Calgary West's new MP returned to Parliament Hill, now as a caucus colleague of Deb Grey. Reform's fifty-two seats were almost enough to make the party the Official Opposition, but it just trailed the Bloc Québécois whose fifty-four separatist and anti-monarchist MPs constituted Her Majesty's Loyal Opposition instead.

In 1994, at the Reform Party's policy convention, MP Harper was part of a small minority of delegates who voted against a policy to restrict the definition of marriage to "the union of one man and one woman." Although personally opposed to same-sex marriage, as well as mandated benefits for same-sex couples, the Calgary MP believed political parties should not take official positions on such "issues of conscience." As time passed, other positions taken by Stephen Harper, from his opposition to a Reform Party expense account for leader Manning's dry cleaning and hair dressing to differences over foreign policy, exacerbated the growing division between the two men even further. The real divide between them, however, was the former's strong commitment to conservative principles and economic policies and the latter's populist inclinations, which, in Stephen Harper's view, was leading Reform to compromise on core ideological matters.

Late in 1996, before even completing his first term in the Commons, MP Harper announced he would not run again in the next general election. On January 14, 1997, he resigned his parliamentary seat. Stephen parted company with the Reform caucus in Parliament.

The very same day he became a vice-president of the National Citizens' Coalition, and later, in 1997, was made NCC's president. This grass-roots organization's advocacy of "more freedom through less government" was as much inspired by libertarian as conservative values. I'd first come to know the National Citizens' Coalition when it was based in London, Ontario, and headed by founder Colin M. Brown of London Life Insurance Company, doing legal work in relation to the Canada Election Act's ban on election-time spending by non-party organizations, which curtailed the NCC's advocacy through newspaper ads.

Freed from party demands and now heading a policy organization, Stephen Harper seemed to have found a sweet spot in public affairs. By spring, he was openly criticizing the Reform Party for embracing social conservatism's "family values" at the expense of the principles of economic conservatism and the need for fiscal responsibility, lowering taxes, reduction of overall government spending to avoid deficits, balancing the budget, and reducing the national debt — not to mention overdue reforms to Canada's governing institutions such as the Senate.

As the National Citizens' Coalition leader, Mr. Harper revisited the core NCC issue of the Canada Election Act restricting non-party advertising during elections, but his court challenge was unsuccessful. He spearheaded an NCC campaign to break the monopoly of the Canadian Wheat Board, something he would later get a chance to accomplish as prime minister. When Liberal finance minister Paul Martin introduced tax cuts in 2000, Stephen Harper supported them as a constructive step. Clearly, he had not lost interest in national politics.

After Jean Charest gave up leading the Progressive Conservative

Party of Canada in 1998 to become the Liberal provincial leader in Québec and take on the separatists, Stephen Harper toyed with running to replace him. He decided doing so would end his relationships with Reformers with whom he'd worked and thus prevent a deeper reunification of conservative parties from taking shape, which he saw as essential. The following year, still thinking in these terms, he expressed skepticism about the Reform Party's evolution into something called the "United Alternative," believing it would only consolidate Preston Manning's leadership, which he now saw as unproductive, while diluting the movement's ideological focus.

From the sidelines, Stephen Harper watched yet another shift in the Reform political entity that was Preston Manning's troubled child. The United Alternative next reformed itself into the Canadian Alliance. When Alberta MP Stockwell Day, a glowing evangelical who earlier had been Alberta's treasurer in a Progressive Conservative government, beat Manning for the Alliance leadership on the first ballot, Harper knew the Alliance would become even more a party of the religious right. He saw the remnant of Reform heading for total eclipse as a regional protest party taken over by extremists, just the way he'd warned.

As Mr. Day's leadership of the Alliance became increasingly troubled throughout the summer of 2001, with several party MPs openly calling for his resignation, NCC president Harper resigned in August to prepare for a political return. On March 20, 2002, after an acrimonious campaign, he was elected Alliance leader on the first ballot with 55 percent support, leaving Stockwell Day and two other challengers behind. Now party leader, Stephen Harper announced he'd run for Parliament in a by-election in Calgary Southwest, the riding Preston Manning had vacated as part of his exit from the smouldering ruins of his political career, leaving behind as his principal legacy splitting the electorate and providing Prime Minister Jean Chrétien's Liberals three easy consecutive majority wins. The Grindstone Group could certainly toast that.

In Calgary Southwest, Ezra Levant, who'd been immersed in conservative politics since joining Reform as a teen, then worked closely for a while with both leaders Manning and Day, already had won the riding's Alliance nomination. I discovered him to be like a firecracker when we engaged in debate at the May 1996 Calgary "Winds of Change" gathering of Reformers and Progressive Conservatives, held to explore common grounds, if any, for reuniting the parties. Although declaring he'd not stand aside for his new leader, Ezra was persuaded to put party ahead of self and went away to set off explosions in forums other than the Commons.

The Liberals honoured the long-standing tradition between Grits and Tories of not fielding a candidate against a new leader seeking entry to the Commons, and Progressive Conservative candidate Jim Prentice similarly stood down so the Alliance leader could run unopposed. The NDP does not honour such comity between parties, however, so fielded Reverend Bill Phillips, who'd been Moderator of the United Church of Canada. He lost by more than ten thousand votes on May 13, 2002, as the new Alliance leader won 71 percent of the ballots. Stephen Harper returned to Ottawa as leader of the Official Opposition.

The following year, the long-sought reunion of Canadian political forces that Preston Manning had rent asunder was accomplished. Canadian Alliance leader Stephen Harper and Progressive Conservative leader Peter MacKay agreed in 2003 to merge both entities into a reconstituted "Conservative Party of Canada," and delegates from each party convened and voted in favour. On January 12, 2004, Mr. Harper resigned as Leader of the Opposition to run for the leadership and was duly elected first leader of the revamped Conservative Party on March 20, claiming a first ballot majority win over MPs Belinda Stronach and Tony Clement.

The Liberals, enjoying a majority government under Prime Minister Paul Martin, called a quick general election to catch the Conservatives still raw and reeling, but by voting night, rewarded for their clever enterprise by Canadian voters, the Liberals came home with only a minority government.

The Conservative Party's inaugural policy convention took place in Montreal in mid-March 2005, when delegates endorsed Stephen Harper as leader by 84 percent, rejected an anti-abortion policy, turned down another resolution against bilingualism, adopted policies in favour of balanced budgets, debt reduction, lower taxes, and an elected Senate.

By this date, the exact nature of Senate reform had become more puzzling to Stephen Harper. He had fully absorbed the tenets of triple-E Senate reform as an Albertan, as a Reform MP, and as Reform's policy chief. Believing, with many others, that a reinvigorated Senate could help address some of Western Canada's many issues, an upgrade of the upper house was an easy plank to build into the new Conservative Party of Canada's platform. As party leader, he simply pledged to "make the Senate more democratic, more accountable" in the campaign that brought him to office.

When Mr. Martin's minority government was defeated in the Commons in late November of 2005, the Conservatives moved swiftly and effectively, outlining an important policy every day and moving up in the polls. The Conservatives won the largest number of seats in the House, though not enough for a majority government. Stephen Harper was sworn in as Canada's twenty-second prime minister on February 6, 2006.

It was time to begin a major reordering of operations and programs of the Government of Canada. It was time to puzzle through in detail what at last to do with Canada's embarrassing upper house of Parliament, which Stephen Harper had already called "a relic."

The pure triple-E Senate proposal had already been forced through the negotiating wringer for the Charlottetown Accord and come out modified. It was hard, really, to see how, in another round of constitutional talks, a negotiated version could ever again achieve even that much consensus. It would be hard, too, for Stephen Harper to head in that direction, questing after something he'd earlier campaigned to defeat. And by this date, even those at the Canada West Foundation, who had originated and championed the elected, equal, and effective Senate makeover, were cooling on the idea, some even beginning to turn their backs on it. The PM needed to find a politically valuable plan somewhere between what zealous Senate reformers dreamed about and whatever shifting political realities now made possible.

He settled, as a pragmatic realist, on a tempered measure of term limits and a version of Senate elections that could fit within existing procedures of the Constitution. Both were specific, and each implemented ideas he'd campaigned on, two goals that were achievable. As well, he would show commitment to electing senators by refusing to appoint any.

The legislation was introduced in his first year in office. It was reintroduced in the second session, after failing to be enacted during the first session. The plan was reiterated once more as a campaign promise in the 2008 general election, which he again won. But the "plan" wasn't working.

For three years Prime Minister Harper stuck with his plan's related tactic of not appointing senators.

Only twice he made principled exceptions. First he appointed Michael Fortier to the Senate to get him in cabinet so Montreal, where no Conservative MP had been elected, could have representation in Canada's national government. Although Conservatives piled up a lot of votes in Montreal, as well as Toronto and Vancouver, the party won no seats in any of these cities because the electoral system served a two-party political universe not the multi-party elections Canada has known since the 1920s.

Lacking a system of proportional representation that would let our House of Commons mirror the popular vote of Canadians, similar distortions likewise had kept Liberals from winning seats in Western Canada. In 1972, after failing to win a single seat west of Manitoba despite a healthy Liberal popular vote in British Columbia, Alberta, and Saskatchewan, Prime Minister Trudeau had been forced to appoint cabinet ministers through the Senate, too. In 1979, even though Progressive Conservatives won plenty of votes in Québec, the PC had no Commons representation from the province and Prime Minister Clark appointed Québec senator Jacques Flynn as Canada's minister of justice. In 2008, honouring a pledge Prime Minister Harper had extracted from minister Fortier, the senator resigned his seat to seek election as an MP in that year's general election, but was defeated.

The second exception was Prime Minister Harper's appointment of Albertan Bert Brown to the Senate in July 2007. Mr. Brown, a farmer who'd created and chaired the Canadian Committee for a Triple-E Senate, first came to national prominence when he climbed onto his tractor and skillfully plowed "Triple E Senate or Else" in huge letters down his neighbour's two-mile long field. Passengers on aircraft high above got the message, and so did readers when an aerial photograph of Brown's grassroots billboard appeared in magazines and newspapers across Canada.

Then, in 1989, in response to the troubling and complex wrangling over the Meech Lake Accord constitutional amendments, Alberta

Premier Don Getty instituted a system for a Senate election in the province. A serious Senate reform attempt that did not require changing the Constitution, it was an improvised way Albertans could implement their democratic project of making the upper house an elected body. This innovation left it to the PM and governor general to complete the necessary constitutional formalities for summoning a senator chosen by the people in a provincial vote.

Bert Brown ran for the Senate under the Alberta Progressive Conservative banner. In 1998 he ran again, this time under the Reform Party of Alberta's colours, losing to Stan Waters, who'd served valiantly in the Canadian army during World War II and reached rank of lieutenant-general before retiring, when he became a founder, with Preston Manning, of the Reform Party. Premier Getty recommended that Prime Minister Mulroney appoint candidate Waters. In the Commons, MP Deborah Grey urged his appointment with bravado, telling the prime minister, "If we don't get this seat, we'll get ten in the next election." Out of consideration for Don Getty, the PM did recommended his candidate to Governor General Ray Hnatyshyn, who in June 1990 duly appointed Stan Waters Canada's first "elected" senator. He also became Reform's first member of the upper house. Senator Waters died a year later, from a heart attack.

Meanwhile, Bert Brown ran again in Alberta and was elected a "senator-in-waiting" in 1998. When the federal Liberals returned to power in the 1993 general election under leader Jean Chrétien, Senate reform was abandoned. Neither he nor his successor Paul Martin recommended appointment of Senate candidates elected by Albertans in 1998 and 2004, when Bert Brown was again re-elected a "senator-in-waiting," on the grounds that elections are not part of the Senate selection process defined by the Constitution.

When he came to office, Stephen Harper saw things differently. He could plausibly even argue that appointing Bert Brown to the Senate was not an exception to his rule, because Mr. Brown had in fact been "elected" through a non-binding provincial Senate election. Senator Brown, three times elected, was at last sworn into the Senate on July 10, 2007.

* * *

The appointment issue was becoming a particularly problematic part of Stephen Harper's puzzling conundrum over Senate reform.

The 105-seat Senate was in major imbalance, with Liberals outnumbering Conservatives three-to-one. The fifty-eight Liberal and twenty Conservative seat tallies were in part the legacy of years of successive Liberal PMs appointing senators. But the imbalance was also due to Mr. Harper's refusal to fill his vacancies, as a way to ramp up political demand for Senate change. In the most recent general election, in October 2008, he'd again identified Senate reform as a priority, but now his prospects of doing anything about the Senate, or about anything else for that matter, seemed in jeopardy. A coalition of all three opposition parties was prepared to bring down his government.

At first he responded by putting a padlock on Parliament's front door on December 8, persuading Governor General Michaëlle Jean to prorogue Parliament in order to stave off defeat of his minority Conservative government. Then, on December 22, his partisanship on full boil because of Liberals plotting with separatists to take power, the PM resolved that, if the opposition parties should form a government, they would at least not be able to claim these Senate prizes.

He moved to fill all vacant Senate seats. As he spoke with each candidate for a senatorship, he extracted a commitment to work for Senate reform, even to resign and run for a Senate seat if the province he or she represented instituted elections for upper house nominees the way Alberta already had, and the way he someday hoped to achieve.

As January 26, 2009 approached, with Parliament about to begin a new session, Prime Minister Harper prepared to face a coalition of Liberal, New Democrat, and Bloc Québécois MPs whose leaders had signed a pact to defeat his government and take power.

Governor General Michaëlle Jean swore into office eighteen new senators whom the PM had recommended to her, the largest number ever appointed at once, since Confederation.

After the PMO announced on December 22 the prime minister's dozen and a half hand-picked Senate reinforcements, they'd had a month to prepare, and time to hear commentators criticize a prime minister who'd opposed appointing senators for now doing so.

Stephen Harper internalized a swirl of thoughts and puzzled feelings. Was he on the brink of forfeiting the prime ministership, and about to see his government defeated? How could he appoint senators the way he'd criticized earlier prime ministers for doing, when said he never would? Still, he was buoyed by this bold manoeuvre; by filling the Senate vacancies himself, with hand-chosen supporters, including some big-name personalities, he would deny his opponents the spoils of office. He geared himself for the imminent challenge of the new parliamentary session.

Those sworn in as Canada's newest senators were Parliament Hill celebrity Mike Duffy, national chief of the Congress of Aboriginal Peoples Patrick Brazeau, and famed broadcaster and diplomat Pamela Wallin. Nancy Greene arrived to warm greetings from those admiring her sporting accomplishments and Olympic gold. Chair of the Conservative Party Fund, successful businessman Irving Gerstein, received solid handshakes from those who respected his accomplishments in amassing a fortune for the party's election coffers.

The thirteen other new senators were well-connected Conservative organizers and supporters and former federal or provincial politicians. From Québec, Michel Rivard had been a politician with the Parti Québécois, Suzanne Fortin-Duplessis, a former Progressive Conservative MP and for several years my seatmate in the House of Commons, and Leo Housakos, a director of Via Rail. A new Ontario senator arrived in the person of Nicole Eaton, member of the prominent Eaton family. Fabian Manning from Newfoundland and Labrador had been an MP. Three Nova Scotia senators being sworn in were businessman Michael L. MacDonald, lawyer Fred Dickson, and Stephen Greene who'd served Conservative Premier Rodney MacDonald.

A duo appeared from New Brunswick, lawyer John D. Wallace, and long-serving member of the provincial legislature and cabinet minister Percy Mockler. From the West were added former member of the Yukon Legislative Assembly Hector Daniel Lang, British Columbia's former minister of energy, mines, and petroleum Richard Neufeld, a provincial Liberal who supported the federal Conservatives, and Yonah Martin, Korean-born co-founder of British Columbia's "Corean Canadian Coactive" Society.

As large as this roster was, it by no means constituted all Prime Minister Harper's 2009 Senate appointments. Later in the year he would name nine more, many of them hard-core partisans, such as campaign chair of the Conservative Party, Doug Finley.

Though Stephen Harper had seemingly resigned himself to the necessity of maintaining the old ways by breaking his vows and making appointments to the Senate, he remained committed to the need for reform of the institution. However, a number of problems began to emerge that complicated even his modest plan for Senate reform, making the puzzle of what to do even more mystifying.

First was eruption of the Senate expenses scandal. It greatly upped the ante on the prime minister to do something serious, significant, and soon.

The second challenge was the drive to declare that his plan for indirect Senate elections did in fact require amending the Constitution. Stephen Harper contended there was no need to formally change the Constitution, nor seek provincial consent, to implement his type of Senate reform. Several provinces, however, disagreed. In 2007, the governments of Ontario, Québec, New Brunswick, and Newfoundland and Labrador each stated that change to the terms and selection of senators would require provincial consent, and requested the PM consult with the provinces before making any alterations to the Senate.

In 2011, the Harper government responded with the Senate Reform Act, a bill to allow indirect "election" of senators for a maximum term of nine years. In reply, and to shore up the Liberal resistance to this measure, the government of Jean Charest in Québec launched a court challenge to the constitutionality of Bill C-7, while the Liberal government of Dalton McGuinty in Ontario, through Intergovernmental Affairs Minister Smith, mused publicly about doing the same.

When Premier Charest was replaced by Parti Québécois premier Pauline Marois in September 2012, the case was allowed to continue. Only the animus behind it changed. The separatists did not anticipate making Senate appointments the way the Liberals did, but they certainly welcomed any challenge to Ottawa over something that affected some dimension of Québec's status, even if just altering the terms and selection of senators. The Bloc Québécois separatists in Parliament stood for complete abolition of the Senate, a far more radical change.

In 2013, the Québec Court of Appeal, after hearing lawyers advance a dazzling yet mind-numbing array of arguments on both sides of the question, opined that the plan embraced by the Harper government's proposed Senate Reform Act, Bill C-7, could only take place with provincial concurrence, and would require approval of seven provinces representing 50 percent of the Canadian people.

Although in all his election campaigns Mr. Harper had called Senate reform "a priority," only in 2013 did his government refer questions to the Supreme Court of Canada about how much Senate reform could be pushed through Parliament without amending the Constitution. At the time, this initiative was also considered as a way to counteract possible interpretations on the issue by the Québec justices. The Harper government asked the Supreme Court of Canada more questions, too, not just about changing the Senate by electing senators, but even on abolishing the upper house, in compliance with the Constitution.

As this book goes to print, the Supreme Court's answers are still awaited. The inevitable action that awaits the Senate will require amendment of the Constitution.

The third problem for Stephen Harper's original plan for Senate reform was that earlier proponents of the measures he'd embraced began deserting the cause and seeking to influence public opinion in a different direction, many calling for a referendum on the Senate, more of them than ever before simply espousing outright Senate abolition.

Addressing an October 2013 conference in Calgary contemplating what to do about the Senate, Albertan Scott Hennig, vice-president for communication with the Canadian Taxpayers' Federation, referred to the province's nomination system, which the Harper government had adopted for electing senators within the existing constitutional provisions. "It was a policy that I supported, at first strongly and then less so, and now, not at all," said Mr. Hennig. "In fact, it was a policy that many in the Canadian Taxpayers' Federation supported for many years. But times have changed. Views have changed and it's time for the government to abandon this policy, like so many former supporters of it have already."

National Director Stephen Taylor of the National Citizen's Coalition, which Stephen Harper formerly headed, stated in 2013, "The timeline for Senate reform and for the prime minister is getting shorter and shorter. A lot of people are getting fed up. A lot of conservatives are actually calling for abolition. If Prime Minister Harper does not have serious Senate reform markers — term limits, elections, accountability every step of the way — in place by the next election, we'll be encouraging him to run on abolition."

The Canada West Foundation, originally a deep well of information and resources that triple-E Senate supporters could draw from, has renounced the concept. It also now rejects the approach taken by Stephen Harper. In a "let's start all over again" paper written by CWF Senior Fellow Dr. Roger Gibbins and CWF Vice-President for Research Robert Roach, the Canada West Foundation now contends, "Canadians need a vision of what a new and improved Senate could do. We have to shift the terms of debate from the problems of Senate reform to its democratic potential." Most pointedly, CWF condemns "the current focus on tactical issues such as term limits and the appointment process" — the heart of Stephen Harper's plan — as "not likely to capture the imagination of Canadians."

Conservatives scratched their heads and puzzled about what to do next.

It seemed the government could only go a short distance with Stephen Harper's incremental, non-constitutional approach to Senate reform — and that with the Senate expenses scandal and the rising public mood for abolition, the horizon they'd been running toward was receding further into the distance.

The Conservative government's reforms — making the Senate democratically accountable by integrating indirect elections into the appointment process and limiting a senator's time in office to nine years — had still not been implemented as Stephen Harper clocked his seventh anniversary as prime minister in February 2014.

Indeed, by early 2014 Stephen Harper, who'd declared a decade before, on March 14, 2004, "I will *not* name appointed people to the Senate," had done so fifty-seven times.

While the PM tried to discern what to do about the upper house, he had been forced to hunker down, suffering loss of personal standing for his response to the scandals involving the celebrity senators he'd appointed and staff he had hired. In the end, what had once been his puzzle with the Senate had somehow become the puzzle of Stephen Harper himself.

CHAPTER 20

Clear Choice Faces Canadians

Canada's political parties currently represented in Parliament offer us clear choices:

Justin Trudeau: *Liberals Want to Keep the Senate but Appoint Better Senators*
Thomas Mulcair: *New Democrats Want to Abolish the Senate*
Daniel Paillé: *The Bloc Québécois Wants to Abolish the Senate*
Elizabeth May: *Greens Want a Referendum on Senate Reform*
Stephen Harper: *Conservatives Want the Senate Elected or Abolished.*

These are not policies created in a vacuum.

For the most part, they come from recognizing that the Senate's significance as a legislative body is negligible, that its reputed role for "sober second thought" is real only in the sense that Santa Claus is real — a lot of attention is paid to what everybody knows is make-believe — and that its other ostensible functions, such as scrutiny of statutes, giving voice to regional needs, and providing deep study of important public issues, are all now done more effectively by others. The unexpected behaviour of so many people in the Senate expenses scandal is an expression of the dysfunctional nature of the institution. All this is reflected in the policies our political parties put forward.

Those who, even now, want to justify keeping the Senate utter only vague approbations of the place. They refuse to concede that the Senate's moving parts are not connected to anything important in Canadian public affairs. Speaker Kinsella offered bromides about the Senate's important work, but ducked hard questions on the immediate reality surrounding him. Former prime minister Joe Clark, interviewed by Ian Hanomansing in Vancouver in late November 2013, said that he "regretted" the current scandal, but thought the Senate was "a valuable institution" for the country. Liberal leader Justin Trudeau wants to keep the Senate, seeing only a need for "upgrading it by appointing better senators."

So long as important players in Canadian public life start, as these three do, from the premise that the Senate is all right, the policies they offer Canadians are more likely to perpetuate than remove the problem of Parliament's second house.

The Senate's cost to taxpayers in now close to $100 million each year for directly budgeted amounts of current operations. Beyond the factored amounts are contingencies that add to the total, from Senate pensions to the cost of recovering the reimbursements for senators Wallin, Duffy, Harb, and Brazeau — so far, an amount five times greater than the total amount of money to be recouped. Then come additional costs arising from the complexity burden of having two legislative assemblies pass the same bills, a redundancy that Canadian provinces and territories prove is unnecessary.

For Canadians considering the parties' policies, making a rough cost-benefit analysis of the intermittent studies by senators on public issues can be helpful. The topics the senators examine are important, but most are simultaneously being reviewed, often in much greater depth, by Canada's dynamic community of existing public policy organizations. For value-per-page, Canadians would be better served, if the Senate were to be abolished, by allocating just a fraction of the current Senate budget to the existing and highly professional operations of the Research Branch of the Library of Parliament to do this work.

Also to be considered is the intangible, non-financial cost to Canada's political life and public affairs from the unnecessary complexity inherent in the Senate set-up. Functioning as a handmaid to prime ministers and the governing political party — whether Liberal or Conservative — draws senators into partisan campaign service that impacts democratic life and electoral performance. In 1974, the Election Finances Reform Act, whose provisions are now incorporated in the Canada Elections Act, established in public law a level playing field for all who participate in Canadian elections. From limitations on financial contributions and disclosure of donors' identities, to spending limits for candidates and political parties, and other rules to clean up the earlier corruption in Canadian elections, policy was fully overhauled. But the role of the Senate has been to subvert that policy. Upwards of a hundred of the best Conservatives and Liberals operating from the Parliament Buildings assist their parties' election preparedness and do so on the public dime. This work by senators for their political parties carries high value but does not show up on the financial statements of the Conservative Party of Canada or the Liberal Party of Canada. It has never been squared with laws designed to make elections in our country fair for all parties.

Senators are paid $132,300 a year, with benefits, allowances for accommodation, daily expenses, and travel. The work is part-time. Most senators have other well-remunerated positions, a number of them acquiring additional lucrative private-sector positions while in office as senators. Generous pensions provide income, after retirement from the Senate, to continue a substantial level of their prior remuneration as senators. For paying out close to $100 million a year, Canadians get almost nothing of value in return.

No topic in Canada has ever been more discussed, by more people, at greater length, with higher cost, and fewer results, than the Senate. It is bad enough that the institution itself is dysfunctional. But Parliament's upper house has made public life for our whole country dysfunctional, too.

The policies of the parties are in direct response to this broad historic tableau. Yet they are also torqued by the energies unleashed by the Senate's ongoing scandals.

The current Senate expenses scandal being probed by politicians, covered extensively by news media, reviewed by the Senate's Internal Economy Committee, investigated by the RCMP's new National Division established in 2013 to handle politically sensitive cases under command of Assistant Commissioner Gilles Michaud, scrutinized by Canada's auditor general, Michael Ferguson, and examined by Parliament's conflict of interest and ethics commissioner Mary Dawson, has scandalized Canadians. People are demanding corrective action.

The action sought today, by a growing number of citizens, is not the old bromide of vague "Senate reform" but the simpler, cleaner solution of abolition. This reflects a matured understanding that reform is not possible — "the reality of October 26, 1992," when the Charlottetown Accord's triple-E Senate plan went down to defeat in a referendum. The national mood, as a result, has steadily progressed from "reform" to "abolition." This shift can be seen in the evolution of the Conservative Party's policy.

Public opinion surveys have tracked this climbing support for getting rid of the upper house. In February 2013, a CP/Harris-Decima survey showed some 32 percent of Canadians wanted the Senate abolished, up from 27 percent two years earlier. By July 2013, some 41 percent of Canadians surveyed by Nanos Research favoured abolition. For the first time, as many people want to abolish the Senate as hope to see it elected.

The dramatic change in thinking of members of such public policy organizations as the Canadian Taxpayers' Federation also registers this historic shift. In 1998, when the Federation surveyed its supporters on their Senate opinions, 46 percent wanted it elected, 45 percent wanted it abolished, and 6 percent wanted it appointed from provincially selected lists. In June of 2013, asking the same question, some 7,600 supporters responded to the survey. Now 65 percent of the Taxpayers' Federation want the Senate abolished, with only 33 percent still favouring electing senators. A whopping 82 percent called for a national referendum on Senate abolition.

In 2015, we Canadians will be voting in a general election for a new parliament.

Between now and election day:

▶ the actions of Canada's national political parties will shape the possibilities of what we do about the Senate;

▶ the ruling by the Supreme Court of Canada on the constitutionality of Senate change or outright abolition will channel future political actions with more precision;

▶ the rising need for a referendum on the Senate will be responded to.

This concluding chapter examines each of these in turn, beginning with the choice a voter might makefrom the menu of what our national parties offer.

LIBERAL PARTY OF CANADA

Keep the Senate but Appoint Better Senators

The Liberal Party of Canada today continues its long-displayed easy ambivalence to maintaining a Senate status quo. Throughout the twentieth century, Liberals were more intimately entwined with the Senate of Canada than members of any other party. They held office 70 percent of the time and the Senate came to play an indispensable role in maintaining the party's partisan prowess across the country and its political control of government in Ottawa.

In September 1885, at a Liberal Party of Canada convention in Toronto, a policy resolution was put forward to reform the Canadian Senate on an elective basis. The policy was adopted, but never implemented. Eighty years later, Lester Pearson's Liberal government changed the retirement age of senators, and though he'd come into office hoping to make the major changes in the Senate that had been long discussed but never implemented, he retired as PM thinking no reform should be attempted, other than perhaps to abolish the place. Over time, noteworthy Liberals have called for abolition, such as Agriculture Minister Eugene Whalen, but nothing came of it, and he himself even ended up a senator.

The current policy of the Liberal Party of Canada was enunciated by leader Justin Trudeau in early May 2013: "We do not need to change the Senate. We need to appoint better senators." His policy reflects the Liberal Party's well-honed, deep respect for the upper chamber as a political tool in gaining, holding, and exercising power.

The initial political appeal of Mr. Trudeau's policy to maintain things as they are had three elements. It kept the public focus on the immediate controversy over the Senate expenses scandal, which was doing more damage to the Conservatives than the Liberals, instead of shifting it to the larger picture of Senate reform generally. It avoided getting the fresh new leader of the Liberals embroiled in the messy restructuring of a hoary institution, using up political capital for no real gain, on an issue having little traction with younger Canadians. And third, this policy maintained the Liberals' ability to continue their opposition to Prime Minister Harper's plans for Senate reform.

But as noted, events in 2013 came to demand more. On January 29, 2014, Liberal leader Justin Trudeau made an important departure. His statement that morning opened with a preamble that Canadians wanted leaders "to come forward with practical solutions that address problems directly." He zeroed in on one. "The Senate is broken, and needs to be fixed." At the same time, he stated, "Canadians do not want to reopen the Constitution. They don't want a long, rancorous, and likely pointless debate with the provinces that would distract us from focusing on more important problems."

In announcing a new Liberal policy on the Senate, that preamble took a swipe at the NDP's solution of Senate abolition, since that would definitely require amending the Constitution, and also was a boxer's jab at the Conservatives' effort to indirectly make senators elected, since that would, if the Liberals had their way, also require constitutional amendment. With his insistence that Canadians do not want to "reopen the Constitution," Justin Trudeau further underscored that he did not want his career drawn into the same vortex that so consumed his father's.

Instead, he proposed "an immediate remedy that will not only quell many of the distractions that the current Senate is causing, but actually improve its capacity to serve all Canadians." Identifying the "two central problems" of the Senate as partisanship and patronage, the Liberal leader advocated that the Senate be non-partisan, "composed merely of thoughtful individuals representing the varied values, perspectives, and identities of this great country — independent from any particular political brand."

Then he explained that the thirty-two Liberal senators would no longer be members of the Liberal National Caucus, as already reviewed. But his attempt to decapitate his hydra-like Liberal senators was coupled with a second key part of his dramatic Senate reform plan. "If I am elected prime minister, I will put in place an open, transparent and non-partisan appointment process for senators. This process will be developed working with experts and informed by other non-partisan appointment processes, such as that of the Supreme Court justices and Order of Canada recipients."

And in so doing, he concluded, "we will remove partisanship and patronage from the Senate, reforming it and improving it in a deep and meaningful way, without ever having to touch the Constitution of Canada."

This policy will remain the position of the Liberal Party into the 2015 election campaign.

NEW DEMOCRATIC PARTY OF CANADA

Abolish the Senate

The New Democratic Party's policy for fifty years has been that the Senate of Canada must be abolished.

As the Official Opposition, following major gains in the House of Commons in the 2011 general election, New Democrats now also feel a pragmatic urgency about Senate abolition, as NDP prospects of forming a national government are stronger. All legislation enacted in the Commons must also be passed by the Senate. History shows how partisan differences between Liberals and Conservatives can create stalemate between the two houses, so it takes little imagination to picture how an NDP government's legislation would fare in an upper house dominated by Conservatives and Liberals. More than just overwhelming numbers would allow the other two parties to do this. The senators' partisan desire to vote them down, amend them significantly, and stall them, would be just as real.

The goal of Senate abolition guided the party's strong performance in the Commons during 2013 when raising the profile of the Senate expenses scandal. From the steady work of NDP ethics critic, MP Charlie Angus, to the barrage of daily questioning unleashed by Thomas Mulcair, NDP leader and leader of the Official Opposition, the social democrats used the rising public outrage to ignite a larger fire under the Senate itself.

The same policy goal has consistently guided the NDP.

In 2005, the party's hard-line position saw New Democrats refuse Lillian Dyck of Saskatchewan a place in their caucus when she was appointed to the Senate by Prime Minister Paul Martin. In 2007, at a

Winnipeg gathering of party organizers in November, NDP leader Jack Layton called for a referendum to abolish the "outdated and obsolete" Senate. "It's a nineteenth-century institution that has no place in a modern democracy in the twenty-first century," he stated. Mr. Layton highlighted the time-lapse effect. "It's undemocratic because senators are appointed by prime ministers who then are turfed out of office but end up leaving their long shadow with the continued presence of those senators in the legislative context." He insisted a referendum was well worth the effort. "Why don't we start by finding out how Canadians feel about it?" he asked. "That seems to be to be a democratic approach."

In 2011, when the Conservatives introduced the Senate Reform Act, Mr. Layton said the proposed changes merely reinforced his party's view that the Senate should be abolished. "They are going to create a monster here, because you will have at the end of the day an elected body that may or may not be elected, because the Prime Minister may or may not accept the recommendations that come out of an election," Layton said. "It's going to be one ugly scene, and throughout the years we will spend $100 million every year feeding this beast which will, by and large, stand in the way of democracy in this country. It's a disaster for Canadian democracy, all wrapped up in the guise of Senate reform."

In 2013, the party's "Roll Up the Red Carpet!" campaign launched a website giving the financial cost of the red-carpeted upper house, describing the reversal of Stephen Harper's position on appointing senators, the idea that senators do not represent Canadians but the party that appointed them, and establishing a petition to abolish the Red Chamber, which visitors to the NDP site can sign online. The party ran a series of paid advertisements in prime time to focus the public mind on the need for abolition. The party's many MPs took up the cause in their speeches across the country, whether at the constituency level to local organizations or when addressing provincial or national bodies. During the summer, Mr. Mulcair reinforced this work by touring Canada to speak with provincial premiers, one by one, to advance his plan for abolition and seek their support, cooperation, or at least non-resistance.

This policy will remain the position of the New Democratic Party into the 2015 election. NDP leader Thomas Mulcair has pledged to make

Senate abolition a centrepiece of his party's general election campaign.

BLOC QUÉBÉCOIS

Abolish the Senate

The Bloc Québécois succinctly enunciated its policy in the 2011 general election: *Le Bloc Québécois estime toujours que le Sénat est une institution archaïque et qu'il devrait être aboli.* "The Bloc has always seen the Senate as an archaic institution that should be abolished."

At that time, the party platform also criticized Stephen Harper's partisan nominations to the upper house, noting how the PM had promised to put an end to political favouritism and institute an elected Senate, but had instead appointed twenty-seven senators, including many Conservative militants such as Doug Finley, Conservative Party campaign director in 2006 and 2008; Irving Gerstein, chair of the Conservative Fund of Canada; Don Plett, president of the Conservative Party; Carolyn Stewart-Olsen, director of strategic communication in the Prime Minister's Office; Michel Rivard and Leo Housakos, Conservative organizers in Québec; Michael L. MacDonald, vice-president of the Conservative Party; Stephen Greene, former chief of staff to Reform leader Preston Manning; and Claude Carignan, Suzanne Duplessis, Fabian Manning, Yonah Martin, and Percy Mockler who'd each been Conservative MPs or candidates.

This policy will remain the position of the Bloc Québécois into the 2015 election campaign, provided the Québec-based party remains in existence and fields candidates.

GREEN PARTY OF CANADA

Hold a Referendum on Senate Reform

The Green Party of Canada has, since its inception, expressed unclear or vague policies regarding the Senate.

For some time the Green stance was to favour a referendum on what form Senate reform should take. A referendum, though, is not a focus group but a decision-making process between two alternative courses.

Presumably, if there were to be a national referendum on whether or not to abolish the Senate of Canada, Greens would welcome it.

Other party statements on what to do about the Senate differ, however. One, from the Prince Edward Island Greens, came out against abolition, advocating "sober second thought" on Senate reform.

In early 2014, the party's platform for "True Democracy" deals broadly with topics such as the electoral system and access to information, but not the Senate. However, a slightly specific motion was adopted by the party to support "the election of senators through a system that ensures proportional representation."

With the Senate issue rising up the public agenda, leader Elizabeth May will likely address it more fully. It did not feature in her autumn 2013 "democracy tour," which was focused on prime ministerial power and how she saw democracy "slipping away" in the Commons. Nor did the Senate come up in her feature interview with *Toronto Star* political writer Susan Delacourt at year's end.

This policy of the Green Party could be further developed before or during the 2015 election campaign.

CONSERVATIVE PARTY OF CANADA

Either Elect Senators or Abolish the Senate

Conservative policy on the Senate remains a unique work in progress.

Unlike the proposals of parties that are not in power, the Conservative plan is enmeshed in legislation that has undergone revamps and postponements and reflects a hands-on state of evolution. The policy is very much that of Stephen Harper, who has himself evolved, as traced in the preceding chapter, through support of triple-E Senate plans as a Reform MP, opposition to the Charlottetown Accord's negotiated version of triple-E, winning electoral mandates as Conservative party leader for an elected Senate, and his determination to bring about this result without changing the Constitution.

Seven different legislative initiatives have been attempted since Mr. Harper became prime minister in 2006. His government's bills to deal with the upper house — the Senate Appointment Consultations Act, and the Senate Reform Act — have received slight adjustments from one parliamentary session to the next, over the life of three parliaments, although their essence has remained the same. They centre on the idea of an elected Senate and a limited term in office for senators.

One bill, passed by the Commons in 2007, to limit senatorial terms to eight years, was blocked by the Liberal-dominated upper chamber. The most recent measure, embodied in Bill C-7, the Senate Reform Act, was passed in the Commons in 2011 only to be stalled in the Senate again. Most of the objections to the legislation that were voiced by Liberal senators dealt with whether the changes could be made by federal statute alone, or required constitutional amendment. Behind such arguments, of course, was the reality of Liberal policy opposing elections to the Senate in preference to continuing with appointments, something over which the party once restored to office can have more control.

After the Conservatives formed a national government in 2006, progress in dealing with the Senate, especially important to the party's Alberta base and the prime minister's long-time commitment, seemed dawdling at best. Having roundly criticized the Liberals for appointing senators before he became prime minister, Stephen Harper was so dedicated to changing the system that he abstained for three years from making any appointments himself, the only two exceptions in that period being to bring one Quebecer into cabinet for the sake of national perspective and unity, and to name Bert Brown as an "elected" senator from Alberta. But from 2009 on, the PM has appointed many senators, and in politics, as in life, a person is generally remembered for his or her most recent act. As of March 2014, Conservatives outnumber Liberals fifty-seven to thirty-two in the Senate, with nine vacancies the PM could fill when he wishes. The other seven Senate seats are held by so-called Independents.

In the event of Justin Trudeau's election as prime minister in 2015, his government's legislation would face the same fate in the Senate that Stephen Harper's did in his early years of governing. The Liberal leader's plan to convert the upper house into a body of Independents, with no party affiliation, could be expected to encounter similar results to his dramatic but ineffective ouster of those thirty-two Liberal senators.

Having obtained three electoral mandates to reform the Senate, principally by making it an elected body, the Harper government sought to put an end to this debate over constitutionality and the game of legislative ping-pong between Parliament's upper and lower houses, by asking Canada's Supreme Court to clarify the relevant constitutional questions.

While Prime Minister Harper was seeking to turn the Alberta experiment into a nation-wide program by legislation that was stalled in parliament, his Saskatchewan ally Premier Brad Wall meanwhile deconstructed the plan in his province and moved to the cleaner position of outright Senate abolition. Premier Wall's move was not far from what Stephen Harper himself seemed increasingly ready to embrace, and perhaps will influence the redefinition of Conservative policy at the national level by 2015.

His government's Throne Speech on October 16, 2013, made clear the Conservative policy as of that date: "The government continues to believe the status quo in the Senate of Canada is unacceptable. The Senate must be reformed or, as with its provincial counterparts, vanish. The government will proceed upon receiving the advice of the Supreme Court. The Senate of Canada will either be reformed or like its provincial counterparts, dissolved."

The brief statement, though clear, seemed tentative in the poignant venue of the Red Chamber itself. A number of people expected the prime minister, embattled for months by the scandals surrounding senators he'd appointed and the actions of his own staff in the PMO, might leapfrog over the whole mess with a bold new move — announcing a plan and timetable to actually make the Senate "vanish." Evidently, Mr. Harper had another plan in mind, keyed to the pending Supreme Court decision — perhaps an end-run around the entrenched power interests of the Senate and even some provincial premiers to the sovereign Canadian people themselves in a national referendum on Senate abolition.

Even though Stephen Harper feels more at home addressing economic progress than dealing with democratic institutions, his prior Reform Party commitment to Senate reform and his Alberta base, which for thirty years had been Canada's hotbed of reformist drive on the Senate, knew the importance of the issue. He'd decided on a minimalist approach, a decision no doubt reinforced by having witnessed up close the swamp Brian Mulroney had led an earlier Conservative government into by seeking consensus on revamping the Senate through a major constitutional amendment.

Although he'd started with a couple of "reforms" responsive to his Conservative Party base — electing instead of appointing senators, and shortening their time in office to a uniform nine years — the PM abandoned the other two triple-E ideas of "equal" and "effective" because changing the number of senators allocated to each province and increasing powers of the Senate were politically suicidal in light of many deeply entrenched interests.

Mr. Harper sought to do a minimalist deed in a minimalist manner — by a simple bill in Parliament, changing membership attributes of senators, not switching their numbers between provinces or altering their powers in office. Where Prime Minister Pearson's change told senators: *You can only remain in office to age seventy-five*, Mr. Harper's bill would tell them: *You can only get in if people first elect you, instead of me or my successors choosing you ourselves, and you can only stay for nine years.* Mr. Harper had a modest precedent, established by Brian Mulroney's Conservative government and his own, of the appointment of several provincially elected Albertans as senators — an innovation that was accepted without challenge.

Rather than calling for direct elections to the Senate, which surely would require constitutional amendment with provincial consent, the Senate Reform Act instead supports the Alberta model of provinces holding electoral consultations with voters on who should be appointed to the Senate.

Each senator appointed by Mr. Harper agreed, as a condition of receiving his or her senatorship, to support the Conservative project for Senate reform; and in many if not all cases these new senators even agreed to resign their seat and run for a position in the Senate if provincial elections for this purpose would be instituted.

For the Conservatives, Stephen Harper had synthesized what initially seemed an efficient plan for Senate reform. In a world of many conflicting proposals to modernize the upper house, he'd opted just to change the way senators reached office and limit their time of service. His political base found the idea of "term limits" appealing. Senators would have eight or nine years to make their mark, rather than being in the upper house for as little as three years or as many as thirty, either not getting the hang of the place in time or relaxing into complacency on the job. For him, term of office was not contingent on one's age at the time of appointment.

Coupling indirect democratic election with the existing constitutional role of the PM in recommending to the governor general those to be appointed to the Senate, he believed he could avoid the political complexity, time delays, and negotiations that would be required if reform to the Senate tackled more major features of the institution such as altering its law-making powers. Legitimizing the Senate by making it elected would mean its existing unused powers, which are considerable, could be taken up with less restraint than was the case by appointed senators who operated more tentatively most of the time.

Although Mr. Harper believed his clean and efficient approach could modernize Canada's Senate and bypass the need for constitutional amendment, he nevertheless faced strong opposition to his Senate legislation and the fact that since 1981 dealing with constitutional provisions had become exceedingly onerous.

To his supporters, the political appeal of Mr. Harper's policy was that it maintained the institution but democratized its membership. It addressed a real and long-standing need in Canada to do something about an institution so dramatically out of date that it festered as unfinished business over the lifetimes of two dozen governments. It placed a premium on democratic values, which resonated in Canada's democratic society. It took the essence of key Senate reform proposals, most of which originated from the Conservative Party's political base in Alberta, and embraced Alberta's procedure for electing senators-in-waiting for the prime minister to officially appoint, extending the model as a workable solution for the whole country.

The Harper government, having in February 2013 referred questions to the Supreme Court of Canada about the constitutional framework within which changes to the Senate may be made, in July 2013 submitted legal arguments to the court. The government's view, of course, is that the proposed Senate reforms embodied in Bill C-7, the Senate Reform Act, which it introduced in June 2011, do not require consent of the provinces.

Looking past difficulties it still might encounter with Bill C-7, the government's reference in February also asked the Supreme Court to clarify the constitutionality of several ways by which the Senate could be abolished.

The Harper government believes Parliament can alter the term in office of senators, modify the property requirements for becoming a senator, and provide a democratic vote resulting in popularly recommended senators for the upper chamber, without triggering an amending formula that would require provincial consent to such tweaking of the Constitution.

The inescapable difficulty of making any change to the Senate, however, has reminded Conservatives of the realities of October 26, 1992, and has led inexorably to the conclusion that the only way to reform the Senate is to abolish it. Between the 2011 general election, when the Conservatives pledged to reform the Senate by making it an elected body, and today, the option of abolition has been rising in Tory skies like the morning sun.

The malleable policy of the Conservative Party will doubtless continue to evolve heading toward the 2015 election, with a possible full embrace of Senate abolition, which in part will be determined by the constitutional ruling by the Supreme Court of Canada.

SUPREME COURT OF CANADA

A Ruling of Constitutional Questions Pertaining to the Senate of Canada

Justices of the Supreme Court of Canada are deliberating on constitutional questions referred to the court by the Government of Canada regarding proposed changes to the Senate, having heard argument and received written briefs pro and con from a battery of our country's top constitutional lawyers representing a number of different governments in the Canadian federation.

The questions asked of the court, though six in number, with many sub-parts to several, fall into two broad categories — what is constitutional about the Harper government's current legislative plan for electing senators and limiting their term of office, and what is required to abolish the Senate?

To abolish the Senate of Canada requires nullifying the constitutional provisions that created it in 1867. To do so requires consent from Parliament and provincial legislatures. The Supreme Court ruling, when handed down, will provide details.

NATIONAL REFERENDUM

Ballot Question on the Senate's Future

Abolition of the Senate will require approval by Parliament and provincial legislatures. The still-awaited ruling by the Supreme Court will provide a guide in terms of constitutional law.

The last Canada-wide referendum was on the 1992 Charlottetown Accord constitutional package and took place under the current amending formula adopted in 1981. It therefore provides a clear model and useful precedent.

The difference between 1992 and today is two-fold. First, a single ballot question on what to do with the Senate is direct, clean, and comprehensible, whereas the Charlottetown Accord required approval or rejection of a complex and interrelated set of far-reaching proposals. Second, the 1992 referendum came at the end of years of expensive and time-consuming constitutional negotiations and sent all that effort down the drain; a referendum on the Senate today can precede any detailed work and, indeed, would provide clear guidance for it.

The necessary first step in this process of resolving what to do about the upper house of Parliament is obtaining a clear verdict from the sovereign people of Canada:

"Are you in favour of abolishing the Senate of Canada? YES [ ] NO [ ]"

A referendum forces choice. It does not canvass a range of options nor seek to rank preferences. Some issues may seem complex, multi-dimensional, nuanced. But at the end of the day, whether for an individual or the cabinet or Parliament, every decision comes down to making a clear choice: Do I marry him? Will we build that pipeline? Are we going to war? The exercise of power, and the responsibility of being, is to confront "Yes" and "No" and make a decision between one or the other and then proceed as committed.

Many calls are now being made for a national referendum on the Senate.

In 2007, NDP leader Jack Layton urged a referendum to abolish the Senate, and then introduced a bill in the Commons prior to the 2011 general election for a referendum on Senate abolition. The Green Party, though uncertain how it wants to deal with the Senate, has adopted a policy plank to hold a national referendum to ask Canadians about Senate reform. Conservative Senator Hugh Segal in October 2007 called for a referendum on Senate abolition, believing that a majority "No" vote would propel overdue changes needed to help the Senate overcome what Mr. Segal called its "democratic deficit."

Prime Minister Stephen Harper has repeatedly said, most recently in his government's October 2013 Throne Speech, that if the Senate cannot be reformed it must "vanish," which requires eliminating the provisions in our Constitution that created it.

Leader of the Official Opposition Thomas Mulcair advocates abolition of the Senate, as do several provincial premiers and legislative assemblies.

All of them know full well that abolition requires constitutional amendment. Public policy organizations such as the Canadian Taxpayers' Federation have also joined those calling for a national referendum on Senate abolition. A critical mass of political force has now been generated around a referendum and constitutional amendment on the Senate's future.

A number of Canadians have already grasped the importance of *starting* the constitutional amendment step with the referendum.

The rules require major constitutional change to be approved by a majority of our representatives in most or all Canadian legislatures before it can take effect. Again, this is where the Supreme Court justices will provide timely guidance to a waiting nation.

No rule stipulates that constitutional change must be approved by citizens who live under the Constitution and whose lives are governed by it, but voting in a referendum to ratify or reject constitutional change is what many democratic countries do. In Canada today, while a referendum may not be legally required, it is politically necessary for a couple reasons.

The first reason is to respect the spirit of Canada as a democratic country, a *free and democratic* society in the words of our Constitution. The Charter lists the rights and freedoms of Canadians, but specific acts are needed to turn abstract concepts into living reality in the small daily places where each of us lives. Charter rights must be realized in concrete ways.

The Charter includes the right to vote for our elected representatives, and though it does not also expressly stipulate that we have the right to vote on measures, the Charter is not a closed list. Some democratic rights are also granted by statute law. We have acquired the right to cast ballots on transcending issues of public importance, for example, under a number of provincial statutes across Canada, including those that empower citizens to initiate votes on particular issues. This is currently happening in a number of municipalities, where balloting is taking place on the fluoridation of municipal water supplies.

The second reason for holding a referendum is that some Canadians will vote on any proposed constitutional amendment pertaining to the Senate because their provincial legislatures enacted laws to stipulate that, before the elected representatives in the assembly vote on a resolution to approve a constitutional amendment, a province-wide referendum must first take place. Those provinces recognize the sovereignty of the people, understand that the Constitution belongs to the people and not to governments, and seek as their delegated representatives to take guidance from them. More than a "representative sample" for an opinion poll that may or may not be accurate, the deliberately cast votes of all citizens provide truer participation and a more accurate voice for the people to guide politicians.

Prime Minister Mulroney noted, when instituting a Canada-wide ballot question in 1992, it was "intolerable to have two classes of Canadian citizens" — those who could directly express themselves on a constitutional amendment (in British Columbia, Alberta, and Québec), and those who could only sit on the sidelines and watch. That reasoning remains valid today, but added to it is the precedent of the 1992 constitutional referendum that solicited the people's verdict. How could Canada in 2015 be less democratic than a quarter century earlier?

In the 2015 general election, when we citizens are handed a ballot to choose one candidate from among several in the process of electing our forty-second Parliament, we can also be handed a second ballot, on which to record our individual choice on retaining or abolishing the Senate.

The cost of the 2011 general election was $288 million and the 2015 election will run to at least that much money. Combining the Senate referendum with the election of MPs will add little more to that inescapable cost than the printer's bill for twenty-five million ballots.

Before conducting a 2015 Senate referendum contemporaneously with the general election, the Referendum Act enacted by Parliament in 1992 for voting on the Charlottetown Accord, since amended, needs to be revisited again by the current forty-first Parliament in order to revise it in certain respects. Specifically, the act requires adjustment to accommodate a referendum occurring at the same time as a general election.

Several valid reasons, which I review in my books *Law-Making by the People, The People's Mandate,* and *Direct Democracy in Canada*, suggest it is preferable to hold a referendum at a different time than during a general election. But a number of provinces in the recent past have held referendums in conjunction with the election of representatives and shown it not to be problematic and, in fact, to carry some notable advantages.

In any event, the urgent need to settle for once and for all the fate of the Senate that has been highlighted by the current scandal, plus the financial advantages of conducting a referendum at the same time as a Canada-wide vote, combine to make the 2015 general election the right time, as well as the historic moment, to put "the question" to the people. The 2015 election campaign is going to bring with it substantial debate over the Senate anyway, given the public pressure to address the many scandals about Parliament's second house and the different choices the parties are offering to Canadians.

Some voters may wish to support a particular political party for a host of reasons, but also want to render an opinion on the Senate that is at odds with the policy of their party of choice. Do you grimace and vote NDP just to get rid of the Senate, or happily cross party lines to reward the NDP for a half-century of consistency on abolition? Do you have to not vote for Justin Trudeau just because the Liberals want to keep the Senate? Will the Conservatives stick with their stale plan for indirect election of senators, or realize that conservatism is not about keeping things as they are but knowing when "to lop the moulded branch away," so that Stephen

Harper can realign his policies to provide clarity of choice? There's a lot to sort out, alongside a host of other issues. A second ballot, exclusive to this transcending issue, will place the Senate's future above partisanship and into the realm of an unequivocal verdict from citizens.

The Referendum Act contemplates umbrella committees for both the Yes and No sides, provides fund-raising and campaign spending and broadcasting rules, and generally sets the legal framework for the democratic exercise Canadians expect in contemporary conditions. During the campaign period, those wanting to retain or abolish the Senate can present their best arguments to their fellow citizens.

When Canadians give "the answer," it will provide clear guidance to elected representatives in Ottawa and all provincial capitals when they, in turn, consider any consequent resolution to amend the Constitution about the Senate.

In February 2014, the Canada West Foundation endorsed Liberal leader Justin Trudeau's proposal for an appointed panel to appoint high-calibre Canadians as senators and condemned Conservative Prime Minister Harper's plan to have Canadians elect senators. This showed how those who endorse "democracy" as a concept can mean something quite different as a practice.

This current stance by the same foundation that initiated a groundswell of support in Western Canada for an elected Senate in the 1980s was already telegraphed by its 2010 discussion paper entitled "A New Senate for a More Democratic Canada." The authors of the document, Roger Gibbins and Robert Roach, stated, "an elected Senate would bring its own challenges to efficient government as elected senators would have the legitimacy and, to a degree, the mandate to tackle the government of the day. Thus Canadians with a thirst for efficient government may cast a wary eye on Senate reform, fearing its potential to seriously gum up the works of Parliament." They sought "to shift the terms of debate from the problems of Senate reform to its democratic potential. The current focus on tactical issues such as term limits and the appointment process is not likely to capture the imagination of Canadians."

The Canada West Foundation, by dropping the "E" of elected and focusing on the "E" of effective, and by supporting a different appointment system for senators, was still in a conundrum, though.

Neither Mr. Trudeau nor Mr. Harper contemplates changing the powers or functions of the Senate. Their idea, though not much articulated, is likely that once senators have greater legitimacy — either by virtue of Trudeau-style appointment or Harper-style election — they would use the existing considerable powers already allocated to the Senate by the Constitution. For years, those powers have been unused, or under-utilized, because senators are savvy and know they're balanced on a performance high-wire with no safety net. Neither the Liberal leader nor the Conservative leader wants to touch the Constitution, either to change now how new senators are chosen (which is why each has embraced a plan to bring greater legitimacy to senators by working within existing constitutional provisions), or to change in the future the powers that senators would wield.

Messrs. Gibbins and Roach, though deeply nuanced in conceptual understanding and devoted to making Canada better, still have sights on "Senate reform" as a future ideal, the way a couple of boys might rearrange Lego pieces to build a staircase to the moon. The battles already waged to bring about Senate reform in recent Canadian history, at the core of which was the triple-E idea spawned by the Canada West Foundation, cannot be blithely ignored. Those acts have enduring consequences. The reality of the Charlottetown Accord's fate taught the lesson.

Canadian support for abolition is growing because a restless majority of us feels that Senate "reformers" have had a very long turn at trying their costly best to put a satellite dish on top of the settler's sod hut. Those efforts, sincere and sustained, have all failed.

Because the best predictor of future performance is past behaviour, Canada ought not to waste any more time or money on yet another round of teasing out and trying on nebulous concepts around the non-existent possibility of Senate reform. Patience has run out.

Abolitionists now want our turn.

Once the Senate of Canada is gone, it will not be missed.

If in the future we think about Parliament's appointed, costly, and redundant second house at all, it will only be to puzzle over why it took so long to liberate ourselves from this colonial relic.

ACKNOWLEDGEMENTS

"Do you think there's a book in this?" asked Kirk Howard, for over forty years head of Dundurn, today Canada's largest independent book publisher. We'd been talking about the Senate expenses scandal one morning last summer as yet another day of "breaking news" aroused Canadians to the bizarre events unfolding around Parliament's upper house.

Our Scandalous Senate emerged as my answer. Thank you, Kirk.

My bride Elise Marie Boyer discovered the adventure of bringing life to a book by sharing the work with me, adding new skills to her already extensive repertoire while enriching my life's work in all ways. Merci, Elise!

My lawyer nephew Johnson Billingsley in Edmonton provided counsel about the book's content, to ensure the scandal was with the Senate of Canada, not the way I wrote about it. I am grateful, Johnson.

Dominic Farrell maintained his stellar reputation for intelligence in editing as we completed yet another book together. Thank you, once again, Dominic. Sergey Lobachev assisted me with the index.

Others at Dundurn each played their roles in turn, making me again grateful to Sheila Douglas, Beth Bruder, Livio Copetti, Dick Yu, Diane Young, Carrie Gleason, Jennifer Scott, Courtney Horner, Colleen Wormald, James Hatch, and Margaret Bryant. Thank you for this.

To Prime Minister Brian Mulroney, I am grateful for the fulsome account of behind-closed-doors records of constitutional negotiations, made public years before their secret classification ended, in his *Memoirs*, a Douglas Gibson book published by McClelland & Stewart in 2007.

Many individuals contributed information and insights, now woven into this book, over a number of decades. Their lives and lessons have been incorporated here in ways I hope bring a measure of private satisfaction for public service well rendered. Beyond ability to record here your names and the extent of my indebtedness to you, I am grateful beyond measure to each of you. Please take a well-earned bow.

INDEX

Also by J. Patrick Boyer

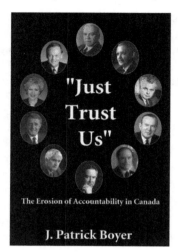

Just Trust Us
The Erosion of Accountability in Canada

Canadians care deeply about our country but nevertheless feel perplexed, angered, and even embarrassed by the way we now govern ourselves. In Just Trust Us: The Erosion of Accountability in Canada, Boyer draws together new patterns of thought to help explain why.

Since the late 1700s "representative government" has been part of our Canadian birthright, and since the 1800s "responsible government" has, additionally, been a part of the constitutional foundation of our country. That the forms of both endure, but not their substance, is the thesis of Boyer's book. The result? An absence of accountability in Canadian government.

Most of our country's pressing concerns and complex problems — from regional economic disparities to the Quebec and Western Canadian separatist movements, from tax evasion to voter apathy — can be traced back to this fundamental lack of accountability. A citizen who understands this absence sees that it makes sense to step back from a dysfunctional system. Making this accountability connection is critical, Boyer concludes, because only when we clearly understand the root cause of the problems we face as a nation can we begin to develop workable, long-term solutions.

Also by J. Patrick Boyer

The People's Mandate
Referendums and a More Democratic Canada

Direct democracy — the occasional use of referendums, plebiscites, and other such initiatives — can play an important role, in concert with our existing institutions of representative democracy, for Canadians seeking a greater say in the matters that affect them.

Nor is this concept alien to our country, says Boyer, pointing to the two national plebiscites (on the prohibition of alcohol in 1898 and on conscription for overseas military service in 1942), approximately sixty provincial plebiscites (on everything from sovereignty-association to abortion, medicare, and women's suffrage), and several thousand that have been held at the municipal level.

The People's Mandate is a helpful guide to understanding the distinctions between plebiscites and referendums in a purely Canadian context. It addresses some of the concerns about this unparliamentary practice, and makes a powerful and logical statement about their necessity for democracy.

Also by J. Patrick Boyer

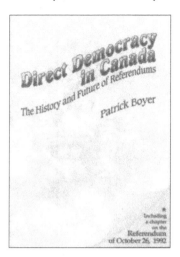

Direct Democracy in Canada
The History and Future of Referendums

Direct Democracy in Canada: The History and Future of Referendums surveys Canada's century-long record of plebiscites and referendums. J. Patrick Boyer analyzes the effects of the three national referendums and the development of a consensus. This companion volume to *The People's Mandate* studies some of the major provincial and municipal referendums, examines existing legal frameworks and speculates on the future of direct democracy in Canada.

Also by J. Patrick Boyer

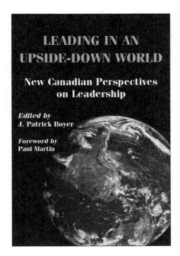

Leading in an Upside-Down World
New Canadian Perspectives on Leadership

The world as we know it has been turned upside down by recent events but it's still a place where leadership is needed more than ever.

Fifteen Canadians with highly diverse perspectives and richly different experience explore this timely question in *Leading in an Upside-Down World*.

Chapter by chapter, stories of Canada unfold and future prospects for leadership grow clearer as these eminent Canadians explain how to "recognize leadership" in an age where old institutions and behaviours are being left behind. They also identify leadership attributes that endure. *Leading in an Upside-Down World* gives voice to both scholars and practitioners of Canadian-style leadership.

Also by J. Patrick Boyer

Another Country, Another Life
Calumny, Love, and the Secrets of Isaac Jelfs

Quiet Isaac Jelfs led many lives: a scapegoated law clerk in England; a soldier in the mad Crimean War; a lawyer on swirling Broadway Avenue in New York. His escape from each was wrapped in deep secrecy. He eventually reached Canada, in 1869, with a new wife and a changed name. In his new home — the remote wilderness of Muskoka — he crafted yet another persona for himself. In *Another Country, Another Life*, his great-grandson traces that long-hidden journey, exposing Isaac Jelfs's covered tracks and the reasons for his double life.

Available at your favourite bookseller

 DUNDURN

Visit us at
Dundurn.com | @dundurnpress
Facebook.com/dundurnpress | Pinterest.com/dundurnpress